Praise for *Water from a Deep Well*

"Ever since that day at noon when a Samaritan woman asked for living water, people have turned to Jesus for the water that satisfies the thirst of the human condition and wells up to eternal life. In *Water from a Deep Well*, Gerald Sittser has followed the lives of significant Christians down through the centuries who have tasted the water, shared it with others and, in some cases, carried it to foreign lands. This book will serve as an excellent resource in the classroom, in our personal libraries and in our prayerful consideration of the 'great cloud of witnesses' who have drunk from the well before us."

ALBERT HAASE, O.F.M., DIRECTOR, SCHOOL OF SPIRITUALITY AT
MAYSLAKE MINISTRIES AND AUTHOR OF *COMING HOME TO YOUR TRUE SELF*

"Gerald Sittser opens up windows into worlds of spiritual practice that we truly need both because they intensify our thirst for God and because they stimulate our imaginations for the varied ways God meets and leads the people of God. While this book feeds me, it also does something even more important: it leaves me hungry, which is where I need to be in order to grow as a disciple, husband, father, friend and pastor."

MARK LABBERTON, PASTOR AND AUTHOR OF *THE DANGEROUS ACT OF WORSHIP*

"What Gerald Sittser gives us is not a guidebook . . . but something which reads more like an extended declaration of love. A history of Christian spirituality it may be, but such spirituality is understood less as a benefit to be acquired neutrally through detachment than a matter of being enthralled and enticed by the beauty which is Christ. Each chapter is instructive and informed, and Gerald Sittser provides the kind of clarity and simplicity which only grows out of deep knowledge."

IAIN TORRANCE, PRESIDENT, PRINCETON THEOLOGICAL SEMINARY, AND FORMER
MODERATOR OF THE CHURCH OF SCOTLAND

"Gerald Sittser offers us two enormous gifts in this compelling history of Christian spirituality—a wonderfully flowing narrative that catches us up into the lives and practices of great saints, and voluminous endnotes so that we can pursue more thoroughly the topics and characters he describes. This beautiful book will widen everyone's spirituality, for Sittser introduces us to an extensive range of eras and their greatest contributions. Taste and see—this book will deepen you!"

MARVA DAWN, AUTHOR OF *KEEPING THE SABBATH WHOLLY*

"Much of the current interest in 'spirituality' suffers from a kind of amnesia—forgetful or oblivious that there is indeed a centuries-long well to draw from, full of an inheritance which can enrich our lives. Jerry Sittser has provided a bucket by which we can draw from that well, whether simply to taste, or better to drink deeply. This is a book to humble us, discovering how much more there is to know, but also to bring fresh hope that God works beyond our small personal experiences, and beyond our own lifetime. Read it—enjoy, and be stretched."

LEIGHTON FORD, AUTHOR OF *TRANSFORMING LEADERSHIP*

"Jerry Sittser is a rare kind of writer: a scholar with a scholar's depth, and a man with the spiritual health of his readers ever before him. . . .The chapters are full of anecdotes that inspire and amuse, and practical suggestions to help us appropriate the wisdom that is the deposit of the church's great men and women through the ages. *Water from a Deep Well* is a thoroughly worthwhile read."

BEN PATTERSON, AUTHOR OF *WAITING*

Water from a Deep Well

CHRISTIAN SPIRITUALITY FROM
EARLY MARTYRS TO MODERN MISSIONARIES

Gerald L. Sittser

FOREWORD BY EUGENE H. PETERSON

IVP Books

An imprint of InterVarsity Press
Downers Grove, Illinois

InterVarsity Press
P.O. Box 1400, Downers Grove, IL 60515-1426
World Wide Web: www.ivpress.com
E-mail: email@ivpress.com

InterVarsity Press® is the book-publishing division of InterVarsity Christian Fellowship/USA®, a movement of students and faculty active on campus at hundreds of universities, colleges and schools of nursing in the United States of America, and a member movement of the International Fellowship of Evangelical Students. For information about local and regional activities, write Public Relations Dept., InterVarsity Christian Fellowship/USA, 6400 Schroeder Rd., P.O. Box 7895, Madison, WI 53707-7895, or visit the IVCF website at <www.intervarsity.org>.

Scripture quotations, unless otherwise noted, are from the New Revised Standard Version of the Bible, *copyright 1989 by the Division of Christian Education of the National Council of Churches of Christ in the USA. Used by permission. All rights reserved.*

Photographs are reprinted with permission. See illustration credits at the end of the book.

Design: Cindy Kiple
Images: Grant V. Faint/Getty Images

ISBN 978-0-8308-3745-8

Printed in the United States of America ∞

Library of Congress Cataloging-in-Publication Data

Sittser, Gerald Lawson, 1950-
  Water from a deep well: spirituality from early martyrs to modern
  missionaries/Gerald L. Sittser.
    p. cm.
  Includes bibliographical references and index.
  ISBN-13: 978-0-8308-3493-8 (cloth: alk. paper)
  1. Spirituality—History. I. Title.
  BV4501.3.S5848 2007
  248.09—dc22
                                                                          2007031454

P	21	20	19	18	17	16	15	14	13	12	11	10	9	8	7	6	5	4	3	2
Y	27	26	25	24	23	22	21	20	19	18	17	16	15	14	13	12				

To

Rachel Johnson

Sister Florence

Harold Korver

Rits Tadema

—my Abbas and Ammas—

with affection and gratitude

Contents

Foreword by Eugene Peterson   9

Acknowledgments   11

Introduction: There Is More!   15

1 WITNESS: *The Spirituality of the Early Christian Martyrs*   27

2 BELONGING: *The Spirituality of Early Christian Community*   50

3 STRUGGLE: *The Spirituality of the Desert Saints*   73

4 RHYTHM: *The Spirituality of Monasticism*   96

5 HOLY HEROES: *The Spirituality of Icons and Saints*   118

6 WINDOWS: *The Spirituality of the Sacraments*   139

7 UNION: *The Spirituality of the Mystics*   163

8 ORDINARINESS: *The Spirituality of the Medieval Laity*   187

9 WORD: *The Spirituality of the Reformers*   209

10 CONVERSION: *The Spirituality of Evangelicals*   231

11 RISK: *The Spirituality of Pioneer Missionaries*   256

Conclusion: *Where Do We Go from Here?*   281

Discussion Questions   296

Annotated Reading List   303

Illustration Credits   310

Notes   314

Index   360

Foreword

I was standing with a friend on the shore of an alpine lake in Montana. It was a clear, moonless night. The late autumn air was crisp. Every star was sharply etched on the domed firmament—the sky didn't have to compete with town lights.

My friend said, "I can hardly wait to get to heaven and learn the names of all the stars!"

I said, "I know how you feel. But why wait? I can tell you of a few of their names right now. Look. Right over there is Deneb. And that bright one off to the left is Betelgeuse. Just over that pine tree—see that tight cluster of seven stars?—that's the Pleiades that are mentioned in Job. A lot of them have stories that go with them. Let me tell you about the hunter, Orion . . ."

That was enough for my friend. She impatiently brushed me off and changed the subject. "I'll wait for heaven."

Dr. Jerry Sittser doesn't want us to wait for heaven to get to know the names and stories of our brothers and sisters, parents and grandparents, uncles and aunts and cousins, this firmament of saints, this family of faith into which we have been baptized. He tells us their names and stories in this book, *Water from a Deep Well*. The book is a bucket lowered into a well that brings up stories that get me in touch with my family. When I take my place in a pew each Sunday morning with my local congregation, the people I don't see far outnumber the people I do see, this "cloud of witnesses" that provides much-needed depth and texture and companionship as I follow Jesus. Their bones have been placed in cemeteries for twenty centuries on every continent. Their names are written in the "book of life." I worship with them.

There is more. This book is a timely antidote to the amnesiac, one-generational world that we live in. A one-generational church is capable of generating energy but there are no roots. When the emotions wear off or difficulty arrives it withers. Soon there is nothing to show for it. Without a cultivated memory we live from hand to mouth on fad and novelty. But Christians don't sprint out of the starting blocks in each generation in a race for heaven. We are on a relay team. We have a heritage, a richly composted family history. We need to know these members of our family who lived lives similar to what we are living and lived them well. As we get to know them, we are less isolated, less alone. We are not orphans. We are not misfits.

And there is also this: *Water from a Deep Well* is a part of the answer to the longest of the recorded prayers of Jesus (Jn 17). On the night before his death by crucifixion, Jesus prayed to the Father for his disciples ". . . that they may be one, even as we are one" (Jn 17:11). It is imperative that we recognize that he specifically included us in his prayer: "I ask not only on behalf of these, but also on behalf of those who will believe in me . . . that they may all be one" (Jn 17:20-21). That means us.

Jesus prayed in intercession for his disciples "that they may become completely one" (Jn 17:23) and for all of us who continue to follow Jesus today, at one with Jesus, at one with the Father, and at one with one with one another. A family, "one body," held together relationally in love and obedience by the prayers of Jesus. That prayer of Jesus, who "always lives to make intercession" for us (Heb 7:25), continues to do its work, bringing his people into an intimate praying oneness in the same way that the beloved son Jesus is one with the Father.

Water from a Deep Well is a detailed documentation of the unity that Jesus' prayers have brought about through these centuries of Christian living. The oneness is not yet complete. Some Christians look on others as rivals. Some compete for dominance. Willfulness and pride are roadside bombs responsible for considerable fragmentation. Meanwhile, we have these names and stories of the many in our family who have entered into the prayers that Jesus continues to pray for us that we "become completely one, so that the world may know that you have sent me and have loved them even as you have loved me" (Jn 17:23).

Eugene H. Peterson
Professor Emeritus of Spiritual Theology, Regent College, Vancouver, B.C.

Acknowledgments

I started working on this book many years ago, long before I had any idea that I would actually write it. In 1993 I took fifteen students to Tall Timber, a camp located in a remote area of the Cascades, where for a month I introduced them to the history of spirituality. It was a new world to them, as it was in many ways to me too. I soon became fascinated by that world and so began to study it in earnest. I read dozens and then hundreds of books, accumulated pages and pages of notes, and eventually started to scratch out a thesis and outline. Two years ago, almost to the day, I began to write. This book is the final product.

I learned along the way that I am a very rich man, for I belong to a community of faith that gives me a deep sense of belonging. That community includes two groups of people in particular. This book is *about* the one group; it is *for* the other group.

The former group includes believers—the *saints*, as I will call them—who have lived over the past two thousand years. These saints have bequeathed to us a rich legacy of faith, sacrifice and service. Many of the books we read, the hymns we sing, the art we view, the rituals we observe and the disciplines we practice are reminders and repositories of this legacy. We owe them a debt of gratitude. I write this book at least in part to honor them and to tell their stories.

The latter group includes the hundreds of millions of believers who live today. They are my Christian contemporaries, my brothers and sisters in Christ, to whom I want to introduce the first group, their spiritual family, the saints who have gone before us. It would be an incalculable loss if this legacy of faith was forgotten, like some precious heirloom stored for too long in an attic chest.

Another group of people deserve special mention too. It includes the people who helped me in the writing of this book, which is clearly the better for the contributions they so generously made. I am deeply grateful to all of them. Carolyn Browning Helsel, Shelby Dresback Miles, David Lincicum, Kyle Dresback, Erin Dung, Gabe Schmidt and Matt Kaemingk, former Whitworth students who have graduated and now gone on to other things, assisted in the research. Katie Wisenor, Kathy Watts, Paige McIlraith, Howard Wilcox, Bill Yakely and John Weller, fellow members of Whitworth Community Presbyterian Church, read most of the chapters and met with me as a small group to discuss the book from a lay perspective. Dick Avery, Rob Eyman, Matt Thomas, Rob Fairbanks, Joe Wittwer and John Underhill, who meet monthly with me in a pastors' study group, read the manuscript and commented on it from a pastoral perspective. Julie Canlis and Jerry Root, fellow scholars, offered a thorough critique of selected chapters.

Three colleagues from Whitworth, Jim Edwards, Adam Neder and Terry McGonigal, read every chapter and offered helpful comments from beginning to end. Their investment in this book has been immeasurably valuable to me. They challenged me to settle for nothing less than the best that I could do. Gail Fielding, a reference librarian at Whitworth, procured books and articles from around the country, often on short notice. I am grateful too for the faculty, administration and students at Whitworth—especially those students who enrolled in Christian Spirituality at Tall Timber—who have, over the years, provided such a warm and supportive academic home for me. Stan and Becky Fishburn, the directors of Tall Timber Ranch, also deserve special recognition. Cindy Bunch, an editor at InterVarsity Press, pushed me to write with focus, to keep the intended audience in mind and to cut until it hurt. Lorraine Caulton devoted a great deal of time to finding just the right art images for the book; her eye and instincts are superb. In fact, the entire team at InterVarsity Press provided excellent support throughout the project. I am deeply grateful for them all.

I dedicate this book to four dear friends, all a generation older than me, to whom I owe so much. They are my Abbas and Ammas, as I like to call them. Harold Korver, the senior pastor under whom I worked as a young man fresh out of seminary, challenged me to work as if the success of ministry depended entirely on me and to pray as if it depended entirely on God. I still enjoy our occasional telephone conversations. Rachel Johnson has been a gracious friend, guide and mentor for many years. I am sad that she no longer lives in Spokane. Sister Florence always welcomes me as an honored guest into her community of sisters, listens well, asks good questions and allows me to enjoy the solitude of the hermitage. Finally, Rits Tadema, a monthly breakfast companion, inspires me to want to love God with heart, soul, mind and strength. I dedicate this book to them with affection and gratitude.

Introduction

There Is More!

Everyone who drinks of this water will be thirsty again,
but those who drink of the water
that I will give them will never be thirsty.
The water that I will give will become in them a
spring of water gushing up to eternal life.

JN 4:13-14

O f all the books I have read, one stands above them all. It is *The Confessions* of St. Augustine, who served as bishop of Hippo in North Africa in the early fifth century. What about this book makes it tower over the rest, even over other spiritual classics? Why do I return to it year after year and always seem to find new insights? What makes it so timeless and compelling? Its genius comes, I think, from Augustine's ability to reflect so brilliantly on his own conversion experience, which he wrote in the form of a prayer, as if he were having an intimate conversation with God about his soul's journey to God.

Casting off the faith of his mother when he was only a teenager, Augustine (A.D. 354-430) sampled various philosophies and lifestyles before realizing that only God could answer the deepest questions of his mind and satisfy the deepest desires of his heart. He indulged himself in physical pleasure, but it failed to deliver what it promised. No matter how much he enjoyed the lusts of the flesh, he always ended up wanting more. He strove for success, fame and recognition, but these too led to bitter disappointment. He discovered over time that he had become a prisoner to his base desires and ambitions, which threatened to destroy his life. What he truly desired, of course, was to know God. "I was hankering after honors, wealth and marriage," he prayed to God, "but you were laughing at me. Very bitter were the frustrations I endured in chasing my desires, but all the greater was your kindness in being less and less prepared to let anything other than yourself grow sweet to me."[1] Not that pleasure and beauty and ambition are evil in themselves. They become evil only when pursued apart from God. God must always be first in our lives because God is the center, source and end of all existence. "Sin gains entrance through these and similar good things when we turn to them with immoderate desire, since they are the lowest kind of goods and we thereby turn away from the better and

Augustine, *The Confessions*

Late have I loved you, Beauty so ancient and so new,
late have I loved you!
Lo, you were within,
but I outside, seeking there for you,
and upon the shapely things you have made I rushed headlong,
I, misshapen.
You were with me, but I was not with you.
They held me back far from you,
those things which would have no being
were they not in you.
You called, shouted, broke through my deafness;
you flared, blazed, banished my blindness;
you lavished your fragrance, I gasped, and now I pant for you;
I tasted you, and I hunger and thirst;
you touched me, and I burned for your peace.

higher: from you yourself, O Lord our God, and your truth and your law."[2] Augustine eventually surrendered his life to God, but only after a long and tumultuous struggle.

CAN WE LEARN FROM HISTORY?

Augustine

The power of Augustine's story explains why I have chosen to write a book on the history of Christian spirituality. *The Confessions* is about one's man journey to God. It still speaks, even though it was written 1,600 years ago. Augustine is one saint among hundreds whose stories need to be told, remembered and cherished, for they remind us that we are not alone, that we do not know it all, that we have not exhausted the depths of the Christian faith. Their voices echo to us across the centuries, saying, "There is more, so much more!" They invite us to drink more deeply from the well of living water available in the Christian faith, which promises to satisfy the deepest thirst in all of us, a thirst that is part of our very nature as human beings who have been created by God and for God but who have rebelled against God and tried to find satisfaction in something less worthy. This insatiable thirst can only be quenched in one way—in a more intimate relationship with God as we know him in the face of his Son, Jesus Christ, and through the life-giving power of the Holy Spirit. Only the triune God can satisfy our deepest longings.

Much of what we see and experience in contemporary Christianity is not leading us into the depths of God. If anything, it is making us feel restless and dissatisfied. *There must be more than this!* we say to ourselves. We grow weary of trivial controversies and petty jealousies that divide the church, massive buildings and glittery programs that dazzle but do not make disciples, self-help sermons that gloss over the great truths of the biblical faith, styles of worship that pander to popular tastes, Christian leaders who strive for political influence at the cost of faithfulness to the gospel. Not that all things contemporary are uniformly and unequivocally bad. American Christianity in particular is thriving; it boasts of high rates of church attendance and exercises broad influence in our culture. Still, success itself can deceive us into thinking we know it all and have it all, as if the world has been breathlessly waiting for us to arrive on the scene.

Every generation of believers faces the risk of becoming a prisoner to its own myopic vision of the Christian faith, assuming that how it understands and practices faith is always the best. C. S. Lewis cited this problem as a reason for reading old books. "None of us," he wrote, "can fully escape this blindness, but we shall certainly increase it, and weaken our guard against it, if we read only modern books," for modern books (as well as the ideas and practices they convey) only tell us what we already know and thus reinforce our blind spots and prejudices. "The only palliative is to keep the clean sea breeze of the centuries blowing through our minds, and this can be done only by reading old books." Of course people from the past did not get everything right. "People were no cleverer then than they are now; they made as many mistakes as we. But not the same mistakes." Their successes will teach us; their failures will warn us. "Two heads are better than one, not because either is infallible, but because they are unlikely to go wrong in the same direction."[3]

History can be a valuable resource for us, especially in the spiritual life, for it provides examples of how believers who lived in other times and places understood what it means to seek, know and experience God, which captures the essential meaning of "spirituality."[4] As different as they are from us, these believers can teach us truths about the Christian faith that we have not yet learned or do not consider important.[5] It could be that returning to the old ways will enable us to live a new way for God, a way characterized by deeper knowledge, richer experience and greater faithfulness to the gospel. It could be that discovering old truths will enable us to live as new people, a people devoted to serving God's kingdom. It could be that by looking back we will be able to look ahead and set a new course for our lives. History will show us that there is more to the Christian faith than what we think and have experienced. It will teach us truths that our contemporary religious blind spots prevent us from seeing, challenge us to read Scripture with new eyes, beckon us to practice spiritual disciplines we never tried before, and enable us to view our own time and place from a fresh perspective. The Holy Spirit will use the knowledge of history to send us on a journey that could lead us into the depths of God.

Why history? History is fundamental to the faith because Christianity itself tells a story—a true story as it turns out—about how God plans to redeem the world. At its barest and simplest, this story recounts how God created the world good, how the world went bad through human sin, and how God is now restoring the world to goodness again through Jesus Christ. The most important part of that story has been recorded in the Bible, which provides the record of salvation history. But that redemptive story did not end at the close of the New Testament. It has continued to this day, and it will not end until God brings history to a glorious ending. How God is working today is as relevant and vital as it was during the time of the apostles, for God remains active in the world. His plan is still unfolding; his commitment to redeem the world is as firm now as it ever was. History has always been the arena of God's activity.[6] What God initiated with Abraham and accomplished in Jesus he promises to continue in and through people like us, until all things are made well and whole again. We too can play a part in this epic story.

History exposes us to people who, though often different from us, have valuable things to teach us. Some suffered martyrdom, which is virtually unheard of in the Western church (though not in the Two-Thirds World church); others spent years in desert solitude before assuming positions of leadership in the church; still others sailed to distant lands to preach the gospel and serve the poor, never to return to their homelands. They read the same Bible we read, worshiped the same God we worship and followed the same Lord we follow, though often in ways that differ from us. These differences do not necessarily make them better than modern believers. They were sinners too; their record of spiritual achievement was not unstained; their ventures did not always succeed. They were as flawed as we are. Not everything that has occurred in the history of the church has been true, right and good. Much said in the name of God has been errant; much done in the name of God has been abhorrent. *Strange* and *different* are not always the right words to use. Sometimes *misguided* and *destructive* are.

Any movement can go bad, like good food that spoils. But corruption does not imply worthlessness. *Abusus non tollit usus*, reads a famous Latin phrase. "Abuses do not destroy uses." History tells the story of many abuses. But these obvious abuses should not distract or detract us. Eastern Orthodox iconography can be gaudy and obtrusive, but it also depicts in artistic form the future glory of believers; Catholic sacramentalism can lead to a purely external and formal faith, but it also reminds us that God uses the material—water, oil, bread and wine—to communicate grace; Reformation doctrine can engender a faith that exalts head above heart, but it also affirms the importance of biblical fidelity. No tradition has it all right or all wrong. Still, we, the offspring and heirs of these saints and the great traditions they represent, enjoy one huge advantage. We can learn from them because we come later in the story. Chronology works in our favor. The saints could not see us, but we can see them, study the past they helped to create and learn from their feats and errors. We will be the better for it if we do, for they have much to teach us.

We have much to learn too, but only if we are humble and teachable. Augustine once wrote that the only way to understand something is to love it first, that is, to study it with sympathy, patience and appreciation. True understanding requires the courage to surrender ourselves to the subject and let it have its way with us.[7] In his wonderful essay "Meditations in a Toolshed," C. S. Lewis observed that there are essentially two ways to learn something. We can look *at* the subject from another—and usually alien—point of view, which gives us ultimate authority over the subject; or we can look *along* it, allowing the subject itself to illumine the world for us.[8] Obviously both are legitimate methods of study. Still, I prefer the latter. This book therefore travels *along* the beam of spiritual light that streams from the martyrs and mystics, Puritans and pioneer missionaries, ascetics and artists. That beam of light will shine into our lives too. It will expose us for the shallow Christians we sometimes are; it will also inspire us to persevere. It will illumine the pathway lying before us, drawing us ever closer to the light that is God himself, thus fulfilling what the psalmist said, "In thy light shall we see light" (KJV).

Unfortunately, history is not a subject we naturally turn to for spiritual help. There is a bias against history in our culture, especially religious history. We tend to be preoccupied with the present, captured by the contemporary, attracted to anything that is immediate and current. We assume for some reason that what has happened most recently is always—or at least usually—the most important. We therefore view the past with a certain degree of indifference, suspicion, even snobbery, thinking it obsolete and irrelevant, like a piece of outdated technology, before we have given it a chance to teach us anything. Consequently, we criticize or ignore before we have even bothered to listen and understand. We might be missing out on more than we know.[9]

I teach in the department of theology at Whitworth University, a private liberal-arts university located in Spokane, Washington. The university's academic calendar includes a January term during which students enroll in just one three credit course. Many professors use the time to take the students off-campus to such faraway places as South Africa, Thailand, Germany, Turkey and Honduras. About ten years ago I started to teach a course at a camp located in a remote area of the Cascade Mountain Range. The students and I stay there for a month. There are no distractions—no telephones, radios, televisions, cell phones, e-mail or computers. We live in community and follow a modified Benedictine Rule, which includes worship four times a day, four hours of quiet for prayer and study, small group discussion, mutual service and, of course, play (e.g., cross-country skiing). The purpose of the course is to expose students to the history of Christian spirituality.

Something happens to those students during that month away. It is not the setting alone that changes them, however beautiful it is. It is the subject matter. The history of spirituality becomes their history, and the characters they meet along the way become members of their spiritual family. At first students are put off by the unfamiliarity and strangeness of what they learn, for the history of Christian spirituality introduces them to a whole new world. But over time the students find the stories of the saints compelling, holy and beautiful. The strangeness no longer offends them; if anything, it fascinates, captures and moves them. This history inspires them to dare to be different, only in a way that is appropriate and relevant to their own time and place.[10]

IS THE CHRISTIAN FAITH REALLY TRUE?

But there is another reason why *The Confessions* speak so powerfully. Augustine did more than tell his story. He also used his story to proclaim the pivotal truth of the Christian faith, which has been ultimately revealed to us through Jesus Christ, the one who reveals God and unites us with God. "Accordingly I looked for a way to gain the strength I need to enjoy you," Augustine prayed to God, "but I did not find it until I embraced the mediator between God and humankind, the man Jesus Christ, who also is God, supreme over all things and blessed forever."[11]

Many religions claim to speak truth about God or the gods or some ultimate reality. But such a claim raises a question. How do we know it is true? The Christian faith provides an answer. God chose to tell us the truth about himself by revealing himself to us as a human being. The first followers of Jesus could not have arrived at this conclusion through their own ingenuity, intelligence and creativity alone, for it was simply outside the realm of possibility for any devout Jew. Thomas's unthinkable confession of faith illustrates the transformation that occurred in the disciples. Hearing that Jesus was alive again after the crucifixion, Thomas refused to believe the preposterous rumor unless he could touch the nail prints on Jesus' hands and feet. Appearing before Thomas, Jesus invited him to do just that. Thomas immediately fell to his knees and exclaimed, "My Lord and my God" (Jn 20:28). Jews reserve such a confession only for God, whom they believe is one, holy and transcendent. But here was Thomas, using the divine name for Jesus, thereby proving that the disciples believed that Jesus is truly God, the divine self-portrait in human flesh. In their minds Jesus Christ makes God visible, human and knowable. They worshiped him, prayed to him and surrendered their lives to him, though as Jews they held strictly to a monotheistic faith.

This belief in what Christians call the incarnation set in motion a long, complex debate about how to understand the nature of God and the nature of Christ, assuming, as the first disciples did, that Jesus truly was divine. Over roughly four hundred years Christians came to two startling conclusions. First, they concluded that God is a relationship of love; God is one in community, or a tri-unity. God is love not simply because he loves his creation but because he is love within himself. The Father loves the Son;

the Son loves the Father. The Holy Spirit, who lives in our hearts, is the perfect, pure and personal essence of that relationship, thus drawing us into the love that exists within the very being of God.

Second, they concluded that Christ is both perfectly divine and perfectly human. His divine nature does not overwhelm his human nature, nor does his human nature diminish his divine nature. He is God and man simultaneously. Thus, if we want to know who God truly is, we must look at Jesus Christ; if we want to know what a human being truly is, we must likewise look at Jesus Christ.[12] As Augustine discovered, ultimate reality has come to earth, God has become human, immortality has submitted to mortality, all for our sake. "This mediator between God and humankind, the man Jesus Christ, appeared to stand between mortal sinners and the God who is immortal and just: like us he was mortal, but like God he was just." It was this Jesus, perfectly divine and human, who won our salvation. "How you loved us, for whose sake he who deemed it no robbery to be your equal was made subservient, even to the point of dying on the cross. . . . For our sake he stood to you as both victor and victim, and victor because victim; for us he stood to you as priest and sacrifice, and priest because sacrifice."[13]

This firm confidence that the Christian faith is actually and absolutely true runs contrary to much of contemporary spirituality. Spirituality itself has become something of a cultural fad. Politicians, celebrities, scholars and the media frequently use the term without bothering to define it. If anything, the ambiguity serves a useful purpose. In modern American culture we can be "spiritual" without actually believing in a particular faith tradition and belonging to a particular faith community, especially Christianity. This kind of fuzzy spirituality allows us to fashion a spiritual life that suits our immediate interests and consumer tastes. But such spirituality often lacks substance, integrity and discipline. It means everything and nothing at the same time; it is as vacuous as Hollywood's definition of love.

The history of Christian spirituality will not let us settle for such vacuity, emptiness and relativism. Not that there is complete uniformity in the church. The purpose of this book, after all, is to explore the *diversity* of Christian spirituality. Still, however diverse these various traditions are, there is an underlying truth that unites them. From the apostolic age to the present, the vast majority of Christians have believed that God has revealed himself in Jesus Christ, that Jesus Christ is both divine and human, and that God is therefore one in community. My goal is to explore how these various spiritual traditions—ascetic, monastic, sacramental, evangelical and the like—reveal who God is, how we can know him intimately, and what we can become in and through him.

The book follows a historical chronology; it begins with the spirituality of early Christian martyrdom and ends with the spirituality of pioneer missionaries. Each chapter contains a seminal idea, captured in a word or phrase. We will explore how each of these ideas grew out of a particular set of historical circumstances and unfolded over time, eventually contributing to the rich history of Christian spirituality we have at our disposal today. For example, one idea, "witness," captures the spirituality of the early martyrs, "rhythm" the spirituality of early medieval monasticism, "Word" the spirituality of the Reformers and "risk" the spirituality of pioneer missionaries. Typical of any work on a historical subject, this book will provide a collage of anecdotes and introduce a cast of magnetic, if sometimes eccentric, characters along the way. I hope that there will be enough information contained in these pages to stretch the most learned person, but not so much to frustrate the person who is tackling the topic for the first time. The endnotes contain references for readers who want to know more about the sources, and they provide suggestions for further reading. My aim is to write a usable and accessible history, one that is fair to the past and relevant to the present.

"All things are yours," Paul said to the believers in Corinth, who had formed exclusive religious parties around the teachings of prominent leaders in the church, obviously without the approval of the leaders themselves. There was the Apollos group, the Peter group, the Paul group, even the Jesus group. Each group claimed certain distinctives that made it feel superior to the others. Paul argued that they were depriving themselves of the benefits of learning from *all* the teachers, who had been called to use their gifts for the common good of the whole church. "So let no one boast about human leaders. For all things are yours, whether Paul or Apollos or Cephas [Peter] or the world or life or death or the present or the future—all belong to you, and you belong to Christ, and Christ belongs to God" (1 Cor 3:21-23).

"All things are ours," including the rich history of the church. I invite you to embark on this journey through history with me, to meet and befriend the family of faith that has lived through the ages, and to learn from this "great cloud of witnesses." These people, our brothers and sisters in Christ, loved, served and followed God as best they could in their own time and place. Their examples can help us do the same. As they would want to say to us, "There is more, so much more."

1

Witness

The Spirituality of the Early Christian Martyrs

"There is salvation in no one else,
for there is no other name under heaven given among mortals
by which we must be saved."

ACTS 4:12

A visit to the Roman arena might seem like a strange place to begin this book. Yet it is where we must begin, for the ancient arena is the place where early Christians bore courageous witness to their faith in Jesus Christ and demonstrated their determination to remain faithful to him, no matter what the cost. Arenas in the ancient world functioned much like our modern arenas do, as places of entertainment. But the entertainment back then was cruel, brutal and bloody. Gladiators fought to the death, charioteers raced to victory or died trying, wild beasts mauled slaves, prisoners and enemies of the state. Victors won the crowd's admiration, and perhaps even achieved fame or freedom; losers were maimed for life, if they survived at all.

Christians met their death in the arena too. Their suffering satiated the bloodlust of the mob, which assembled to watch them being torn apart by animals or run through with a gladiator's sword. The martyrdom of Chris-

The Christian martyrs' last prayer

tians was a public event that provided entertainment for average citizens and warned the faithful that they could be next.[1] Ironically, this persecution achieved the opposite result for which it was intended. Rather than snuff out the Christian movement, persecution fanned it. The blood of the Christians, as Tertullian said so long ago, became seed, inspiring believers and impressing—or enraging—pagans (that is, those who practiced the ancient religions or participated in foreign cults). Spectators wondered where these Christians found their courage and what kind of religion could inspire such sacrifice.[2]

We will never understand Christian spirituality—what it is and what makes it unique—unless we grasp the significance of martyrdom. The early Christians died because they confessed Jesus Christ as Lord. His lordship challenged all other ultimate claims on their lives—wealth, status, power and Rome itself. They believed that Jesus tolerates no rivals. When forced to choose, they chose to follow Jesus, no matter what the price. The early martyrs paid an extreme price, their very lives. But the value of their example is not in the martyrdom itself, however noble and courageous, but in their commitment to Christ's lordship. That we might not have to die for Christ is irrelevant. How we *live* for Christ is the real issue.

PERSECUTION IN THE NEW TESTAMENT

Considering the story line of the New Testament, the martyrdom of Christians during the early Christian period should not come as a complete surprise to us. Persecution, suffering and death are at the heart of the Christian message. The cross, an instrument of gruesome execution, became by A.D. 500 the primary symbol of the faith because it reminded believers then, as it does to this day, of Jesus' ignominious sacrifice on the cross. The New Testament recounts story after story of persecution and suffering, not only in the Gospel accounts, which narrate the story of Jesus' life, but also in the book of Acts, which tells the story of the early church. Stephen was the first Christian to be martyred, and the apostle James faced a similar fate only a few years later. Paul encountered opposition wherever he traveled. His life was one long experience of suffering—beatings, imprisonment, shipwrecks, betrayals, sleeplessness and deprivations of every kind, all for the sake of the gospel.[3]

The New Testament addresses the issue of persecution so often that it begins to sound like static on a radio, always buzzing in the background. It is easy to grow accustomed to the noise and thus to ignore it, especially if we find it difficult to identify personally with the actual experience of persecution. Jesus taught his disciples, "Blessed are you when people revile you and persecute you and utter all kinds of evil against you falsely on my account" (Mt 5:11-12). Before sending his disciples out on their first missionary journey, he warned them:

> See, I am sending you out like sheep into the midst of wolves. . . . Beware of them, for they will hand you over to councils and flog you in their synagogues; and you will be dragged before governors and kings because of me as a testimony to them and the Gentiles. . . . and you will be hated by all for my name. (Mt 10:16-18, 22)

Paul reminded the Christians of his day that they should regard persecution as a necessary aspect of discipleship. "Indeed, all who want to live a godly life in Christ Jesus will be persecuted" (2 Tim 3:12). Paul even suggested that his suffering somehow helped to complete the sufferings of Christ. "I am now rejoicing in my sufferings for your sake, and in my flesh I am completing what is lacking in Christ's afflictions for the sake of his body, that is, the church" (Col 1:24). He claimed that his entire life embodied a kind of martyrdom. "I have been crucified with Christ; and it is no longer I who live, but it is Christ who lives in me" (Gal 2:19-20). He saw life in Christ as nothing but gain, even if it required death. "For to me, living is Christ and dying is gain" (Phil 1:21). Peter exhorted the churches in Asia Minor to prepare for the inevitable. "Beloved, do not be surprised at the fiery ordeal that is taking place among you to test you, as though something strange were happening to you." He referred to the suffering of Jesus as an example worthy of imitation. "But rejoice insofar as you are sharing Christ's sufferings, so that you may also be glad and shout for joy when his glory is revealed. . . . Yet if any of you suffers as a Christian, do not consider it a disgrace, but glorify God because you bear his name" (1 Pet 4:12-13, 16).

We are often at a loss to know how to respond to these texts, largely because our faith has followed a drastically different course, one far more agreeable to our creature comforts. Most of us rarely think about persecution and martyrdom, and for an understandable reason. We have never had to face it, nor have the vast majority of Christians living in the West. Thus when we read contemporary accounts of persecutions in countries like Indonesia, Vietnam, India or Nepal, we are never quite sure what to think about them. Two Whitworth students recently attended a graduation ceremony of a seminary located in a non-Western country. Several of the graduates performed a dramatization of the biblical story of the stoning of Stephen, the first Christian martyr. They were not being playful or irreverent but solemn and serious. At the end of the ceremony the students with one voice pledged to remain faithful to God even in the face of the threat of martyrdom, for they knew that at least a few of them would most likely suffer a fate similar to Stephen's. Our experience is far different. Considering the suffering of Christians around the world today, it is probably the exception too. Discipleship implies suffering, leads to persecution, tests mettle, demands steadfastness, requires endurance and even leads to death. It demands that we confess Jesus as Lord.

Not that we should glorify or seek martyrdom as a good in itself, as if the Christian faith validates or even encourages the use of violence. Much of the martyrdom we read about today, especially in the form of suicide bombing, is the complete opposite of the martyrdom that Christians suffered in the first few centuries. These modern "martyrs"—if we dare even use the word to describe such horrific acts—bear witness to a God of vengeance, hate and murder, not a God of love. The early Christian martyrs were victims of such hate, not perpetrators. They absorbed violence; they did not inflict it. They were called to martyrdom; they did not force it on innocent people, which is what suicide bombers do today. In early Christianity martyrdom was only one of many ways to bear witness to the truth of the gospel. Not every Christian was—and is—called to literal martyrdom; still, every Christian is called to surrender his or her life to God.

I have never known a person who suffered martyrdom. But I am acquainted with people who have personally known martyrs, and I have heard their stories. For some reason these stories linger in my memory like vivid dreams that refuse to fade over time. In one case two young pastors, traveling on motor scooters to do their pastoral work in a neighboring village, were accosted by a mob and beaten to death for no other reason than that they were Christians. Their story does not make me want to die a martyr's death; it is too gruesome and horrible for that. But it does make me want to live a martyr's life, for they had the courage to give their lives completely to Jesus Christ. Their faith in Christ puts a fire in me to honor Christ, "whether by life or by death," as the apostle Paul put it. It is that passion to live for Christ that makes the stories of martyrdoms, both ancient and modern, so compelling and convicting.

STORIES OF THE MARTYRS

The Christian movement got its start in the Roman world, a massive empire wrapping itself like a garment around the Mediterranean Sea. At first Christianity appeared to be little more than a sect within the ancient religion of Judaism. After all, both religions claimed the same holy city, quoted the same Scripture, spoke the same language and followed many of the same rituals. But Christianity soon reached out to Gentiles and spread throughout the Roman world, gradually separating from Judaism. By the year A.D. 100 this fledgling faith had planted a church in most of the major cities of the Roman Empire. Unlike Judaism, Christianity was from the very beginning a missionary faith, intent on winning converts. Its mem-

bers were so exhilarated by the message of the incarnation, death and resurrection of Jesus that they could not keep quiet. What the movement
lacked in size, prestige and power it made up for in enthusiasm and courage. This was good news—gospel—that had to be shared!

Christianity was not the only new religion to arrive on the scene, not by
far. The Roman Empire became a grudging host to dozens of new religions, most of which came from the East. Christianity was perhaps the
newest, but certainly not the wealthiest or largest. It is hard to imagine,
therefore, why people in positions of power even bothered with it, let alone
thought it deserving of persecution. As late as the year A.D. 200, scholars
say, the church did not comprise much more than 1 percent of the population. Rome was actually quite tolerant of these new religions. Yet Rome
persecuted the Christians. There was something about this one religion
that set it apart, making it an obvious target.[4]

The earliest nonbiblical stories of martyrdoms, which date from the
second century, serve as powerful reminders of how Christians in the early
centuries were willing to pay a high price to bear witness to a faith they
considered priceless. Eyewitnesses recorded the events as they saw them,
and then church officials (usually bishops) edited, expanded and sometimes embellished these stories before circulating them among the
churches. Their purpose was to inspire Christians to be faithful, courageous and bold, to remind them of the truth of the gospel, and to challenge
them to live for Christ.[5] Scholars are unsure of the exact number of Christians executed during this early period, from the close of the apostolic age
to A.D. 313, when Emperor Constantine issued an edict that gave Christianity legal protection. Estimates vary from perhaps three thousand to ten
thousand. In any case, the number does not appear to be very high, if numbers alone concern us. Then again, the total number of Christians was not
very high either. Besides, Rome tended to target church leaders for martyrdom, hoping that their deaths would intimidate their fellow Christians
and break apart the movement.[6]

The accounts are both terrifying and holy. As we reflect on these stories
in armchair security, we run the risk of treating them as little more than a
curiosity or a spectacle. It is easy to gawk but not learn, listen but not sym-
pathize and thus trivialize what is sacred. These stories are not fanciful, fic-

tional accounts that have been recorded and passed down for our entertainment. The martyrs were real people who did in fact die horribly. They had families and friends, hopes and longings, and they wanted to live a long, peaceful and prosperous life, just like us. They chose to accept death rather than renounce their faith because they believed something was more valuable than the long and happy life for which they longed, for "whatever gain" they had they "counted as loss for the sake of Christ" (Phil 3:8 NASB).

It was their witness to Christ that led to martyrdom, which in turn provided opportunities for witness. But witness was always primary because the martyrs held the conviction that the gospel is indeed true. They wanted to tell the world about Christ, and not even the threat of death could stop them. Ironically, the word for "witness" in the Greek language—*martyria*—is the root word for "martyr" in the English language. Witness and martyrdom became, over time, virtually synonymous, for Christian witness often led to death, which in turn allowed for greater witness. The great historian of early Christianity, W. H. C. Frend, observes that "the distinction between witnessing and suffering on account of that witness was becoming a fine one, and it could only be a matter of time before actual persecution would equate them."[7]

Justin Martyr, a noteworthy second-century theologian and apologist, became a Christian after he had watched the brutal execution of several Christians in Rome. He was moved by their courage and serenity, and he was intrigued by a faith that could engender such uncompromising conviction. After his conversion he attempted to explain to secular critics why Christians were willing to die.

> We do not give up our confession though we be executed by the sword, though we be crucified, thrown to wild beasts, put in chains, and exposed to fire and every other kind of torture. Everyone knows this. On the contrary, the more we are persecuted and martyred, the more do others in ever increasing numbers become believers and God-fearing people through the name of Jesus.[8]

Justin knew what he was talking about; he too died for his faith in the middle of the second century. Like other martyrs, he bore witness to Christ through his death.

Consider just one example from the pen of Justin; it is typical of what occurred in early Christianity. In A.D. 165, two men, Carpus and Papylus, were brought before the proconsul of Pergamum, charged with the crime of being Christian. When urged to sacrifice to the gods, Carpus replied, "I am a Christian. I honor Christ, the son of God, who has come in the latter times to save us and has delivered us from the madness of the devil. I will not sacrifice to these devils." Not even torture could persuade him to change his mind. He simply kept repeating, "I am a Christian." Then the proconsul turned to Papylus, who said, "I have served God since my youth. I have never sacrificed to idols. I am a Christian. You cannot learn anything else from me. There is nothing I can say which is greater or more wonderful than this." As the two were being burned alive, Carpus said, "Praise be to thee, O Lord, Jesus Christ, Son of God, that thou didst deem me, a sinner, also worthy of this part in thee!"[9]

Carpus and Papylus never committed an actual crime. Why then were Christians like them singled out for such brutal punishment? It seems to make little sense, for it was common knowledge that Christians espoused a religion of love and peace, served the common good of society and prayed for the emperor. Far from posing a threat to the empire, Christians demonstrated that they were good citizens of the empire. What was so threatening about Christianity?

Comforted by the joy of martyrdom. There are four reasons why Rome persecuted Christians. First, pagans viewed Christians with suspicion because they considered Christianity a strange and threatening foreign cult. Roman officials did not like anything that was non-Roman, especially if it was religious in nature. Christianity was both. Not surprisingly, then, critics called Christianity a "superstition," and thus "depraved, excessive, foreign, and new," as the Roman governor Pliny stated in a letter to the Emperor Trajan, written in A.D. 112.[10]

"The Martyrs of Lyons" tells the story of the gruesome deaths of a number of Christians living in Lyons, a city in Gaul (modern-day France). The account is long and rich in detail, and it tells us much about why Roman officials and pagan mobs hated, tortured and killed Christians. In addition to the story itself, it also includes spiritual commentary, biblical quotations and exhortations along the way. In A.D. 177 an angry, resentful group of pagans began to abuse Christians living in Lyons.[11] "The Adversary swooped down with full force," the account reads, inciting the mob to beat, stone and imprison them. Eventually a prefect leveled charges against them. Christians, he said, participated in orgies, practiced cannibalism and indulged in incest. That Christians kept to themselves and practiced their rituals in secret only exacerbated the problem. These accusations might sound ridiculous to us now, knowing what we do about early Christian belief and practice, but back then they demonstrated the ignorance of pagans, who confused the Christian love feast with orgies, the Eucharist with cannibalism and the use of terms of endearment—*brother* and *sister*—with incest.

Prison guards began to beat and torture the Christian prisoners, hoping to force them to deny that they were Christian; but no one would compromise. To the contrary, some who had initially denied the faith to spare their lives later stepped forward and admitted they were Christians, which only infuriated the officials even more. Day after day the abuse continued, and deaths began to mount up. One man, Pothinus, bore the indignities with unusual courage and serenity, considering his age, for he was ninety years old. "He was brought to the tribunal by the soldiers, accompanied by some of the civil magistrates and the entire mob, who raised all kinds of shouts at him as though he were Christ himself. He gave a noble witness."

There were miracles too, but of a very peculiar kind. In one instance Christians discovered that they had been confined in prison with common criminals, which gave them an opportunity to tell these fellow prisoners about Christ. The guards and mob also noticed the clear difference between the two groups. "For [the Christians] were comforted by the joy of martyrdom, their hope in the promises, their love for Christ, and the Spirit of the Father; whereas the other [pagan prisoners] were greatly tormented by their conscience, so that as they passed by they were easily distinguished by their looks from all the others." The "miracle" was their witness, not some spectacular deliverance, which leads John D. Ziziouslas to the conclusion that "those who possess the Spirit are not so much the Christians who prophesy and perform supernatural acts as the martyrs who give their lives for Christ."[12]

Finally, those few who had survived torture and deprivation in prison were led into the arena, where they were torn apart by beasts or killed by the gladiator's sword. But not even martyrdom could silence them. Their courage in the face of death left an impression long after they were gone. Pagans wondered about the source of the inspiration and confidence of the martyrs. How could they endure such pain? What kind of religious belief could produce such conviction? What seemed most striking was their motivation. The martyrs were "intensely eager to imitate and emulate Christ." Amazingly, they even refused to accept the title of martyr, for "it was their joy to yield the title of martyr to Christ alone." He alone was worthy of honor and glory. Their deaths served only as a witness to the power of the gospel to transform human life. "They made a defense of their faith to all, but accused no one; they loosed all, but bound none. Indeed, they prayed for those who had used them so cruelly."[13]

The wild accusations leveled against Christians seem outrageous, hard to take seriously, both then and now, for the courage and love they demonstrated in the face of suffering showed them to be people of upright character, not the kind who would commit such vile acts.[14] That Christianity was viewed as foreign, strange and immoral, therefore, probably diverted attention from more important concerns. Rome was alarmed about things that were far more threatening than the peculiar rituals that Christians practiced.

The day of their victory dawned. Christians practiced a way of life that passed implicit judgment on Roman society, which is the second reason why Christians were persecuted. Christians believed that life in this world is not the only or the most important life there is. They considered themselves citizens of heaven, and they tried to live consistently with that conviction.[15] Life in the world to come mattered more to them than life in this world. This orientation toward heaven separated Christians from Roman society and kept them from participating in popular forms of Roman entertainment. Christian leaders in particular considered Roman entertainment—the "games" and the theater, for example—corrupt, and thus off limits for the community. Early Christian documents spoke harshly against these popular activities and warned Christians to avoid them.[16] Pagan writers also observed that Christians tended to remain somewhat separate from society. For example, Tacitus, a Roman historian, commented cynically that Christians were "haters of humankind" because they refused to participate in popular Roman culture, which left the impression that they were anti-Roman.[17]

The story of Perpetua's martyrdom, perhaps the most famous of all early martyr stories, illustrates how firmly Christians resisted the encroachment of Roman culture. In the early third century the emperor Septimius Severus established a policy that disallowed conversions to Christianity. Soon a severe persecution broke out in Carthage, North Africa. Vibia Perpetua (A.D. 181-203), young, married and mother to a newborn, was arrested with several others (including her brother and a servant) and thrown into prison. She was probably singled out because she came from a prominent family, which made her conversion more public and her faith more threatening.

Perpetua

Shortly after her imprisonment Perpetua learned in a vision that she was soon to die. In the vision she saw a ladder reaching to heaven. She had to climb it, which she did with ease, in spite of the dragon guarding it. When she arrived at the summit she saw an immense garden; in the center sat a tall, gray-haired man dressed like a shepherd, surrounded by thousands of people dressed in white robes. He said to her, "Welcome, my child." Then he invited her to approach and gave her a morsel of cheese, which tasted sweet to her. When she awoke she described the vision to her brother. "We realized that we would have to suffer, and that from now on we would no longer have any hope in this life."

Court hearings followed; family passions flared. Her father kept pleading with her. "Do not abandon me to be the reproach of men. Think of your brothers, think of your mother and your aunt, think of your child, who will not be able to live once you are gone. Give up your pride! You will destroy all of us!" Others urged her to sacrifice to the emperor and gods. "Perform the sacrifice—have pity on your baby!" But Perpetua would not yield. "I am a Christian," she kept repeating. Finally the governor condemned her to the beasts. Far from being enraged or terrified, Perpetua

Perpetua's Martyrdom

"The day of their victory dawned, and they marched from the prison to the amphitheatre joyfully as though they were going to heaven, with calm faces, trembling, if at all, with joy rather than fear. Perpetua went along with shining countenance and calm step, as the beloved of God, as a wife of Christ, putting down everyone's stare by her own intense gaze. . . . Perpetua began to sing a psalm: she was already treading on the head of the Egyptian. . . . Then when they came within sight of Hilarianus, they suggested by their motions and gestures: 'You have condemned us, but God will condemn you' was what they were saying. At this the crowds became enraged and demanded that they be scourged before a line of gladiators. And they rejoiced at this that they had obtained a share in the Lord's sufferings. . . . The others took the sword in silence and without moving, especially Saturus, who being the first to climb the stairway was the first to die. For once again he was waiting for Perpetua. Perpetua, however, had yet to taste more pain. She screamed as she was struck on the bone; then she took the trembling hand of the young gladiator and guided it to her throat. It was as though so great a woman, feared as she was by the unclean spirit, could not be dispatched unless she herself were willing." (The Acts of the Christian Martyrs)

"returned to prison in high spirits." Again, people began to take notice. One prison guard was so moved that he "began to show us great honor, realizing that we possessed some great power within us."

Perpetua cared little about what she would lose, however severe the loss seemed to be. Instead, she fixed her eyes on heaven, which she considered a greater reality than life in this world. Just before her death she had a vision that reminded her of the victory that was sure to be hers: a man came to her prison door and escorted her to the arena. She noticed that a huge crowd was watching her. Then she saw a fierce Egyptian who was about to attack her. Suddenly she became a great warrior ready to do combat with the enemy. She started to fight the Egyptian, whom she defeated by stepping on his head. The crowds shouted their approval, while a man clad in a purple robe said to her, "Peace be with you, my daughter!" "Then I woke up realizing that I would be contending not with wild animals but with the devil himself. I knew, however, that I would win."

The account makes clear that Perpetua was not a hero but a witness to Christ.

> Ah, most valiant and blessed martyrs! Truly you are called and chosen for the glory of Christ Jesus our Lord! . . . For these new manifestations of virtue will bear witness to one and the same Spirit who still operates, and to God the Father almighty, and to his Son Jesus Christ our Lord, to whom is splendor and immeasurable power for all the ages. Amen.[18]

What inspired Perpetua to be so courageous and joyful? Her story is especially troubling to me because I have a twenty-two-year-old daughter. I know that I would have been tempted to respond as Perpetua's father did and beg my daughter Catherine to forsake faith in Christ, for surely in such dire circumstances life would seem preferable to death. How could I bear losing my daughter, however noble and right the cause? Yet Perpetua refused to yield, even to the pleas of her father, the cries of her baby and the scorn of the crowds. For the sake of Christ she happily submitted to death. She made a decision, not between life and death but between Christ and Rome. Her courage and determination only reminded them that perhaps there was more to these Christians than meets the eye. Could it be that what they believed was actually true? If so, then the state itself would have to face competition that it had never had to face before.

Are you a Christian? In fact, Christian allegiance to the lordship of Christ threatened Rome's hegemony, which provides a third reason why Rome persecuted Christians. Surprisingly, Rome was quite tolerant of religion, and Romans considered themselves to be a very religious and pious people. One of their greatest philosophers, Cicero, once commented that, though in many respects Rome was much like other civilizations, "yet in the sense of religion, that is in the worship of the gods, we are far superior."[19] They dutifully observed cultic activities, maintained public monuments and temples, and participated in religious ceremonies, all for the purpose of establishing good order and ensuring the prosperity of Rome. A wide variety of religious beliefs was considered acceptable, provided that they served the interests of the state, contributed to the well-being of the empire and honored the ultimate authority of the emperor. In short, Rome tolerated religious diversity as long as the real religion of Rome was honored, which was Rome itself.[20] The rise of emperor worship, which occurred late in the first century, only reinforced this idea. The emperor became a symbol of the religion of Rome, the religion that *was* Rome.

Justin Martyr's *Second Apology* tells the story of an unnamed woman who had been converted out of a pagan background. She wanted her husband to embrace the new faith with her and so gently tried to persuade him to become a Christian. But he persisted in unbelief and immoral behavior. So she filed for a divorce. Enraged, her husband brought charges against her in a Roman court, claiming that she had left him without his consent. He also mentioned that she was a Christian, which was probably the more serious charge. He then singled out her pastor too, holding Ptolemaeus responsible for her conversion. So Ptolemaeus was also arrested. After being tortured for some time, Ptolemaeus was brought before a Roman judge, Urbicus, who asked him just one question, "Are you a Christian?" When he confessed that he was, Urbicus ordered his execution. Then another man, Lucius, also present in the courtroom, stood up and protested the judge's arbitrary and unfair judgment. "What is the charge? He has not been convicted of adultery, fornication, murder . . . or of any crime whatsoever; yet you have punished this man because he confesses the name of Christian?" Urbicus replied, "I think you too are one of them." Lucius responded, "Indeed, I am." So he ordered Lucius's execution too. The account ends with one final—and very telling—observation. "Lucius then acknowledged his gratitude," it reads, "realizing that he would now be set free of such evil masters, and would depart for the Father and the king of heaven."[21]

What was it about the name *Christian* that caused such offense? Early Christian writers observed the irony and absurdity of the accusation. Philosopher and apologist Athenagoras, writing a defense of Christianity to the emperor Marcus Aurelius, asked incredulously, "Why is a mere name odious to you? Names are not deserving of hatred; it is the unjust act that calls for penalty and punishment."[22] Tertullian, another late-second-century apologist, protested the legal travesty of the charge. "No name of a crime stands against us, but only the crime of a name. What crime, what offence, what fault is there in a name? . . . All that is cared about is having what the public hatred demands—the confession of a name, not examination of the charge."[23]

It is true that Christians did not commit crimes against the state, like murder. But that did not absolve Christians of guilt, for simply being Christian posed a peculiar kind of threat to Rome. Christians were martyred because they would not bow the knee to Rome, sacrifice to the emperor as a god and treat the empire as if it had ultimate authority. Forced to choose between Jesus and Caesar, Christians for the most part chose Jesus, confessing him as Lord. In nearly every one of the early accounts of martyrdom, this conflict between Christianity and the state surfaces as a major issue. Christian belief had public consequences; Christian practice challenged Rome's quest for dominance. Christianity made claims that threatened the empire.[24] Such conviction was bound to upset the state.

The destroyer of our gods! There is one final reason why Rome persecuted Christianity, and it is the most important. The early Christians viewed their faith as ultimately and exclusively true, which threatened the popular pluralism of the day. "The Romans tolerated a remarkable degree of religious liberty," notes historian Stephen Benko, "and they therefore found the Christians' exclusive claims to truth disconcerting." Pagans assumed that religious truth was by nature ambiguous and obscure, and thus best left open to debate. Christians thought otherwise, for they were certain that God chose to come to earth as Jesus Christ to bring salvation to the world because all other attempts to reach God had failed. "The Christian, however, was convinced that he was in possession of the truth, because Jesus Christ embodied the ultimate revelation about God," concludes Benko.[25]

In the end, therefore, the Christian belief in Jesus as Savior and Lord caused the greatest offense. Critics indicated that they were willing to accept Jesus as *a* way to God, just as they accepted most other ways to God, but only under the condition that Christians would abandon the belief that Jesus was *the* way to God. The Christian confession that Jesus is Lord simply flew in the face of Rome's pluralism and tolerance. It also infuriated the intellectual elite, who understood Christianity well enough to recognize that it would not fit comfortably, if at all, into Roman culture.

S. POLYCARP
BISHOP of SMYRNA.

S. POLYCARPUS.

The martyrdom of the venerable bishop Polycarp, who served the church in Smyrna (located in modern-day Turkey) for many decades, illustrates how offensive Christian belief proved to be. As the story goes, a mob, which had already put several Christians to death, started to call for Polycarp's death too, for he was a well-known leader in the region. His friends persuaded him to withdraw from the city, and he complied, finding a place to hide in the country. Writing an account of the story in the fourth century, Eusebius notes, "There he remained with a few companions, devoting himself night and day to constant prayer to the Lord, pleading and imploring as he had always done that God would grant peace to the churches throughout the world." Officials eventually hunted him down, transported him to the city, and ushered him into the arena, where a huge crowd began to call for his death. As the account reads, a voice from heaven cried, "Be strong, Polycarp, and play the man."

The proconsul pressured him to deny Christ and swear to Caesar, but Polycarp refused. "For eighty-six years I have been His servant, and He has never done me wrong: how can I blaspheme my King who saved me."

"Swear by Caesar's fortune," the proconsul shouted.

"If you imagine that I will swear by Caesar's fortune, as you put it, pretending not to know who I am, I will tell you plainly, I am a Christian."

The proconsul threatened. "I have wild beasts. I shall throw you to them, if you don't change your attitude."

"Call them."

"If you make light of the beasts, I'll have you destroyed by fire."

"The fire you threaten burns for a time and is soon extinguished: there is a fire you know nothing about—the fire of the judgment to come and of eternal punishment, the fire reserved for the ungodly. But why do you hesitate? Do what you want."

"Polycarp has confessed that he is a Christian," the proconsul announced to the crowd. "This fellow is the teacher of Asia, the father of the Christians, the destroyer of our gods, who teaches numbers of people not to sacrifice or even worship."

Enraged, the crowd called for his death. They bound Polycarp to a stake, stacked wood around him and set it on fire. Meanwhile, Polycarp prayed, "I bless Thee for counting me worthy of this day and hour, that in the number of the martyrs I may partake of Christ's cup, to the resurrection of both soul and body ." After his death a public official requested that Polycarp's body be withheld from the church, lest Christians make him an object of veneration, "not realizing," as the account reads, "that we can never forsake Christ, who suffered for the salvation of those who are being saved in the entire world, or worship anyone else." The story ends by offering praise to Christ, the one for whom Polycarp was willing to die. "For to Him, as the Son of God, we offer adoration; but to the martyrs, as disciples and imitators of the Lord, we give the love that they deserved for their unsurpassable devotion to their own King and Teacher."[26]

JESUS, THE ONLY SAVIOR?

The accusations against Polycarp—"the teacher of Asia, the father of the Christians, the destroyer of our gods, who teaches numbers of people not to sacrifice or even worship"—are noteworthy. Polycarp's influence, it would seem, undermined the heart and soul of Rome's religious philosophy. Not only did he refuse to yield to the power of the state, dangerous enough in itself, but he also challenged Rome's religious pluralism. He would not acknowledge the legitimacy of Rome's gods and participate in Rome's religious ceremonies. Polycarp believed that there was only one way to know God, and that was through Jesus Christ. By preaching that faith in all of Asia, he was joining battle with Rome's entire worldview. Polycarp's belief in Jesus as Lord was the real problem.

The ancient record at this point sounds curiously modern. Modern pluralism resembles Rome's; modern rejection of Jesus' lordship repeats Rome's rejection of Jesus. In the academic world, for example, Christian exclusivity—the idea that Jesus is the only way to God—offends the pluralistic assumptions of the day, just as it did two thousand years ago. Now, as then, the idea that there is one religious truth runs contrary to the spirit of the age. It is assumed that religious belief could be and often is valuable for any number of reasons, but there is no way of knowing which religion is actually true. Christians challenge this cultural assumption when they claim that Jesus is Savior and Lord.[27] Christians have been causing such offense for two thousand years.

The incarnation—God becoming human in Jesus Christ—violated the religious sensibilities of the day, for it was widely believed that the transcendent God of the universe could not become a human being. Celsus, a second-century philosopher and opponent of Christianity, recoiled at the very idea. He argued that God could not undergo such change, God could not become a man. "It is the nature only of a mortal being to undergo change and remolding, whereas it is the nature of an immortal being to remain the same without alteration. Accordingly, God was not capable of undergoing this change."[28] How could the eternal God of the universe be a mortal man too? If Christians "worshiped no other God but one, perhaps they would have had a valid argument against others. But in fact they worship to an extravagant degree this man who appeared recently, and yet think it does not offend God if they also worship his servant."[29]

But Christians did not stop there. Christians erred even more grievously by worshiping a human being whose entire life proved to be unworthy of such attribution. Far from being an impressive, imposing figure, which the ancients would have expected of a God who had chosen for whatever reason to come to earth, this man whom Christians called Lord was an abject failure. Born under suspicious circumstances, raised in total obscurity, deprived of education and proper training, executed for claiming that he was divine—this was hardly a person whose claims to deity could be taken seriously. Celsus could hardly hold back the laughter. He ridiculed Christians for glorying in something as crude and ignominious as a cross.[30] That Christians called Jesus God was unthinkable, an affront to sane religion and sound reason.

Porphyry, a well known third-century pagan philosopher, suggested that Jesus did not *have* to be a problem. He found Jesus an attractive figure, worthy of admiration, but only if he were viewed as one among many gods. Porphyry was even willing to welcome Jesus into the pantheon of Rome. "What I am about to say seems surprising to some, namely, that the gods have proclaimed Christ to be most pious and immortal, and that they remember him in a laudatory way."[31] But Porphyry could not comprehend— and would not accept—the Christian claim that Jesus was God incarnate. "We cannot attain to so great a mystery by one way."[32] Desperate to undermine Christian belief, he tried to provide an alternative explanation, one that sounds curiously modern. The disciples, he suggested, had fabricated the idea that Jesus was God incarnate, claiming "more for their master than he really was, so much more indeed that they even called him the Son of God, and the Word of God, by whom all things were made, and affirmed that he and God are one."[33]

In one sense, pagan critics were right. Even the disciples themselves were not predisposed to believe in the unique person Jesus eventually proved himself to be. They inherited from their Judaic background an expectation that the Messiah would emerge as a great leader to drive out the hated Romans, reestablish Israel's independence and usher in a golden age. Jesus' death on the cross put an end to their hopes. If Jesus had remained in the grave, then the movement would have quickly faded, as earlier messianic movements had. But the disciples claimed that Jesus was raised from the dead, not as a resuscitated corpse that would surely die again but as a resurrected being who would live and reign forever. The resurrection convinced them that Jesus was the Son of God. They called him Lord and worshiped him as God, and rightly so.[34] Their belief in the bodily resurrection of Christ, which emerged out of the many postresurrection encounters they had with Jesus, had a profound impact on how they viewed life in this world. Far from disparaging it, they saw life in this world as a prelude and preparation for life in the next world, which they viewed as a completion and perfection of this world. It made them value life as it is, but it also gave them courage to sacrifice their lives in anticipation of another, greater one.[35]

This belief in God's "condescension," as Athanasius, the courageous fourth-century bishop of Alexandria, described it, implied that other religions, which emphasized the necessity of an "ascent" to God or the gods, were wrong. If humans could get to God through law, ritual or special knowledge, as every ancient religion prescribed, then God would not have had to come to earth. But the disciples proclaimed that God did come to earth, thus exposing these other religions as vain and false. Christianity had succeeded where other religions had failed because God had accomplished what fallen people, left to their own schemes and efforts, could not do—win their salvation. This was good news to the early Christians, and they could not keep it to themselves. Polycarp was called "the teacher of Asia" and "the father of Christians" because he preached this message to the masses, as did so many others. This eagerness to spread the news won converts, but it also attracted enemies. "The Christians were seen as religious fanatics," Robert Wilken concludes, "self-righteous outsiders, arrogant innovators, who thought that only their beliefs were true."[36] As witnesses, they would not be intimidated into silence or forced to compromise their convictions.

Their witness led to martyrdom, as Polycarp's story shows. They thought it a small price to pay. What was persecution to them, considering the privilege they had of telling others about the one who promised eternal life? For that matter, what was death to them, considering that they belonged to the one who conquered death? "Twelve men, illiterate and unskilled in speaking," Justin Martyr observed, "went out from Jerusalem into the world. Through the power of God they revealed to the whole of humankind that they were sent by Christ to proclaim the word of God to everyone. . . . We meet death cheerfully for confessing to Christ."[37] Ironically, other religions in ancient Rome—the "mystery religions," as they were called, the emperor cults and various Gnostic sects—did not produce many martyrs (Judaism being the one exception). It was Christians who died for their faith. That fact alone caught people's attention.

We can only speculate about the pressure they faced to compromise faith under threat of torture and death. We know that many did capitulate to the Romans, hand Scripture over to the officials, betray fellow Christians, sacrifice to the gods and swear allegiance to the emperor as a divine being. Roman officials tried to make it easy, assuring them that they could continue to believe in Jesus, just a lesser Jesus, not the martyrs' Jesus but Porphyry's Jesus, one god among many gods. But at least some refused, for they believed that Jesus truly was the Son of God and the only way to God. As Pliny complained to the Emperor Trajan, Christians were obstinate, which in his mind was reason enough to punish them. But that obstinacy was rooted in a conviction; Christians believed that Jesus was Savior and Lord.[38]

MARTYRDOM AS A WAY OF LIFE

Christians still die for their faith, now more than ever.[39] Martyrdom is as terrifying today as it was then, if not more so. In some parts of the world Christians disappear from their homes during the night; they are warned that if they persist in faith their relatives will die; they are beaten and dismembered by hostile mobs. Missiologist David B. Barrett estimates that 160,000 Christians were martyred in the year 2000 alone.[40] They died in that year for the same basic reason they died in the year 155, when Polycarp was martyred, or in 202, when Perpetua was martyred. The early martyrs believed that if Jesus is Lord and the only Savior, then he accepts no rivals—no person or religion or ideology or empire. They affirmed that the Christian faith requires nothing less than a firm and joyful commitment to this conviction. Jesus came as God in human flesh to show the way to God and to be the way to God for us. This is the only Jesus there is. A lesser Jesus is not the real Jesus at all, at least not according to the testimony of the martyrs, from Stephen to the present.

It turns out, then, that the Roman arena is not such a strange place to begin this book after all. Martyrdom is foundational to our understanding of Christian spirituality, for it highlights what was—and still is—distinctive and essential in Christianity. Not that all true Christians have to be or will be martyrs. Martyrdom is not a choice but a calling and a gift that God gives to some but not to all. In fact, it could be that martyrdom involves something more fundamental than willingness or longing to die. It could be that martyrdom as *literal* death misses the main point. Most of us will not have to die for our faith, though it might come to that, even for those living in the West. But we will all face moments when we will have to choose between Christ and something else that vies for our ultimate allegiance. The early martyrs—Perpetua, Polycarp and many others—did not in fact choose martyrdom, at least not directly. If anything, the early Christian community criticized those who rushed into martyrdom as if it were some kind of badge of honor. They chose to be faithful to Christ; martyrdom just happened to be the result.

G. K. Chesterton said of Francis of Assisi that he turned martyrdom into a way of life. For the sake of Christ he learned to die daily to the gods—ego, pleasure, power, success—that threatened to dominate his life, which was why he lived with such vitality and passion. It was his commitment to *live* for Christ that made him a martyr, though he never suffered literal martyrdom, for commitment to Christ required him to die to self. Death to self gives life. It is life in Christ that might, under some circumstances, actually lead to literal death.

The martyrs did not die to prove something to God or earn something from God but to witness to the life they had received as a gift from God. This gift was so precious and priceless to them that they could not keep it a secret. In the end, martyrdom was—and still is—a witness to grace, which is why, in my mind, it properly serves as the starting point of a book on spirituality. Christian spirituality has little to do with what we do for God. We will never be able to love, pray, think, feel, work, meditate, fast or even die our way into a deeper spiritual life if we rely on human effort or clever schemes alone. There is nothing we can do—nothing we have to do—to find a way to God, because in Jesus Christ God has already made his way to us. The martyrs' fate might not be ours. But their faith and conviction must be. Salvation is a pure gift. God loves us so much that he came to us in Jesus Christ. That is the good news of the gospel; and it is the foundation of Christian spirituality. At Christmas we celebrate who God is as he came to us in human flesh; at Easter we celebrate what God did to win our salvation. In both cases we bear witness to the glorious work God has done, to the glorious God that he is. We declare that we are recipients of grace, beloved of God, prodigals welcomed home. That is good news worth living for, and dying for. Thus we confess, as the early martyrs confessed: "Jesus is Lord!"

PRACTICES

- Read Philippians 3:2-16.
- Meditate on your own death. Ponder the legacy you would like to leave.
- Now write your own obituary in light of how you would like to honor Jesus as Lord of your life. What would you want said about the way you lived your life for Christ?
- What does this say about the choices you make today?

2

Belonging

The Spirituality of Early Christian Community

"I give you a new commandment, that you love one another.
Just as I have loved you, you also should love one another.
By this everyone will know that you are my disciples,
if you have love for one another."

JN 13:34-35

Numbers alone can never tell the whole story, whatever the story is, for sometimes small numbers of people can accomplish great things. Such was certainly the case in the early Christian movement. At the beginning of the second century the church comprised roughly fifty thousand people, most of whom lived in major urban centers of the Roman world. Considering the population of the empire, some sixty million, Christians constituted a tiny minority. Yet several pagan leaders expressed concern that Christians, however small their numbers, were having a noticeable impact in society.[1]

In A.D. 112 Pliny the Younger (62-113), the newly appointed governor of Bithynia and Pontus, two provinces located in modern-day north-central Turkey, wrote a long letter to Trajan, the Roman emperor, to solicit the emperor's advice concerning how to deal with the growing menace of the Christian movement. Pliny was a Roman gentleman, highly educated, a man of means and influence. After receiving his appointment, he set out immediately to tour the territory, to collect information, and to make observations that would allow him to establish a just administration.[2] It soon became obvious that Christianity was one of his biggest problems.

What Pliny heard and subsequently reported in his letter to Trajan provides a fascinating perspective on pagan attitudes toward the early Christian movement. First, he mentioned that Christians had become an economic nuisance. Their commitment to honor and obey Jesus as Lord had the indirect effect of undermining pagan rituals. New converts to Christianity had abandoned temple worship, which led to a loss of revenue among those who sold sacrificial animals and temple merchandise. Merchants complained to Pliny that Christianity posed a threat to their economic livelihood.

Second, Pliny accused Christians of forming a "political club," the best word he could find to describe the Christian church, which was attracting pagan converts. Christians were proclaiming a new message, caring for the sick, organizing social events, providing hospitality, burying the dead, supporting widows and orphans, and raising money for the destitute. Pagan political clubs existed too, of course. But most of these were small and local. Though potentially troublesome, they nevertheless honored the basic values of Roman culture, especially the state religious cult. The Christian church was different. Like some deadly virus, it was spreading beyond local boundaries, as if aspiring to become a universal faith.

Third, Pliny discovered that Christian belief and practice departed sharply from the cultural norm. To learn about the movement, he arrested a number of people who had been accused of being Christian. Some of them denied the faith; others confessed faith in Christ and suffered for it. He mentioned two women leaders in particular whom he identified as "servants" or "ministers" (they were most likely deacons). He tortured them to get information about the movement. He discovered that women held positions of leadership in the church and that people of all kinds appeared to be welcomed into the community. He also learned that Christians met in the early morning to worship "Christ, as to a god," an astonishing observation about early Christian belief, considering the pagan source. Finally, he observed that they followed a strict moral code and met often for a sacred meal.

The influence of the movement was undeniable, though Pliny believed that it could be thwarted if the proper pressure was applied. "The contagion of this superstition has spread not only in the cities, but in the villages and rural districts as well; yet it seems capable of being checked and set right." Pliny had already used harsh measures, and they seemed to be working.[3] Pliny tried to force Christians taken into custody to invoke the name of the gods, to make an offering of wine and incense to Trajan's statue, and to revile the name of Christ. These procedures served as a test of religious allegiance. Some cooperated. But many did not, which infuriated Pliny. "For I do not doubt that, whatever kind of crime it may be to which they have confessed, their pertinacity and inflexible obstinacy should certainly be punished."[4]

LOVE ONE ANOTHER

It is clear that by the early second century the Christian movement was already influencing pagan culture. It was providing a sense of belonging that was not readily available through traditional Roman institutions, thus earning a reputation that reflected what the New Testament teaches about true community. In his letter to the church in Ephesus Paul argued that Christ destroyed old animosities that existed in the ancient world between male and female, citizen and barbarian, slave and free, and especially Jew and Gentile. In Paul's day observant Jews considered themselves superior to Gentiles. They alone had received God's favor—the heritage, the covenant, the law, the land, the temple and the promises. Gentiles were outsiders to this community, alienated "from the commonwealth of Israel, and strangers to the covenants of promise, having no hope and without God in the world." But all that had changed when Jesus came. "But now in Christ Jesus you who once were far off have been brought near in the blood of Christ." Christ established peace and unity by breaking down "the dividing wall, that is, the hostility" that existed between Jew and Gentile. The cross of Christ exposed how Jewish religion had become insular, failing to fulfill its divine purpose. The cross also reconciled Jews and Gentiles, showing by Christ's sacrificial death that neither group had any advantage over the other. Both were sinners who had received grace, both were broken until Christ had healed them, both were enemies who had become friends. Gentiles, therefore, were no longer strangers and sojourners but "citizens with the saints and also members of the household of God" (Eph 2:11-22).

Paul's own journey to faith illustrates the point. His Jewish background, party affiliation and religious accomplishments had made him feel superior to Gentiles. He had risen to the top, from where he could look down smugly on the rest of the world.

> If any one else has reason to be confident in the flesh, I have more: circumcised on the eighth day, a member of the people of Israel, of the tribe of Benjamin, a Hebrew born of Hebrews; as to the law, a Pharisee; as to zeal, a persecutor of the church; as to righteousness under the law, blameless.

But his conversion on the Damascus road taught him that these religious credentials about which he felt so proud were the very things that had kept him from Christ. He discovered that they did not provide him with the spiritual assets that he once thought he had. If anything, they had become spiritual liabilities. "Yet whatever gains I had, these I have come to regard as loss because of Christ. More than that, I regard everything as loss because of the surpassing value of knowing Christ Jesus my Lord" (Phil 3:4-8).

Paul's conversion transformed the way he viewed others too, including the despised Gentiles. He had once evaluated Gentiles only from a "human point of view," as he confessed in a letter to the church in Corinth, despising Gentiles because they did not belong to his party and observe his religion. He had once evaluated Jesus from a human point of view as well, regarding him as a menace to his tradition, a dangerous upstart and a messianic pretender. But when Paul discovered who the real Jesus was, he had to change the way he viewed everyone else too. What mattered was no longer cultural background or religious performance but knowledge of Christ.

> From now on, therefore, we regard no one from a human point of view; even though we once knew Christ from a human point of view, we know him no longer in that way. So if any one is in Christ, there is a new creation: everything old has passed away; see, everything has become new! (2 Cor 5:16-17).

A PECULIAR PEOPLE

The early church grew steadily in the Roman world for over three hundred years, in part because pagans found the message it preached and the belonging it offered both unique and attractive. Christians were a peculiar people. Christians claimed this identity for themselves, and pagans appeared to agree, as Pliny's letter indicates. For example, the "Letter to Diognetus," probably written during the reign of the emperor Hadrian around the year A.D. 130, provides telling evidence of how Christians viewed themselves in contrast to the larger pagan world.[5]

It was an ambiguous identity. On the one hand, Christians appeared to be completely normal, living the same kind of lives as ordinary Romans would; on the other hand, they were peculiar enough to stand out, which was why the emperor Hadrian heard about them, and the Roman Empire turned on them. In short, Christians did not fit the normal categories. Historian Wayne Meeks defines the identity of early Christians as "amphibian"—in the world but not of the world. "For the vast majority, the Christian life was an amphibian life, life at the same time in the old world that was passing away and in the new world that was coming or, to use the language we have encountered in several places, life as resident aliens in the world."[6]

The *Letter to Diognetus* is not the only example we have of a Christian apologist trying to explain and defend the Christian movement to a puzzled and suspicious world. Aristides, an Athenian philosopher who also lived in the second century, listed a number of attributes that distinguished Christians from the rest of the population. Christians, he noted, modeled fidelity, truthfulness, contentment, respect for parents, love for neighbors, purity, patience in the face of persecution and kindness to strangers. They cared for widows and orphans. They treated slaves with unusual kindness too. "Any male or female slaves or dependents whom individuals among them may have, they persuade to become Christians because of the love they feel towards them. If they do become Christians, they are brothers to them without discrimination." Likewise, they also served the poor, often sacrificially. "If anyone among them comes into want while they themselves have nothing to spare, they fast for two or three days for him. In this way they can supply any poor man with the food he needs." After provid-

"Epistle to Diognetus"

"They dwell in their own countries, but only as aliens. As citizens, they share in all things with others, and yet endure all things as foreigners. Every foreign land is to them as their native land, and every land of their birth is as foreign land to them. They marry, as do all. They beget children, but they do not cast away their offspring. They have a common table, but not a common bed. They are 'in the flesh,' but they do not 'live according to the flesh.' They pass their days upon the earth, but they are citizens of heaven. They obey the prescribed laws, and at the same time surpass the laws by their own lives. They love all men, and are persecuted by all. They are unknown and condemned; they are put to death, and restored to life. They are poor, yet make many rich; they are lacking of all things, and yet they live in abundance of all; they are dishonored, and yet in their very dishonor they are glorified. They are spoken evil of, and yet are justified; they are reviled, and bless; they are insulted, and repay the insult with honor; they do good, yet are punished as evil-doers. When punished, they rejoice as if by it they are brought to life." (Invitation to Christian Spirituality)

ing this long and detailed account of the Christian "rule of life," Aristides could not resist pointing out to the emperor how much he unknowingly benefited from the movement. Such behavior, he added, brought prosperity to the whole empire. "And see, because of them, good flows on in the world!"[7]

Were these accurate descriptions or mere exaggerations? It is easy to idealize the early church as the perfect model of community. We know that such is not the case. Paul's letters to the troubled, divided, heretical church in Corinth remind us that all was not well in early Christianity. Subsequent controversies and divisions—to say nothing of oddities—over the next three hundred years provide further evidence that the church has never had a "golden age." The church has always faced troubles, and it always will. Worldliness, cowardice, acrimony, heresy and stupidity have dogged the Christian community since Paul first put pen to paper, exhorting believers in Corinth to discipline errant members, repair their divisions, get their theology straight and repent of their spiritual arrogance.

Yet there is good reason to believe that these second-century accounts of Christian belief and practice are reasonably accurate. For one, the church attracted the attention of pagans because of the quality of life it offered, even though the church suffered persecution during most of those early years. This growth was obvious to all. The late-second-century lawyer and apologist Tertullian noted with sarcasm that Roman elites were worried about the church's success. "Men cry out," he said of pagan critics, "that the state is beset by Christians; that there are Christians in the countryside, in the villages, in the islands. That people of both sexes, of every age and condition, even of high position, are passing over to the Christian society; this they lament as though it were a calamity." Tertullian wondered if they would ever entertain the idea that so many conversions might actually be good for Rome.[8]

For another, pagans themselves observed that Christians were different. As late as the middle of the fourth century the pagan emperor Julian complained that Christians had developed a massive social welfare system with which the pagan empire could not compete because the pagan worldview did not inspire people, as the Christian worldview did, to serve and sacrifice for the common good. He felt nothing but contempt for Christians, though it is clear that he was jealous too. In a letter to a court official he wrote, "I think that when the poor happened to be neglected and overlooked by [pagan] priests, the impious Galileans observed this and devoted themselves to benevolence." Or again, "The impious Galileans support not only their poor, but ours as well, everyone can see that our people lack aid from us."[9]

A WELCOMING COMMUNITY

How did the Christian movement create a sense of belonging that made people feel included, loved and cared for? First, the Christian community welcomed outsiders, regardless of their background, and thus overcame the obvious divisions of gender, ethnicity and class that characterized the Roman world. As the apologist Tatian noted, the church seemed to include everyone, making no "distinctions in rank and outward appearance, or wealth and education, or age and sex."[10] Christians maintained close contact with family, friends, neighbors and coworkers, which provided a large pool of potential converts who found the small but vital movement attractive. Living mostly in cities, Christians bartered in the same markets, drew water from the same wells, worked in the same shops and lived in the same kinds of apartments as everyone else. They did not use organized rallies, high-profile evangelists and big-budget programs to win recruits. If anything, Christians maintained a low profile to avoid public notice. The church thus attracted outsiders through natural networks of relationships.

This subtle method of recruitment infuriated the acerbic philosopher Celsus, who despised Christianity as a lowbrow religion that attracted the underclass. "By the fact that they themselves admit that these people are worthy of the God, they show that they want and are able to convince only the foolish, dishonorable and stupid, and only slaves, women and little children." He noted that Christians won converts not through public debate among elites but through quiet witness in their homes and places of work, which he found disconcerting, though there was little he could do about it. "In private houses also we see wool-workers, cobblers, laundry-workers, and the most bucolic yokels, who would not dare to say anything at all in front of their elders and more intelligent masters."[11]

The Christian movement was especially attractive to women, who achieved higher status in the church than they did in pagan society. Men outnumbered women in the Roman world. There were clear reasons for this imbalanced ratio. Roman men did not value marriage very highly, did not hesitate to divorce if marriage proved to be dissatisfying, and did not refrain from promiscuous behavior. They often pressured women—their wives or mistresses—to get abortions because they did not want to be burdened with children, which led to higher mortality rates among women. They were more inclined to let female infants die of exposure too, largely because female children were less valued than male children.

The church lived by a different ethic, which impressed the very people who suffered the most as victims of Rome's immorality and injustice. The Christian worldview condemned infanticide, abortion and incest, and it disapproved of marital infidelity, divorce and polygamy. Instead, the Christian community valued both chastity and marriage, which applied equally to men and women. Christian women could remain single if they chose, without losing status in the church. If they did marry, Christian women tended to marry later in life than their pagan counterparts, and they received support from the church when they did marry because marriage was viewed as spiritually beneficial to husband, wife and community.[12] Fertility rates among Christian women were higher than among pagans and mortality rates were lower, largely because Christian women were treated better. Whether married or single, women had opportunities to use their gifts in the church. They prayed and prophesied and served the poor, and they held church office too, specifically the office of deacon.[13]

The early Christian movement valued family life too. The second-

Women praying

century apologist Tertullian viewed the family as if it were a little church. In a good Christian marriage, he wrote, a Christian couple should "pray together, fast together, instruct, support, and exhort each other." They should also "share each other's tribulations, persecutions, and revival."[14] Christians viewed family life as a noble calling, and they had the leisure and motivation to raise children. "To the servant of God, forsooth, offspring is necessary," proclaimed Tertullian. "For our own salvation we are secure enough, so that we have leisure for children! Burdens must be sought by us for ourselves which are avoided by the majority of the Gentiles, who are compelled by laws [to have children], who are decimated by abortions."[15]

The church attended to the needs of widows too, viewing widowhood as a spiritual calling. For example, by A.D. 250 the church in Rome had 1,500 "widows and distressed persons" under its care, and Constantinople had over 3,000 widows on its payroll in the year 400. Moreover, the early Christian movement also showed special concern for children, viewing them as people made in the image of God and capable of reflecting the character of Christ. Christian leaders noted that Jesus treated children with kindness, which motivated them to do likewise. They warned against the sin of sexual abuse and insisted children be adequately cared for. They also included children in worship, raised them to become mature Christians ("athletes for God") and prayed diligently for their salvation and growth.[16] For these and other reasons, the church proved itself to be highly inclusive of populations of people that the Roman world neglected or exploited, and thus contributed to the sense of belonging that made the Christian community so attractive.

The church set high standards of membership as well, thus creating a tight-knit community that only reinforced this sense of belonging, making it appear that being a member really meant something.[17] Second-century writer Athenagoras argued that the expectation of a final judgment held Christians accountable to God for their daily conduct in the world. He also believed that Christian moral excellence was directly attributable to the Christian belief in the last judgment. "If we did not think that a God ruled over the human race, would we live in such purity? The idea is impossible. But since we are persuaded that we must give an account of all our life here to God who made us and the world, we adopt a temperate, generous, and despised way of life." Athenagoras reasoned that the Christian conception of God was bound to affect how Christians viewed other people, even those outside the faith. The God whom Christians worship, he suggested, is one in community, a "fellowship of the Father with the Son, along with the Spirit," and thus the unity which "exists between these three."[18] Christians believed that the essential nature of God is love because

God—as Father, Son and Holy Spirit—is a perfect community. The people of God are privileged to belong to this community through the redemptive work of Christ and the indwelling power of the Holy Spirit. Such an experience of love inspired early Christians to share it with others. "We have learned not only not to return blow for blow, nor to sue those who plunder and rob us, but to those who smite us on one cheek to offer the other also, and to those who take away our coat to give our overcoat as well."[19]

As a pagan philosopher, Justin Martyr was deeply moved by the virtuous behavior of Christians. The contrast between their way of life and the pagan way of life was too obvious to overlook and helped to draw him into the Christian fold.

> Those who once rejoiced in fornication now delight in continence alone; those who made use of magic arts have dedicated themselves to the good and unbegotten God; we who once took most pleasure in the means of increasing our wealth and property now bring what we have into a common fund and share with everyone in need.[20]

The church did not try to separate religious ritual and public conduct, as most ancient religions appeared to do. The Christian faith mandated that all of one's life be submitted to God. "That was how the Christian movement differed most visibly from the other cults that fit more easily into the normal expectations of 'religion' in the Roman world," Wayne Meeks notes. "The Christians' practices were not confined to sacred occasions and social locations—shrines, sacrifices, processions—but were integral to the formation of communities with a distinctive self-awareness."[21] Christians believed that God was the creator of all that is good in the world. This good world, however, had fallen into corruption. But they also believed that Jesus Christ had come to redeem and reclaim the fallen world, which involved even the most ordinary and routine matters of life, such as marriage and family, stewardship of money, treatment of friends and enemies, and daily conduct.[22]

STABILITY IN AN UNSTABLE WORLD

Second, the Christian community provided a high degree of social stability, which caught the attention of people who lived in a world that seemed to teeter on the verge of chaos. Christianity began as an urban movement in the ancient world. It is hard for us in the West to imagine what these cities were like. Take Antioch (of Syria), a city of roughly 150,000 in A.D. 100. It is estimated that Antioch had a population density of 117 citizens per acre, which exceeds the population density of Manhattan Island. Moreover, the tallest buildings in Antioch did not exceed three stories, while modern cities build high rises that exceed fifty stories. As it is, the population density of ancient Antioch was probably greater, for upwards of 40 percent of the city property was devoted to public buildings, like monuments and temples. The wealthy lived in larger homes that had atriums or center courtyards. But the vast majority of the population lived in small cubicles on the second and third floors of buildings. These apartments had no chimneys, no indoor plumbing, and no heating, except a small charcoal brazier that was used for both heating and cooking. People used chamber pots and open-pit latrines for disposal.[23]

The population of the Roman world was also mobile. The empire established economic and political order, used a common coin, shared a common language (Greek) and provided new economic opportunities for industrious people. Local tradition and customs were giving way to an emerging Mediterranean culture that allowed for travel and trade. The middle class benefited the most.[24] This growing population of people, cut loose from the obligations and loyalties of the local town, became "citizens of the world," notes historian Peter Brown, though it appears that many "were finding that the world was a lonely and impersonal place."[25]

Cities provided people with new opportunities, but they also created serious problems. Cities like Antioch bordered on social chaos. A considerable proportion of the population consisted of newcomers, mostly from distinct ethnic groups, who moved to the city as displaced persons seeking their fortune. They usually found people from the same ethnic group when they settled into these large urban areas. These ethnic enclaves did little more than exacerbate intraethnic rivalries. For example, there were eighteen identifiable ethnic groups in Antioch, and these groups staked out their own quarters in the city to create a sense of belonging, though such belonging remained fragile. Newcomers to the city had difficulty forming attachments in a city that suffered from a high turnover rate, disease, crime and disasters. In fact, Antioch was afflicted with a natural disaster of one kind or another forty-one times over a six-hundred-year period, which led to loss of life, displacement, homelessness and instability.[26]

The fledgling Christian movement thrived in such an unstable environment. The church became like family to aliens and outsiders who flocked to the cities.[27] The church welcomed people from a wide cross-section of society and taught a message that was easily understandable—more "middlebrow" than sophisticated—which appealed to those who lacked the education to comprehend impenetrable mysteries. The Christian community offered an array of social services too. Christians cared for widows and orphans, visited prisoners, fed the poor, nursed the sick, and buried the dead. Church members gave freely of their money to support these various ministries. "The appeal of Christianity," Peter Brown states, "still lay in its radical sense of community: it absorbed people because the individual could drop from a wide impersonal world into a miniature community, whose demands and relations were explicit."[28]

Christian community

This charitable behavior departed dramatically from pagan values. The contrast between Christian and pagan at this point became more than apparent. Roman culture emphasized reciprocity; helping the poor and homeless, therefore, was simply not the norm.[29] But Christians emphasized stewardship and charity, based on an ethic of love. Speaking of the contributions Christians made to worthy causes, Tertullian noted,

> Rather they are used to feed and to bury the poor; for boys and girls without means and without parents to help them . . . for shipwrecked sailors; and for those doing forced labor in the mines, or banished on islands, or in prison, provided they suffer for the sake of God's fellowship. That

makes them beneficiaries by virtue of their confession of faith. But even such acts of great love set a stain on us in the eyes of some people. "Look," they say, "how they love each other." . . . "See, how ready they are to die for one another."[30]

This quality of life impressed and attracted outsiders who observed the benefit of belonging to a stable community, and it helped to mitigate social tensions within the city and to improve the quality of life for everyone.[31]

SOCIAL CRISES

Third, the church cared for people during periods of intense crises. The Roman world suffered periodic catastrophes throughout its long history, but none worse than two plagues that swept over it, one striking in A.D. 165, the other in 250. It is hard to determine the exact number of deaths, but scholars estimate that up to a quarter of the population died during each plague. At the height of the second epidemic, thousands died daily in the city of Rome. The fatality rate was so high that some cities fell into ruin and military campaigns had to be stopped. It tested the mettle of the empire, and it tested the faith of Christians. Dionysius, bishop of Alexandria, wrote in an Easter message, "out of the blue came this disease, a thing more terrifying . . . than any terror, more frightful than any disaster whatever."[32]

The plague afflicted both pagans and Christians. But the response of the two groups was decidedly different, as observers noted. The Christian worldview offered a more satisfying explanation of the disaster. Bishops in particular used their pulpits to answer the hard questions and to provide comfort and hope. They preached on such themes as God's sovereignty, the suffering of Jesus, the last judgment and the resurrection of the dead. They also interpreted the catastrophe as a kind of divine test. Cyprian, the bishop of Carthage when the plague of 250 struck, asked his congregation whether they would show the same kind of generosity to victims that God extends to the least deserving.

> He continually makes His sun rise and imparts sudden rain to nourish the seeds, showing all these kindnesses not merely to His own friends. Should not one who professes to be a son of God imitate the example of his Father? It is proper for us to correspond to our birth, and it does not become those

who are clearly reborn in God to be degenerate, but, as a son, the descendent of a good father, should rather prove the imitation of his goodness.[33]

But the Christian faith did more than make theological sense of the epidemics; it also made a practical difference in the lives of people, as if theory found a perfect match with practice. In general, Christians faced the plagues with courage, nursed the sick and buried the dead. They believed that because God loved them, as undeserving as they were, they were dutybound to love others. Again, the contrast between Christians and pagans was noticeable. "Equally alien to paganism was the notion that because God loves humanity, Christians cannot please God unless they love one another. Indeed, as God demonstrates his love through sacrifice, humans must demonstrate their love through sacrifice on behalf of one another."[34] For example, Dionysius, bishop of Alexandria, wrote movingly of the sacrifices that Christians had made on behalf of the sick and dying. Christians, he said, "showed unbounded love and loyalty, never sparing themselves and thinking only of one another. Heedless of danger, they took charge of the sick, attending to their every need and ministering to them in Christ, and with them departed this life serenely happy." They discovered soon enough that, however Christlike their behavior, they would not be spared from the same fate that had already taken the lives of others.

Dionysius interpreted their sacrificial deaths in light of the sacrifice of Christ. In fact, a number of the sick had recovered while their caretakers had died. So Dionysius reasoned that perhaps the caretakers had suffered vicariously, dying in the place of those who had survived. However misguided from a purely scientific perspective, his theology must surely have left an impression.

> For they were infected by others with the disease, drawing on themselves the sickness of their neighbors and cheerfully accepting their pains. Many, in nursing and curing others, transferred their death to themselves and died in their stead, turning the common formula that is normally an empty courtesy into a reality.

Dionysius also mentioned that Christians buried the dead, and they showed great tenderness by first washing their bodies and wrapping them in grave clothes. Again, these actions set Christians apart from pagans, who would have nothing to do with the dead. "The heathens behaved in the very opposite way. At the first onset of the disease, they pushed the sufferers away and fled from their dearest, throwing them into the roads before they were dead and treating unburied corpses as dirt."[35]

Ironically, Christians survived the plagues at higher rates than pagans, even though Christians were more willing to be exposed to the deadly contagion. Why? First, they cared for the sick. Such care ensured that a higher percentage of the afflicted would survive, even if there was no actual cure available. Basic nursing care—sips of broth, cold rags on the forehead, tender backrubs, a change of bedding, visits from loving friends—strengthened the sick and helped at least some of them to overcome the disease. Second, Christians who survived became immune and thus provided a work force of healthy people who were no longer susceptible to the disease. These survivors made themselves available to the sick, which in turn increased survival rates even more. Finally, Christians believed in, prayed for and experienced miracles. Miraculous cures and demon exorcisms occurred with enough frequency to leave an impression on pagans, who interpreted these manifestations of power as evidence that the Christian God was real, thus making "physically and dramatically visible the superiority of the Christian's patron power over all things."[36]

PASTORAL CARE

Finally, pastors helped to create a sense of belonging by functioning as shepherds of the flock, providing pastoral care from cradle to grave.[37] The role of the pastor had no counterparts in the pagan world (the one exception was the Jewish rabbi). Pastors practiced the "cure of souls," as it was called back then, to help believers make progress in the faith. Unlike pagan priests and cult leaders, who presided over various rituals or who taught obscure and esoteric "mysteries," Christian pastors attended to the practical concerns of everyday life, striving to create a seamless unity between creed and conduct, religion and life. They taught the Scriptures, visited the sick, provided for the destitute, comforted the afflicted, maintained church unity, administered the sacraments and disciplined errant church members.

Speaking like a parent, John Chrysostom, archbishop of Constantino-

ple in the late fourth century, said that to love all members alike, pastors
had to love them all uniquely. "It is impossible to treat all his people in
one way, any more than it would be right for the doctors to deal with all
their patients alike."[38] A pastor was called to function as "a teacher, a
guide, a friend" for the members of the flock, the great third-century
teacher Origen wrote. The pastor's work depended on setting a good example or demonstrating "perfection" (maturity of faith), for how could a
pastor nurture in others what was lacking in his own life? "There is no
moral progress without the person of the spiritual helper, without the living example and the loving participation of someone who is perfect."[39]
Gregory of Nazianzus, a fourth-century bishop, added, "A man must
himself be cleansed before cleansing others; himself become wise, that he
may make others wise; become light, and then give light; draw near to
God, and so bring others near."[40]

Pastors presided over the worship life of the church too. By the middle
of the second century, pastors were already following an established liturgy of worship. On Sundays they called believers together for worship,
which was usually held in large homes. They read from the "memoirs of
the apostles," preached a sermon and led the church in singing and corporate prayers. Then they distributed the bread and wine to the faithful.
They also collected funds and appointed deacons to distribute those
funds, and thus provided "for the orphans and widows, those who are in
need on account of sickness or some other cause, those who are in bonds,
strangers who are sojourning." The deacons became the "protector of all
who are in need."[41]

Pastors enrolled new believers in a training program to prepare them for
church membership. Hippolytus of Rome (A.D. 170-236) wrote *On the
Apostolic Tradition* in A.D. 215 to provide a manual that instructed bishops
and presbyters about how to teach new believers the essentials of the faith.
The period of instruction lasted up to three years. Amazingly, most of the
church fathers—Origen, John Chrysostom, Augustine of Hippo, Theo-
philus of Jerusalem, for example—taught those classes, demonstrating that
instruction of new believers was so important that only the best-trained
pastors were qualified to take on the responsibility. These great bishops
and teachers adopted a variety of strategies to train inquirers and converts.

For example, Cyril, bishop of Jerusalem, used the creed as an outline for instruction. "For the present," he said to his pupils,

> just listen and memorize the creed as I recite it, and you will receive in due course the proof from Scripture of each of its propositions. . . . And just as the mustard seed in small grain contains in embryo many future branches, so also the creed embraces in a few words all the religious knowledge in both the Old and the New Testaments.[42]

These manuals provided moral instruction for the Christian community too. One such manual, the *Didache*, states, "There are two ways, one of life and one of death; and between the two ways there is a great difference." Following New Testament guidelines, the *Didache* emphasizes such virtues as love and humility and generosity.

> Do not be one who holds his hand out to take, but shuts it when it comes to giving. If your labor has brought you earnings, pay a ransom for your sins. Do not hesitate to give and do not give with a bad grace. . . . Do not turn your back on the needy, but share everything with your brother and call nothing your own. For if you have what is eternal in common, how much more should you have what is transient.[43]

Such moral instruction was intended to protect the flock from the evil influence of pagan culture by erecting clear moral boundaries. For example, Hippolytus ruled certain jobs as off limits for Christians, such as harlot, sculptor of idols, actor, teacher of "worldly knowledge," charioteer, executioner, charmer, astrologer and military governor.[44]

Pastors and theologians also scrutinized popular forms of entertainment. Tertullian, a moral rigorist if there ever was one, attacked "The Shows" with brutal honesty, warning the flock about their moral danger. Though inclined to take extreme positions, Tertullian did reflect a general consensus, however exaggerated, concerning how the Christian community viewed the immorality of the ancient world. Christians kept their distance from the culture, which sometimes undermined their efforts to reach it. Thus Tertullian used words like *incite* and *arouse* and *excite* to describe the way these popular forms of entertainment awakened ungodly passions in people. "See the masses thronging to the circus, their violent emotions already aroused! They are already riotous, already blind with hysteria, already agitated about their bets!" In a description that sounds like he is writing about behavior at modern athletic events, he wrote, "There is the united shout of a common madness. . . . Then there is cursing and booing—with no real cause for hatred. There are shouts of applause, with nothing to merit them!" He concludes with this clever play on words: "I wish that we did not even inhabit the same world as these wicked men! And although that wish cannot be realized, yet even now we are separate from them in what is of the world. For the world is God's. But the worldly is the devil's."[45]

Baptism

Finally, pastors administered the sacraments to the Christian community to nurture them in the faith. They considered the administration of the sacraments one of their primary duties, for they believed that God imparts grace through the sacraments. Baptism in particular functioned as an important rite of passage; it symbolized believers' clear break with the world and inclusion into the Christian family.[46] Pastors required candidates to make a formal confession of faith and to submit to a moral examination. When they were satisfied that candidates were sorry for their sins, understood the faith, trusted in Christ and purposed to obey Christ's commands, pastors followed a ritual that lasted four days, culminating in the sacrament of baptism on Easter Sunday morning. As part of the liturgy, they anointed candidates with oil, prayed over them and exorcized any demons that might be afflicting them. After baptism they dressed the initiated in white robes, joyously welcomed them into the community of faith and then encouraged them to follow a strict routine of spiritual discipline. This routine included sabbath worship; various fasts; private prayers at the third, sixth and ninth hours; and regular meetings with fellow Christians. Fellowship with other believers would protect new Christians from capitulating to the evils of popular culture. "But having prayed with the church he will be able to avoid all the evils of that day."[47]

THE WITNESS OF THE COMMUNITY

The circumstances in which we live today seem so very different, at least in America. Christians in America enjoy the privilege of living in a free society. We are in large measure spoiled by the cultural privileges we have as Christians. We have large numbers, access to power and cultural influence. We have lots of money too, and thus can build massive churches, publish thousands of books, operate radio and television stations, and run Christian schools and colleges. We also have opportunity to flex our religious and political muscles. We vote candidates into office, lobby Congress and the White House, form nonprofits to promote our favorite causes, engage in public policy debates, and pursue vocations that serve the common good.

But it is easy for us to ignore one fundamental truth. God calls the church to be a community of belonging for broken people. The church's message matters a great deal, for the truth it proclaims is the precious, eternal message of the gospel. But the church's "life together," as Dietrich Bonhoeffer called it, matters just as much, for such a community is proof that the gospel still has power to transform people's lives, to heal divisions and to provide a sense of belonging for rootless people. The world longs to hear the gospel; it also wants to see it in action. Christians living in the Two-Thirds (or Majority) World, especially those living under persecution, have much to teach us because they have in many ways surpassed Christians living in the West in forming communities of faith that more closely resemble the early Christian church.

Early on in my pastoral career I served as an associate pastor of Emmanuel Reformed Church in Southern California. It was not a "successful" church as we often understand that term—big-budgeted, consumer-oriented and program-driven. The church's pastor, Harold Korver, has not written any books; his ministry will not garner the attention of Christian magazines. The church building is no architectural masterpiece. The church is as ordinary as the low-income, multiethnic community in which it resides. Yet this midsize congregation embodies, however imperfectly, what the church is supposed to be and do. Members speak English and Spanish; they drive BMWs and old Vegas; they dress in suits and blue jeans; they earn big salaries, little paychecks or nothing at all; they work as executives, teachers, secretaries, salespersons and janitors—if they work at all. The church serves the needs of the entire community, even when there is no payoff in membership growth and publicity. It holds worship services in Spanish and English. It offers computer classes for the unemployed, after-school programs for latchkey kids, basketball leagues for people who lack the means to join a health club, premarriage and marriage classes, and counseling services for the community. Its latest project is to start a series of house churches in some of the poorest neighborhoods in the Los Angeles area and to found a medical clinic for people who cannot afford health insurance. It functions as salt, leaven and light in its little corner of the world.

Can the church be renewed? We must believe it can because it is God's church and it has a great history. Our knowledge of the early church can point the way. First, the church today can strive to become as inclusive as the early church was, welcoming one and all into a body of believers whose only reason for being together is Jesus Christ. The church is not—and should not be—an arm of the Republican or Democratic parties, not a country club without a golf course or a health club without a pool, not a venue for rock, country or classical music concerts, not even a therapist's office or a twelve-step recovery group. The church is a community of sinners who have found salvation through Christ, who care deeply for one another as saints in the making, who proclaim in word and deed that God plans to restore the entire world to himself through Jesus Christ.

Just last week our local newspaper ran a front-page article on a local church that recently moved into a new facility. Surprisingly, the article did not emphasize the new building but the church's ministry. It told the story of one of its members, Kerry Sides, to illustrate what makes this church so attractive and successful. Homeless, penniless and addicted to meth, Sides made her way to the church one day almost as a last resort, desperate to meet someone who could help her. The first person she met was the senior pastor, Joe Wittwer, who greeted her warmly and asked her what she needed. She received immediate assistance. She started to attend worship because she could understand and apply the simple, biblical messages he preached. She found community there too. "They've cared for me from day one," she said to the reporter. When Sides was diagnosed with cancer just a few months ago, the members of her "life group" provided her with daily meals and attended to other needs too, like transportation. "They're my biggest cheerleaders. I can count on them for anything. These are the kinds of relationships I have always wanted in my life."[48] No wonder why Sides has become an active member at the church.

Second, the church can respond with compassion and action to catastrophic suffering, just as the early Christian community did when plagues swept through the Roman world. There is no lack of opportunity in the world today: natural disasters, genocide, epidemics and massive poverty, which seem more the rule than the exception. No community on earth has the network, resources, institutions and motivation that the church has. Its influence reaches everywhere; it operates hundreds of charitable organizations that provide a wide array of services to the needy; it believes in a message and way of life that the world needs and wants. Never before has the church had such opportunities for influence. The biggest problem it faces is its own complacency and worldliness.

Here church leaders must take charge, not by doing more but by doing less. They must surrender all desire for political, economic, social and cultural influence in the larger society to devote their energies to enabling the church to become a community of belonging. Church leaders are called to serve the church; the church in turn is called to serve the world. Harold Korver has served the same church for thirty-five years. He has baptized, married and buried hundreds of people, preached the Word in season and out of season, cared for the sick, dealt with every kind of crisis imaginable, encouraged and confronted wayward members, and initiated many programs to meet practical needs. Above all, he has called people to become disciples and the church to become a community of belonging for others. He is not the reason why the church has prospered. The members are the reason. They have caught a vision of what their church can be. He only pointed in the right direction. Once the church started moving, there was no turning back.

PRACTICES

- Read John 13:34-35; Acts 2:42-47; 1 Corinthians 12.
- Identify one community within the larger church to which you belong or would like to join. It could be a small Bible study group, committee, choir, youth group or the like.
- Describe the kind of community it presently is.
- How can you help it become a place of genuine belonging? What steps can you take?
- Begin to pray every day for that community.

3

Struggle

The Spirituality of the Desert Saints

"Athletes exercise self-control in all things;
they do it to receive a perishable wreath, but we an imperishable one.
So I do not run aimlessly, nor do I box as though beating the air;
but I punish my body and enslave it, so that after proclaiming
to others I myself should not be disqualified."

1 COR 9:25-27

W hitworth students often describe their life experiences as a "struggle." They struggle with health issues, family problems, sudden losses and the doubts that invariably follow. These kinds of struggles usually come as a result of unexpected and unwanted circumstances. A student tells me in anger, confusion and distress that her parents are getting a divorce. She did not choose this turn of events. It may serve a good purpose, to be sure; but it was certainly not what she wanted. The struggle was imposed, not chosen, which probably involves the vast majority of struggles we face.

But would it ever be right to *choose* to struggle? To put ourselves in a hard place? To follow a pathway that would make life more difficult for us? Most of us would reject the idea out of hand, especially in matters pertaining to the spiritual life. The Christian faith, we think, is supposed to make life better, happier and easier for us, not harder. It is struggle that often drives us *to* the Christian faith; it seems wrong to suggest that it should come *from* the Christian faith.

THE LIFE OF STRUGGLE

The desert saints, a delightfully peculiar group of Christians who flourished in fourth- and fifth-century Egypt, Palestine and Syria, challenge us to think otherwise. They believed that struggle is normal, necessary and even healthy in the spiritual life. The fallenness of the world imposes it (e.g., physical sickness, mental anguish, death of a loved one), discipleship requires it (e.g., self-sacrifice) and believers must choose to face it. We therefore cannot escape struggle, nor should we try. Rather, we should embrace it as one aspect of our calling to discipleship, for the goal of life in this world is not ease, prosperity and success but intimacy with God, maturity of character, and influence in the world. Struggle proves that we are taking the Christian faith seriously. After all, Jesus himself taught that we must die to ourselves, take up our cross daily and follow him, who is Lord over all. An unknown desert saint once said that if a person knows an Abba (a spiritual father, wise man or mentor, usually a generation older) with whom he would make progress in discipleship, though in a way that would make life hard for him, "he is an atheist if he does not go there."[1] Another famous Abba, St. Mark the Ascetic, summed up this positive view of struggle, "He who does not choose to suffer for the sake of truth will be chastened more painfully by suffering he has not chosen."[2]

Though the deserts saints affirmed that God created the world to be good, they also believed that something has gone desperately wrong. Sin has entered the world and affected everything—every relationship, institution, vocation, personality and pleasure. We are subject to evil powers beyond our control. The "world, the flesh, and the devil" are on the prowl, and they menace us at every turn.[3] There is no safety in this world, no easy path to take, no convenient and comfortable way to live. There is no safety inside us either, for human beings are by nature rebellious, indulgent and lazy. Though Christ has redeemed us from sin, defeated Satan and conquered death, he has not taken us out of this world. God has decided that the place of humanity's temptation and Fall also should be the place of humanity's redemption and restoration.

A battle is now being waged to reclaim what belongs rightfully to God. This world is the battlefield; humanity is the prize. "Not a single person could endure the enemy's clever attack," a saying from the tradition goes,

> nor quench, nor control the leaping fire natural to the body, unless God's grace preserved us in our weakness. In all our prayers we should pray for his grace to save us, so that he may turn aside the scourge. . . . For he makes a man to grieve, and then lifts him up to salvation: he strikes, and his hand heals: he humbles and exalts, mortifies and enlivens: leads to hell and brings back from hell.[4]

This theme of struggle appears often in the *Sayings* of the desert saints, that mosaic of teachings from the great spiritual masters. "This is the great task of man," Antony said to his disciples, "that he should hold his sin before the face of God, and count upon temptation until his last breath." "Take away the temptation," he continued, "and no one will find salvation."[5] A young novice in the community confessed that he battled constantly against the temptation of lust. An old master asked him, "Do you want me to ask the Lord to release you from your trouble," to which the young man replied, "Abba, I see that although it is a painful struggle, I am profiting from having to carry the burden." Then he added, "But ask God in your prayers, that he will give me long-suffering, to enable me to endure." The master was humbled by his apprentice's wisdom and courage. "Now I know that you are far advanced, my son, and beyond me."[6] Abba Pocmen once told Abba John the Short, another spiritual master, that he had asked God to take away his passions. His prayer had been answered, and his heart had become tranquil. So he said to himself, "I find that I am at rest, with no war of flesh and spirit." But Abba John warned him, "Go, ask the Lord to stir a new war in you. Fighting is good for the soul."[7] On another occasion Poemen said, "If temptations come in, and you deal with them there, they will prove you."[8] Or again, "Just as you cannot stop air coming into your breast, you cannot stop [evil] thoughts coming into your mind. Your part is to resist them."[9]

THE LIFE OF ST. ANTONY

The most famous of the desert saints is Antony of Egypt.[10] We know his story so well because his friend and protégé, Athanasius, bishop of Alexandria, wrote his biography shortly after Antony died. It became one of the most popular and influential books of the Middle Ages and has remained in print to this day. Born in A.D. 251, Antony grew up in a prosperous Egyptian home. After the death of his parents, he took over the management of household affairs, which included responsibility for a younger sister. He also became more earnest about the Christian faith of his parents. While walking to church one day, Antony began to consider what it would mean for him to live more like the apostles, forsaking everything to follow Christ. That very morning the gospel text in the worship service read, "If you wish to be perfect, go, sell your possessions, and give the money to the poor, and you will have treasure in heaven" (Mt 19:21). Antony did exactly what the text commanded: he sold the family's possessions and distributed the money to the poor, keeping only enough for his sister and him to live on comfortably.

Several months later he had a similar experience, except this time he decided to make a clean break with his past. He distributed the rest of his wealth and possessions to the poor, entrusted his sister to the care of friends, and withdrew into the wilderness to seek God. He found a mentor, or Abba, in a nearby village, and practiced what his biographer, Athanasius, the revered bishop of Alexandria, called "the discipline," which included such ascetic exercises as vigils, fasting, celibacy, poverty and solitude. "All the desire and all the energy he possessed," Athanasius wrote, "concerned the exertion of the discipline." He memorized Scripture too, so that "in him the memory took the place of books." To provide for his physical needs, he worked with his hands by weaving mats.[11]

According to the account provided by Athanasius, as the public began to admire him, the devil, "who despises and envies good, could not bear seeing such purpose in a youth," and thus set to work to destroy him. So Antony entered a period of intense conflict with the devil.[12] To combat these demonic attacks, he practiced "the discipline" with ever greater severity and withdrew ever deeper into the desert, settling first among tombs and eventually taking up residence in an abandoned fortress, where he lived for twenty years in almost total isolation. The devil tempted him with the desires of the flesh, but Antony resisted, thus making the devil look like a "buffoon." Then the devil tempted him with wealth and fame, but again

Antony rebuffed him. As Athanasius reports, the devil even assumed the form of wild beasts and physically attacked Antony, but Antony would not be intimidated. Antony attributed his success to the help of Jesus and to the ascetic exercises he practiced, assuming that "the soul's intensity is strong when the pleasures of the body are weakened."[13] Ironically, in his struggle against the devil Antony found God.

Meanwhile, Antony's reputation as a spiritual master spread.

Antony tormented

People became fascinated by stories about a man who had the courage to live alone in the wilderness and to seek God. Curious to see what had become of him, his admirers tracked him down, hoping he would teach them the way of salvation. Antony begged them to leave him alone, but they refused, tearing down the doors of the remote and abandoned fortress in which he was living so that they could catch a glimpse of him. He finally relented under pressure and appeared before them. "Antony came forth as though from some shrine, having been led into divine mysteries and inspired by God." They were amazed to observe that his body was strong and lean, his soul pure and peaceful, his demeanor quiet and humble. He maintained "utter equilibrium," whether combating the devil or welcoming the crowd. He began to heal the sick, to cast out demons, to console the distressed, to reconcile enemies and to impart wisdom to anyone who would listen, "urging everyone to prefer nothing in the world above the love of Christ." He became an adviser to hundreds who hoped to achieve the spiritual depth he exhibited, whom he exhorted to die daily, discard their possessions and prepare themselves for the day of judgment.[14]

Antony spent the last decades of his life practicing "the discipline," serving those who had suffered for their faith, healing the sick, debating heretics and mentoring disciples. He preferred living in solitude, but his popularity prevented him from pursuing it to the degree he wanted. He longed for martyrdom too, hoping thereby to identify with Christ, but he was not given that gift. Still, his commitment to asceticism—that is, vigorous self-denial through the practice of discipline—allowed him to become "a bloodless martyr," as the desert saints were called. "Antony departed and withdrew once again to the cell, and was there daily being martyred by his conscience, and doing battle in the contests of the faith. He subjected himself to an even greater and more strenuous asceticism, for he was always fasting, and had clothing with hair on the interior and skin on the exterior that he kept until he died [A.D. 356]."[15]

ECCENTRICITY WITH A PURPOSE

Antony's story captures the essence of this peculiar spiritual tradition, for he spent years in the desert fighting the devil and seeking after God.[16] How can we make sense of such an idiosyncratic movement? What can we learn from it? Antony's behavior was so unusual that it is easy for us to dismiss him, ridicule him and even call him crazy, which would only have the unfortunate consequence of depriving us of an opportunity to learn from this unique man. What would motivate a man to sell everything he possessed, withdraw into the desert, spend twenty years in isolation and fight the devil? Antony was by no means the only desert saint, nor the most fanatical one. The movement attracted thousands, especially in the fourth and fifth centuries. Many followed Antony's example, though in a less extreme form. But some surpassed it. Simeon the Stylite, for example, ascended a pillar of an old Roman ruin and remained there for some thirty years, never once coming down. Others lived in trees or caves, refusing to lie down or to protect themselves from the elements. In short, they were eccentric to the extreme.

Still, sometimes eccentricity serves a useful purpose, for it functions like a cartoon that intentionally exaggerates certain features on a person's face to highlight what makes it interesting and unique. We know who the person is, even though the image before us is distorted for effect. Perhaps the desert saints went too far in giving up everything to follow Jesus. It certainly appears to be that way in an age like our own when Christianity blends so comfortably into the cultural status quo. The desert saints were aware of this problem of strangeness even in their own day. As Abba Antony once said, with considerable irony, "A time is coming when people will go insane. And when they see someone who is not insane, they will attack that person saying, 'You are crazy; you are not like us.' "[17] However crazy, they deserve our admiration, for they dared to take a stand against the compromised Christianity of their day.[18]

Their heroic efforts at spiritual discipline manifested a deep respect for the example Jesus set. They withdrew into the desert to honor the God "incarnated in Christ."[19] The incarnation, in their minds, was not intended to spare them from suffering but to inspire them to choose suffering because through the incarnation suffering had become redemptive. "The more profound our personal misery," John Chryssavgis writes, "the more abundant God's eternal mercy. The deeper the abyss of our human corruption, the greater the grace of heavenly compassion. The more involved our exposure to the way of the cross, the more intense our experience of the light of resurrection."[20]

BLOODLESS MARTYRS

How did this strange movement ever get started? Christianity was born in the hostile world of the Roman Empire, and Christians suffered periodic persecution for nearly three hundred years. The last official persecution was the worst. The emperor Diocletian assumed the throne in Rome in A.D. 285. Diocletian's advisers urged him to restore Rome's old glory, which mandated that he marshal public support. One group of people stood in the way. At first public officials targeted Christians in the military for persecution, whose loyalty to Rome seemed questionable. Then they singled out clergy and, finally, church members. They confiscated Bibles, ordered the faithful to offer sacrifices to the gods, and mandated worship of the emperor. In short, they tried to force Christians to deny Christ. Thousands died as a result of this empire-wide persecution; thousands more capitulated under pressure and either forged documents claiming they had sacrificed to the gods, handed Bibles over to public officials or committed open apostasy.

Diocletian retired from public service in 305. Several years later Constantine, the son of a Roman general, raised an army, marched on Rome, and defeated his chief rival, Maxentius, at the battle at Milvian Bridge. After assuming the throne he issued the Edict of Milan (A.D. 313), which granted Christianity legal status in the empire. But Constantine did not stop there. For the next twenty-five years he showed increasing favoritism toward Christianity. Both his religious interests and political instincts supported such a policy. Constantine understood that Christianity was on the rise and that the church's support for his government was necessary—for the church's success and for his survival. He built churches, honored bishops, called church councils and passed laws that showed at least some deference to Christian moral teachings. In less than a generation, therefore, Christianity ceased to be a persecuted faith and became a privileged faith.[21]

Constantine's faith in Christ and favoritism toward the church had an irreversible impact on Christianity. Suddenly it became almost fashionable to be Christian. Church attendance grew at an unprecedented pace; meanwhile, standards of discipleship appeared to decline. Some scholars estimate that in A.D. 300 Christians comprised no more than 10 percent of the empire, if that; but by the year 360 Christians comprised over 50 percent of the empire.[22] Christianity and Rome gradually became fused until the church of the martyrs became the church of the empire, a dramatic reversal of what had previously been the case. Eusebius, a bishop from Asia Minor and a friend of Constantine's, argued that Constantine's emergence as the Christian emperor was a direct result of the providence of God, allowing Christianity to triumph.[23]

The desert saints constituted a movement of serious Christians who wanted to reclaim the old standards of discipleship, only under very different conditions.[24] Ironically, the enemy they had to face was not an evil empire but a worldly church, not persecution but privilege. They became known as "bloodless martyrs" and "athletes of God."[25] They fled into the desert to protest the church's compromise and to start a countermovement of discipleship. "The flight to the desert represented both a protest and an affirmation—a protest against a decadent and overly institutionalized ecclesiastical body and a restatement of the gospel teaching to fit the changed conditions of the times."[26] They withdrew not so much to escape problems but to engage them. The desert became a place of combat. They fought the devil and found God, purged themselves of sin and cultivated holiness, practiced ascetic disciplines and prayed unceasingly to God. As Antony's story reveals, they obeyed Jesus' words literally: they sold their possessions, gave the money to the poor and followed Jesus. They were zealous, even fanatical. Still, they were on a clear mission to save the church from its own power and success.[27]

WHY THE DESERT?

The desert saints believed that the desert itself is a fitting place to engage in this struggle, for it forces us to face our weaknesses squarely, strips away illusion and pretension, and enables us to recognize our absolute need for God. Antony spent much of his life in the desert because he believed it was a place well suited for struggle and growth. His withdrawal into the desert became the pattern for literally thousands of other desert saints to follow. They cited biblical texts and stories to justify the pattern they followed.[28] The people of Israel spent forty years in the wilderness. Elijah lived in the wilderness for many years too, as did John the Baptist. There they weaned themselves from earthly attachments, practiced the ascetic disciplines, sought the face of God, honed their prophetic

Sinai Desert, Egypt

message and lived by God's provision. Jesus was driven into the wilderness by the Spirit, where he fasted for forty days and resisted the temptations of the devil. Jesus found other occasions to seek "lonely places" too, as the Gospels describe them, usually before he was about to make an important decision. The apostle Paul withdrew into the desert of Arabia to contemplate his conversion, meditate on the gospel and pray to God before being launched into his vocation as a missionary. The desert, of course, is not the only setting for a life of serious discipleship. Jesus did ministry in public places, Isaiah served in the royal court, and Paul planted churches in several of the largest cities of the Roman world. It is therefore not the only setting in which to be a disciple, but it is still a necessary one.

The desert is barren, stark and lonely, thus symbolizing a life that is stripped of distractions, possessions and pleasures. It is a place of extremes—frigid cold at night, unbearable heat during the day, endless sand and rock, dangerous animals, utter emptiness. There are no provisions to meet physical needs, no conveniences to make life run more smoothly, no friendships to dull the edge of loneliness, no settlements to welcome hungry, thirsty travelers. People who face catastrophic difficulties usually use terms like *desert* or *wilderness* to describe their experience. The desert implies isolation, loneliness, temptation and combat—"a barren place, a secret place, a place that humans can make nothing of themselves, where only God can do anything."[29] It is the domain of the devil, useful for his evil purposes; but in an ironic way it is equally the landscape of God, which God uses to make us mature disciples. "Here man takes responsibility for fostering his own inner life and his ability to hear that Word of God when it is spoken. The solitary faces the full mystery of this inner life, in the presence of the invisible God."[30]

The desert saints chose to live in the desert to reclaim a faith that had become too easy and convenient. They read the same Bible we read, but they focused on texts that we tend to ignore.[31] They identified themselves as aliens in this world. "Foxes have holes, and birds of the air have nests; but the Son of man has nowhere to lay his head" (Lk 9:58). They believed that discipleship requires renunciation of everything. "So therefore, none of you can become my disciple if you do not give up all your possessions" (Lk 14:33). They also believed that discipleship engenders conflict and difficulty because it demands a way of life that contradicts natural desires. The desert invited them to train themselves in discipleship, as the apostle Paul enjoined, and thus become mature Christians (1 Tim 4:7-8). Clearly the goal was right, even if the means they used were excessively severe.

The desert saints believed solitude was necessary for spiritual growth. In Scetis, one of the places in Egypt where the desert saints lived, a brother once asked Abba Moses for a word of wisdom. Moses said to him, "Go and sit in your cell, and your cell will teach you everything."[32] Involvement in the world has its place, for God calls us to serve him in the world. But we need distance and quiet too, or the busyness, noise, demands and pressures of the world will consume us. This kind of solitude, however, does not necessarily require absolute separation from society. The desert saints were aware of the dangers and limitations of the cell too. It did not provide a magical

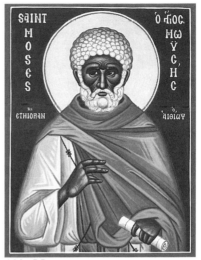

Abba Moses

cure. Amma Matrona taught, "Many people living secluded lives on the mountain have perished by living like people in the world. It is better to live in a crowd and want to live a solitary life than to live a solitary life but all the time be longing for company."[33] Still, regardless of location, the desert forced these saints to fight the most important battle there is—the battle for the soul. The world, the flesh and the devil are formidable foes, as the *Sayings of the Desert Fathers* indicate. The desert saints took those enemies seriously and resisted them. But they also recognized that they were vulnerable to these external forces for a reason, and that reason was an internal one.

THE DARKNESS WITHIN

It was the battle for the soul that mattered the most to them. The desert saints believed that the Christian life requires struggle against the darkness that resides in the heart, epitomized by the egoism that runs rampant in every human being. Only by facing that darkness will we find true life and freedom.[34] One desert saint in particular explored this idea with particular insight. He is now known as the great psychologist of the desert tradition. Precocious and confident, Evagrius Ponticus made his way to Constantinople as a young man. There he met the most famous political and ecclesiastical leaders of his day and was drawn into the intellectual and spiritual

affairs of that great city. But his rapid rise to power had a negative impact
on his spiritual life. An early biographer commented that he was "great in
pomp, made a great deal of caring for his body and had himself ministered
to by slaves." He eventually fell in love with the wife of a prominent member of high society. Horrified by his carelessness and vulnerability, he fled
the city and traveled to the Holy Land, where he met a famous abbess,
Melania the Elder, who invited him to join a monastery and develop discipline in his life. But once again he became complacent. "Satan made the
heart of Evagrius as hard as the heart of Pharaoh." This time a serious illness broke him of his pride. After his recovery Melania suggested that he
journey to the Egyptian desert to practice "the discipline." He spent the
last sixteen years of his life there, and he became a renowned holy man,
miracle worker, writer and teacher. He died in 399.[35]

Evagrius explored why humans are so vulnerable to temptation and so
quick to commit sin. All of us, he said, are subject to certain "thoughts" (logismoi in Greek) that make us susceptible to temptation. He classified
eight kinds of "thoughts," which correspond roughly to the seven deadly
sins that became popular during the Middle Ages. "There are eight general
and basic categories of thoughts in which are included every thought. First
is that of gluttony, then impurity, avarice, sadness [envy], anger, acedia [a
Greek term that means restlessness and boredom], vainglory, and last of
all, pride." Evagrius did not define these sins exclusively in terms of behaviors; he identified them as motives or inclinations too. In essence, he described the problem of the darkness within, the tendency of all human beings, regardless of background and personality, to be egoistic. "It is not in
our power," he wrote, "to determine whether we are disturbed by these
thoughts, but it is up to us to decide if they are to linger within us or not
and whether or not they are to stir up our passions."[36]

For example, he said that gluttony consists of obsession with food,
whether or not we actually eat too much of it. Vainglory tempts us to angle
for attention and honor, regardless of how it can be attained. Pride causes
us to claim credit for our virtues and successes rather than acknowledge our
indebtedness to others and to God. Thus the proud person "gets a big head
in regard to the brethren, considering them stupid because they do not all
have this same opinion of him."[37] But Evagrius did not stop there. As if sin

is not bad enough, he said that the *memory* of sin is even worse, causing us to cling to the pleasures of the past in our minds. "Whatever experience we now undergo while under the influence of passion will in the future persist in us in the form of passionate memories."[38]

The remedy to overcome these thoughts is not simple or easy. Evagrius advised his desert disciples to own up to their vulnerability, resist temptation with courage and practice spiritual discipline, or what he called *ascesis*. "The time of temptation is not the time to leave one's cell, devising plausible pretexts. Rather, stand there firmly and be patient. Bravely take all that the demon brings upon you."[39] Over time such discipline would engender a spirit of calm, peace and serenity, or what Evagrius called *apatheia* (from which we get the word *apathy*, though Evagrius does not use it in that way). Finally, he told them that these "thoughts" cannot be overcome simply by resisting them. They must be replaced by positive virtues—gratitude instead of gluttony, humility in the place of pride and especially love *(agape)*. "*Agape* is the progeny of *apatheia*. *Apatheia* is the very flower of *ascesis*. *Ascesis* consists in keeping the commandments."[40] In the end, however, victory is possible only through the grace and love of God. As Evagrius observed, though passions of the body can be controlled through the exercise of discipline, those of the soul can be overcome only through "spiritual love."

ASCESIS: DISCIPLINE WITH A PURPOSE

The desert saints recognized how perilous it is to live in the fallen world where temptation seems to lurk everywhere. Amma Syncletica taught, "When the devil does not use the goads of poverty to tempt, he uses wealth for the purpose. When he cannot win by scorn and mockery, he tries praise and flattery."[41] They identified comfort and prosperity as enemies of the spiritual life. One Abba warned, "Just as bees are driven out by smoke, and their honey is taken away from them, so a life of ease drives out the fear of the Lord from man's soul and takes away all his good works."[42] The desert saints thus practiced spiritual discipline or *ascesis*, which required daily self-denial and obedience to God in all things, but which also promised to help wean them from worldliness and resist temptation. They became masters of spiritual discipline for this very reason.[43] The desert saints labored to invert the hierarchy of values that usually dominates society. Macarius once taught, "This is the truth, if a monk regards contempt as praise, poverty as riches, and hunger as a feast, he will never die."[44] It was therefore not unusual for them to go to extreme measures to detach themselves from the world. They ate a Spartan diet, slept as little as they could (sometimes refusing to lie down) and lived in isolation. One monk even carried a stone in his mouth for three years to overcome the temptation of gossip and frivolous talk.

They considered marriage and sex as virtual enemies of the spiritual life.[45] They tried to avoid marriage altogether, if they could. Some even resorted to manipulation and craftiness to overcome parental expectations. At this point Syncletica's story comes to mind. Born into a wealthy home in Constantinople, Syncletica was promised in marriage to an illustrious citizen of the same city. She asked her father if she could go on a pilgrimage to the Holy Land before her wedding to fulfill a vow she had made to God. "I have promised to worship my Master there while I am still a virgin. Therefore, if you desire my well-being, do not cut me off from what I aim to do, my father, or something evil might happen to me on account of this."[46] So her father consented. A large entourage accompanied her. She worshiped at many of the holy sites, including caves where desert saints lived, and she distributed a large sum of money to the poor.

Meanwhile, she plotted her escape, hoping "to put an end to the deceit of a frivolous life."[47] She wrote two letters, one to her parents and the other to her servant. "I have offered myself to the God of the universe. Do not, therefore, search for me any longer, for you will not find me. I am leaving here to go where God will lead me."[48] She slipped away from her retinue, fled the city and found an Abba, asking him to help her live a solitary life. The old man prayed for her, provided her with books and clothed her in a habit. Then he sent her off into the desert. "I cast all my concern upon the Lord and prayed that I be veiled from human sight, having given myself to that desert."[49] She found a cave, where she lived for twenty-eight years before being discovered by a wandering Abba, who described her as radiating light and holiness.

For the vast majority of desert saints, however, this pattern of *ascesis* was far more humane and normal than would at first appear.[50] Every desert saint came under the influence of a mentor or Abba, including the famous Antony.[51] Abbas introduced their spiritual apprentices to the rigors of discipleship and instructed them in Christian doctrine. They were not to impose their own will on disciples, as if they were the superior; instead, they were to offer suggestions, provide encouragement, impart the wisdom of the desert and, above all, set an example.[52] Poemen, an Abba almost as famous as Antony, warned Abbas to practice what they preached. "Teach your heart to keep what your tongue teaches others. . . . Men try to appear excellent in their preaching, they are less excellent in practicing what they preach."[53]

Antony preaching

The communication between master and disciples was entirely oral, which engendered a vast network of relationships, a useful corrective to the isolation they valued and sought. In fact, in the areas of Egypt where the largest concentration of desert saints congregated—Scetis, Nitria and the Cells—disciples would gather on Sunday to worship, receive the sacraments and listen to instruction. Young disciples would ask questions, and Abbas would answer them. Over time this teaching—memorized and meditated on, studied and passed on—became an oral tradition. Its authority was based on faithfulness to Scripture and association with the name of famous Abbas or Ammas. As Esias of Scetis said, "Brothers, whatever I heard and saw in the company of those old men I have handed on to you; adding nothing, taking nothing away; so that, walking in their footsteps, we may be judged worthy to share their inheritance."[54]

When the great masters began to die off, these sayings were collected and put into writing, becoming known as *The Sayings of the Desert Fathers* (and Mothers).[55] Other writers, like John Cassian, wrote more elaborate theological works *(The Conferences)* to preserve and explain the same tradition of teaching in a more sophisticated and systematic form.[56] The movement eventually produced several generations of leaders for the church. Many famous bishops who served the church during the fourth and fifth centuries—Augustine of Hippo, Martin of Tours, Hilary of Poitiers, Athanasius of Alexandria, John Chrysostom—spent considerable time in isolation and practiced "the discipline," even after they assumed church office. Their experience in the desert helped to prepare them for the lofty position. Weaned of ambition, greed and desire for power, they carried out their episcopal duties as servants of the church. Their influence bears witness to the power of the desert.[57] Women too achieved high status in the church by becoming desert saints, thereby transcending the traditional roles imposed on them by society. They served as advisers, patrons, founders of monasteries and servants to the poor.[58]

The desert saints followed a rhythm of work, prayer and solitude. They lived in small stone huts or caves, and they practiced some kind of trade— for example, weaving mats or baskets—to provide for basic necessities. What they did not use or eat they gave away, thus supporting the poor, though they were usually poorer. They prayed too, even while they worked, thus fulfilling the biblical command to "pray without ceasing." Their diet consisted of dry bread, which could last up to six months, water, salt, a little oil, fresh vegetables and lentils. They fasted according to the church year and listened to, memorized, and meditated on Scripture. The Bible had to be committed to memory because there were so few copies available. On Sundays they gathered for worship and received the Eucharist if a priest was present. In short, the practice of *ascesis*, whether in severity or in moderation, characterized their daily life.

APATHEIA: IMPERTURBABLE CALM

Yet such *ascesis*, however well-intended, could cause as much harm as good. Some of the desert saints became fanatics, thus tarnishing the reputation of the movement as a whole. Some ransacked or destroyed pagan temples and started riots. Others built huts that never allowed them to stretch out or to stand up, went without sleep for days at a time and fasted until they became emaciated.[59] Ironically, the desert saints had to guard against temptations associated with the very disciplines they practiced so assiduously. The great teachers of the movement were well aware of this fanaticism and often criticized it. Discipline of the body was not the goal. At best it was a means. Passion was the real enemy. To master passion, they had to reach a state of "imperturbable calm," as Evagrius called it, or perfect "equilibrium," as it was referred to in the biography of St. Antony.

They prized moderation over excess for this very reason. Some of the old men were fond of saying, "If you see a young man climbing up to heaven by his own will, catch him by the foot and pull him down to earth: it is not good for him."[60] They were not above poking fun at those who appeared to be too earnest about the spiritual life. In one of many humorous stories found in the *Sayings*, a young man approached Abba Silvanus on Mount Sinai to express concern about brothers who were wasting time doing something as undignified, unnecessary and unspiritual as common labor. The young man quoted several Scriptures to prove that true disciples should pray, not waste time doing ordinary chores, for "Mary has chosen the better part" (Lk 10:42). Abba Silvanus summoned an assistant, saying to him, "Put this brother in a cell where there is nothing." The day passed without incident. But by late afternoon the young disciple was hungry, and he wondered why no one had brought him anything to eat. So he found Abba Silvanus and asked if the brothers had eaten yet. "Yes, they have eaten already," replied Silvanus. "Why did you not call me?" Silvanus replied, "You are a spiritual person and do not need food. We are earthly, and since we want to eat, we work with our hands." Then, to drive the point home, he quoted (perhaps playfully) the very text the young brother had used to prove his superiority. "But you have chosen the good part, reading all day, and not wanting to take earthly food." The apprentice was pierced to the heart, bowed before Silvanus and repented. Silvanus commented, "I think Mary always needs Martha, and by Martha's help Mary is praised."[61]

They criticized exaggerated use of *ascesis* too. Abba Poemen said that true fasting does not necessarily require going without food. "I would have everyone eat a little less than he wants, every day." Referring to his behavior as a young man, he told a fellow disciple that he used to fast for days on end. "But the great elders have tested all these things, and they found that it is good to eat something every day, but on some days a little less. And they have shown us that this is the king's highway, for it is easy and light."[62] In another story from the desert tradition, three zealous disciples visited an old man in Scetis. The first bragged that he could recite the entire Bible, to which the old man said, "You have filled the air with words." The second claimed that he had copied the whole Bible with his own hand, but the old man retorted that he had only produced more books to line a shelf. The third said that his chimney had grass growing in it, thus proving that he refused to heat his little hermitage even in the winter. "You have driven away hospitality," the old man replied.[63] No movement in the history of Christianity exceeded the desert saints in asceticism; yet the masters in the movement acknowledged the dangers of excess (i.e., achieving great feats rather than great virtue) and reminded the community to keep the proper goal in mind. Perhaps Abba Moses summed it up best: "As the fathers have said, all extremes are equally harmful," whether the extreme of fasting or of gluttony, of vigils or of too much sleep.[64]

Surprisingly, the *Sayings* contain a number of stories that indicate that the desert is not necessarily the only place, or even the best place, to train oneself in the faith, and that the practice of rigorous discipline is not the only way, or even the best way, to become a mature disciple. God can use virtually any setting to do his deeper work in us in order to help us reach a state of imperturbable calm. The true test of discipleship involves how believers live for God wherever they are, whether in the desert or in the city, whether celibate or married, whether in solitude or in community. One of the greatest of the desert stories tells how Abba Macarius heard a voice telling him that he had not yet attained the standard of maturity of two women who lived in a nearby city. He immediately went to the city and found the two women. He asked them, "Tell me how you live a religious life." Surprised by his question, they told Macarius that they had been married for fifteen years; in fact, they had had sexual relations with their husbands the night before (a comment that would have shocked and offended Macarius). Asking their husbands if they could live the celibate life, they had been denied. So they purposed to live faithfully for God as wives, choosing to show kindness and speak graciously to everyone they knew, especially to each other. Macarius then said, "Truly, it is not whether you are virgin or a married woman, a monk or a man in the world: God gives his Holy Spirit to everyone, according to their earnestness of purpose."[65]

AGAPE: THE GOAL OF VIRTUE

Struggle itself was not the end but the means. It might be constant, but it would not be permanent. The goal was inner transformation, especially as it found expression in the highest of the virtues—humility and charity (or love). "How do I find God?" a young disciple asked a master. Fasts? Labor? Vigils? Yes, the old man replied, many practice these disciplines, but do not profit because they lack discretion. "Even if our mouths stink with fasting, and we have learned all the Scriptures, and memorized the whole Psalter, we still lack what God wants—humility and charity."[66]

Humility was necessary because it kept the desert saints from becoming proud of their spiritual feats and from assuming that they were more worthy of God's favor than ordinary Christians. A devil once appeared to a disciple as an angel of light, announcing that he was the angel Gabriel. But the disciple said, "See whether you were not sent to someone else. I am not worthy that an angel should be sent to me."[67] On one occasion Macarius was accused of seducing a young woman, which ruined both her and his reputation. Though the accusation was false, Macarius refused to defend himself. Instead, he provided for her needs, which gave the impression that he was in fact guilty. Some time later the truth came out, thus vindicating Macarius. But Macarius fled in order to avoid the praise he was about to receive.[68]

Charity was the ultimate goal, and sacrificial service its primary manifestation. Serapion, for example, sold a book containing the four Gospels to give the money to the poor and hungry. Later he said, "I have sold the book which told me to sell all that I had and give to the poor."[69] A young disciple once asked an Abba which of two men was more acceptable to God—the man who fasted six days at a time or the man who cared for the sick. The old man replied, "If the brother, who fasts six days, even hung himself up by his nostrils, he could never be the equal of him who ministers to the sick."[70] Hospitality was considered of special value because it provided a concrete way of showing charity. Accused of breaking his fast during Lent, one old man said, "Fasting is ever with me. I cannot keep you here for ever. Fasting is useful and necessary, but we can choose to fast or not fast. God's law demands from us perfect charity. In you I receive Christ: and so I must do all I can to show you the offices of charity."[71] The fifth-century Abba St. Mark the Ascetic stated how *ascesis* and *apatheia* have as their ultimate goal *agape*. "Of all the commandments, therefore, the most comprehensive is to love God and our neighbor. This love is

Sayings of the Desert Fathers

"Abbot Anastasius had a book written on very fine parchment which was worth eighteen pence, and had in it both the Old and New Testaments in full. Once a certain brother came to visit him, and seeing the book made off with it. So that day when Abbot Anastasius went to read his book, and found that it was gone, he realized that the brother had taken it. But he did not send after him to inquire about it for fear that the brother might add perjury to theft. Well, the brother went down into the nearby city in order to sell the book. And the price he asked was sixteen pence. The buyer said: Give me the book that I may find out whether it is worth that much. With that, the buyer took the book to the holy Anastasius and said: Father, take a look at this book, please, and tell me whether you think I ought to buy it for sixteen pence. Is it worth that much? Abbot Anastasius said: Yes, it is a fine book, it is worth that much. So the buyer went back to the brother and said: Here is your money. I showed the book to Abbot Anastasius and he said it is a fine book and is worth at least sixteen pence. But the brother asked: Was that all he said? Did he make any other remarks? No, said the buyer, he did not say another word. Well, said the brother, I have changed my mind and I don't want to sell this book after all. Then he hastened to Abbot Anastasius and begged him with tears to take back his book, but the Abbot would not accept it, saying: Go in peace, brother, I make you a present of it. But the brother said: If you do not take it back I shall never have any peace. After that the brother dwelt with Abbot Anastasius for the rest of his life." (Thomas Merton, ed., The Wisdom of the Desert)

made firm through abstaining from material things *[ascesis]*, and through stillness of thoughts *[apatheia]*."[72]

These expressions of *agape* did not stay confined to the desert. Surprisingly, the desert saints exercised considerable influence over the wider population, which proves once again that physical isolation did not always lead to social ostracism or spiritual irrelevance. People became fascinated by these strange men and women who left behind everything to seek God in the desert. Many joined the movement, so many in fact that contemporary observers commented that the desert became as populated as the city. Others sought their advice, believing that the desert saints, as detached as they were from the world, would serve as trustworthy advisers. Thus even the great Simeon the Stylite, who lived atop a Roman pillar for some thirty years, became adviser and mentor to the wealthy and powerful. From time to time the desert saints even traveled to cities to serve the needy, protest injustice, battle heretics and witness against the compromised state of the church. Remaining on the margins of society, they nevertheless challenged, comforted and served the mainstream.[73]

THE MODERN DESERT

Is this strange movement still relevant to us who will not—and probably cannot—live in a literal desert? Few of us will become desert saints. Our place of engagement will be different. It will be in our homes and schools and places of work. But the struggles we face are the same. We too must battle against the world, the flesh and the devil. We too must confront the darkness within, our persistent egoism. The desert saints challenge us to dare to face these struggles squarely by entering some kind of desert where, stripped of security, distraction and comfort, we will confront the devil and meet the living God, just as Jesus did. Such a hard place of struggle might actually spare us from having to face more serious problems, such as the devastating consequences of unrestrained sin. "Life is difficult," psychiatrist M. Scott Peck wrote many years ago in his bestselling *The Road Less Traveled*. Peck could have added that human nature is difficult too. The darkness of the human soul is the real and ultimate enemy.

The desert will also enable us to see how unfriendly modern culture is to the spiritual life. It seduces us into being too busy, too ambitious and too self-indulgent. We never seem to be satisfied; we always seem to want more. Thomas Merton, a convert to Catholicism, a Trappist monk and a devoted student of the desert saints, observed that people seem to be in constant need of activity and success. The frenzied pace of their lives poses a threat to spiritual health. Many people fail to make progress in the spiritual life, he said, because "they are attached to activities and enterprises that seem to be important." Thus

> blinded by their desire for ceaseless motion, for a constant sense of achievement, famished with a crude hunger for results, for visible and tangible success, they work themselves into a state in which they cannot believe that they are pleasing God unless they are busy with a dozen jobs at the same time.[74]

The desert saints call us to resist these cultural values by seeking solitude, which might separate us just enough from modern culture to allow us to recognize, expose and combat our vulnerability to its seductive power. Abba Antony once said, "The man who abides in solitude and is quiet, is delivered from fighting three battles—those of hearing, speech and sight. Then he will have but one battle to fight—the battle of the heart."[75] Like the desert saints, we too must withdraw into the desert. But it will most likely be a different kind of desert, and it will most likely require a different kind of sacrifice, one less obvious but no less necessary and significant. Heroic feats are not as useful as the subtle and deliberate choices we make every day to submit ourselves to God. The desert will force us to hold our appetites in check, to resist the temptations of the devil and to seek the face of God.

We should start modestly—sit in an empty church sanctuary for an hour in total silence just to listen to God, pray for a half hour in the morning before leaving for work, go without dessert during Lent, fast from watching TV for a month, serve in an inner-city ministry one Saturday a month, donate another 2 to 3 percent of our income to charitable causes, or set aside one evening a week to invite people into our homes who rarely receive such invitations. Jesus said that the person who is faithful in little will also be faithful in much. These "little" gestures might engender big changes over time. Who knows where it will all end?

"The self always dies hard," Martin Luther once said. It dies hard because it resists giving up habits of mind and body that satisfy immediate desires but in the long run destroy the life of the soul. However much it resists, the self must still die. It will die as we struggle against the world, the flesh, the devil and the darkness within. We must *submit* to this struggle when it is imposed on us through difficult circumstances; we must *choose* to struggle when God calls us to discipline our appetites, resist temptations that threaten to undermine the good work he wants to do in us, and confess our egoism. Above all, we must pray daily what the psalmist prayed,

> Search me, O God, and know my heart;
> test me and know my thoughts.
> See if there is any wicked way in me,
> and lead me in the way everlasting. (Ps 139:23-24)

PRACTICES

- Read Luke 4:1-13.
- God created us with appetites. But God did not intend that we be ruled by these appetites, as we often are. Identify an appetite that seems to be dominating your life. (It could be food or gadgets or TV or shopping or golf or gossip.)
- Commit yourself to fasting from it for a period of time.
- In place of that appetite, memorize an appropriate passage of Scripture and pray for areas of the world that lack what you so desperately crave.

4

Rhythm

The Spirituality of Monasticism

"All who believed were together and had all things in common. . . .
Day by day, as they spent much time together in the temple,
they broke bread at home and ate their food with glad and generous hearts,
praising God and having the goodwill of all the people."

ACTS 2:44, 46-47

Monasteries function today much as they did fifteen hundred years ago. The routine, the worship, the daily labor, the layout of the grounds, the study, the discipline and the practice of lectio divina follow the same pattern that was first established when these institutions were founded in the Roman world. They are the embodiment of tradition, perhaps more than any other institution in Western civilization. Monasteries still dot the landscape too, just as they did in the Middle Ages, not only in Europe, where they are most visible, but also in the United States and around the rest of the Christian world. I live in Spokane, Washington, and I know of half a dozen monasteries in and around the city. To most of us they are invisible institutions. We drive by them every day, but we fail to take notice. We hear their names, but we know little about them, and we probably care even less. Very few Christians in America know a person who belongs to a religious order, very few understand the history of the monastic movement, very few appreciate the rich legacy of these institutions. We treat them as if they were like ancient ruins, a curiosity perhaps, but little more.

It was not always so. The monastic movement peaked in twelfth-century Europe and has steadily declined since then, though there have been a number of significant revivals along the way, including one in the nineteenth century. In what is known as the "high" Middle Ages (1050-1300), several thousand monasteries dotted the European landscape, and they played a dominant role in the culture. Towns grew up around them, which explains why even today monasteries, or at least their ruins, sit in the center of many European cities. Monasteries once owned large tracks of land, and the monks turned that land into prosperous farms, ranches and vineyards. Monks became masters of skilled trades too, and they put those trades to good use, producing items like furniture, wine and cloth. Monks copied, illuminated, cataloged and stored manuscripts in large libraries. They collected paintings, mosaics, sculptures, relics and other cultural artifacts, established schools to teach people to read and write, and deployed missionaries to win barbarian groups to Christianity, thus helping to evangelize Western Europe during its darkest years. In short, monasteries preserved and spread the cultural heritage of Western civilization. We are profoundly indebted to these institutions for preserving this legacy, a legacy we value so much.

But our indebtedness goes deeper than that, touching on something profoundly spiritual. At their very inception monasteries established a daily, weekly and yearly rhythm based on a Christian view of time, and they have continued to do so ever since. Monasteries sanctify time, as if to show that all time belongs to God and our use of time finds meaning only if we do our tasks, both religious and secular, to honor and serve God.[1] Monastic rhythm strikes a balance between two activities—prayer and work—which constitute the basic purpose for which humans were created. God calls us to seek his face in prayer and to do his work in the world. Monastic spirituality affirms that we must do *both* activities if we hope to fulfill the purpose for which God created us.

Peter Levi, a one-time Jesuit and professor of poetry at Oxford, claims that this sense of rhythm sets monasteries apart as unique institutions. When Levi was first exposed to such rhythm he thought it oppressive. But eventually he changed his mind, recognizing that the intent is to set a person free. "If one spends a week or a month [in a monastery], a different scale and pattern of time imposes itself, which at first one resists as if one were in prison. When this new time-scale is accepted, it soaks into one's bones and penetrates one's mind." As Levi observed, monastic rhythm replaces a hectic pace with "a tranquil, unhurried, absolutely dominating rhythm. This specially undisturbed yet specially rhythmical sense of time is the greatest difference between monastic life and any other." In Levi's mind this rhythm is grounded in the monastic liturgy, the most distinctive feature of the monastery. "Beyond the rhythm of days is the underlying rhythm of seasons and festivals. The liturgy sets the pace: above all, the night hours and early morning hours."[2]

I have a vested interest in this chapter, perhaps more than the others. My visits to a monastery saved my life. During a period of difficulty in my life I found solace and recovered my equilibrium by submitting on occasion to a monastic rhythm. Sister Florence, the superior in a local monastic community, heard about my situation and decided to make the services of the monastery available to me. She wrote me a letter and invited me to enter the life of the community whenever I wanted. I took her up on the offer. My first visit felt like I was returning to a familiar place. Over the next few years I visited the monastery many times. I spent hours in one of its little hermitages on a wooded hillside. I sat in silence, wept, prayed, wrestled with God, evaluated the direction of my life. On occasion I met with Sister Florence for conversation and prayer. I can remember conversations with her in which not a word was spoken. That little monastery became like a second home to me, though I did not really visit it that often. It helped me to find a new rhythm for my life. My "work" was obvious—to reconstruct my life and care for my children. But my experience at the monastery invited me to commit myself to a life of prayer as well, even though for a time I had no idea how to pray. The nuns prayed for me too, as they do to this day. That rhythm of work and prayer enabled me to make it through the hardest and loneliest months of my life.

BIBLICAL RHYTHMS

Rhythm is at the very heart of biblical faith. God established a rhythm from the first moment of creation. The creation story itself follows a rhythmic pattern. God created a day—the first of seven—to provide temporal space to do his mighty work. "And there was evening and there was morning, the first day." Then a second day, followed by a third day, through six days, as if creation was a kind of symphony in six movements (Gen 1). God established a second kind of rhythm when he completed creation; this was the rhythm of the week, the only division of time we know of that is not based on the movements of heavenly bodies. The week as seven days exists because God created it. Nature does not provide a reason why it must be seven days. It could be five, or ten, or even more.

> Thus the heavens and the earth were finished, and all their multitude. And on the seventh day God finished his work that he had done, and he rested on the seventh day from all his work which he had done. So God blessed the seventh day and hallowed it, because on it God rested from all his work that he had done in creation. (Gen 2:1-3)

Thus God established the rhythm of seven days—six days for work and one for rest, worship and prayer. God rested after he created the world; God expects his human creation to do the same. The fourth commandment mandates that God's people follow this divine rhythm too (Ex 20:8-11).

The Hebrews also followed a yearly rhythm, again based on religious principles. They celebrated the Passover to remember how God delivered them from slavery in Egypt, and they used various symbols (blood on the doorposts, unleavened bread, bitter herbs) to remind them of God's mighty acts. They celebrated the Feast of Weeks (later known as Pentecost) in the spring and New Years in the fall to remind them of God's provision, both at the beginning of harvest and at the end. Finally, they observed Yom Kippur, the Day of Atonement, to confess sin, to purge the community of wrongdoing and to thank God for cleansing (see Deuteronomy). Other annual festivals were added later, largely as a result of God's continued work in their history. The Feast of Purim, for example, commemorates how God used Esther to protect the Jews from certain annihilation, and Hanukkah marks how God used the Maccabees to win Israel's independence. In this way the people of Israel followed a yearly cycle of religious ceremonies that reminded them of what God had done for them and who they were as God's chosen people.

The early church continued to follow this Jewish rhythm.[3] As faithful Jews they observed the sabbath, though they also began to worship God on Sundays as well, the day on which Jesus was raised from the dead. The church eventually added other days to its calendar, too—Easter and Holy Week, Pentecost, Christmas, and the like. This Christianization of the calendar was intended to establish an annual rhythm for the Christian community. Such a rhythm reminded the community of God's gracious work on their behalf, created a sense of unity around the most important events of their history, like the resurrection, and assured them that the God who had worked in the past to accomplish his redemptive purposes would continue to do so in the future until his redemptive plan was completed. The early Christian calendar enabled the church to see time as a medium that belongs to God and unfolds according to God's purposes.[4]

The early church followed a daily rhythm too, especially in the first years of its existence, when the church was still flush with the excitement of Pentecost. Luke tells us that believers gathered together daily for prayer and fellowship, and they held all things in common. In what appears to be an expression of voluntary communism, believers sold their possessions and distributed the money to the needy, a discipline which the desert saints practiced later on. They attended the temple every day for worship, and in the evenings they met in private homes for common meals. They listened to the teachings of the apostles and shared their faith freely with anyone who would listen (Acts 2:42-47; 4:32-37). Again, though this rhythm borrowed heavily from Judaism, it was clearly adapted to the new reality of Jesus Christ. The history and practices of Judaism receded into the background; the incarnation, death and resurrection of Jesus became the center piece. The entire life of the believing community became reoriented and reorganized around him. "With great power the apostles gave their testimony to the resurrection of the Lord Jesus, and great grace was upon them all" (Acts 4:33).

MONASTIC ROOTS

The monastic movement adapted this biblical rhythm to a unique set of circumstances, the same circumstances, as it turns out, that also gave birth to desert spirituality. The growth of the church under the emperor Constantine did not please everyone. A group of zealous believers, who had not forgotten the persecution under Diocletian, wanted to uphold the old standards of discipleship that the martyrs had established, for they believed that the Christian faith requires the sacrifice of one's life to God. A few decided to establish communities of faith in the desert to witness against and to create an alternative to the churches of the city, which were being overrun by people who were joining the Christian movement because it seemed the fashion and promised immediate—and worldly—benefits.[5] Opposing the "material advantage" that the new Christianity under Constantine provided, the monks decided to launch a countermovement. "Under such conditions," David Knowles, the great historian of monasticism, writes, "there has always occurred a revolt of some or many against what seems to them prevailing laxity; they choose the narrow way, in the words of Jesus, leading to eternal life."[6]

The structure of these monasteries evolved over time, though the foundation laid at the very beginning has endured to this day. The rhythm of prayer and work has always characterized the movement. The impetus no doubt came from the desert saints, who, as we have already observed, did not live in the kind of complete isolation that romanticized accounts indicate. Most followed a pattern of prayer and work. Abbas would gather a group of disciples around them, and these disciples would live in close proximity to each other. The disciples would spend time alone—praying, practicing "the discipline" and doing common labor. Then they would gather on Sundays for worship, instruction and conversation. This pattern established by the first generation of desert saints gave rise to the more formal monastic movement that emerged later.[7]

The official founder of Egyptian monasticism was Pachomius (c. 290-346). The son of pagans, Pachomius was conscripted to serve in the Roman army. While stationed in Thebes, he met a group of Christians, who were described as doing "all manner of good to everyone." "They treat us with love for the sake of the God of heaven." He was so impressed by their

Pachomius

behavior that he purposed to convert to Christianity after his release from the army and to serve the poor and needy just as they did. When his tour of duty came to an end, he joined a Christian community, received instruction and submitted to baptism. On the eve of his baptism he had a vision in which he saw dew falling from heaven, turning to honey in his hands. A voice from heaven told him that so his future would be. At first he was content to remain under the guidance of a local church. But then he withdrew into the desert and practiced asceticism under the supervision of an abba. Eventually Pachomius was told in a vision to "serve mankind" and "to fashion the souls of men so as to present them pure to God."[8]

Curiously, Pachomius chose to obey this command by starting the first monastery, which included his brother, Palamon (who was his mentor) and a handful of other followers. The first experiment failed; subsequent efforts succeeded, but only gradually. By the end of the fourth century the communities started under Pachomius's leadership included some seven thousand monks. Though the process of formation was fluid, the goal of the movement was clear from the beginning. "What we do see," comments Philip Rousseau, "is a man who tried gradually to define the best setting in which ascetics might support each other both spiritually and materially. He saw the enterprise as the necessary fulfillment of New Testament demands of brotherly love."[9]

Over time the movement became more carefully organized. Pachomian monasteries assigned two monks to a small room or "cell," as it was called; ten cells constituted a house, organized according to the skills and duties of the monks and supervised by a "superior." The monks followed a regular routine. The morning began with prayers, followed by labor, which changed from week to week so that the monks could rotate such duties as tailoring, weaving, carpentry, gardening and baking. In the evening the monks listened to instruction, recited verses and discussed theology. Again, they prayed before retiring to their cells for sleep. They ate two meals a day, which consisted of bread, cooked vegetables and dried fruit.

The purpose of these monasteries was not merely to establish a regimen of discipline but to nurture spiritual—and therefore interior—growth. The example of Christ—his incarnation and sacrificial death, love and service, lowliness and kindness—set the pattern for behavior.[10] But the example of Pachomius as the ideal monk played a role too. He exhibited humility, kindness and wisdom, and he was genuinely concerned about the spiritual welfare of the monks in the community. As one biographer writes, "We used to think that all the saints were made holy and unswerving by God without regard to their free will, from their mothers' womb, and that sinners were not able to have life because they had been created that way." Pachomius provided an alternative to such a fatalistic assumption. "But now we see the goodness of God manifested in our father who, although born from pagan parents, has become so dear to God and has clothed himself with all God's commandments."[11] Pachomius wanted to encourage that same kind of transformation in others. The goal of his monasteries was to help facilitate the restoration of the image of God in sinful humans. "When you see a man who is pure and humble, that is a vision great enough. For what is greater than such a vision, to see the invisible God in a visible man, his temple?"[12] Pachomius followed a routine of prayer and work, which was used by the Holy Spirit to make him such a formidable Christian leader. That discipline set the standard for his followers.

Prominent leaders also began to organize communities outside Egypt that built on this Egyptian foundation.[13] Two founders stand out. Basil the Great (330-379), bishop of Caesarea, grew up in a wealthy, Christian home in Cappadocia, Asia Minor, a region which had then only recently been introduced to Christianity.[14] He received his formal education in Antioch and Athens. For a brief period of time his native intelligence and advanced education made him worldly and arrogant, but his older sister, Macrina, confronted him and called him back to faith in Christ. He then embarked on a tour of monasteries in Egypt, where he was exposed to the desert saints and to the mystical writings of Origen. Returning to Cappadocia, he was ordained as presbyter in 364 and bishop of Caesarea in 370. At that point he joined himself in battle against the Arians over the question of the nature of Christ, and he helped to shape the theological position of the orthodox party that has prevailed to this day. He also wrote perhaps the most formative book on the Holy Spirit to come out of early Christianity.[15]

Basil laid the foundation, both written and institutional, for Eastern Orthodox monasticism. His "Shorter Rule" and "Longer Rule" (both written in question and answer form) established guidelines for the monasteries he founded.[16] Like other monastic founders, he struck a balance between prayer and work. He believed that monasteries had a responsibility to serve the common good of society. He required all monks to perform hard labor, for "we must not treat the ideal of piety as an excuse for idleness or a means of escaping toil." He directed monks to care for the needy too, arguing that "it is God's will that we should nourish the hungry, give the thirsty to drink, clothe the naked."[17] Consequently, Basil started hostels, soup kitchens, hospitals for those who suffered from infectious diseases and other ministries to the poor, and he used his pulpit to preach against exploitation, conspicuous consumption, profiteering and avarice. His efforts were so successful that a virtual city of charity grew up around the church.

Basil argued that monks should pray too, not simply for themselves but for others. How, he wondered, could monks ever learn to pray if they lived in isolation? Up to this point most monastic leaders viewed the "cenobitical" life (that is, monks living in community) as a concession to the weakness and frivolity of human nature. They viewed the "eremitical" life (monks living alone) as superior because it required heroic discipline, such as living for long periods of time alone. Basil challenged that assumption. He reasoned that while the solitary life leads to self-discipline, "this is plainly in conflict with the law of love which the apostle fulfilled when he sought not his own advantage, but that of the many which might be saved." Living in community forces people to learn how to get along with others, which, considering fallen human nature, is no easy task. In his mind praying for the community was an expression of love, assuming that acts of charity followed. So Basil encouraged leaders (whom he called "superiors") to function as guides and physicians of the soul, "not being angry with the sick but fighting the disease. . . . Let him face the illness and by more laborious regime if necessary, cure the soul's sickness."[18]

Augustine (354-430), bishop of Hippo, played a pivotal role too, though less directly. After his conversion under the influence of Ambrose, the bishop of Milan, Augustine returned to his native North Africa to start a monastic community of study and prayer with his dearest friends. He was appointed the bishop of Hippo against his will a few years later. But even as a bishop he organized a quasi-monastic community for pastors of the church. He sketched a Rule for monasteries too, though not by intention. While serving as bishop he wrote a letter to a group of women whose nunnery was being torn apart by dissension. In the letter Augustine outlined principles that a community should follow if it hopes to be healthy. Like Basil, he believed that living with others is necessary for the cultivation of spiritual maturity, for life in community provides the best—in fact, the only—setting in which the most important of all virtues can be formed, and that is the virtue of love. "Perfection" in the spiritual life is impossible to attain as long as a person lives alone, for how can that person learn how to love? Over time this "Rule of St. Augustine," as it came to be called, was adapted to a variety of settings. For example, priests applied it to the small, intimate communities they formed while serving as parish pastors, which later became known as the Canons Regular.

Rome's decline and eventual collapse created a vacuum that the monastic movement was poised to fill. In 410 a migrant people (formerly known as "barbarians") invaded Italy and marched toward Rome. Under the leadership of Alaric they sacked the city and carried away much of its wealth. Rome recovered, but not for long. In 476 the last emperor to rule in the West abandoned the throne (until Charlemagne was crowned Holy Roman Emperor in the year 800). The western half of the empire fell into ruins—cities declined in population, trade routes were cut off, the economy suffered, agricultural production fell. Thus began the period in the history of Western Europe known as the "Dark Ages." It would last for several hundred years, though not without significant periods of cultural revival. The fall of Rome catapulted the West into a major crisis. "Those who had welcomed the alliance between Christianity and the power of the world were given pause," states Anthony C. Meisel and M. L. del Mastro, two scholars of Benedictine monasticism.

> Suddenly the illusion of stability and solid security that political and economic prosperity had created shimmered and started to dissolve. Transience and impermanence were once again operative realities. Christians were forcibly reminded that their Kingdom was not of this world.[19]

The monastery emerged as a force for good in a world that seemed to be falling apart. Over the next several centuries literally hundreds of monasteries were founded; they became the most stable feature of the European landscape. The combination of monastic prayer and work helped to establish stability during a period of cultural chaos.

THE RULE OF ST. BENEDICT

The stage was finally set for Benedict of Nursia (c. 480-c. 550), the most influential monastic leader in the Western church.[20] Benedict grew up on an estate in Italy, which was at the time occupied by Ostrogoths. Attending school in Rome, he recoiled from the worldly behavior he observed in his fellow students. Disillusioned by the experience, he left Rome at the age of twenty to pursue the life of a hermit, and, living in a cave, he practiced severe asceticism for several years. Eventually a handful of young, zealous believers heard about his ascetic exploits and asked that he organize them into a monastic community. His first attempt to start a monastery failed because the monks under his charge resented his rigorous demands. According to his biographer, Gregory the Great, who served as pope in Rome from 590-604, they actually tried to poison him. So Benedict withdrew once more into solitude. Then another group of disciples approached him to found a monastery. Benedict tried again, this time moving to Monte Cassino, a place so remote that pagans still used a sacred grove of trees there as a site for worship. Benedict cut down the sacred trees, overturned the pagan altar and built a monastery. Then he wrote a Rule to lay down guidelines for the community. Now known as "The Rule of St. Benedict," these guidelines are still used around the world today. The reason for its success is obvious. The Rule strikes a balance between severity and moderation, structure and flexibility, general principles and specific rules, and it uses Scripture throughout the entire document to support the guidelines it lays out. It has become one of the most influential documents in Western civilization.[21]

Benedictine work. Like his predecessors, Benedict required monasteries to practice both work and prayer. The most important kind of work was done by the abbot, who was called to provide competent leadership for the monastery. It was not what the abbot *said* that ultimately mattered, though

Benedictine meal

his instruction did carry authority, but how the abbot *lived*. Consequently, the abbot was to show the monks "by deeds, more than by words, what is good and holy." The abbot was accountable directly to God for the spiritual health of the monks. "The abbot should always remember that he will be held accountable on Judgment Day for his teaching and the obedience of his charges. The abbot must be led to understand that any lack of good in his monks will be held as his fault." The abbot was commanded to love the monks, treating them all alike, whether they came from aristocratic backgrounds or from peasant families. It was a weighty responsibility that required vigilance, humility and discernment. "He should recognize the difficulty of his position—to care for and guide the spiritual development of many different characters. One must be led by friendliness, another by sharp rebukes, another by persuasion. The abbot must adapt himself to cope with individuality so that no member of the community leaves and he may celebrate the monastery's growth."[22]

The abbot was responsible for discipline in the monastery, too. Benedictine discipline was moderate and redemptive, aiming for the restoration and growth of the monks. It followed a series of steps. Abbots issued a warning to errant monks first (say, if they were guilty of excessive talking). Then, if a warning did not succeed, abbots rebuked the guilty monks before the entire community. If there was still no change, abbots excommunicated them, which meant that they would be barred from the Eucharist and worship. Failing that, abbots beat stubborn monks. Only then were monks expelled from the community. Even so, readmission was allowed if they showed sorrow for their sins and were willing to submit to a regimen of penance. The degree of gravity of the misdeed determined the severity of the punishment. A minor infraction required a mild rebuke, a major infraction something much stronger. In any case, the purpose was clear. "The abbot must take care, with diligence and cautious practical wisdom, not to lose any of his flock. He must remember that he has undertaken the care of sick souls, not the repression of healthy ones. . . . He should follow the lead of the Good Shepherd who left ninety-nine sheep behind to search for the lost one."[23] This special attention extended far beyond the exercise of discipline too. The abbot also cared for the needs of the sick, the very young and the very old.[24]

The Rule outlined a simple way of life for the monks. All monks had to perform common labor. They developed specialties, like copying manuscripts or making wine, but they also did chores in common, like working in the kitchen, which assured that every monk—abbot and novice alike—would remain humble, doing mundane tasks that served the common good of the community. However productive and successful their labor, monks were not allowed to own anything. Instead, they held all property and goods in common. "The vice of private ownership must be uprooted from the monastery. No one, without the abbot's permission, shall dare give, receive or keep *anything*—not book, tablet or pen—nothing at all. Monks have nei-

The Rule of St. Benedict

"The brothers should wait on one another. No one is to be excused from kitchen duty unless he is ill or he is engaged in a task of greater import, for he can thus obtain great charity and commendation. Depending on the size of the monastery and the convenient arrangement of the kitchen, let the weaker brothers have help to keep them from worry. The cellarer may be exempted from kitchen service in a large monastery, as may those engaged in more vital jobs as we have said. Let the remainder serve each other in charity. After completing his weekly kitchen chores, the monk should clean on Saturday. He must wash the towels the brothers use for drying hands and feet. Everyone's feet are to be washed by the monk finishing his week's service and the one starting his. The monk ending service should return the utensils he has used clean and in good order, to the cellarer, who will then give them to the new kitchen staff. This is done so the cellarer may keep track of his inventory. One hour before the meal each server may have a portion of drink and bread over his daily allowance, so he may serve his brothers without complaining or fatigue. The servers should wait until after Mass on feast days, however."

ther free will nor free body, but must receive all they need from the abbot." The "cellarer" and his assistants were responsible for the distribution of goods. For this reason the position of cellarer held great authority, and the person occupying that position was to be chosen carefully. The cellarer had to exercise wise judgment, taking into account the needs of each monk.

> We do not mean by this that personal preference should play a part, but rather that individual weaknesses should be taken into account. He who has lesser need ought to thank God and not lament. He who has great need should show greater humility because of his weakness and not gloat over the allowance made him. Then everyone will be content.[25]

Monks had to attend to the work of the soul too. The cultivation of virtue was primary. Benedict considered three virtues in particular as sine qua non for the spiritual life of the monastery. The work of *silence* forced monks to discipline the most dangerous weapon the monks had—the tongue. Gossip, foul talk, judgment and even idle chatter were strictly forbidden.

Monks were not allowed to speak unless spoken to. "We always condemn and ban all small talk and jokes; no disciple shall speak such things." The work of *obedience* helped monks to become subservient to Christ, to Scripture, to the Rule and to the Abbot, in that order, which would protect them from self-will and unruly behavior. The work of *humility* made them lowly in spirit, broke them of pride and set them on a course toward heaven. Benedict outlined twelve steps that would enable monks to grow in humility.[26]

Benedictine prayer. The Rule mandated that monks pray too. The primary vehicle for prayer was the observance of the Divine Office, which consisted of eight short worship services a day, each of which had an individual name (matins was the first, which began at 2:00 a.m., followed by lauds at dawn, then prime, terce, sext, and none, vespers at sundown, and finally compline, which ended the day).[27] Every day the monks would gather in the oratory (chapel) for prayer. On each occasion they would chant psalms, listen to readings from Scripture, sit in silence and pray. The Divine Office focused their attention on God, and it reminded them of their ultimate purpose in life—to know God as their Creator, Savior and Provider, to trust God's providence for daily needs, and to perform even perfunctory tasks to his glory.

Finally, the monks studied. Monastic study united the two tasks of the monastery—prayer and work—into a seamless whole, for monks did the hard work of study with a prayerful attitude. They learned to read and write in the monastery, if they were illiterate when they first joined. They read John Cassian's *Conferences*, the *Lives of the Saints* and patristic theology. Above all, they studied Scripture. The primary method of study was lectio divina, which involved a reflective, repetitive and meditative reading of texts, especially the biblical text.[28] This method became standard practice in Benedictine monasteries; it was based on the assumption that study itself had to be kept subordinate to spiritual concerns. "All the monk's activities," writes Jean Leclercq, "including his literary activity, can have no motivation other than spiritual, and spiritual motives are always called upon to justify his actions."[29] Thus monastic study, as with all other monastic activities, was intended "to further the salvation of the monk, his search for God, and not for any practical or social end."[30] The goal was transformation of the monk's entire life, not merely the accumulation of information in the head. Benedict did not consider knowledge an end in itself, as if it were a virtue. At best, it was a means to the end of holiness, humility and contemplation of God. Benedictine monasticism always had this tension running through it—"on the one hand, the study of letters [literature]; on the other, the exclusive search for God, the love of eternal life, and the consequent detachment from all else, including the study of letters." This tension could only be transcended by "raising it to the spiritual order," namely, by doing the work of study in a spirit of prayer.[31]

The monks followed this rhythm every day but Sunday—they prayed and they worked. Prayer protected them from turning their work into an idol; work kept their prayers from becoming an empty exercise. This alternation of prayer and work choreographed each monastic day. The day was ordered and busy, but never hurried and frantic. The monks prayed for their work, and they worked out their prayers. They worshiped God, and they served the common good of the community.

THE IMPACT OF BENEDICTINE MONASTICISM

Benedict was not an innovator. Other monastic leaders, like Pachomius, Basil, Cassian and Augustine, had already developed most of the ideas and practices that Benedict spelled out in the Rule. Benedict merely synthesized those ideas. Still, Benedictine monasticism prevailed over other forms, and for two reasons. First, the Rule provided a clear, orderly, concise way of life. Other monasteries adopted it because it was the best available and simplest to use. Second, Benedict added an additional vow to the three traditional vows of poverty, chastity and obedience; this new one was a vow of stability. Once monks joined a monastery—and he prescribed a long trial period, called the novitiate, to prevent monks from making a rash decision—they were expected to stay for life, which kept them from flitting from one monastery to the next, depending on the popularity of the monastery or its abbot. "More important, by the vow of stability," asserts Meisel and Mastro,

> Benedict had brought mobility—the physical expression of a man's pride, independence and self-will—under the healing influence of obedience. The course of perfection, as Benedict saw it, could only be completed success-

fully if self-will were annihilated and replaced by the Divine will. To this
end, stability proved a remarkably effective means.[32]

This commitment to stability became one of the hallmarks of Benedictine
monasticism.

The influence of the Rule of St. Benedict spread slowly but steadily until it became the norm in the Western church, though even then its dominance was never universal. It contributed significantly to the growth and
success of Christianity during the Middle Ages. Abbots adapted the Rule
as they saw fit, sometimes by emphasizing work, sometimes by emphasizing prayer, whichever was more needed. At times the need for the work of
monks prevailed. For example, from its inception Benedictine monasticism excelled in doing missionary work. Monks developed an effective
method of Christianizing tribal groups that had invaded Europe. They
would travel to some remote corner of Europe, build a monastery there,
make contact with local tribal groups, learn the language and over time introduce them to the Christian faith. The story of Boniface provides a good
example. Known as the "apostle to Germany," Boniface (680-754) joined
a Benedictine monastery in Ireland. He traveled to Germany to do mission
work but met with little success. Then he traveled to Rome, where he received papal approval and support. His second trip to Germany proved to
be more successful. He witnessed many conversions to Christianity, helped
to organize the church in Germany and contributed to the reform of the
Frankish church. He was martyred doing mission work among the Fri-
sians. Boniface's story is typical. The monastic movement supplied pla-
toons of missionaries for centuries.[33]

The work of education and scholarship became an important priority
too. Many Benedictine monasteries became centers of education. Two of
the most famous early Benedictine scholars were the Venerable Bede and
Alcuin of York. Bede (673-735), who was influenced by Celtic monasticism, spent almost his entire life in the monastery of St. Paul at Jarrow,
England. He became a master educator of young monks, teaching Scripture and its interpretation. He also translated several important Latin
works into the vernacular, and he wrote commentaries on Scripture and
the early fathers. But his most significant book was his *Ecclesiastical History*

of the English Nation. The work is characterized by careful collection and analysis of sources, by verification of the reliability of documents and by measured interpretation, which enabled him to avoid the pitfall of partisan scholarship. Alcuin of York (c. 735-804) spent his early years in a Benedictine monastery in York, England. Hearing of his reputation for learnedness, Charlemagne summoned him to his court in Aachen (France) to start a school for children of nobility, though it eventually accepted able students from the lower classes as well. Alcuin designed the curriculum of the school. He also helped to develop a uniform liturgy, revised the Vulgate Bible and wrote several treatises on theology.[34]

At other times prayer dominated the life of the monastery. Observance of the Divine Office became the centerpiece of the community's life. No monastic house did this better than Cluny, which was founded in 909. Cluny became a nursery of reform during the Middle Ages, and it provided ecclesiastical leadership for the entire church. At the heart of Cluny was its practice of the liturgy. Cluny and its sister houses were devoted to the observance of the Divine Office, which they turned into an art. Monks worshiped eight hours a day, and they established new posts of liturgical leadership—the cantor, for example—to enhance and enrich their performance of the liturgy. They built architectural masterpieces too, including one of the first Gothic chapels (under the able leadership of Abbot Suger). The Cluny movement assumed that humanity was created to worship God. This assumption, however, led to the faulty conclusion that doing secular work is of secondary value, if even that. Only monks could be assured of heaven, though they could help others achieve salvation by interceding on their behalf, especially in worship.[35]

The Benedictines were not immune from corruption. Cluny in particular became a victim of its own success. The sprawling empire of Cluniac houses collected art, built huge, ornate chapels and charged fees for their religious services, which contradicted the original vision of monasticism as outlined in the Rule. But the monastic movement spawned renewal movements too. These movements were often inspired by a rediscovery of and return to the original principles of the Rule, and thus to the simple rhythm of prayer and work. For example, the Cistercians, which was founded by Robert of Molesme in 1098, embodied one such attempt to return to the simplicity, austerity and purity of the Rule. The towering leader of the movement was Bernard, the abbot of Clairvaux for over thirty years. A man of deep passion, Bernard of Clairvaux advocated a return to the original principles—work and prayer—of monasticism. Bernard rejected anything indulgent and ostentatious, always favoring the basic disciplines that had characterized the early Benedictine movement. Bernard's leadership was effective. He started sixty-eight houses himself; by the time of his death in 1153 the Cistercian order included some 343 monasteries. By the eve of the Reformation, the Cistercians operated 738 houses for men, another 654 for women.[36]

The Cistercians emerged at the right time. Monasticism peaked in the twelfth century and then began, ever so slowly, to decline. The growth of cities and commerce, the emergence of universities and the interests and needs of a growing middle class required a new expression of spiritual life, one that was less compatible with traditional monasticism. New movements—the military orders, the Franciscans and Dominicans, the Canons Regular, various lay orders (to which we will return in chap. 8)—captured a popular following because they addressed the new conditions and concerns of a Europe in transition.

RHYTHMS IN MODERN LIFE

But the movement never died. Monasteries—thousands of them—still exist around the world. To be sure, they no longer serve as art galleries, schools, hostels and libraries, at least not as they once did. But most of them still abide by the Rule, and they still follow a rhythm that alternates between prayer and work.[37] It is that rhythm that has much to teach us in the modern world, as desperate as we are to find and follow healthier rhythms. Monasteries create rhythm for a spiritual reason. God calls his people to two principle duties—prayer and work. Prayer draws us to God; work sends us into the world. Prayer centers and quiets us; work energizes us. Prayer restores us to God; work allows us to participate in God's restoration of the world. Jesus himself followed this rhythm: he withdrew into the wilderness to pray, and then returned to the world to preach the good news, heal the sick, cast out demons, confront injustice, and eventually suffer and die for the sins of the world.

We divide these two activities at our peril. On the one hand, without work, prayer becomes rote, vacuous and irrelevant, an empty discipline that shows little evidence of a deep concern for the world. It loses its purpose, lacks passion, turns inward, serves the self. We mouth the words, but there is nothing at stake. It does not seem to matter much whether our prayers are answered or ignored. On the other hand, without prayer, work becomes an idol. We work to make money, to gain power and prestige, to advance in our careers. We become presumptuous too, thinking that our work can accomplish good things without actually relying on God for wisdom and power. But work that pleases God and serves the common good of humanity must have God involved in it, for only God can accomplish what has transcendent value and eternal significance. Human effort is necessary, but it is not sufficient. Strangely, even churches and Christian organizations fail to grasp this fundamental truth, and therefore find it difficult to practice a regular discipline of prayer. They do the work of God, but they neglect to seek the face of God. Monastic rhythm, rooted in the liturgy, forces us to strike a balance. "The prayers of the liturgy," says Susan J. White, "become models for the prayer which occupies the rest of our lives."[38] All work, regardless of who does it—pastors, parents, teachers, coaches, scholars, executives, secretaries, engineers, scientists, social workers, computer technicians—needs God's help for lasting impact. Without God, even our best efforts are in vain.

The monastic rhythm of prayer and work establishes a routine that monasteries have followed for centuries. Routine means repeating the same activities time and time again: we pray and then we work, day in and day out. Such routine creates the conditions for God to do a subtle, deep and transformative work in our souls and in the world. It requires patience and endurance. It should come as no surprise, therefore, that one of the greatest temptations we will face once we settle into a routine of prayer and work is, as Evagrius pointed out to monks sixteen hundred years ago, *acedia*, a Greek word that does not translate easily. "Sloth" is not quite right because it connotes laziness, which is more a result of *acedia* than the meaning of it. *Acedia* is better defined as boredom, restlessness, inattentiveness. Routine can make us impatient; we wish that there was an easier and faster way to maturity of faith and fruitfulness of life. We want to take

shortcuts; we look for entertainment along the way; we expect to be dazzled by the rapid speed of our progress. Known as the "noonday demon" in
monasteries, *acedia* tempts us to quit at midcourse, just when we have followed a routine of prayer and work long enough to be weary of the same-
ness and tediousness. Musicians contend with this problem when they are
sick of practicing scales, athletes when they have had enough of shooting
free throws or swimming laps, scholars when they have reached a point of
exhaustion doing the exhaustive research required of them. But there is no
getting around it. Routine, however boring and wearisome, is necessary.
Mastery comes from persisting in some endeavor when everything in us
wants to quit. That is true in music, athletics, scholarship and many other
earthly pursuits; it is also true in the spiritual life.

Very few of us will ever live in a monastery, and perhaps will never even
visit one. But there are ways of developing a monastic rhythm all the same.
We should begin by asking questions about how we view time. We tend to
view time, at least in the West, as a commodity we can either consume or
perhaps waste. We keep schedules and create "to do" lists so that we can
squeeze the most out of the time we have, using it as efficiently and pro-
ductively as we can. But there is only so much we can do. As it is, we face
severe limits, suspended, as we are, between a past we cannot change and
a future we cannot control. In truth, we only have *this present moment* in
which to live. The rhythm of prayer and work will enable us to relish the
present moment as a gift from God, give ourselves completely to the one
thing at hand and surrender our work to God through prayer.[39]

How can we develop a monastic-like rhythm without living in a monastery? First, there is the importance and dignity of work. Study, chores,
jobs, volunteer work, hospitality, service to neighbor and stewardship are
examples of work, which we should strive to do with excellence and humility. But we should never work so much that we neglect prayer, which in my
mind seems the more urgent discipline, at least in our culture. We can rise
half an hour earlier in the morning to pray over the day and practice lectio
divina. Families can set aside time for regular meals and family devotions.
Husband and wife can pray before bedtime for their children, friends,
neighbors and coworkers. Roommates can invite a group of friends over
for a weekly meal and Bible study. Christian teachers can gather together

before or after school once a week to pray for administrators, fellow teachers, students and families. Business leaders can meet over lunch to pray for the needs of the city. Above all, every one of us can try to observe the sabbath as a day of worship, rest, hospitality, reflection and play. These are examples of healthy rhythms—praying and working, seeking God and serving God, offering ourselves to God in an act of worship and doing the will of God in ordinary life. It is the great legacy that the monastic movement has left us, a legacy that we need to reclaim and apply to modern life.

A month ago I visited the monastery that had become a home of healing for me some fifteen years ago. I had not walked the grounds, prayed in a hermitage or talked with Sister Florence for several years. I realized that it had been too long. I did not need to return for the reason that initially drove me there. I have long since recovered my equilibrium and found a new life. But I discovered in my recent visit that I still need that monastery, or better to say, I need the rhythm that is practiced there. God calls me to two principle duties. My tendency is to work at the expense of prayer. That visit to the monastery reminded me of the importance of prayer too, lest I turn my work into an idol and fail to seek the face of God. I returned home from that beloved place renewed in my desire to follow the rhythm that God himself has established for my own good.

PRACTICES

- Read Luke 6:12-19.
- Carefully analyze how you schedule your time over a typical week. How can you develop a healthier rhythm that reflects the monastic integration of prayer and work? For example, try to pause briefly three times during the day to pray (for the people with whom you work, the projects you are doing, the mundane activities you have to perform). In addition, pray over your day's schedule first thing in the morning. Then, at the end of the day, review the day's activities, thanking God for his provision, confessing your sin and surrendering areas of concern to God. Finally, try to protect the Lord's Day, if you can, by turning it into a day of worship, celebration, community and rest. Plan next Sunday with that in mind.

5

Holy Heroes

The Spirituality of Icons and Saints

"And all of us, with unveiled faces,
seeing the glory of the Lord as though reflected in a mirror,
are being transformed into the same image from one degree of glory to another;
for this comes from the Lord, the Spirit."

2 COR 3:18

It seems a strange world, at least to outsiders. Its churches are adorned with portraits of people who appear to belong to another world; worship follows customs and rituals that take us back to a former age; liturgical incantations sound archaic. The entire tradition transports us to another time and to a different place, one far removed from our world. The contrast between then and now, there and here is so startling that we wonder if we could ever view this tradition as anything other than a relic of the past. Does it offer us anything relevant and useful for today?

Eastern Orthodoxy is perhaps the most unfamiliar of the Christian traditions explored in this book.[1] Its art, architecture, liturgy, theology and saints seem exotic and mysterious, as foreign to us as the languages—Greek and Russian, for example—spoken in Orthodox churches. Still, it might not be as foreign as it at first appears. Its most sacred term—

deification—not only describes what in fact the incarnation of God in Jesus Christ was intended to accomplish in believers, which is to make us holy, but also reflects a central truth found in the New Testament.[2] As Eastern Orthodox Christians have confessed for centuries, "God became man so that man could become God." The phrase itself needs parsing. It does not mean that we as believers will literally become God; it is more accurate to say that we will become *like* God through the saving work of Jesus Christ. In other words, believers will some day share in Christ's resurrection glory—his power, beauty and perfection. The divine image will be completely restored in us, and we will reflect God's ineffable light and love. But that is not all. The Eastern Orthodox faith teaches that this process of transformation has already begun. Even now believers are being transformed "from one degree of glory to another," as the apostle Paul described it. Sainthood is not a distant hope that awaits us after death. God's power is already at work in us, restoring the divine image. Deification is a present reality; Christians are saints in the making.

SAINTS IN THE MAKING

But it is not an easy journey, however certain and glorious the outcome. Believers therefore need help along the way, which God so graciously provides. First, God empowers us through the gift of his Holy Spirit; but he also provides examples for us to follow, heroes for us to imitate. In the New Testament the title "saint" refers to all believers, but it also refers to those who have demonstrated unusual faith and holiness of life. The writer of the book of Hebrews devotes an entire chapter to the stories of holy heroes, showing how they lived exemplary lives of faith under difficult circumstances. It was by faith that Abraham, Moses and a host of others "conquered kingdoms, administered justice, obtained promises, shut the mouths of lions, quenched raging fire, escaped the edge of the sword, won strength out of weakness, became mighty in war, put foreign armies to flight." It was also by faith that they "were tortured, refusing to accept release in order to obtain a better resurrection. Others suffered mocking and flogging, and even chains and imprisonment. They were stoned to death, they were sawn in two, they were killed by the sword" (Heb 11:33-34, 35-37). The deeds of these great "saints" are recorded in Scripture to inspire us to live by faith—and to endure in faith—when we face similar difficulties. "Therefore," the author concludes, "since we are surrounded by so great a cloud of witnesses, let us also lay aside every weight and the sin that clings so closely, and let us run with perseverance the race that is set before us" (Heb 12:1).

The text does not end there. The author exhorts us to look to Jesus, "who for the sake of the joy that was set before him endured the cross, disregarding its shame, and has taken his seat at the right hand of the throne of God" (v. 2). Jesus Christ is the reason why Christians can be confident of their glorious destiny. Jesus took on human nature so that fallen humans could share in God's nature. Athanasius argued that Christ became incarnate to repair the damage that was done to God's creation and to restore the divine image in fallen humanity. Facing the consequences of the Fall, which led to human misery and eventually to death, God faced a terrible dilemma. God did not want to see his creation waste away, nor witness the corruption of his image. He wanted to see human nature rejoined to the divine so that there could be complete restoration. "What else could He possibly do, being God, but renew His Image in mankind, so that through it men might once more come to know Him?" God had only one option. "And how could this be done save by the coming of the very Image Himself, our Savior Jesus Christ? . . . The Word of God came in His own Person, because it was He alone, the Image of the Father, Who could recreate man made after the Image."[3]

So Christians are in fact destined for perfection and glory. Christ is not only the means of this restoration; he is also the end. He is the image of God in human form, God's perfect self-portrait and humanity's perfect prototype. What Jesus was on earth by natural endowment and perfect obedience we will become through the gift of God's grace, the infusion of the Holy Spirit and the practice of spiritual discipline. The stories of saints in Eastern Orthodoxy remind us that such transformation is possible. If it happened to them, sinful as they were, it can happen to us. They show us what the followers of Jesus can and will become.

The purpose of this chapter is to use three examples to explore the concept of "deification" in the Eastern Orthodox tradition, which emphasizes the important role that saints have played and will continue to play in the life of the church. This great tradition uses two mediums in particular—icons and spiritual biographies—to draw us into the world of the saints and to provide us with examples to follow. *Icons* are paintings that accomplish this purpose by inviting us to gaze upon the portraits of people whose human nature has already been transformed into something unspeakably glorious. As works of art they might look peculiar to us, bearing little resemblance to more familiar and realistic paintings. But the peculiarity is necessary in this case because the purpose is to portray realities that transcend what the eye can naturally see and to transport us into another world, a world where matter is transformed by spirit, where the human is infused with the divine. They show us in symbolic form what the spiritual transformation of a person's life actually accomplishes.[4]

Spiritual biographies or *hagiographies* serve a slightly different purpose. They tell the stories of saints to show how this transformation actually takes place in people who know and trust Christ as Savior and Lord. They do not read like normal biographies, because their central purpose is not simply to communicate historical information but to inspire the faithful to imitate the saints and to embark on the same journey of faith. If icons reveal the *results* of this transformation, engendering in us a longing to enter into that transformed state, then spiritual biographies show the *process* of transformation.[5] The intent is not to "tell the facts" of the saint's life in a straightforward way but to trace the spiritual transformation of the saint over time. In a sense, the stories of saints function as written icons, showing us what it means to grow into the likeness of Christ.[6]

THE ICON OF ST. MACRINA THE YOUNGER

Deification points to the ultimate destiny of believers, who will someday share in Christ's resurrection glory and become "like him, for we shall see him as he is" (1 Jn 3:2). Iconography is intended to provide an artistic vision of that destiny. Take, for example, the icon of St. Macrina the Younger (c. 327-379).[7] Her large eyes gaze toward us, as if she is simultaneously looking at us, through us and beyond us, seeing some larger reality that envelopes us. Her face is calm and serene, like one who, having weathered fierce storms, basks in the bright light of day. The dull and flat background gives the impression that she serves as a portal between her world and ours.

She almost seems to be calling out to us, inviting us to enter into a reality greater than our own. Finally, the icon has a translucent quality about it, as if the light that illumines it comes from within her. She appears to be aglow with an inner beauty and a heavenly radiance.

Macrina the Younger is one of three siblings who have been canonized as saints in the Eastern Orthodox tradition, the others being Basil the Great, bishop of Caesarea, and Gregory, bishop of Nyssa. All three lived in the second half of the fourth century in the region of Cappadocia, located in what is today central Turkey. Macrina was the founder of a monastery, a woman of deep prayer and piety, a teacher of Christian faith, and a mystic. She was largely responsible for Basil's conversion, and she helped to shape Eastern Orthodox spirituality. Her icon is revered because she embodies the primary values of sainthood.

Macrina

The first icons were painted in the fifth century, at about the same time the church was spelling out how the divine and human natures of Christ cohere in one person.[8] The Council of Chalcedon (451) explained this mystery theologically; icons portrayed it artistically. So important was the icon in Eastern Orthodoxy during this early period that, when the Eastern Emperor, Leo III, condemned icons as idolatrous and ordered their destruction, thousands of priests and monks protested, even though it cost many of them their lives. Two theologians, John of Damascus (c. 675-c. 749) and Theodore of Studios (759-826), wrote tracts and treatises to explain and defend the use of icons in worship. This Iconoclastic Controversy, as it is now known, was finally resolved at the Second Council of Nicea, held in 787. The Council stated that icons are useful and valuable because they portray in artistic form both the unity and distinction of the divine and human natures of Jesus Christ.

The central icon, then, is and always has been Christ, whose depiction in the form of a painted image was made possible, permissible, even necessary in the incarnation.[9] As any iconographer will say, all icons of Christ depict a person, Jesus of Nazareth, who has two distinct but related natures, one divine and the other human. They show that Jesus was not simply divine, not a mere abstraction, nor a phantom, but a real person—Jesus of Nazareth, the perfect God-man.

The image we see in the icon points beyond itself to the reality of the person, the incarnate Son of God, who transformed the material creation into a vessel for the divine. The icon of Christ depicts the results of this transformation of earthly matter. John of Damascus states: "Of old, God the incorporeal and formless was never depicted, but now that God has been seen in the flesh and has associated with human kind, I depict what I have seen of God . . . who became matter for my sake and accepted to dwell in matter and through matter worked my salvation."[10] We see the Maker through the material world, the Creator through the creation. Ultimately, we see God's very nature through a human being, Jesus Christ. The incarnation fuses these two worlds together in one person. The icon of Christ portrays this glorious reality in a painting.

Jesus, Pantocrator

Icons of saints like Macrina serve a slightly different purpose. They demonstrate that, as God became truly human for the sake of our salvation, human beings can likewise share in the divine nature and reflect the divine glory, and thus be restored to what God always intended human beings to be, bearers of the divine image. Thus their human nature becomes infused with the Spirit of God, transforming them into Christlike people.[11] If the icon of Christ depicts the divine *descent*, God becoming human, then the icons of saints depict the human *ascent*, humans reflecting the very nature of God, which is made possible through the incarnation and the work of the Spirit. But human nature is not lost in the process of transformation any more than the divine nature is lost in the incarnation. The saints have glorified bodies, infused with light, a revelation of things hidden. They show what the incarnation of God in Jesus Christ was intended to accomplish through the work of the Holy Spirit in fallen humanity. The process of sanctification begins in the saint's earthly life. The Holy Spirit fills and illumines and transforms ordinary persons, conforming them to the image of Christ.[12] Thus saints are not suddenly changed, as if by magic; they grow into sainthood through the work of the Holy Spirit.

The dual nature of saints poses a significant problem for the iconographer. The depiction of the unity of these two natures—material and spiritual, human and divine—cannot be done directly, for how can one communicate such a reality in a painting? It is for this reason that icons should not be viewed in the same way we would view any other kind of portrait, for icons do not portray people as we ordinarily see them. Icons are not so much works of art as works of devotion. They function as a window that allows us to see spiritual qualities in addition to mere earthly beings. "The second reality, the presence of the all-sanctifying grace of the Holy Spirit, holiness, cannot be depicted by any human means, since it is invisible to external physical sight."[13] Icons must therefore use symbols to communicate the glory, luminosity and inner beauty of a saint, one whose human nature has not been diminished but transformed by the work of the Holy Spirit.

The "unreality" is therefore intentional and necessary, not the result of inferior artistry. The distortions are not meant to deceive but to enlarge our perspective, to expose us to these spiritual realities and to illumine us so that we see the glory of God's existence in and through the icon.[14] Even at first glance we see that the icon portrays a real person. The saint has a name, an identity, a story, a role in the history of the church, for the saint is a person who lived an earthly life. For example, we know Macrina's name; we know that she founded monasteries, that she served as a mentor and teacher, that she was a woman of unusual spiritual depth and discipline.[15]

Yet the spiritual nature of the person is primary, and thus receives special artistic attention, which makes the image appear odd, strange, even bizarre. If we take the time to gaze at icons, we will immediately observe certain physical features that seem exaggerated or distorted, all of which symbolize various aspects of holiness. For example, a high forehead symbolizes wisdom; large eyes, luminosity; a gaunt face, discipline and self-sacrifice; intense stillness, perfect inner equilibrium. The halo conveys holiness, the gold background timelessness. The source of light—which seems to come from *inside* the saint rather than from some outside source—represents the divine radiance. This radiance makes the painting seem haunting and otherworldly.

Finally, unlike most paintings, in which the point of convergence lies *behind* the subject, thus allowing onlookers to peer into the world of the painting, icons push the point of convergence *in front of* the saint, as if the saint were staring into *our* world. We can no longer pretend to be mere objective and neutral observers, studying the painting in the security of our own world. If anything, the roles are reversed. We become part of the foreground, and the saint studies us. As if standing between two worlds, the saint beckons us to enter into the greater reality of their world.[16] Speaking less as a theologian and more as a pastor, John of Damascus confessed:

> I have not many books nor time for study and I go into a church, the common refuge of souls, my mind wearied with conflicting thoughts. I see before me a beautiful picture and the sight refreshes me and induces me to glorify God. . . . The representations of the saints are not our gods, but books which lie open and are venerated in churches in order to remind us of God and lead us to worship him.[17]

The icon symbolizes the reality of the kingdom of God and invites us to enter in. "There is more," it seems to be saying to us. "So much more."

Eastern Orthodoxy calls iconography "theological" or "spiritual" art, and Eastern Orthodox iconographers view their art as a spiritual exercise. Not just *anyone* can become an iconographer, for true iconographers follow a rigor of discipline to prepare themselves for such a holy calling. They develop and demonstrate both artistic and spiritual competence, and they nurture their spiritual sensibilities through fasting, prayer, meditation and contemplation so that they have the necessary maturity to convey the spiritual nature of the art. Mere artistic excellence is not enough. Moreover, they follow strict guidelines in their artistic endeavors. The materials they use, the colors they mix, the symbols they employ and the saints they portray must honor the ancient tradition, though differences in style and composition are allowed. When a work is completed, it is not simply admired as a work of art but used in worship. Eastern Orthodox believers adorn their churches with icons, using them to venerate the saints, to seek their guidance and help, and to ponder the heavenly realm that the saints now occupy. They remind the faithful that this world is not the only reality there is.[18]

THE BIOGRAPHY OF MELANIA THE YOUNGER

While icons manifest the *results* of sainthood, depicting the saints as already having been transformed by the spirit of God, spiritual biographies show the *process*. If icons provide a portrait of perfection, spiritual biographies tell a story of growth and change. Their purpose is to inspire ordinary

Melania the Younger

people like us to renounce the world, the flesh and the devil, to pursue a life of holiness and virtue, and to follow Christ. In early Christianity the most popular subjects were apostles, martyrs, desert saints and bishops. These saints were lifted up as examples to follow, and their stories set a standard for the flood of literature that followed.[19] In medieval Christianity the subjects stayed the same, but the purpose changed. Saints were seen less as examples and more as intercessors who had the power and authority to function as spiritual patrons for the faithful. Lawrence Cunningham notes, "The intercession of the martyrs or the application of the martyr's relics could cure illness, forestall disaster, shield from antipathetic forces, engender conversion, forgive sins, or avert calamity."[20] The stories of the saints became ever more fanciful and fictional. They described how the relics of saints healed the sick, how water blessed by the saints washed away sins, how pilgrimages to the tombs of saints won the special favor of God.

We must therefore turn to an early account to recover the original purpose of these biographies. The story of Melania the Younger (c. 383-438) provides a good example.[21] Her biographer, Gerontius, a priest who spent many years by her side in Jerusalem, wrote the account between 452 and 453. Melania came from a Roman family of senatorial rank and enormous wealth. From an early age she longed for Christ and purity of life (which she defined as celibacy). But her parents wanted heirs and so forced her to marry Pinian, a family friend, when she was fourteen and he was seventeen. Pinian too insisted on having children. Melania eventually gave birth to two children, but she remained steadfast in her longing. After both children died and Melania became very ill, she resumed her appeal. She begged and finally persuaded her father to release her and Pinian, now in full support of her aspirations, to pursue a life of holiness.

Together they practiced the ascetic discipline of renunciation. They wore cheap clothing and eliminated the use of luxuries. They treated each other as brother and sister, called on the sick, provided hospitality to strangers and visited prisons and mines, setting free those who were in debt. They also began to distribute their enormous wealth to the poor and to divest themselves of their substantial properties, which were scattered around the Roman world.

In due time Melania and Pinian sailed for Africa, where they owned still more properties and an estate. Blown off course, they landed on an island where some leading citizens were being held for ransom by barbarians. They paid the ransom and provided for the material needs of the people. After arriving in Africa, they sold their property and gave the money to the poor. They also met and sought the advice of Augustine, then bishop of Hippo, and eventually settled for several years in Thagaste, where they worked under Bishop Alypius, Augustine's dear friend. There they founded a monastery and practiced ever more vigorous forms of asceticism, finally living only on moldy bread. Melania also excelled as a theologian. She copied Scripture, read treatises of saints and other theological works, and studied both Greek and Latin. Her study and zeal for learning turned her into a great defender of the faith.[22]

After living in Africa for seven years, Melania and Pinian departed for the Holy Land. They visited Alexandria and the Egyptian desert on the

way, where Melania conferred with several desert saints and contributed
to their needs. She finally settled in Jerusalem, "carrying a full cargo of
piety" with her. After Pinian died, she withdrew into seclusion for a
time. She eventually built a monastery in Jerusalem for ninety women,
though she refused out of humility to serve as its abbess. She rescued
women of ill-repute, housed them in the monastery and taught them the
way of salvation. On one occasion she traveled to Constantinople to
meet with the emperor, whom she exhorted to follow Christ. "I beg you,
approach the bath of immortality, so that you may obtain eternal goods,
just as you have enjoyed temporal things."[23] While staying in Constantinople she taught Scripture, virtually "night and day," and routed heretics
in debates. Due at least in part to her influence, the emperor was baptized before he died. She spent much time with the empress, Eudoxia,
too, becoming like a spiritual mother to her. By this time she also started
to perform miracles. But her health began to decline. Sensing that the
end was near, she returned to Jerusalem, where she died after receiving
the Eucharist one last time.

How should we interpret this unusual story? First, it is clear that the author had an evangelical purpose in mind. Gerontius states at the very beginning of his book that he wanted to use Melania's life to inspire belief in
and imitation of Christ.

> I shall approach the spiritual meadow of our holy mother Melania's deeds,
> and gathering there what can be readily plucked, I shall offer those flowers
> to the ones who are fond of hearing recitations that inflame their virtue and
> to those who wishing the greatest benefit, offer their souls to God, the savior
> of us all.[24]

He quotes Melania on her deathbed to reinforce this point. Melania
prayed to God, "May I be deemed worthy of your heavenly bridal chamber.
. . . For to you belongs inexpressible compassion and abundant pity; you
will save all those who hope in you."[25] Gerontius was as zealous for the
Christian faith as his saintly subject. He wrote as an apologist, using the
biography as a means to an end. He wanted to persuade his readers to trust
and obey Jesus, too, no matter what the cost.

Second, the biography of Melania describes the process of her transformation. She gave up comfort and security to follow Christ, trusting that

she would receive hundredfold in return, if not in this life then certainly in the next. This pattern of devotion started early on in Melania's life. After receiving permission to pursue a life of radical discipleship, Melania and Pinian began to renounce their privileged past and to disperse their wealth among the poor. "They clearly recognized that it was impossible for them to offer pure worship to God unless they made themselves enemies to the confusions of secular life."[26] Melania spoke with urgency about the necessity of these efforts. "Let us quickly lay aside our goods, so that we may gain Christ."[27] She recruited women to join the monastery, cared for the needy and pursued a life of solitude. "Such was her burning love for God, even though she had been delicately raised as a member of such an important senatorial family."[28] Still, what seems most important in the story is not the cost of her sacrifices but the one who was worthy of the sacrifices, not the greatness of her deeds but the one who commanded her to follow him. In the end the biography sheds light on what it means to know and follow Christ.

Third, it is obvious that Melania the Younger was *not* a typical believer. Melania's devotion exceeded the norm, her accomplishments challenged traditional notions of how Christian women should function in society, and her influence made her the equal of desert saints, bishops and emperors. She achieved a status that appeared to transcend gender roles, social distinctions and ecclesiastical office. Her entire life seems almost unbelievable. But the strangeness is essential to the portrait, as necessary to the writing of these stories as it is to the painting of icons, for the Christian faith, if taken seriously, promises to change a person's life. The earthly must yield to the heavenly, the real must give way to the reality of the kingdom. The strangeness thus serves an important function. It draws attention to the mysterious process that leads to sainthood. God plans to transform us into glorious creatures. Melania's story is not a fabrication. The person we come to know in the biography really existed. But neither is her strangeness meant to serve as a template. Not everyone can live just like Melania, and not everyone should. But everyone should take the Christian faith as seriously as she did. Our pathway will no doubt be different from Melania's, but the goal is the same—complete transformation.

THE PREACHING OF JOHN CHRYSOSTOM

Deification is not a mere abstract idea. It is meant to challenge and inspire believers today. Here icons and spiritual biographies face a clear limitation. The saints do not and cannot speak for themselves. We learn of them through the artistic vision of painters and writers, who function as their interpreters. We therefore come to know the saints only indirectly, through the eyes of their creators. That is good, as far as it goes. But these artistic media do not create the conditions for genuine communication. We can

John Chrysostom

see the saints; we can read about the saints. But we cannot listen to them speak to us. So it is easy to keep them at arm's distance. Over the years I have tried to meet regularly with a "saint"—some believer a generation older than I who has followed Christ faithfully for a long time. I listen to their stories, seek their counsel and enjoy their friendship. I invite them to speak into my life. For the past year I have been meeting with Rits Tadema, a retired pastor who grew up in the Netherlands and, as a teenager, joined the resistance movement against the Nazis. He has light in his eyes and depth of spirit, like some old warrior still ready for battle. He is more than an icon and story; he is a living person with a voice of his own.

The ancient saints have voices of their own too. They can still speak directly to us through their writings and thus challenge us to surrender our lives to the same God they knew and followed. Fortunately, many have left us a legacy in print. In the Eastern Orthodox tradition one of the greatest of the saints was—and still is—John Chrysostom (c. 347-407). He was patriarch of Constantinople around the turn of the fifth century, as well as a noteworthy Bible scholar, pastor, leader and preacher. Known as "Golden Mouth" (the meaning of Chrysostom in Greek) because of his brilliant preaching, he has been the subject of several icons and spiritual biographies over the centuries. His writings have also been preserved, including commentaries on the Bible, treatises, letters and sermons. His powerful preaching illustrates why the saints still have an important role to play. Far from being irrelevant relics of the past, saints like Chrysostom have much to teach us. Chrysostom in particular has a timeless quality about his writings, especially when he addresses practical Christian living.[29]

Born in Syrian Antioch, Chrysostom lost his father when he was a young boy. His pious mother, Anthusa, shunned remarriage, deciding to devote herself to raising her son and his younger sister. He received the best education available in Antioch, studying under the famous master of rhetoric, Libanius, an atheist who disdained Christianity. Chrysostom was planning to pursue a career in law, but for some reason he changed his mind and determined to devote himself to the service of God. He wanted to retreat into monastic seclusion, but his mother begged him to wait. After her death in the early 370s Chrysostom joined a monastery for two years and then withdrew into total isolation for four more years. He practiced ascetic discipline, prayed diligently and memorized almost the entire New Testament. This period of seclusion deepened his spiritual resolve, focused his calling and weaned him from worldly desires. Later on he said of this period in his life: "For what purpose did Christ go up into the mountains? To teach us that loneliness and retirement is good when we are to pray to God. . . . For the wilderness is the mother of quiet; it is a calm and a harbor, delivering us from all turmoils."[30]

Returning from this long period of isolation (largely for health reasons), Chrysostom became active in the church in Antioch. At first he refused church office, considering himself unworthy, but eventually he decided to submit to ordination, first as deacon (381) and then as priest (386). For the next twelve years Chrysostom did ministry in Antioch, a city known for its Olympic Games, theater and festivals. He also honed his preaching skills.

Those preaching skills were tested almost immediately when, in 387, a riot broke out in the city over an increase in the imperial tax. The rioters desecrated the statues of the emperor and other members of the imperial family. Outraged officials of the empire made arrests and began punishing city leaders, torturing some and executing others. The archbishop, Flavian, then eighty years old, was dispatched to Constantinople to beg mercy from the emperor, though it was in the dead of winter and the capital was 800 miles away. Chrysostom remained behind to preach and provide pastoral care. "There is a silence," he wrote, "huge with terror, and utter loneliness everywhere." After spending a week in prayer and fasting, he mounted the pulpit and preached every day until the crisis was averted. He spoke eloquently of God's mercy, judgment and providence, and he exhorted believers to prepare for spiritual battle. "Strip yourselves, for it is the season of wrestling. Clothe yourselves, for we are engaged in a fierce warfare with devils. Whet your sickles which are blunted with long surfeiting, and then sharpen them with fasting."[31] He excoriated them for their desire for luxury and greed, which he believed was the real cause of the disturbance. After eight weeks, Flavian returned, the day before Easter, to announce the good news that the emperor had pardoned the city. That one crisis established Chrysostom as the premier preacher of his day.

In 398 Chrysostom was escorted by a senior military official to a secret meeting in a chapel outside the city walls, where he was seized by soldiers and transported to Constantinople. The kidnapping was arranged by Eutropius, a government official, who wanted the most famous preacher in the empire to serve the church in the capital. Contrary to his wishes, Chrysostom was ordained as patriarch of Constantinople, the center of the empire. Thus began the most difficult and tumultuous years of his life.

Chrysostom embraced the office with enthusiasm, rigor and zeal, doing what he could to provide pastoral care and oversight for a church of 100,000 people, a huge staff and the imperial family. Though surrounded by people who were hungry for power, he refused to serve as a mere religious ornament of the court. Far from being accommodating, Chrysostom proved to be uncompromising, if not stubborn and intolerant. He used his office to serve the needs of the entire city, not simply those who sat in positions of power. He fed the poor, built hospitals and supported widows. He also took on the task of reforming the clergy. He disciplined celibate clergy who were living with "spiritual sisters"—single women who lived in clergy residences to tend to domestic matters, like household servants. Some of those spiritual sisters had become "spiritual mothers," as Chrysostom called them, which scandalized the church. He ordered reforms in the care and support of widows too, advising second marriages in some cases and instituting stricter standards for those who remained celibate. He confronted bishops in Asia Minor for financial mismanagement, preached against popular culture and indulgent use of wealth, and threatened to withhold communion from those who continued in immorality. "If you shudder with horror at this judgment, then let the guilty ones simply show repentance, and the judgment will be lifted."[32]

He became enormously popular with the people. It is not difficult to see why. In a sermon he preached after his return from a long trip, he said, "Did you even think of me as long as I was away from you? For my part, I have never been able to forget you. Rather your image was always before my eyes."[33] He paid special attention to those who worked secular jobs, who had to raise families, and who faced the dull routine and difficulties of living in the world. The Bible, he said, was intended for them, not for clergy and monks.

> You stand continuously in the front rank, and you receive continual blows. So you need more remedies. Your wife provokes you, for example, your son grieves you, your servant angers you, your enemy plots against you, . . . poverty troubles you, loss of your property gives you grief, prosperity puffs you up, misfortune depresses you. . . . Therefore you have a continuous need for the full armor of God.[34]

He often preached about God's compassion. It was never too late, he said, to repent and to receive God's forgiveness. "Even if you are in extreme old age, and have sinned, go in, repent! For here there is a physician's office, not a courtroom. The Church is not a place where punishment of sin is exacted, but where the forgiveness of sin is granted."[35]

But he could be harsh as well, especially in the way he addressed the upper classes. He did not hesitate to castigate them for their immorality. Sounding like a modern-day prophet haranguing against the sin of pornography, Chrysostom warned them that attending the theater (which had a reputation for being shamelessly immoral) would ruin them. It was like wantonly exposing themselves to a deadly virus.

> If you see a shameless woman in the theater, who treads the stage with uncovered head and bold attitudes, dressed in garments adorned with gold, flaunting her soft sensuality, singing immoral songs, throwing her limbs about in the dance, and making shameless speeches . . . do you still dare to say that nothing human happens to you then?

He warned them that those images would not suddenly disappear after they left the show and returned home.

> Long after the theater is closed and everyone is gone away, those images still float before your soul, their words, their conduct, their glances, their walk, their positions, their excitation, their unchaste limbs—and as for you, you go home covered with a thousand wounds! But not alone—the whore goes with you—although not openly and visibly . . . but in your heart, and in your conscience, and there within you she kindles the Babylonian furnace . . . in which the peace of your home, the purity of your heart, the happiness of your marriage will be burnt up![36]

Chrysostom was no less forthright when he addressed the abuse of wealth. It is astonishing that he would dare preach such prophetic sermons to a congregation that included wealthy citizens and members of the court.

> It is foolishness and a public madness to fill the cupboards with clothing and allow men who are created in God's image and our likeness to stand naked and trembling with the cold so that they can hardly hold themselves upright. . . . You are large and fat, you hold drinking parties until late at night, and sleep in a warm, soft bed. And do you not think of how you must give an account of your misuse of the gifts of God?[37]

John Chrysostom: Sermon

"We who are disciples of Christ claim that our purpose on earth is to lay up treasures in heaven. But our actions often belie our words. Many Christians build for themselves fine houses, lay out splendid gardens, construct bathhouses, and buy fields. It is small wonder, then, that many pagans refuse to believe what we say. 'If their eyes are set on mansions in heaven,' they ask, 'why are they building mansions on earth? If they put their words into practice, they would give their riches and live in simple huts.' So these pagans conclude that we do not sincerely believe in the religion we profess; and as a result they refuse to take this religion seriously. You may say that the words of Christ on these matters are too hard for you to follow; and that while your spirit is willing, your flesh is weak. My answer is that the judgment of pagans about you is more accurate than your judgment of yourself. When the pagans accuse us of hypocrisy, many of us should plead guilty." (from On Living Simply)

He redefined what it meant to be rich and poor. "Rather, if we are to tell the truth, the rich man is not the one who has collected many possessions but the one who needs few possessions; and the poor man is not the one who has no possessions but the one who has many desires."[38] Chrysostom encouraged the wealthy to be good stewards. Their possessions and money were not their own. Thinking so was tantamount to theft. Their resources were God's, and it was God who required the rich to invest those resources in his work, especially for the sake of the poor.

> For our money is the Lord's, however we may have gathered it. If we provide for those in need, we shall obtain great plenty. This is why God has allowed you to have more; not for you to waste on prostitutes, drink, fancy food, expensive clothes, and all the other kinds of indolence, but for you to distribute to those in need.[39]

Such preaching made enemies. His fiery sermons and zeal for reform was bound to conflict with power-mongers. A jealous bishop from Alexandria brought charges against Chrysostom for harboring heretics and abusing power. Chrysostom was brought before a tribunal, convicted of the charges (though he was clearly innocent), deposed from office and removed from the city. When the news spread, a riot broke out in the city, which forced officials to bring him back and reinstate him. But within a year he fell into disfavor again, this time with the imperial family. The emperor, Arcadius, sent Chrysostom into exile. To avert another riot, Chrysostom left through the side door of the church immediately after worship, pausing only long enough to say goodbye to his priests and deacons. But the people rioted anyway. They set fire to the cathedral, and it spread to several other public buildings. Troops were dispatched to put down the resistance.

Meanwhile, Chrysostom departed for the remote shores of the western Black Sea. Old, feeble and exhausted, he was forced to walk over rough terrain during the heat of summer. Everywhere he traveled he met loyal followers who welcomed him into their homes. He also wrote many letters to his closest friends. But his body could take only so much. Nearing a remote village on the eastern shore of the Black Sea, he collapsed in exhaustion and was taken to a small chapel. After being dressed in a baptismal robe, he gave away his clothes to local villagers. He received the Eucharist and offered a final prayer that ended with his usual closing words: "Glory be to God in all things. Amen." He died only hours later, on September 14, 407.

Many mourned his passing. An ancient story says that one bishop, Adelphios of Arabessos, suffered profound grief after Chrysostom died, for he knew him well and admired him greatly. He prayed to God to learn whether the beloved leader of the Eastern Church was included in the circle of the great patriarchs already in heaven. One day he fell into a trance. A heavenly guide led him to the "bright and glorious place" where all the great preachers and doctors of the church dwelt. The guide named every one of them and spoke of their deeds. Adelphios was distressed because he did not see Chrysostom. He said, "This grief is upon me because I have not seen my most dear John, Bishop of Constantinople, among the other doctors." The guide responded, "Do you mean John [the prince] of repentance? A man in the flesh cannot see him, for he stands in the presence of the Lord's throne."[40]

HOLY HEROES AS EXAMPLES

These three examples provide us with a vision of deification, which explains why their stories seem so unusual. Icons, spiritual biographies and voices from the past remind us that the destiny awaiting believers is beyond earthly imagination and human achievement. They reflect the reality of the kingdom, where martyrs are glorified and ascetics honored. The least becomes the greatest, the servant becomes the master, the lowliest becomes exalted. If the stories of their lives appear subversive, it is only because the gospel itself is subversive. What we are inclined to dismiss as fanciful or distorted or ridiculous is, at least in the saints, nothing less than what is true and right from a Christian perspective. The saints call us to abandon our worldliness and to follow Jesus Christ with reckless abandon, and they beckon us to enter a world that is infused with the light of the incarnate Son of God, founded on the principles of the kingdom of God and animated by a call to radical sacrifice and service.[41]

C. S. Lewis wrote that Christians should realize that they are destined for absolute perfection. The saints remind us of that destiny. "No possible degree of holiness or heroism which has ever been recorded of the greatest saints is beyond what He is determined to produce in every one of us in the end. The job will not be completed in this life: but He means to get us as far as possible before death." The process is as important as the outcome. It is for this reason, Lewis warns, that a Christian should not expect an easy life. Why?

> Because God is forcing him on, or up, to a higher level: putting him into situations where he will have to be very much braver, or more patient, or more loving, than he ever dreamed of being before. It seems to us all unnecessary: but that is because we have not yet had the slightest notion of the tremendous thing He means to make of us.

In the end, Christians will become "dazzling, radiant, immortal creatures, pulsating all through with such energy and joy and wisdom and love as we cannot now imagine, a bright stainless mirror which reflects back to God perfectly His own boundless power and delight and goodness"—in short, deified, as the Eastern Orthodox tradition teaches.[42]

For some reason we seem to think that genuine faith is supposed to spare us from or to help us escape these difficult "situations" to which Lewis refers, as if faith were intended to make life convenient for us. A popular religious movement in Western Christianity promises us that, if we have enough faith, we will be able to overcome all our problems and achieve complete victory. There is little mention in this movement of the sacrifice of the martyrs, desert saints and great leaders like Chrysostom. It is all crown, no cross; all promise, no demand; all success, no suffering, at least not chosen suffering. It is hard for us to imagine that faith might push us *into* such difficulties and actually keep us there, where God will make us more like Christ, both in character and in influence.

Years ago I read Peter Kreeft's *Heaven: The Heart's Deepest Longing*. One paragraph in particular struck me as so insightful that I memorized it. Kreeft argues that God promises to work all things out for our good. Nothing falls outside God's ultimate sovereignty and creative purposes; he will accomplish what he says. "Galaxies revolve and dinosaurs breed and rain falls and people fall in love and uncles smoke cheap cigars and people lose their jobs and we all die—all for our good, the finished product, God's work of art, the Kingdom of Heaven. There's nothing outside heaven except hell. Earth is not outside heaven; it is heaven's workshop, heaven's womb."[43]

Earth is heaven's workshop, Kreeft says, which implies that God uses all things to change us for the better. It follows that how we respond to our circumstances, however unwelcomed, carries significant weight. Life in this world is like a divine workshop; the stuff of daily experience—marriage and children, responsibilities and opportunities, interruptions and problems and suffering—the tools that God uses; the artist is God himself, who will sculpt the block of marble that we are into something extraordinary.

This divine plan requires us to be attentive to the process of deification. Daily we should ask, What is God trying to do in my life? How is God using the stuff of ordinary experience to change me? What choices can I make to give him freedom to work? The Christian faith is not a self-help religion, and mature Christians are not self-made people. The powers we have to change ourselves are severely limited. True maturity must be God's doing. Not that we are left with nothing at all to do. God calls us to trust him, pray to him, surrender ourselves to him, respond to his initiative and obey his commands. Above all, we should remind ourselves daily of the goal, which is complete transformation. What God has started, God will surely finish (Phil 1:6). We can be sure that this is true because we have works of art from the past to inspire us and to show us the way. The lives of the saints prove that God will transform us, perfect us, *deify* us, as the Eastern Orthodox say. We will become living icons; our biographies will tell stories of transformation; our lives will bear witness, in word and deed, to the power of the gospel.

PRACTICES

- Read Luke 9:28-36 and 2 Corinthians 3.
- Gaze at the icons printed in the chapter. Ponder the resurrected glory of Jesus Christ and of the saints. Consider that you too will someday share in Christ's resurrection glory. Even now believers are being "changed from one degree of glory to another." God is doing this work through the normal circumstances of life (God's "workshop," as Kreeft called it), which is where the Christian life ought to be lived.
- What circumstances is God trying to use to transform you?
- How can you be prayerfully submissive to God in those circumstances?

6

Windows

The Spirituality of the Sacraments

"For I received from the Lord what I also handed on to you,
that the Lord Jesus on the night when he was betrayed took a loaf of bread,
and when he had given thanks, he broke it and said,
'This is my body that is for you. Do this in remembrance of me.'
In the same way he took the cup also, after supper, saying,
'This cup is the new covenant in my blood.
Do this, as often as you drink it, in remembrance of me.' "

1 COR 11:23-25

⧫

The size alone staggers the mind. It can be seen from miles around, like a great stone monument that dominates the landscape. It rises to a height of over 150 feet, not including the towers and spires, which rise much higher. It appears so weighty that it makes us wonder how it sits on the surface of the earth instead of sinking into oblivion. As we draw nearer, the edifice becomes even more imposing. The thick walls, flying buttresses, dark stone and massive size make it appear like a sculpted mountain. Perched high on the roof, gargoyles set a brooding tone, as does the scene of the last judgment, carved in stone, which sits above the front entrance, making us want to flee inside to find safety.

Once inside, we feel like we have walked into another world. Even though it appears larger on the inside than it did on the outside, which seems almost impossible, the interior seems bright, airy, even weightless, as if it were floating in space. It is quiet and peaceful, beckoning us to stop and simply gaze in reverence. Huge columns shoot straight up and then fan out as ribbed vaulting on the ceiling, like a canopy of tree branches, drawing our eyes heavenward. Light streams in through the stained-glass windows that stand like great sentinels halfway up the walls, casting a hue of colors that makes the interior come alive. The symmetry of the building gives an impression of perfect order and harmony. The rose window and high altar, located at the front (always to the east), invite us to move forward. We cannot help but raise our hearts in worship to God.

GOTHIC CATHEDRALS

The Gothic church I just described is Chartres Cathedral, located an hour

Chartres Cathedral

from Paris, France, which my wife and I visited on our honeymoon. It captures the essence of the Gothic style, a revolution in architecture that began to appear in twelfth-century Europe.[1] By the mid-fourteenth century several thousand Gothic cathedrals and churches dotted the European landscape, especially in England and France. France boasted of more than five hundred, and the English cities of York and Lincoln had over fifteen Gothic churches each, though the population of each city was small, somewhere between five and ten thousand. One scholar estimates that between the years 1050 and 1350 more stone was quarried for Gothic buildings in Europe than during any major building period in the entire history of Egypt, and that says nothing about the huge timbers that were cut for beams and scaffolding, the glass that was formed, colored, cut and shaped into beautiful windows, the lead that was mined, melted and used for glass work, water spouts, and roof, and other materials that were needed along the way. Entire guilds of workers—stone masons, woodcarvers, cloth makers, stained glass artists—were founded and fostered to build these architectural behemoths. Not every church or chapel was of the massive size of the great cathedrals at Salisbury, Notre Dame and Chartres, but they still reflected the unique style and the profound vision of Gothic architecture.

The new style of Gothic adopted, improved and expanded the Romanesque architecture that had immediately preceded it. But what made Gothic architecture truly new was the vision of reality that it portrayed. Gothic churches were intended to represent in earthly form an image of heaven. The first great visionary of the Gothic style, Suger (c. 1081-1151), abbot of St.-Denis monastery, wanted the design of his abbey church, the first known Gothic building, to depict in material form the spiritual reality of heaven, as if it were a kind of earthly incarnation of the celestial city, a window that opened up into another world. Suger attempted to combine architecture and theology into a seamless whole. In a sense, he was, according to Otto von Simson (a renowned historian of Gothic architecture), "an architect who *built* theology."[2] Whereas Romanesque churches created the setting in which certain divine realities could be *displayed*—say, by hanging tapestries and paintings that told the biblical story—"the Gothic builder applied the very laws that order heaven and earth."[3] The Gothic cathedral was therefore more than a symbol; it was a literal representation of the kingdom of God on earth.

How could a mere building, however majestic, be transformed into something so transcendent? Two qualities in Gothic architecture enabled it to serve this lofty purpose. The first was its geometric design. Medieval theologians believed that God had fashioned creation to reflect certain aspects of heavenly reality, among them what medieval theologians called "harmonious proportion." Human beings could do the same thing when they created works of art, provided they uphold that principle. What made something beautiful was not the subjective impression it left on the beholder but the objective qualities—like perfect symmetry—that reflected the beauty of creation as God had designed it.[4] Architecture in particular provided an ideal opportunity to exhibit the harmonious proportion of creation because it was the most mathematical of art forms (sharing much in common with music, according to medieval thinkers). In the medieval worldview, geometry had a kind of cosmic significance because it embodied in mathematical form the rules of symmetry. "Perfect proportion," Robert A. Scott explains, "led builders of great churches to conceive of architecture as applied geometry, geometry as applied theology, and the designer of a Gothic cathedral as an imitator of the divine Master."[5] Gothic buildings, therefore, were mathematical wonders, exhibiting the principle of harmonious proportion from top to bottom.

The second was the use of light. In medieval theology, light served as a symbol of God's revelation. It was the medium by which the invisible, concealed God of heaven revealed himself to material people, leading to spiritual illumination. Gothic cathedrals were designed, therefore, to let in as much light as possible. This posed a problem for architects, however, because Romanesque buildings—the immediate precursor to Gothic—were required to have thick walls to hold up the heavy roof, which did not leave adequate space for large windows. But architectural innovations like flying buttresses, load-bearing columns, ribbed vaulting and pointed arches allowed builders to open up larger spaces in the walls, which were then filled with huge stained glass windows. These massive windows made the walls seem diaphanous and luminous, allowing light to fill the cavernous sanctuary and to shine down on worshipers, as if God himself was illuminating them, making his presence known to them, pouring his grace upon them. Stained glass became the ideal symbol of the Gothic vision of reality because it is the one artistic medium that allows light to shine *through* it, which creates the conditions for luminosity. Thus, if harmonious proportion manifested the perfect order of heaven, then luminosity reflected the light of God shining into the dark world of fallen humanity.[6]

SACRAMENTAL LIFE

The central purpose of these Gothic buildings was to provide a proper setting for the administration of the sacraments, which, according to the Roman Catholic Church, total seven in number (baptism, penance, confirmation, ordination, marriage, the Eucharist and extreme unction).[7] The faithful viewed the sacraments with great reverence, if not fear, for they believed that the sacraments served as the primary means of grace. They assumed, therefore, that churches (especially cathedrals, where the bishop presided) had to be worthy of such a sacred function. The more magnificent the building, the more worthy it would be. Just as the cathedral was a mirror of heavenly realities, so the sacraments were tangible means of grace that had the power to draw people into communion with Christ.

Gothic cathedrals were constructed to direct attention to the altar, the place where the sacraments—especially the Eucharist, which was offered weekly as the culminating act of worship—were administered to the believing community. The medieval church was a sacramental church; the sacraments were the primary means by which believers came to know and experience God. It was not in the preaching of the Word, as the Reformed tradition advocates, nor in the experience of conversion, as evangelicals emphasize, that people encountered God, not even in worship proper, as we would understand it today. Medieval worship was in Latin, which many people could not understand; sermons were short, if that; worship was formal, a performance done by the choir and the priest, all of which seems lamentable to

Eucharist

us now, and rightly so. The cathedral, however, provided the place and the sacraments the means by which God blessed his people with grace. It is no surprise, therefore, that cathedrals were designed to convey the sacredness and power of the sacraments themselves. They became like a holy ship that would carry believers to salvation, which is why the back of the cathedral, where the people actually stood (there were no pews or chairs in the Middle Ages), was called the "nave" (which is closely related to the word *navy*).

There is an understandable reason why the sacraments became so important in the medieval church. Beginning in the fifth century, the Roman Empire started to collapse due, at least in part, to successive waves of tribal migrations that disrupted the social order. Literacy rates, average life span, mobility and economic prosperity all declined. Such a crisis forced the church to adapt its ministry to new—and difficult—conditions. One result was that the faith of the Middle Ages became increasingly tangible and concrete, and thus accessible to people whose world teetered on the edge of chaos. At the heart of this tangible faith was the administration of the sacraments. But there was more to it than that. The medieval church embodied a sacramental approach to religion itself. The church used tangible things to lead people to the reality of the gospel, which was based on the belief that God himself became physical for our salvation. The church adhered to this same pattern. It used a formal liturgy and followed the church year, provided opportunities for pilgrimages, displayed relics and religious art, and honored the saints. The Gothic cathedral played a central role in this concrete, complex religious landscape.

Controversies have swirled around the sacraments for many centuries. Throughout most of the history of the church Christians have debated the theological meaning of the sacraments, disagreed over their proper number, fought over whether baptism should be administered to believers only or to infants as well, contended over what Jesus meant by "This is my body," and argued over the role that the pastor or priest should play in the administration of the sacraments. Theologians have also tried to do what the Bible itself does not do: explain exactly how the sacraments work metaphysically. More often than not they have missed the point. We might not be able to understand their operation, but we can understand their effect. The sacraments are a source of genuine spiritual life and an objective means of grace. The tangible, concrete, material nature of the sacraments reminds us of the reality of Christ's saving work. The sacraments join material and spiritual together into a seamless whole, just as the incarnation does. They are windows that allow us to gaze into another world and receive the grace that pours from that world into ours.

It is all a profound mystery. As I file forward with my children on a Sunday morning to receive the bread and the cup, I meditate on the blessing of God that rests on our family, a blessing that has nothing to do with us—the kind of father I am, the kind of children they are, the kind of Christians we are. I reflect on the journey we have taken together as a family, and I ponder the challenges and difficulties we have faced in the past and will continue to face in the future. I realize that, as God has given us grace in the past, he will continue to in the future. The evidence of that grace is in the bread and cup. "These are the gifts of God for the people of God," our pastor says. I watch my children receive the Eucharist (which means "thanksgiving," an appropriate designation considering the bounty of grace we have experienced as a family). In that moment I see that they are no longer my children but God's children, recipients of his grace, beloved of the Father. Then I step forward. I take a piece of bread as an elder says, "The body of Christ broken for you." Then I dip it in the cup. "The blood of Christ shed for you." God is at work in that moment to cleanse me, renew me and transform me, always in and through Jesus Christ, who suffered and died to unite me—all of us—to himself. I say, "Thanks be to God."

SACRAMENTAL MATERIALS

The role the sacraments play in the Christian faith raises an important question about the role of material objects in religion, including the religion of Christianity. On the one hand, most religions affirm the existence of a spiritual, transcendent, holy God, a being who is completely "Other." On the other hand, we as human beings are material creatures who depend on the physical senses to live, communicate and survive. If anything, we are bound by our senses; without them, we are helpless.

How can material creatures comprehend spiritual reality? Some religions teach that we must learn to leave the senses and material world entirely behind in order to perceive and experience divine reality. Materiality, in other words, is a problem that must be overcome. Other religions set aside and use material mediums for spiritual purposes. These material mediums—sacred objects, sacred places and sacred rituals—create spaces in which earthly creatures can encounter the transcendent God. Muslims use mosques, Hindus have their temples, Jews meet in synagogues. These buildings, the holy objects found inside and the sacred rituals practiced in them function like windows that connect two worlds, the world of material reality and the world of spiritual reality, and they share properties of both, as if they were permeable objects that can mediate to us the spiritual life of God.[8] Christianity, in fact, could be considered the most material of religions because it is shot through with material objects that provide a medium in which we can come to know God.[9] In short, the Christian faith is in essence a sacramental faith.

But there is risk in all this—the risk of idolatry. Though the Pentateuch prescribed the use of sacred objects, places and rituals so that God and humanity could safely and meaningfully meet, it also warned against the sin of idolatry, which consists of reducing God to something less than what God is or replacing God with something else.[10] The Old Testament addresses this problem. The Ark of the Covenant provided a space for an encounter between divine and human. Yet even in the case of this sacred object, God himself was not portrayed directly. The space reserved for God—the "mercy seat," as it was called—was left empty, as if to demonstrate that God could not be reduced to a concrete object. Likewise, the second commandment warns, "You shall not make for yourself an idol, whether in the form of anything that is in heaven above, or that is in the earth beneath, or that is in the water under the earth. You shall not bow down to them or worship them; for I the Lord your God am a jealous God" (Ex 20:4-5).

SACRAMENTAL INCARNATION

It is a problem which most religions face—using material means to make God known, though the use of these material objects can lead to idolatry. Here Christianity stands apart as different. In the Christian faith the ultimate place of encounter between God and humanity is not an altar or a statue or a temple or a ritual but a person, Jesus Christ, who is the incarnation of God. "In the Christian approach to life, however," Catholic theologian Kenan B. Osborne observes, "Jesus, the incarnate Word, has revealed to us precisely the kind of God in whom we believe and for whom we live."[11] Christianity claims that the transcendent, holy God of the universe actually became a human being in order to demonstrate how far God would go to reveal himself to us, win our salvation and unite us with him through Christ.

Christianity is unique in this claim. Jesus "is the image of the invisible

God," the apostle Paul writes. Likewise, "in him all the fullness of God was pleased to dwell" (Col 1:15, 19). Jesus Christ is God's self-portrait, God in human flesh, God as a real person, neighbor, friend. Jesus makes the God of the universe visible, tangible, concrete and accessible. "Long ago God spoke to our ancestors in many and various ways by the prophets," writes the author of the book of Hebrews, "but in these last days he has spoken to us by a Son. . . . He is the reflection of God's glory and the exact imprint of God's very being, and he sustains all things by his powerful word" (Heb 1:1-3).The incarnation thus functions as a kind of stained-glass window that reveals to us ultimate, heavenly reality.[12] In short, Jesus *reveals* God by *being* God. He is both revealer and revelation itself.

The incarnation alters the way Christians should view the spiritual purpose of the material. The material objects that Christians use in worship should point to Jesus Christ, who is the ultimate, perfect and final intersection between human and divine, material and spiritual.[13] In Christ God and humanity come together in a seamless whole. God takes on materiality, the material is united with the divine; God becomes a man, a man embodies God; God embraces humanity, humanity surrenders to God. Together they become a perfect unity, the great God-man. "Since Christ is the word made flesh, true God and true man, as he is confessed by the whole church, Christ is the meeting place of God and humanity, spirit and matter, invisible and visible."[14]

But God came to earth in Jesus Christ to do more than reveal who God is in material form. He also came to share his life with us. Christ ordained the sacraments as material mediums that God uses to give grace to needy people. Again, they are like stained-glass windows that reveal something of eternity: we see God in all his glory and goodness, and God sees us in all our need and sinfulness. His light pours in on us, his grace restores us, his love fills us. "In him a whole new creation is formed, a new humanity is inaugurated in which we are now sons and daughters of God, partakers of the divine nature, and citizens of heaven."[15] The sacraments are not ends but means, the material means of the grace of Christ. *How* God uses the sacraments as a means of grace remains a mystery. *That* God commands us to receive them and offers us grace through them is God's promise. We live in the tension between the mystery and the promise.

THE TEXTURE OF MEDIEVAL RELIGION

The sacraments. The sacraments served as the primary means of grace in the Middle Ages. *Baptism* was administered to infants, a practice which began in the late second century, if not earlier. One of the first to mention infant baptism was Cyprian, bishop of Carthage (d. 258), who noted that by his day infant baptism was universally practiced in the church in North Africa. Cyprian supported infant baptism for three reasons. First, though acknowledging that infants were innocent of committing personal sins, they were not thereby free from the guilt of Adam. Infants still bore the burden of sin, not their own but their ancestors'. Thus, if the church administered baptism to the worst of sinners, "how much less right do we have to deny it to an infant, who, having been born recently, has not sinned, except in that, being born physically according to Adam, he has contracted the contagion of the ancient death by his first birth!"[16] Second, Cyprian argued that infants, no less than adults, are important in God's sight, recipients of grace, beloved of God. Like adults, infants bear the divine image; again like adults, infants are in need of God's mercy. God offers mercy to all, "not according to measure, but according to love and fatherly mercy equal for all. For God does not make such distinction of person or of age since He offers Himself as a Father to all to obtain celestial grace with balanced equality."[17] Finally, Cyprian viewed the church as if it were like Noah's ark. Only those within the church can be saved, for "there is no salvation outside the church." He viewed baptism as the rite of initiation, nurture and protection. If God is the Father of all believers, then the church is their mother.

In the Middle Ages babies were born at home, usually with the assistance of a midwife.[18] Infants were immediately baptized, even by a layperson if a priest was not available. Newborns would be washed, wrapped in swaddling clothes and taken to the church. Godparents offered the infant for baptism; the mother was never present, nor allowed to be present, for she was considered unclean. The priest followed a simple baptismal rite: he recited the liturgy, exorcized the devil, gave the infant a pinch of salt and anointed him or her with oil for spiritual protection, interrogated the godparents, and then immersed the infant. The baby would then be brought back to its parents who were responsible to nurture the child in the faith.

The sacrament of *confirmation* became the means by which baptized believers, upon reaching the age of discretion, took ownership of the faith, claiming it for themselves and affirming the baptismal vows that the community had said on their behalf. It began almost by accident. The church baptized infants as soon after birth as possible. Bishops were ultimately responsible to administer the sacraments. But bishops often lived at a great distance from many of the parishes within their diocese, which led to long delays between birth and baptism. To solve the problem, the responsibility of baptism fell on the shoulders of priests, deacons and sometimes even laypeople. When bishops visited the parish, which sometimes happened only once in a person's lifetime, they then "confirmed" the baptism of the child. This simple solution evolved into the practice of confirmation that many churches, both Catholic and at least some Protestant, follow today. While infant baptism affirms that God is the initiator of salvation, confirmation stresses the importance of human response.[19] Confirmation thus emerged as the sacrament that complemented and completed infant baptism.

The church administered the sacraments of baptism and confirmation to every believer, but only once. The purpose of these two sacraments was to confer the gift of salvation and provide a point of entry into the church. The church administered two other sacraments to nurture believers in the faith, and for this reason the church administered these repeatedly. The first was *penance,* the sacrament of repentance. The early church was serious and strict about baptism as a rite of confession, repentance and forgiveness. The question soon arose as to whether there could be forgiveness of mortal sins, like murder, adultery and apostasy, after baptism was administered. Some believers actually put off baptism until they were near death because they feared losing their salvation if they committed postbaptismal sins. Because baptism could be administered only once, "it soon became apparent that some supplementary sacrament was needed, and what eventually became the sacrament of penance was introduced to meet the need."[20]

The sacrament of penance allowed baptized believers to remain faithful members of the Christian community even after they had sinned, provided they repented, demonstrated genuine sorrow and submitted to a public ritual of discipline, such as wearing penitential clothing, standing at the back of the church during worship, and begging fellow believers to pray for them. Over time the church provided penitential manuals for clergy to use, an innovation developed and passed on by the Irish. If a believer sinned by, say, cheating someone in a business transaction, the priest would administer the sacrament of penance. The person would make confession to the priest and then the priest would assign some penitential exercise before pronouncing the words of absolution. Thus penance served to extend the effects of baptism beyond the initial rite, as if penance were a kind of "damage-limitation exercise, designed to deal with the problem of post-baptismal sins." Not surprisingly, it was sometimes called a "second baptism."

The second sacrament of nurture was the *Eucharist*. Great mystery was attached to this sacrament. The bread and cup were brought into the church with solemnity, handled by the priest with care and confirmed through the words of institution. "This is Christ's body broken for you; this is Christ's blood shed for you." Medieval Christians believed that once consecrated by the priest the bread and wine somehow became the body and blood of Christ. The rite was so holy, in fact, that only the priest could drink the cup; the laity had to be content with receiving the bread alone. They adored the host as a re-presentation of the death of Christ on their behalf. Such veneration of the host eventually gave rise to the festival of *Corpus Christi*, which was celebrated on the Thursday after Trinity Sunday (in late spring). The festival would begin with a special Mass. Then the people would form two long lines through which a great procession of clergy, town officials and members of guilds and religious orders passed, marching in procession behind the consecrated host, displayed in a magnificent vessel. People would decorate homes and businesses along the parade route, and they would kneel when the host passed because they believed that they were adoring the body of the Lord himself.

When common people reached the age of adulthood, which occurred during the early teen years, they had to choose between marriage, church office or the monastic life. *Marriage* was considered sacramental because Paul identified it as a great mystery (*sacramentum* in Latin), comparing it with the mystical union between Christ and the church. The priest performed marriages outside the church doors. Rings were exchanged, a dowry was provided, vows were spoken. After the marriage ceremony the couple received the Eucharist and then attended a reception held in their honor. Marriage vows were considered sacred, the union between husband and wife binding during their lifetime. Those joining monasteries committed themselves to marriage too, only in this case it was marriage to Christ. Their vows were considered as binding as the vows spoken at a normal marriage ceremony.

Ordination or *holy orders* was understood as sacramental because it endowed the clergy with the authority to consecrate all the other sacraments, thereby setting those sacraments apart as means of grace. "The sacrament of holy orders, therefore, was basic to the other sacraments, which were, as a rule, dependent on it for their valid administration."[21] Only men could be ordained to church office, though both men and women could join a monastery. Thus, when children reached adulthood they found the church ready to solemnize marriage, ordain them to office or welcome them into a monastery, which constituted the three pathways open to them, though the vast majority of common people in the Middle Ages chose marriage.

There were few hospitals in the Middle Ages, especially for common people, who were therefore forced to rely mostly on home remedies to deal with sickness and disease, such as various herbal treatments, dietary measures and bloodletting. The sacrament of *extreme unction* served as the spiritual means of healing. To administer this sacrament, the priest would visit the sick, anoint them with oil and, using the liturgical prayers of the church, call on God for healing mercy. As it is, life was short. Many children died in infancy, many women died in childbirth, many people died of diseases for which there was no cure. If people survived to adulthood, they rarely lived past the age of fifty. Last rites were administered to people who were on the verge of death. When death was imminent, the priest would be sent for. Wearing surplice and stole, the priest would administer the Eucharist, penance (when possible) and extreme unction, only this time extreme unction was intended to prepare the person for death.

Village funerals were simple. The body would be sewn in a shroud, carried to the church and draped with a black pall. The priest would then say the Mass and on occasion even deliver a brief funeral homily. "Good men," one exhortation reads, "as ye all see, here is a mirror to us all: a corpse brought to the church. God have mercy on him, and bring him into his bliss that shall last for ever. . . . Wherefore each man and woman that is wise, make him ready thereto; for we all shall die, and we know not how soon."[22] The body was then buried in the church cemetery, the sleeping place of the dead, which was usually located in the center of the village. There the dead would serve as a silent witness to the living, reminding them that this world is not the only reality there is.[23]

PILGRIMAGES

Thus from cradle to grave clergy administered the sacraments as a means of grace to ordinary believers. But the church presided over a wide range of other religious rituals too, which were intended to convict, inspire, heal and nurture the faith of common people. For example, some people embarked on pilgrimages to major religious centers, most often to perform some kind of penance, to pray for a miracle, to recover from some catastrophic loss or to visit places that were renowned for their holiness. Pilgrimage was a popular activity in the Middle Ages. The wealthy and powerful often embarked on long pilgrimages to famous, faraway places. Common people had to be content with staying closer to home. Even so, local pilgrimages were considered spiritually meritorious too, provided the place of destination possessed some quality that made it worthy as a pilgrimage site.[24]

Jerusalem map

The primary place of pilgrimage, of course, was the Holy Land. Several early accounts of pilgrimages to the Holy Land have survived, none more famous than the account written by Egeria, a wealthy and prominent woman from Spain who visited the Holy Land sometime between A.D. 404 and 417.[25] Her story is especially illuminating because it provides a detailed description of famous Christian leaders, landscapes, buildings,

Egeria's Pilgrimage

"When noon comes, they go before the Cross, rain or shine, because the place is out-
doors and like a large and very beautiful atrium, between the Cross and the Anas-
tasis [tomb]. All the people are so crowded there that one cannot even open a door.
The bishop's chair is placed before the Cross, and from noon to three nothing is done
except that Biblical passages are read. . . . And so from noon to three either there
are readings or hymns so that all the people may be shown that whatever the
prophets foretold of the Passion of the Lord is done either in the Gospels or the Ap-
ostolic writings. And thus during this three hours the people are taught that noth-
ing happened which was not first foretold and nothing was foretold which was not
completed. Prayers are always interspersed, and those prayers are always fitting to
the day. At each reading and prayer there is such emotion and weeping by all the
people that it is a wonder. . . . The dismissal having been given, they go from the
Martyrium to the Anastasis. And when they have come there, the passage of the
Gospel is read where Joseph asks Pilate for the body of the Lord, that he might place
it in a new tomb. . . . Those among the people who wish, or who can, keep vigil.
. . . [Through] the whole night, hymns and antiphons are sung there until morn-
ing. A great crowd keep vigil, some from evening, others from midnight, but all
doing what they can." (From Patricia Wilson-Kaster et al., A Lost Tradition)

institutions and liturgy. She wrote an account of her pilgrimage for her
"holy sisters," which indicates that she might have been a member of a
community of learned and devout women. Her observations provide invaluable details about the Holy Land in the early fifth century, rich descriptions of the landscape, including the layout of the city of Jerusalem
and the buildings that had been constructed during the reign of Constantine. Her explanation of the liturgy of Holy Week indicates that the Jerusalem church followed a highly choreographed and stylized ritual of worship, culminating in the celebration of the resurrection on Easter morning.

As Egeria noted, the Holy Week rituals made the life and ministry of
Christ come alive to her. She saw where Christ had walked, ate, slept,
preached, healed, suffered and died. The city itself stood as a witness to the
saving work of God through Christ. The pilgrimage astonished and moved

her, providing living proof of the reality of Christ's earthly life and redeeming work. She was not the only one who came to this conclusion. In a sermon to baptismal candidates, Cyril, who served as the bishop of Jerusalem in the late fourth century, extolled the sacredness of the Martyrium, the building that was constructed on the site where Christ was crucified, as living proof of the power of Christ's ministry. "Christ was truly crucified for our sins. Even supposing you were disposed to contest this, your surroundings rise up before your eyes to refute you, this sacred Golgotha where we now come together because of him who was crucified here."[26]

A pilgrimage to Santiago de Compostela, located in northwest Spain, was nearly as sacred as one to the Holy Land. According to legend, James traveled to Spain after the day of Pentecost to preach the gospel. After a decade of fruitful service he returned to Jerusalem, where he was martyred. Two disciples, Athanasius and Theodore, transported James's body back to

Pilgrimage

Spain. There they found a field in the hills, laid the relics of the apostle in a marble sarcophagus and buried him. Then they built an altar and a small chapel over his tomb. All traces of the mausoleum disappeared for eight hundred years. In the ninth century, however, a saintly hermit, Pelayo, saw a star that had settled over some hills near his cave and heard voices of angels who were singing praises to God. He reported the experience to Theodomir, the local bishop, who interpreted the events as a sign from God.

After three days of prayer and fasting, Theodomir dispatched workmen to travel to the place where Pelayo had seen the star. They cleared away brush and discovered the forgotten mausoleum. After a short investigation the bishop concluded that the mausoleum contained the body of James, or Santiago (St. James in Spanish). Several subsequent military victories over the Moors only reinforced the belief that the body was indeed that of James, for how else could these surprising victories be explained? Santiago de Compostela soon became an important pilgrimage site, with churches, hostels and monasteries dotting the route that led to the shrine. Even today it is still considered one of the most famous pilgrimages in the Christian world. Each year thousands of pilgrims follow a route on foot that covers hundreds of miles. Along the way they pray in various chapels and follow other religious exercises that prepare them for their arrival at the tomb of St. James.[27]

SAINTS AND RELICS

Pilgrimages were popular because it allowed believers to view and even touch the relics of the saints, which played a significant role in medieval religious life. Medieval Christians believed that the saints, situated in heaven, served as intercessors for those who still lived on earth. Their remains, held in the church, assumed a kind of power of proxy, as if their bones represented the living presence of the saints and conveyed their merits to the faithful. Thus the church became a kind of repository of saintly power, a point of contact between the almighty God and needy humanity, functioning like a lightning rod that channeled the extraordinary power of heaven to earth. The relics of saints (their hair, bones, teeth, Bibles, swords, sandals and the like) symbolized and embodied the efficacious presence of the saint, which explains why they became objects of so much value (including monetary value) and why they were kept under lock and key.

The importance of relics originated in the early church. Early Christians believed that the bones of the martyrs had sacred power. The relics of these saints reminded the faithful of the ongoing witness of their sacrificial death. For example, after Polycarp was martyred in the middle of the second century, his friends "took up his bones which are more valuable than refined gold and laid them in a suitable place where, the Lord willing, . . . we may gather together in gladness and celebrate the anniversary of his martyrdom."[28] St. Cyril of Jerusalem believed that the body of a saint had power to work miracles. The body itself was venerable and powerful "on account of the virtuous soul that once inhabited it. For it is well known that such external objects as handkerchiefs and aprons have cured the sick after touching the martyr's body; how much more then will the body itself heal them."[29]

Relics therefore became important material objects to medieval believers. They bought, sold and stole them, dismembered the bodies of saints for distribution to churches and monasteries, and housed them in beautiful works of art known as reliquaries, all because they attributed so much power to them.[30] Even educated elites believed that relics could work miracles. Writing just a few weeks after Thomas Becket (d. 1170) had been murdered and then buried in Canterbury, which became a popular pilgrimage site, theologian John of Salisbury observed, almost incredulously:

> And there many mighty wonders are performed, to God's glory: great throngs of people gather to feel in themselves and witness in others the power and mercy of Him who always shows His wonder and His glory in His saints. . . . I should not have dreamt to write such words on any account had not my eyes been witness to the certainty of this.[31]

Consequently, laypeople expected and sometimes experienced miracles when they prayed to God in the presence of these relics.[32]

Of all the saints, the virgin Mary, the "Queen of Heaven," as she was called, occupied a place of eminence in the medieval church, especially after Jesus began to be viewed less as a good Shepherd and more as a remote, heavenly King. As early as the late fourth century theologians argued for her perpetual virginity. During the Middle Ages believers viewed Mary as a tender mother who had nursed her Son, wept for him at the foot of the cross, held his lifeless body in her arms after he was taken down from the cross. As the mother of Jesus and the perfect example of submission to the divine will, she had special power to intercede on behalf of the faithful. Her relics had power too, though in her case the relics did not come from her body (medieval Christians believed that she had been bodily assumed into heaven) but from her dutiful work as the Mother of God (say, her veil, a piece of straw from the manger, or a drop of milk from her breast, held in a precious vial). They dedicated churches to her, sang hymns to her, prayed to her and lit candles in her honor. They celebrated Marian feast days, used Marian liturgical texts, read Marian devotionals, venerated Marian art works and observed Marian rituals, such as the repetition of

"Hail Mary" and the use of Marian prayer beads. "Virtually anything that could be sung, displayed or thought in Mary's honor found its place in the mélange," observes Richard Kieckhefer.[33]

THE CHURCH YEAR

Common people in the Middle Ages followed an annual calendar that was saturated with religious holidays, festivals and saint days. Time itself reflected a Christian view of reality. The process of Christianizing the calendar took centuries because the pagan calendar was so entrenched in Roman society. By the early medieval period, however, the better part of the church year had been established. Churches followed this calendar as a matter of course. Priests, abbots and bishops used the church year as a means of teaching common people, most of whom were illiterate, about the biblical story, especially the life of Christ.[34]

The center of the church year was the celebration of the Pascha, which was a Christian adaptation of the Passover. The festival included instruction, fasting, repentance, processions, prayers, vigils and worship from Maundy Thursday to Easter Sunday. Bishops baptized catechumens on Sunday morning, which was followed by the celebration of the Eucharist. Over time the Pascha was extended to the previous Sunday. Thus Palm Sunday began an eight-day series of liturgical events, known as Holy Week, which culminated on Easter Sunday. Lent was added later as a forty-day period of fasting and repentance leading up to Holy Week.

The earliest evidence for the celebration of Christmas dates to the middle of the fourth century, perhaps as early as A.D. 336. The date itself was borrowed from a pagan festival, *Natalis Solis Invicti*, established by the Emperor Aurelian in A.D. 274 to mark the winter solstice, which was calculated to occur in late December. Christians recognized the close connection between the pagan holiday, which celebrated the birth of the sun, and the Christian celebration of the birth of Christ. They thus adapted the pagan holiday as the date for the festival of the Nativity. Over time the four weeks of Advent were set aside as a period of preparation for Christmas, and January 6 was established as the festival of Epiphany, the day which commemorates the first time that the earthly Jesus was made manifest to the Gentiles (the Magi who visited him). Bishops exhorted the flock to observe Christmas not as a pagan holiday but as a Christian celebration of Christ's birth. "This is our present festival," Gregory of Nazianzus preached,

> this is what we are celebrating today—the coming of God to man . . . so that we might return to God. . . . So let us keep the feast, not like a heathen festival, but in a godly way—not in a way of the world, but in a way above the world—not as if it were ours, but as it belongs to him who is ours, our Master's—not as of weakness, but as of healing—not as of creation, but of re-creation.[35]

Thus the church year evolved into what we know of it today. The year began with Advent, which culminated in the birth of Christ on December 25. This was followed by the twelve days of Christmas, then Epiphany, Ash Wednesday, Lent, Holy Week, Easter Sunday, Ascension Day and Pentecost. Other festivals and saint days were added along the way, such as Corpus Christi, the Feast of Transfiguration and All Saints Day. These holy days and seasons created an annual rhythm that reminded the faithful of salvation history and sanctified time. Ignorant peasants in particular came to know the biblical story through these annual events. "The goal is a life that participates in Christ's life," concludes Philip H. Pfatteicher. "It is a real life—his and ours—that ultimately is, or should be, one. The purpose is not chronology but identification."[36]

RECLAIMING THE SACRAMENTS

Gothic cathedrals thus functioned like a stage where the drama of salvation was played out. They displayed works of art, like stained glass windows, that told the story of salvation and the lives of the saints; they housed relics and reliquaries and tombs that allowed laypeople to brush up against the holiness of the saints; they provided the proper setting where the clergy could administer the sacraments. Churches absorbed the power of the realities they housed, thus helping people know Christ, participate in his story and receive his life. Many believers could not read or write. They suffered much and died young. Yet they found in the church the story of salvation, the truth about Christ, the holiness of the saints, the comfort of Mary and the rhythm of the church year. Their world was saturated with the Christian faith. There were abuses, of course. Common people sometimes worshiped the saints instead of Christ, observed rituals more out of superstition than genuine faith, functioned as religious spectators rather than faithful disciples and received grace as if they were spiritual consumers. Many had the form of religion but denied the power of it.

Still, *abusus non tollit usus*. For all its shortcomings, the medieval emphasis on a sacramental faith has something valuable to teach us. Medieval Christians tried to Christianize their world. We are in the process of doing the opposite. Many churches today, especially in the West, are fast becoming little more than empty monuments. I recently read an article in our local newspaper about a crisis concerning church buildings in Great Britain. Officials of the Church of England are responsible for hundreds of church buildings that have fallen into disrepair because they are no longer being used. Officials say that the church cannot afford to keep them up or open. So they have decided to sell them to developers, who are converting them to other uses—upscale apartments, condominiums, pubs, recreation centers with climbing walls, businesses, even a school to train people for the circus. In short, these buildings are being paganized. No longer used for worship and the administration of the sacraments, they have become the tools of modern capitalism. Perhaps the church in America is following the same course. Today many churches preach self-help principles, peddle a variety of clever religious products, offer various programs to religious consumers and cater to the "felt needs" of people. Ironically, while England is paganizing church buildings, Americans could be "paganizing" the faith itself. When the church is functioning at its best, it communicates the grace and love and power of God so completely that the faithful are enabled to live for God wherever they are, and thus to claim the "secular" world—theaters, bowling allies, schools, businesses, neighborhoods—for God's kingdom purposes. At its worst, it does the opposite; the secular world encroaches on the church until it finally takes over.

The faith of the medieval church was essentially sacramental. It reminded people that the gospel is objective, rooted in the events of salvation history and offered to us through the means of grace that Christ himself established. How can we reclaim the sacraments for the church today? First, the sacraments are quintessentially material, which reminds us of the material nature of the Christian faith. Christianity affirms that God created the material universe, and that he created it good. Everything in it somehow manifests his greatness and glory. "The heavens are telling the glory of God; and the firmament proclaims his handiwork," Psalm 19 reads. Human beings are material too—embodied creatures, sensory bound, made of flesh and blood. We were created to live in the material world, and we are called to take care of that material world.

Jesus used examples from the material world to illustrate his kingdom teaching. He mentioned sower and seed, vine and branches, nets and fish, shepherd and sheep, hen and brood, father and son. He was an earthy teacher, refusing to talk in abstractions. He was earthy in the way he lived too: he slept and ate and cried and bled and died. The incarnation is final proof of the material nature of Christianity. Jesus Christ is God come in person, true flesh and blood. The sacraments are symbols of the ongoing presence of the material Christ who lived, suffered and died for our sake. Every time we see a person baptized, we are physically reminded of the cleansing that Jesus offers through his death; every time we touch, taste and swallow the bread and wine, we are reminded of the sustenance that Christ provides for us. This is no abstract, ambiguous, sentimental, ephemeral kind of spirituality. It is body and blood; it is water, bread and wine. In the Christian faith the spiritual and material are mysteriously, perfectly and ultimately united in Christ, in the sacraments, and in God's plan of redemption.

Second, the sacraments also teach us that grace comes to us as an objective reality. It might not be a quantifiable substance, which some medieval theologians taught, as if it could be measured, weighed, packaged, marketed and sold to the highest bidder. But it is real all the same, manifested as genuine power and life that comes to us from the outside and changes how we stand before God and how we live in the world. It is primarily God's doing; our responsibility is to receive grace by active and sincere faith. The Bible does not tell us *how* the sacraments actually communicate grace, only *that* they do. It is all a mystery.

My local church—a Presbyterian church—uses the method of intinction to distribute the eucharistic elements: every member who is able stands up, walks to the front of the church, tears off a piece of bread, dips the bread in the cup, says a prayer, and then puts the sacrament—bread and wine, body and blood—into his or her mouth. We have nothing to say but a word of thanks, nothing to claim but mercy, nothing to pay for the grace that is lavished on us. We receive the Eucharist—a hunk of bread, soaked in the cup—as if we were little birds, utterly dependent and desperate, who simply need to open our mouths and hearts to receive God's gift. There is no variation in the "sacramental menu" either, to satisfy our culinary tastes. It is the same basic stuff, week in and week out. It is physical food and spiritual food, all wrapped up together, offered to us as something that is objective, tangible and concrete. Grace is just that way. It is God's gift to us. But we must admit our need, confess our sins and believe the good news of the gospel. That is all we must do, all we can do. Our wealth, status, profession, background, accomplishments and righteousness matter nothing. In the Eucharist, only faith counts, and faith turns away from self to find God.

I am acquainted well enough with people at our church to know something about their stories. I think about those stories when I see people standing in line to receive the Eucharist. I know of strained marriages, wayward children, failed businesses, mental anguish, habits of indulgence, doubts and anger, and monumental failures. Every person brings his or her own story to the sacrament and finds grace to keep believing, hoping and enduring for another week because in the end the Christian faith concerns what God has done—and continues to do—for us and in us, not what we do for God.

Third, the sacraments have the power to transform us into living sacraments to the world. Which leads us back to where we started—the Gothic cathedral. Gothic cathedrals were intended to represent in material form the reality of heaven, especially through two fundamental qualities—harmonious proportion and luminosity. As sacraments to the world, we are called to exhibit those same qualities. Harmonious proportion has to do with how we order our lives under God's will and rule. We put first things first, live according to proper priorities, channel our resources toward worthy ends, and hallow the world as God's good creation. Luminosity in turn has to do with how we let God's light shine through us. At night stained-glass windows appear colorless, dark, ominous. But during the day they come alive with color and radiance. We were created to be like stained-glass windows, luminous and resplendent, manifesting the beauty and holiness and love of God. As God came to us in Jesus Christ, revealing the divine glory, so God calls us, as people redeemed by Christ, to reveal the divine glory to a fallen, desperate world.

It is all a mystery. How did God become a human being? The first disciples were certainly not expecting the incarnation. It was only the bodily resurrection of Christ that persuaded them of the truth of it. How do water, bread and wine feed us with the grace of God? It is a truth beyond our ability to understand. How can we become a sacrament to the world? It is a task beyond our ability to accomplish. Yet God can and will transform us by his grace so that we become living sacraments to the world. Christ joined material and spiritual together into a perfect, seamless whole. He nourishes us with the material and spiritual stuff of the sacraments. He calls us to be material and spiritual agents of redemption in the world.

PRACTICES
- Read Luke 22:14-30; John 1:1-18.
- Try fasting the twenty-four hours before you know you will receive communion at your church.
- Spend Saturday evening in prayer and meditation, perhaps reading the entire Gospel of Mark.
- Ponder the significance of the bread and cup as fitting symbols of Christ's body and blood.
- Rise early on Sunday morning to worship God alone.
- When you receive communion during public worship at your church, embrace by faith the gift of God's grace. Keep repeating: "There is therefore now no condemnation for those who are in Christ Jesus."
- After worship enjoy a feast with family or friends. In the later afternoon devote time to reading Romans 5 and 8.

7

Union

The Spirituality of the Mystics

For God alone my soul waits in silence;
from him comes my salvation.
He alone is my rock and my salvation,
my fortress; I shall never be shaken.

PS 62:1-2

O n the surface of things mystical spirituality and sacramental spirituality seem to share little in common. Sacramental spirituality glories in the material stuff of creation. It uses water, bread, wine and oil as means of grace and sets aside ordinary things as the fundamental tools God uses to do his extraordinary work. Mystical spirituality leaves behind the material in order to experience union with God. The sacraments appeal to the senses, mysticism to intuition; the sacraments emphasize the means of grace, mysticism the end; the sacraments remain firmly rooted in the concreteness of earthly reality, mysticism soars into the ephemeral and ethereal realm of heavenly reality.

Of all the traditions explored in this book, the mystical way is the most foreign to my temperament. I am by nature and nurture more sacramental than mystical, a man of flesh more than a man of pure spirit. It is for this very reason that mystical spirituality has the most to teach me, for the tradition to which I am least attracted is the one about which I should be most curious. History itself bears witness to the significance of this tradition. Some of the wisest and deepest writers in the history of the church have been mystics who reached summits of spiritual insight and experience that I have been able to glimpse only from afar. It could be that by studying their writings I will be able to follow in their footsteps.

Mystical experiences often come as a complete surprise. One of the most formidable theologians of the Middle Ages had a mystical experience

Thomas Aquinas

that he did not expect and probably did not want, for he was not naturally inclined toward mysticism. His experience introduces us to the wonder, ambiguity and power of mystical spirituality. Though his contemporaries called him a "dumb ox," probably because he was heavy, slow and quiet, in truth he had one of the greatest minds of his generation. His books became standard fare in the medieval university curriculum. Even today every Catholic seminarian reads him and every Catholic student of philosophy studies his major works. It is impossible to understand the history of theology unless one grapples with Thomas Aquinas. He was—and still is—an intellectual giant.

Born around 1225 into a wealthy home, Thomas entered the famous Benedictine Abbey of Monte Cassino as a young boy and later studied at the University of Naples, all to prepare for a monastic vocation. While at Naples he was exposed to a controversial new movement, the Order of Preachers, which had only recently been founded by Dominic. Thomas was captured by its fresh vision of the Christian faith and joined the order, thus defying his father's wishes. His father, however, was not willing to give up so easily. Expecting that Thomas would outgrow his youthful idealism, he ordered Thomas's older brothers to abduct him and hold him as a prisoner in the family castle until he would change his mind. Thomas remained there for a year, refusing to compromise his commitment to live the apostolic life of a Dominican. After being released from confinement (by his sister), he immediately traveled to Paris to study under a master theologian, Albert the Great (c. 1200-1280), who introduced Thomas to the philosophy of Aristotle. After completing his studies Thomas became a professor of theology. He wrote two massive volumes of theology, the *Summa Contra Gentiles*, which addresses non-Christian religions, and the *Summa Theologica*, which provides an overview of theology. His books are as precise, clear and logical as the writings of a scientist. Indeed, Thomas thought theology *is* a science, the science of God.

The entire course of his life changed, however, on December 6, 1273, the Feast of St. Nicholas. Thomas attended Mass that day, as he did every day. But during the eucharistic service something extraordinary happened to him. He could not speak about the experience, nor could he resume his scholarly work. It is as if he was struck blind, deaf and dumb. His good friend and secretary, Reginald of Piperno, asked him, "Father, how can you want to stop such a great work?" Aquinas replied, "I can write no more." Reginald wondered if Thomas had reached a state of exhaustion. So he inquired once again what had happened to his master. Thomas replied, as before, "Reginald, I can write no more." But then he added, "All that I have hitherto written seems to me nothing but straw." He retreated once again into silence. Later Thomas visited his sister, who also noticed the change. She asked Reginald what was wrong with her beloved brother, what had caused the deep disturbance. This time Thomas said more. "All that I have written seems to me nothing but straw . . . compared to what I have seen and what has been revealed to me." A short while later he left for a Dominican General Council meeting at Lyons. He died in a Cistercian abbey on the way there. The date was March 7, 1274.[1]

THE ROOTS OF CHRISTIAN MYSTICISM

Thomas was not in fact a mystic, although clearly he had a mystical experience, for his encounter with God was ineffable and transcendent. It led him into some kind of mysterious union with God, which is the goal of mysticism. Mystical spirituality is concerned with one basic question: how can we truly know God? One way of knowing involves learning information about God; it is doctrinal. Another way of knowing leads to union with God; it is mystical. Mystical writing often seems impenetrable and incomprehensible, eluding precise definition, as if it were an unknown and unknowable foreign language. Mystics relish paradox, speak in abstractions and metaphors, and love mystery. They tell us that knowing God is intuitive as well as rational, heart in addition to head, and utterly ineffable. They say that knowledge of doctrine is necessary but not sufficient, for the goal of the Christian life is not knowledge *about* God but knowledge *of* God and union *with* God. Thus mystics remind us that true knowledge of God is not like any other kind of knowledge. God is the subject, not the object; the knower, not the known; the one who initiates the relationship. God is the one who reveals himself to believers and the one who unites believers to himself in perfect bliss and harmony.

Christian mysticism reached its pinnacle in the Middle Ages. It was during this period that many of the greatest Christian mystics lived, the most formative ideas of mystical spirituality emerged and the various "schools" of mystical thought developed. Of course the early church had mystics; so did the Reformation church. The modern church has had its share of mystics too. Christian mysticism has always found a way to explain its vision of spiritual reality to the larger church, though often with a quiet voice. That voice spoke with greatest authority and clarity during the medieval period.

Christian mysticism can trace its roots to the ancient philosopher Plato. According to Plato, the human soul is preexistent. In its original state of bliss, it contemplates the eternal truth of God in perfect purity. But creation, birth and embodiment causes the soul to forget its true, original, primal knowledge, engulfing it in materiality. Because the soul is still divine, containing some spark and memory of true being, beauty, goodness and oneness, it longs to return to the divine realm, as if it were a lost child wanting to return home. This process of return requires detachment from everything material so that, released from its earthly imprisonment, the soul can ascend to its divine source, contemplate ultimate reality in pure ecstasy and gain a knowledge that is beyond all knowledge.

The Neo-Platonic philosopher Plotinus developed Plato's ideas. He reasoned that God, the *One*, is absolute and simple, beyond being, beyond knowledge, beyond comprehension. "Generative of all, the Unity is none of all; neither thing nor quality nor quantity nor intellect nor soul; not in motion, nor at rest, not in place, not in time; it is the self-defined, unique in form, or better, formless."[2] Emanating from the One is *Mind*, which constitutes the realm of ideas about God. The *Psyche*, in turn, functions as the link between the perfect eternal world and the material world. Finally, the *Soul* lives as an extension of the psyche in each person. Plotinus asserted that the soul originated in God, but it has become separated from God by being encompassed in creation, as if the material world were a kind of weight dragging the soul downward. Like Plato, Plotinus believed that the soul still remembers its original state; it longs to ascend through the "chain of becoming" back to its source, the One. By turning inward, it can find the One within itself. This requires a process of purification, detachment and contemplation as the soul, imbued with longing for the One, recollects its identity with the One.

> The soul is anxious to be free, so that we may attach ourselves to [the One] by the whole of our being; no part of it not touching God. Then it will be possible for the soul to see both God and herself divinely, and she will see herself illumined, full of intelligible light; or rather she will be light itself—pure, unfettered, agile, become a God or rather being a God, and wholly aflame.[3]

At that point all self-awareness fades, all sense of duality melts away. The soul experiences perfect union. "Here is contained all that is immortal: nothing here but is Divine Mind, all is God. This is the place of every soul."[4]

Perhaps the most influential Platonic Christian mystic in the Middle Ages was an unknown Syrian bishop or monk who lived in the late fifth century. He called himself Dionysius the Areopagite, a name he borrowed from Acts 17 to give the impression he wrote during the apostolic age and had apostolic authority. His strategy seemed to work, for medieval Christians assumed that his writings came from early Christianity. That he used a pseudonym was not discovered until centuries later. He is now known as the Pseudo-Dionysius (or simply Dionysius or Denys). Whoever he was, he played a key role in shaping mystical thought during the entire medieval period.[5]

Dionysius believed that God is pure being whose trinitarian life pulsates and overflows. In fact, creation itself in all its diversity is the result of the overflowing of God's self-giving, trinitarian love. All of created reality has descended from God to earth in a perfect and orderly procession. First comes the heavenly hierarchy of seraphim, cherubim and "thrones"; then comes the earthly hierarchy of bishops, priests and deacons who preside over the divine mysteries of the church and, using liturgy and sacraments, communicate the divine life to the faithful. Creation manifests God's goodness and provides a way for humanity to know God and commune with God for, "being Goodness Himself, He extends His goodness, simply by being good to all that exists."[6] Creation also reveals God's desire to share his life with humanity. Humanity desires to know God too, and thus to participate in the divine life. For this to happen, however, humanity must *ascend* to God, using the created order as a kind of ladder. Fundamental to Dionysius's thought, therefore, is this scheme of *procession* and *return*, as if all of creation participates in a kind of glorious journey. "For it is quite impossible that we humans should, in any material way, rise up to imitate and to contemplate the heavenly hierarchies without the aid of those material means capable of guiding us as our nature requires."[7] The created hierarchy is thus not the end but the means. The end is a vision of "a truth which is simple and one."[8] Unlike the Platonists, therefore, Dionysius had a positive view of creation. Salvation does not consist of escaping creation but ascending through it until we arrive at God.

Still, God is other and greater than the creation, above and beyond it, and thus, from an earthly point of view, unknowable. In the end all the means we use to describe God, ascend to God and commune with God simply fall short and fail. As the soul ascends, "language falters, and when it has passed up and beyond the ascent, it will turn silent completely, since it will finally be at one with Him who is indescribable."[9] To know, therefore, we must abandon all earthly knowledge and enter into the darkness of *unknowing*. Thus, when the soul plunges "into that darkness which is beyond intellect, we shall find ourselves not simply running short of words but actually speechless and unknowing."[10] There are two kinds of knowing. One is direct, rational and revelatory; it depends on the created order or symbols to know God. The other is intuitive, by which "we ascend step by step, so far as we can follow the way, to the transcendent, by negating and transcending everything and by seeking the cause of all. . . . Therefore, God is known in all, and apart from all." This second kind of knowing is truer to the nature of God; it leads to union with God. When this union occurs, our understanding "withdraws from all, and abandons itself, and is united with the dazzling rays and in them and from them is enlightened by the unsearchable depths of wisdom."[11]

Dionysius argued that when it comes to this deeper kind of knowing, we cannot use language to describe God with any degree of accuracy. In calling God good, for example, it would be better to say that God is *not* good, for our understanding of the word *good* is limited by our earthly experience of the good, which falls short of the depth of God's goodness. God is above good, or "hyper-good"; God is above beauty, above being, above eternity, above transcendence, even above Trinity. Thus in the end we can only speak of God in negative terms, or what is called "apophatic" theology, though Dionysius never rejected out of hand the use of affirmative language, or "cataphatic" theology.

Dionysius and his followers believed that to experience union with God even Jesus Christ must be left behind. He is the means, to be sure; but he is not the end. There is something above and beyond Jesus Christ, which can be reached only through mystical experience. Christ is therefore not God's perfect, complete and final revelation. There is an indefinable and unknowable God behind the revealed God, which explains why Dionysius relegated Jesus to the margins of his mystical vision and why many scholars, including myself, find his theology suspect. How can we even know Dionysius's God? Does it all depend on our intuition? What, then, is the revelatory significance of Jesus as the incarnation of God? Scholar Paul Rorem comments on this neglect: "The incarnation, death, resurrection, and ascension of Jesus Christ are not even the principal examples of this motif, much less its indispensable ground, source, or cause. . . . His program of religious epistemology overshadows the historical particularity of orthodox Christology."[12]

However complex, impenetrable and even at times questionable, Dionysius still has something valuable to teach us. He believed that all people long to know God, for God has put that longing in us. This longing goes deeper than what knowledge of doctrine, use of liturgy, reception of the sacraments and ascetic discipline can give us. Ultimately we long to experience union with God, which by definition transcends all earthly categories. Mysticism seems impenetrable because it deals with a reality that in the end cannot be described. It is possible to tell the Christian story, to spell out Christian doctrine, to prescribe a regimen of Christian discipline and to administer the sacraments. It is not possible to explain what it means to reach union with God. Though the experience is real enough, words and concepts simply fail. It is all a profound mystery. Dionysius's vision gives us a glimpse of this great mystery, a mystery that, according to the New Testament, becomes known in Jesus Christ.

Mystics invite us to embark on a journey that leads to union with God. This journey moves through three stages (though it is not possible to graduate from one stage to the next). First, there is the way of *purgation*, which requires confession, repentance and rigorous discipline. All sin must be rooted out and cast aside. Still, however helpful and necessary, ascetic discipline will only get us so far. Second, there is the way of *illumination*, which engenders deep knowledge and insight into the essential truths of the Christian faith. Mystical knowledge is unique because it involves a Being who is transcendent, holy and perfect; it thus requires more than mastery of Scripture and doctrine. Meditation is the right discipline to use. But again, though such discipline is necessary, it will only get us so far. Third, there is the way of *union*. In this stage, knower and known become united and the soul experiences the bliss of communing with God.

THE WAY OF PURGATION

The first stage in the mystical way is purgation. One of the first mystics who taught the way of purgation was John Climacus (c. 579-c. 649), who wrote *The Ladder of Divine Ascent*.[13] At the age of sixteen he journeyed to Mt. Sinai, home to several monastic communities. After living for several years in St. Catherine's Monastery, the oldest continually inhabited monastery in the Christian world, he withdrew from the community and lived as a hermit at Tholas, located some five miles away. After forty years of living in relative seclusion, he was elected abbot of the monastery. The monks considered him like a second Moses. He wrote *The Ladder of Divine Ascent* at the request of a fellow abbot, John of Raithu. "Tell us in our ignorance," he said to Climacus, "what like Moses of old you have seen in divine vision upon the mountain; write it down in a book and send it to us as if it were the tables of the Law, written by God."[14] John Climacus at first resisted, claiming that he was "still among the learners." But he eventually consented.

John's "Ladder" explains the way of purgation in great detail. Much of the book addresses the problem of vice. It warns, for example, against talkativeness, which is "the throne of vainglory on which it loves to preen itself

St. Catherine's Monastery

and show off."[15] It mentions the danger of despondency or tedium, which consists of "a paralysis of the soul, a slackness of the mind, a neglect of religious exercises, a hostility of vows taken."[16] It exposes the problem of gluttony, the "hypocrisy of the stomach." Even when filled, the stomach "moans about scarcity; stuffed and crammed, it wails about its hunger; . . . it eats moderately but wants to gobble everything at the same time."[17]

The "Ladder" assigns a wide variety of spiritual exercises to purge these deadly vices. It demands vigorous self-denial to curb appetites and root out sin, for John believed that attachment to the world—"anxiety, concern for money, for possessions, for family relationships, for worldly glory"—prevents believers from making progress in the spiritual life. "Stripped of all thought of these, caring nothing about them, one will turn freely to Christ."[18] The "Ladder" urges repentance too, which leads to "the renewal of baptism and provides for a fresh start in life," and obedience, "the burial place of the will and the resurrection of lowliness." In short, repentance curbs the desire to rule one's own life.[19]

These ascetic practices are not for the faint of heart. The book contains passages that make chilling demands. "Mortification of the appetite, nightlong toil, a ration of water, a short measure of bread, the bitter cup of dishonor—these will show you the narrow way."[20] What if we fail? At this point John appears surprisingly kind and compassionate for, once restored, those who have fallen can help the weak.

> Even if they tumble into every pit, even if they are trapped by every snare, even if they suffer every disease, still after their return to health they become a light to all, they prove to be doctors, beacons, pilots. They teach us the characteristics of every malady and out of their own experience they can rescue those about to lapse.[21]

Such is the purgative way, which marks the beginning of the mystical ascent to God. But it is not the end, as John himself acknowledged. In fact, it has its own dangers and limitations, for purgation can deceive us into thinking that we can succeed in overcoming vices by human effort alone. John used a humorous example to make just this point. "When we draw water from a well, it can happen that we inadvertently also bring up a frog. When we acquire virtues we can sometimes find ourselves involved with vices which are imperceptibly interwoven with them."[22] Here Thomas Merton, the modern mystic and monk, offers a stern warning. "However, it is relatively simple to get rid of faults that we recognize as faults—although that too can be terribly hard. But the crucial problem of perfection and interior purity is in the renunciation and uprooting of all our *unconscious* attachments to created things and to our own will and desires." It is possible, in other words, to purge ourselves of obvious problems but fail to see—to say nothing of root out—deeper problems, like pride. Our own discipline is preparatory. Only God can purge us of the deepest sins of the

heart. Sometimes he uses what we most dread—darkness and suffering—
to accomplish this work. "We need to leave the initiative in the hands of
God working in our souls either directly in the night of aridity and suffering, or through events and other men."[23]

THE WAY OF ILLUMINATION

The way of purgation is essentially negative; it focuses attention on sins that
need to be expunged from our lives and thus gets us started on the mystical
way. The next stage is illumination, which enables us to come to know God
as God is, to live in the light of God's presence, and to behold the glory of
God. Here we must turn to John Bonaventure—a thirteenth-century Franciscan theologian, church leader and mystic—for guidance, for Bonaventure wrote a great deal about the way of illumination. Born in Bagnoregio,
Italy, around 1217, Bonaventure grew up in a prosperous Italian household.
At the age of seventeen he traveled to Paris to begin his studies at the university. There he was exposed to the Franciscan movement, which, though
founded only a few years earlier (in 1209), had already attracted thousands
into its ranks. Bonaventure joined the order, became apprenticed to the
great Franciscan scholar Alexander of Hales and eventually became a professor of theology. In 1257 he was elected Minister General of the Franciscans. He set out to reorganize the order, to urge members to attend
school and to honor the spirit of St. Francis. He was so successful that he
became known as the "Second Founder of the Order." In 1273 he was appointed a cardinal and, in that capacity, assisted the pope in preparation for
a major church council. He died in 1274 while attending the council.

In addition to his ecclesiastical responsibilities, Bonaventure served the
church as a first-rate theologian. His most famous work is *The Soul's Journey into God*. Before writing it, he decided to go on a pilgrimage to Mount
La Verna, the very place where Francis had received the gift of the "stigmata," the wounds of Christ. It left a profound impression on him. In the
introduction to *The Soul's Journey*, he writes:

> While I was there reflecting on various ways by which the soul ascends into
> God, there came to mind, among other things, the miracle which had oc-
> curred to blessed Francis in this very place. . . . While reflecting on this, I
> saw at once that this vision represented [Francis's] rapture in contemplation

and the road by which this rapture is reached.[24]

In the wake of the vision Bonaventure wrote *The Soul's Journey*, now considered a classic in spiritual writing.

Bonaventure argued that the soul progresses toward illumination through a series of stages. Illumination comes, first of all, by looking *outside* ourselves, at the created world. There we discover "things in themselves," their purpose and their meaning. These created things serve as "vestiges" or "symbols" that point beyond themselves to the character of God. Francis himself taught that nature reflects the greatness and love of God. Our senses function like a door that opens into the great reality of God's existence, and thus they help us see God, "primordial reality," who is Truth and Beauty. It is impossible *not* to behold God through creation, unless we simply refuse out of the hardness of our hearts. "Whoever, therefore, is not enlightened by such splendor of created things is blind; whoever is not awakened by such outcries is deaf; whoever does not praise God because of all these effects is dumb; whoever does not discover the First Principle from such clear signs is a fool."[25]

Illumination comes, second, by looking *inside* ourselves. Following Augustine, Bonaventure argued that when we turn our gaze within we observe a kind of trinitarian dimension to our nature. Our memory, understanding and will all point beyond themselves to the trinitarian nature of God. "See, therefore," Bonaventure exclaimed, "how close the soul is to God, and how, in their operations, the memory leads to eternity, the understanding to truth and the power of choice to the highest good." The result is that, by turning inward, we eventually encounter the triune God as that reality is reflected in the human soul.

Illumination comes, finally, by turning our eyes to see what is *above* us, which leads to a vision of the being of God and the goodness of God, as Dionysius had taught. The *being* of God is eternal, simple, actual, unique and one. It is "most perfect and most immense; it is supremely one and yet all-inclusive."[26] The *goodness* of God consists of "self-diffusion," which manifests itself in the perfect community of the Trinity. There we see distinction and unity, plurality and oneness, perfect love and blessedness. It is the pure light of God. But we cannot see that light directly. As the brightness of the sun blinds our eyes if we look at it, so the light of God blinds the soul. The only way to see God, therefore, is in the darkness. Thus the soul "does not realize that this very darkness is the supreme illumination of our mind, just as when the eye sees pure light, it seems to itself to see nothing."[27] This illumination gives way to pure ecstasy and rapture; the soul journeys into God and becomes united with God. Not surprisingly, Bonaventure's

Bonaventure, *The Soul's Journey into God*

"After our mind has beheld God
outside itself
through his vestiges and in his vestiges
within itself
through his image and in his image,
and above itself
through the similitude of the divine Light shining above us
and in the Light itself,
insofar as this is possible in our state as wayfarers
and through the exercise of our mind,
when finally . . . our mind reaches the point
where it contemplates
in the First and Supreme Principle
and in the mediator of God and men,
Jesus Christ,
those things whose likenesses can in no way be found
in creatures
and which surpass all penetration
by the human intellect,
it now remains for our mind,
by contemplating these things,
to transcend and pass over not only this sense world
but even itself.
In this passing over,
Christ is the way and the door;
Christ is the ladder and the vehicle."

description of this experience borrows much from Dionysius.

Unlike Dionysius, however, Bonaventure saturated his mystical writing with Jesus Christ, especially Christ's Passion.[28] His description of Christ's suffering is nothing short of magnificent.

> God is mocked, so that you may be honored; flogged, so that you may be consoled; crucified, so that you may be set free; the spotless Lamb is slaughtered, so that you may be fed; the lance brings forth water and blood from his side, so that you may drink. . . . O Lord Jesus Christ, who for my sake did not spare yourself: wound my heart through your wounds, inebriate my spirit with your blood, so that wherever I may go, I may continually have you before my eyes as the crucified . . . and may be able to find nothing else but you.[29]

As Bonaventure argued, through Christ we are cleansed of sin, restored to God and empowered to make progress in the spiritual life. "So our soul could not rise completely from these things of sense to see itself and the Eternal Truth in itself unless Truth, assuming human nature in Christ, had become a ladder, restoring the first ladder that had been broken in Adam." We will never taste of the delights of knowing God unless we have faith, hope and love, all qualities that are relational in nature and found in Christ. Thus, if we wish to enjoy God in paradise, "we must enter through faith in, hope in and love of Jesus Christ, the mediator between God and men."[30] Through the "superwonderful union of God and man in the unity of the Person of Christ" we receive God's gift of salvation and see God for who God is.[31] The meeting point between God and humanity is and can only be Jesus Christ.

THE WAY OF UNION

Illumination leads to union with God. But what kind of union? One alternative is a *union of absorption*. In this case the self is simply lost in the divine as a drop of water is lost in the ocean. The soul's journey to God becomes what Plotinus called, "The flight of the alone to the Alone." The distinction between material and spiritual, time and eternity, self and God, even good and evil dissolves. All becomes one. The other alternative is a *union of relationship*. A relationship implies communication, trust and love. It allows for genuine intimacy between persons. Such a union preserves the distinction between self and other, lover and beloved. God is Creator, we the created. God is Savior, we the saved. God is Lord, we his subjects. God is the one who reveals, we the ones to whom he is revealed.

In my mind the most profound and helpful Christian mystics affirm this union of relationship, for they emphasize union with God through Jesus Christ, who is God's self-portrait in human flesh. In Jesus Christ we behold the glory of God, we see the suffering of God, we receive the forgiveness of God, we experience the love of God, and we come to know God, intimately so, as he really is. Jesus Christ is not only the means of salvation but the end, the way to God, the truth about God, the life of God. Karl Barth describes the union in this way:

> There is no disappearance nor destruction of the one in favor of the other. Christ remains the One who speaks, commands and gives as the Lord. And the Christian remains the one who hears and answers and receives as the slave of the Lord. In their fellowship both become and are genuinely what they are, not confounding or exchanging their functions and roles nor losing their totally dissimilar persons.[32]

THE GOSPEL OF JOHN

The Gospel of John shows how the transcendent God of the universe revealed himself once and for all in Jesus Christ. The mystery of the divine identity—the *divine Word* of Greek philosophy and the *I AM* of Judaism—become concrete revelation in the incarnation.

> And the Word became flesh and lived among us; and we have seen his glory, the glory as of a father's only son, full of grace and truth. . . . The law indeed was given through Moses; grace and truth came through Jesus Christ. No one has ever seen God. It is God the only Son, who is close to the Father's heart, who has made him known. (Jn 1:14, 17-18)

John tells a series of stories about people—a woman of ill-repute, a blind man, a grieving friend, a doubting disciple—whose encounters with the human Jesus turns into encounters with God. At first they think that Jesus is only a man. But by the end of the story they confess that he is much more. In Jesus Christ they encounter the living God, for Jesus, they discover, *is* God in human flesh. The man Jesus is seen as the divine Word and the great I AM. Thus the Samaritan woman invites her friends and neighbors to meet the man who "told me everything I have ever done." After meeting Jesus, they say to her, "It is no longer because of what you said that we believe, for we have heard for ourselves, and we know that this is truly the Savior of the world" (Jn 4:39, 42). A man healed of blindness says to his interrogators, "Never since the world began has it been heard that anyone opened the eyes of a man born blind. If this man were not from God, he could do nothing" (Jn 9:32-33). Martha discovers in the raising of her brother Lazarus, who had been dead for four days, that Jesus himself is the resurrection and the life; if one believes in him that person will never die (Jn 11:25-26). Thomas puts his fingers into Jesus' wounds and then falls on his knees, confessing, "My Lord and my God!" (Jn 20:28).

But John does not stop even there. He leaves no room for doubt when he quotes Jesus referring to himself with the divine Name. "I am the bread of life." "I am the light of the world." "I am the good shepherd." "Before Abraham was, I am." Or again, "I and the Father are one."[33] Jesus of Nazareth is the Word made flesh. Such will always be the case. "Beloved," says the author of 1 John, "we are God's children now; what we will be has not been revealed. What we do know is this: when he is revealed, we will be like him, for we will see him as he is" (1 Jn 3:2).

BERNARD OF CLAIRVAUX

Bernard of Clairvaux believed that Jesus Christ makes a union of relationship possible, which he discovered through personal experience and subsequently explored in his many books.[34] Imaginative, generous, magnetic, intense and sometimes ruthless, Bernard (1090-1153) was perhaps the most visible and influential churchman in twelfth-century Europe. He became the major leader of the Cistercians, a monastic renewal movement, serving as the abbot of its most important house at Clairvaux. He studied the church fathers and loved the church's liturgy. He absorbed the Bible so completely that his writing breathes with it.[35] He could stir controversy too. He carried on feuds with several of his contemporaries, including the infamous Abelard, and supported a second Crusade, which ended in failure.[36] Finally, he was a prolific writer. His eighty-six published sermons on the Song of Songs set the standard for the allegorical interpretation of the book, which he used to extol the love relationship between Christ and his church. He was a giant of a man, for good and sometimes for ill.

Bernard's mysticism pulsates with love—God's love for us, our love for God. Bernard believed that, as fallen, helpless, unworthy people, we need God's love. "I am voluptuous," Bernard said of himself. "I am curious. I am ambitious. There is no part of me which is free from this threefold ulcer, from the soles of my feet to the stop of my head."[37] Still, in spite of our unworthiness, God loves us, passionately so. "It is not wretchedness but mercy that makes a man happy, so that humiliation turns to humility and need to strength."[38] Bernard argued that God's love engenders in us the desire to love God in return.

Our love for God, however, is far from perfect. It must grow by degree. In fact, our first impulse of love is not directed toward God at all. It focuses on the self. We manifest this *first* and lowest degree of love when we love ourselves for our own sake. As fragile and finite creatures, we naturally think almost exclusively about ourselves; we clamor to have our needs and wants met, which God graciously does through his providential care. Yet these gifts do not in the end satisfy us because we long for something more, for a relationship with God. Thus we pass to the *second* degree of love, which is to love God, though still for our own sake. We discover that God cares about us and meets our needs, which draws us to God as the source of everything we truly long for. We love God; but it is a love that has self as its primary motive and concern. In the *third* degree of love we adore God for the goodness that he is, not simply for the good things he gives. We love God for God's sake. "This intimacy with God becomes sweet as he learns to discover how wonderful God is. This experience thus promotes the love of God, so that it transcends over all our needs."[39] Surprisingly, Bernard believed that such unselfish love for God is not the highest degree of love. We experience the *fourth* degree of love when we love ourselves for God's sake. We cherish the image of God that is being restored in us and the reflection of God's perfection and beauty that transforms us. Here Bernard exults in the union of relationship that exists between lover and beloved, the one giving life and the other receiving it. "Just as air becomes so radiant with the light of the sun that it appears to be the very sunlight itself, so it is with the saints whose human love is transmuted by the will of God himself."[40]

We know and experience God's love through Jesus Christ. "All love begins in the debt of gratitude," Rowan Williams writes of Bernard's mysticism. "So love of God begins in a recognition of what God has given to the human race. And the greatest gift, the greatest manifestation of God's love, is Jesus the incarnate Word."[41] Bernard thus adored the Christ of the Bible, the Christ of Nicea and Chalcedon, the Christ of the liturgy, the Christ who truly lived in perfection, loved in purity, suffered for the sins of the world, and conquered death itself. True union with God consists in knowing, worshiping, enjoying and loving Jesus Christ.

Julian of Norwich

JULIAN OF NORWICH

Not all mystics were famous males. The woman known as Julian of Norwich (the name of her church) left brilliant writing for posterity. Born during a tumultuous period in the Middle Ages, Julian (c. 1342-c. 1420) witnessed a great deal of suffering in her lifetime, including the Black Death and the Hundred Years War between France and England.[42] We know very little about her early years. She was probably a layperson, for she makes no mention of monastic life in her writing. In her early twenties Julian became an anchoress, which required her to attach herself to a church, live in almost total isolation, pray for the community and offer spiritual counsel to people who sought her out. Her living quarters consisted of several rooms adjacent to the church in Norwich; one window opened into the sanctuary, thus allowing her to participate in the Mass, another to the outside world, thus making her accessible to the citizens of Norwich.[43] Unlike the desert saints, she did not practice severe asceticism.[44] A hired domestic served her, which gave her time and freedom to spend her days praying and giving counsel.

Julian asked God for three gifts—an understanding of the Passion of Christ, a severe physical illness and "three wounds" (true contrition, loving

Julian of Norwich, *Showings*

"I saw three kinds of longing in God, and all to the same end, and we have the same in us, and from the same power, and for the same end. The first is because he longs to teach us to know him and to love him always more and more, as is suitable and profitable to us. The second is that he longs to bring us up into bliss, as souls are when they are taken out of pain into heaven. The third is to fill us with bliss, and that will be fulfilled on the last day, to last forever. For I saw what is known in our faith, that pain and sorrow will be ended then for those who will be saved. And not only shall we receive the same bliss which souls have had already in heaven, but also we shall receive a new bliss, which will be plenteously flowing out of God into us, and will fill us full."

compassion and longing for God). She believed that the experience of suffering would allow her to identify with the Passion of Christ and comprehend something of the magnitude of God's love for her and the world. Her prayer was answered when, at the age of thirty, she fell gravely ill. For three days her life hung in the balance. Under the spiritual guidance of a priest, she meditated on the suffering of Christ, as if sitting at the foot of the cross to witness the agony of the crucifixion. After her recovery she received sixteen "showings" or revelations, all associated, however loosely, with the Passion of Christ. For example, one "showing" focused on the meaning of the crown of thorns, another on the wonders of heaven, still another on God's pure love for humankind.

Julian believed that God took the initiative to establish a relationship with us, which was borne out of God's deep sense of longing for us. God demonstrated that longing by creating the world. Even the most insignificant object reflects God's love and concern for the world. In one of her visions, Julian eyed something small, "no bigger than a hazelnut." She wondered what it could be, what it could signify. "It is everything which is made. I was amazed that it could last, for I thought that it was so little that it could suddenly fall into nothing. . . . [But] it lasts and always will, because God loves it; and thus everything has being through the love of God."[45] God expressed that same longing by coming to us as Jesus Christ, who endured the Passion for our sake, thus proving the length to which God would go to repair the damage of the Fall and to restore the broken relationship.

Like Bernard, Julian affirmed a union of relationship, not absorption. God is one kind of being; we are another. We know him in a relationship of love; God himself initiates, sustains and perfects that relationship.

> What, do you wish to know your Lord's meaning in this thing? Know it well, love was his meaning. Who reveals it to you? Love. What did he reveal to you? Love. Why does he reveal it to you? For love. Remain in this, and you will know more of the same. But you will never know different, without me.[46]

Julian relished this intimate relationship. She felt secure, confident and serene because she knew that she was loved. Even in her doubts, questions, sin, pain and suffering, she heard God say, time and again, "I may make all things well, and I can make all things well, and I shall make all things well, and I will make all things well; and you will see yourself that every kind of thing will be well."[47] Her vision of God was not blinded by darkness or obscured in a cloud of unknowing but illumined by the loving face of Jesus Christ, whom she loved in return as God's Son, her Savior and Lord. Thus the last sentence in *Showings* reads, "Here end the sublime and wonderful revelations of the unutterable love of God, in Jesus Christ vouchsafed to a dear lover of his, and in her to all his dear friends and lovers whose hearts like hers do flame in the love of our dearest Jesus."[48]

THE WAY OF PRAYER

If this union of relationship is possible, how can we begin to experience it as a pattern of life, not someday in the future but today, not when we live in the light of God's goodness but while we struggle in the darkness of this world? Through the discipline of prayer. God himself, Julian argued, prompts us to pray. Prayer is simply the human response to the prior call of God, which we hear in Jesus Christ. God speaks to us; his voice reverberates in our souls like an echo. The sound of his voice makes us want to reply. "I am the ground of your beseeching," Julian wrote, as if God were speaking. "First, it is my will that you should have it, and then I make you to wish it, and then I make you to beseech it. If you beseech it, how could it be that you would not have what you beseech?"[49] Prayer is not a complete leap into the dark. The Christian faith teaches that we do not pray as if speaking into an empty, nameless void. We pray to a God we know, for God made himself known in Jesus Christ. In Jesus we see the face of God. This God cares for the poor, he loves the outcast, he forgives the sinner, he judges the proud, he understands our humanness. Jesus Christ demystifies God; he also demystifies prayer. He turns it into the most human and ordinary of activities.

The most natural and familiar expression of prayer is petition. The Lord's Prayer provides us with the perfect model. "Thy kingdom come, Thy will be done in earth as it is in heaven." "Give us this day our daily bread." "And forgive us our debts, as we forgive our debtors." "Lead us not into temptation, but deliver us from evil." It is a practical prayer that addresses daily life. Our best prayers, therefore, are simply extended conversations with God about life as we live it from day to day in all of its sublime ordinariness. The routine of life presents us with a grand opportunity to learn how to pray, the world a laboratory to teach us to pray.

There is nothing magical about petitionary prayer. It involves little more than inviting God to become active in our lives. If we took a few moments to ponder the weightiness of what happens in a normal day, we would be overwhelmed with a deep sense of helplessness and vulnerability. We would cry out to God in utter desperation. How could any of us think to raise our children, build a good marriage, do our work with energy and integrity, survive a crisis, or care for a needy neighbor, to say nothing of solve world problems, without God's help? We need God, whether or not we feel it; we long to know God, whether or not we are aware of it. "Pray wholeheartedly," Julian wrote, again as if God were speaking through her, "though you may feel nothing, though you see nothing, yes, though you think that you could not, for in dryness and barrenness, in sickness and in weakness, then is your prayer most pleasing to me, though you think it almost tasteless to you. And so is all your living prayer in my sight."[50]

But there is another kind of prayer, which, though less familiar to us, is far more central to mystical spirituality. It is contemplative or wordless prayer, which flows out of darkness, silence and a deep awareness of the supremacy, beauty and purity of God. Thomas Merton writes of such prayer, "It is a vivid realization of that fact that life and being in us proceed from an invisible, transcendent and infinitely abundant Source. Contemplation is, above all, awareness of the reality of that Source." Like most mystics, Merton believed that contemplative prayer is not a spiritual technique or intellectual exercise or natural process, as if we could learn to master it in the same way we learn to speak a language or to play a sport. "It is not the fruit of our own effort. It is the gift of God Who, in His mercy, completes the hidden and mysterious work of creation in us by enlightening our minds and hearts."[51]

Mystics argue, in fact, that the way to contemplation is not through effort but through darkness. John of the Cross, a Catholic mystical writer, explained this way of darkness with exceptional insight. Though from a noble family, John (1542-1591) grew up in relative poverty. After taking his monastic vows, he assisted Teresa of Ávila in founding the Discalced (shoeless) Carmelites, a monastic renewal movement. John wrote several books on spirituality, including *Ascent of Mount Carmel* and *Dark Night of the Soul*. In these books he argued that the great enemy of the spiritual life is our natural inclination to become attached to things that, however good in themselves, keep us from God. Surprisingly, even religious rituals, exercises and beliefs can have a negative effect on the spiritual life. "Hence in the same way it comes to pass that the soul that loves anything else becomes incapable of pure union with God and transformation in Him. For the low estate of the creature is much less capable of union with the high estate of the Creator than is darkness with light."[52] To be weaned from these attachments, therefore, John taught that we must pass through the "dark night of the senses" and the "dark night of the soul," which will break us from these attachments and drive us toward God, with whom we long to be united. Describing what God does to accomplish this in believers, John wrote:

> He strips their faculties, affections, and feelings, both spiritual and sensual, both outward and inward, leaving the understanding dark, the will dry, the memory empty, and the affections in the deepest affliction, bitterness and constraint, taking from the soul the pleasure and experience of spiritual blessings which it had aforetime, . . . so that there may be introduced into it and united with it the spiritual form of the spirit, which is the union of love.[53]

We cannot, therefore, reach union with God through human effort alone. Still, we do not have to be entirely passive either. We can, for example, surrender ourselves daily to God as he does his deep work in us. We can practice the spiritual disciplines, like fasting and meditation. We can also trust that, when we do pass through periods of darkness, God has not abandoned us but is in fact drawing us into more intimate communion with him. Finally, we can learn to wait in prayerful silence. "For God alone my soul waits in silence," the Psalmist writes, "for my hope is from him. He only is my rock and my salvation, my fortress; I shall not be shaken. On God rests my deliverance and my honor; my mighty rock, my refuge is God" (Psalm 62:5-7).

The prayer of silence is not natural. Our attempts to pray this kind of prayer will expose how trivial and superficial our thoughts are, how noisy our world is, how inattentive we are to the reality of God's presence. Mystics urge us to turn these distractions into prayers and to repeat a line from Scripture to quiet the soul and direct our thoughts to God. "Jesus Christ, Son of God, have mercy on me a sinner." "The Lord is my shepherd." "My Lord and my God!" "I believe; help my unbelief." "For God alone my soul waits in silence." It takes time and practice. Even then, we will discover that consistent practive is not enough. Only God can make himself known to us. Contemplative prayer, then, is both means and end. It is a discipline we practice; it is a gift we receive. Such prayer—wordless, silent, patient, confident, secure—will empty us and fill us, break us and restore us, plunge us into the darkness and draw us into the light, separate us from God as we know him through creation so that we can be united with God as we know him in Christ, and thus experience the union with him for which our souls truly long.[54]

PRACTICES

- Read Psalm 62:1-8; Matthew 6:5-15; Romans 8:26-27.
- Spend a week praying through the Lord's Prayer, petition by petition. Repeat each petition, and then pause to pray more specifically in light of that petition. What does it mean, for example, to ask for "daily bread" when we already have it? What does it mean to ask God not to lead us into temptation?

- Spend a second week practicing silent prayer, both in the morning and in the evening. Sit in a quiet place and still the soul. If distractions arise, as they surely will, then surrender them to God in the form of a prayer. Repeat a verse like, "For God alone my soul waits in silence."
- Ask the Holy Spirit to intervene for you in sighs too deep for words. Learn to rest in the grace of God.

8

Ordinariness

The Spirituality of the Medieval Laity

*"And whatever you do, in word or deed,
do everything in the name of the Lord Jesus,
giving thanks to God the Father through him."*

COL 3:17

I t seems that in every generation a few Christians rise above the rest of us. Their courage, sacrifice and extraordinary accomplishments set them apart as worthy of special commendation, which is why the church calls them *saints*. The church has been doing this, both officially and unofficially, for two thousand years. In this book I have already told a few of their stories. Their names—Perpetua, Antony, Augustine, Benedict, Bernard, Aquinas—read like a Who's Who of Christian heroes. I love to tell the stories of these saints to my students, who are fascinated if not dazzled by them. But then it always happens. Some student blurts out, "So what?" That simple and stark question drives the discussion in a different direction. Students begin to ponder the *problem* of sainthood. Who can imitate these extraordinary people? Most of us will *not* suffer martyrdom or live as ascetics in the desert or serve as bishops or travel to far-off places as missionaries. Is it possible for ordinary people to be true disciples too?

THE WORLD OF THE LAITY

For this reason, I have decided to write a chapter on the spirituality of the late medieval laity, which focuses attention on the people who did not reach the level of "sainthood." Most Christians, after all, live as ordinary people who attend church and marry and buy homes and raise families and work regular jobs. Surprisingly, the church has often failed to address the needs and concerns of this large number of people. So much time and energy is put into *religious* concerns—church buildings, church committees, church programs and activities—that the *secular* world suffers from pure neglect. But it is in that very world Christians spend most of their time. If the Christian faith is going to have any kind of impact at all, it must address how believers live in the secular world. Ordinary people must learn to live as disciples of Jesus when they are *not* at church. Perhaps we need a new category of saint—a "secular" saint who lives passionately for Christ while serving as a banker or teacher or construction worker or artist.

The history of Christianity teaches us that the Christian movement thrives when the needs, interests and concerns of ordinary people are taken seriously. The early church lacked most of the material resources and cultural advantages that the Western church enjoys today, yet in very short order it spread throughout the Roman world because it appealed to and attracted everyday people. In the second and third centuries the church continued to grow, even under difficult circumstances, because ordinary Christians proved to be effective witnesses. They infiltrated Roman society at almost every point. Commenting on the subtle but effective witness of ordinary Christians, second-century apologist Tertullian wrote, "We have the same kind of life as you . . . without taking ourselves out of the forum and the marketplace, without renouncing the baths and the shops and the boutiques and the inns and all the other places of commerce, we live in this world with you." Tertullian wryly observed that though Christianity had only recently arrived on the Roman scene, it was already spreading rapidly, winning people, encroaching on almost every area of Roman life, as if it were some kind of contagion. "We arrived only yesterday, and already we fill the earth as well as all that is yours; cities, islands, towns, municipalities, fields of harvest, and even camps, tribes, the councils, the palace, and the senate. We have left you only your temples."[1]

The movement proved difficult to suppress because nonelites were so successful in spreading the message of Christianity. Roman officials wanted to snuff it out and therefore targeted prominent leaders for persecution, assuming that if they attacked the elites then they would eliminate the problem. But this strategy proved to be ineffective. They did not realize that Christianity was a different kind of religion, one that was less formally religious but more culturally influential. If anything, Christianity was not "religious" at all, at least not in the same way pagan religions were, which confined their religious practices almost exclusively to temples, shrines and religious holidays. That made the Christian movement more difficult to monitor and control, yet it also made it more flexible, adaptable and effective. As Tertullian noted, it was like an epidemic that spread from one person to the next. Rome wanted to control the spread of the disease. Lacking an antidote, it tried to quarantine the more visible carriers. But the most effective carriers, as it turned out, were the laity, not the leaders. So the faith continued to thrive. Rome could not tell how it happened, why it attracted attention or even whom it included. The Christian movement became extraordinarily influential through the work of ordinary people.

THE MEDIEVAL HIERARCHY

The church continued to grow numerically after Constantine seized power in A.D. 312. If anything, its rate of growth increased, outstripping its ability to nurture maturity of faith among ordinary church members. This easy growth, however, came to an end in the fifth century, at least in the western half of the empire. Tribal groups swept across much of the Roman world and carved up territories for settlement. The consequences were catastrophic. The empire became less wealthy, less educated, less cosmopolitan and less stable (though its people often proved themselves to be surprisingly industrious, entrepreneurial and inventive). In the wake of the collapse, churches and monasteries emerged as the most stable institutions in a world that everywhere appeared to be falling apart.

Monks and clergy dominated the religious world of that day.[2] Medieval society attached a value to each class of person in the medieval hierarchy. There were the ordinary believers or the "laity," as they were called, who occupied the lowest position because they spent most of their time doing secular tasks, such as raising children and farming. There were the clergy, "the seculars," who occupied the middle position because, though serving the church, they nevertheless had to live in the world. Then there were "the religious" (monks and nuns), who occupied the highest position because they lived apart from the world and spent their days in worship and prayer. Writing in the middle of the eleventh century, Abbo of Fleury, a well known abbot, explained this three-tiered hierarchy of believers. "Among the Christians of both sexes, we know that there exist three orders and three degrees, so to speak. Although none of the three is exempt from sin, the first is good, the second better, the third excellent. . . . The first is that of the laity, the second that of the clergy, the third that of the monks." Abbo put the laity on the bottom of the social order for several reasons. One reason was that the laity married and had children, which Abbo considered a concession to human weakness. "As for the conjugal state, it is permitted only so that man, at the age when the temptations due to the fragility of the flesh are strongest, does not fall into an even worse situation." It would have been better by far had the laity been able to devote themselves exclusively to living as monks did; but such was not always possible.[3]

Laypeople depended on the monks for their very salvation. The leaders of Cluny, a monastic renewal movement that began in 909, believed that monks comprised the one—and only—group in the social hierarchy that could be completely assured of salvation because they alone had the freedom and opportunity to detach themselves from the evils of the world and devote themselves entirely to the pursuit of God. There was some question, in fact, whether anyone living outside the monastery could be saved at all. Thus the "only recognized hope for those who wished to be fully serious about their conversion to Christ was for them to become monks or canons and largely hide themselves away from the turmoil and life in the world."[4] Fortunately for laypeople, however, monastic discipline was thought to be so meritorious that even laypeople could benefit from it, provided they support the monks in their spiritual endeavors and ask the monks to intercede for them. Cluniac monks, therefore, became the masters of intercessory prayer, which they practiced for the benefit of laypeople. "Convinced that they were sinners," historian André Vauchez concludes, "and that their condition as lay people prevented them from avoiding sin if they had wished to, people of the feudal era delegated the task of salvation to an elite of specialists in spiritual matters, who discharged this obligation for the benefit of society as a whole."[5]

THE MEDIEVAL LAITY

But conditions in Europe began to change in the later Middle Ages (1200 1450). It was during this period that the laity emerged ever so slowly as a visible and influential force in the church. They were becoming more educated, more urban, more prosperous, more traveled and more sophisticated, and they were searching for a more robust spiritual life that would address life as they had to live it in the secular world, a world that not all of them were willing to abandon for a religious vocation. What laypeople wanted was a new model of the Christian life, one more relevant to life outside the church and monastery. Over time the needs of ordinary believers forced the church to set a new course for itself, one that would embrace the secular world as a rightful part of God's domain.

The emergence of the profit economy in the later Middle Ages contributed to this change of landscape, for it engendered significant economic expansion that gave rise to a new class of people that the Middle Ages had not seen before in large numbers—the middle class. Cities became the center of operations for this new economy. In these cities people performed jobs that had been virtually unknown in feudal society, some of whom made a living without actually *producing* anything. They borrowed and loaned money, traded goods, wrote contracts, determined fair prices, competed for profits and educated youth eager to benefit from opportunities that the profit economy provided. Cities, guilds and universities became the dominant social institutions in the new Europe, gradually taking the place of monasteries.[6]

A vintner living in southern France, for example, enjoyed options that had been largely closed to him only a century earlier. He could grow a particular kind of grape that was best suited for the land and climate where he lived. Though he would continue to make, grow and produce what were considered basic necessities, which his family had done for generations, he could also supplement his efforts by buying what he needed—and even what he wanted—at a local market or fair. He could ship his wine on a barge to a city some distance away and sell his wine at a profit, often using the services of a merchant to transport the wine and negotiate the transaction. Then he could use the money to buy wool from England, tools from Germany, silk from China or spices from India. He could expand production too, by borrowing money from a local bank, which would allow him to buy more land, plant more grapes, add more casks, ship more bottles and thus make more money. Instead of assuming his sons would join the family business, he could send them to the university in Paris to study the liberal arts and to prepare for a career in law, medicine or theology. His sons in turn could choose to stay in the city and pursue careers that their father and grandfather had never even dreamed of.

This new class of people sought a spiritual experience that would be relevant to their life in the city, their work in the world, their quest for advancement and success. Not that they rejected the traditional spirituality that had dominated the medieval period up to the thirteenth century. They continued to receive the sacraments, venerate relics, embark on pilgrimages, read biographies of the saints and practice various rituals. But they were looking for something else too. As cosmopolitan people they expected the church to reflect a higher degree of cultural sophistication.[7] It was abhorrent to them to sit in small, drab churches, listen to bad sermons preached by illiterate clergy, follow a liturgy in a language that many of them did not understand (Latin), and care much about a religion that was oblivious to their needs and concerns as citizens of the world.

It did not appear that monasteries would provide the answer. Virtually every monastic renewal movement that emerged in the eleventh and twelfth centuries emphasized ascetic devotion and separation from society.[8] For example, Bernard of Clairvaux urged his fellow Cistercians to "flee Babylon," which referred to the new cities of Europe.[9] Guido, a prominent leader of the Carthusians, stated in his *Customs* that distance from society, poverty of life and the salvation of the monk's soul took priority over all other concerns, including the needs of the world, which explains why the members of the order decided to leave the world in the first place.

For after all, we have taken refuge in the isolation of this hermitage not in order to take worldly care of other people's physical needs but for the eternal welfare of our own souls. Thus no one should be surprised if we show greater openness and concern for those who come on account of their souls than for those who come on account of their bodies. If it were otherwise, then not in harsh and remote and nearly inaccessible places . . . ought we long since to have settled down, but rather in busy streets.[10]

THE MENDICANTS

A new movement emerged in the later Middle Ages, however, that forever altered the course of the Western church. The mendicants (ascetics who lived in the world, begged for food and preached the gospel) introduced a new spirit into the religious life of Europe. Mendicants aspired to follow the example of Jesus, and they invited laypeople to do the same. If monks devoted themselves to *meditating* on the life of Christ, especially through the practice of lectio divina, mendicants devoted themselves to *imitating* the life of Christ. Jesus was poor, so they pursued poverty. Jesus lived with the people; so they chose to move to the city. Jesus lived a simple life; so they gave their possessions to the poor. Jesus preached the gospel to common people and outcasts; so they told the gospel story to anyone who would listen. Jesus sacrificed his life to honor God and serve humanity; they did likewise. They lived in utter simplicity and poverty, all before a watching world.

The mendicant movement began in the thirteenth century. The two most important orders that embraced this mendicant pattern of life were the Franciscans and Dominicans. But this impetus to embrace the world of the laity spread far beyond these new religious orders. Other movements emerged at the same time, demonstrating that laypeople were eager to experiment with and experience new forms of religious life. The Beguines, Tertiaries and Brethren of the Common Life helped to make an active and vital spiritual life accessible to ordinary people. Like the Franciscans and Dominicans, these movements gravitated to the city. They addressed the unique needs and problems of laypeople, who responded to them with enthusiasm. Thousands of people joined them; many more admired them from a distance. Regardless of the response, everyone was affected by what was happening across Europe.

The Franciscans. It is hard to overestimate the impact that Francis of Assisi had on the medieval church.[11] He was so popular in the eyes of his contemporaries that the church canonized him as a saint within two years of his death. Two followers, Thomas of Celano and Bonaventure, wrote major biographies of his life within a generation of his death. Both emphasized that Francis set an example of true discipleship for the common people. "Accordingly, in him and through him," Celano wrote in his biography,

> there arose throughout the world an unlooked for happiness and a holy newness, and a shoot of the ancient religion suddenly brought a great renewal to those who had grown calloused and to the very old. A new spirit was born in the hearts of the elect, and a saving unction was poured out in their midst, when the servant and holy man of Christ, like one of the lights of the heavens, shone brilliantly with a new rite and with new signs.[12]

Francis of Assisi (1182-1226) was born into the home of a wealthy merchant family. In his youth he lived recklessly and frivolously. "Until he was

St. Francis of Assisi

nearly twenty-five," Thomas of Celano wrote, "he squandered his time terribly. Indeed, he outshone all his friends in trivialities, suggested various evils, and was eager for foolishness of every kind."[13] He longed to become a famous knight, but his aspirations were cut short when he was captured in battle and imprisoned for a year before his father could secure his release. He spent another year in convalescence after returning to Assisi. It led to a period of deep reflection and repentance. "He bore the greatest sufferings in mind," Celano wrote, "and was not able to rest until he should have completed in deed what he had conceived in his heart."[14]

Knowing that he had to change his way of life, he left home to live a hermit's life. He wore hermit's clothing and lived in an abandoned church, which he began slowly to rebuild. He also started to distribute his father's wealth to the poor. His father became angry, convinced that Francis's new life was far worse than the old one. Outraged by Francis's reckless generosity, his father held him as a prisoner at the family estate. But Francis showed no signs of remorse and refused to change. Desperate, his father hauled Francis before the local bishop to demand that justice be done and that his fortune be restored. Francis stripped himself of his worldly clothing, renounced his heritage and proclaimed that from that point on his Father in heaven would be his only true father. Bonaventure cited this act as an example of Francis's total identification with Christ. "Thus the Most High's servant was stripped of all possessions; he could now follow his Lover who once hung stripped on the cross. . . . Free of all earthly bonds, Francis left the town and sought for quiet places where he could be alone in solitude and silence to hear the secrets which God would reveal to him."[15]

Francis did not live as a hermit for long. He decided to reenter the world, just as Jesus did after spending forty days in the wilderness, though he purposed to avoid any hint of worldliness in the way he lived. Jesus became his model for everything. "Indeed, he was always occupied with Jesus; Jesus he bore in his heart, Jesus in his mouth, Jesus in his ears, Jesus in his eyes, Jesus in his hands, Jesus in the rest of his members."[16] Francis pursued a life of absolute poverty. "He wanted to have nothing to do with ownership, in order the he might possess all things more fully in God."[17] He ignored distractions, rejected worldliness and repented of his sins, all while living in the world. "Therefore, his greatest concern was to be free from everything of this world, lest the serenity of his mind be disturbed even for an hour by the taint of anything that was mere dust."[18] He chose to live among the poor, the sick and the outcast, just as Jesus did. Lepers posed the biggest challenge. He overcame his revulsion, however, when he dared to kiss a leper's face. "From then on he began to despise himself more and more, until, by the mercy of the Redeemer, he came to perfect victory over himself."[19] He purposed to preach the gospel to everyone, even to Muslims. He actually traveled to Egypt where, during the Crusades, he crossed enemy lines and spent a month with the Sultan, trying to convert him to the Christian faith. Francis embraced the entire world with a kind of reckless joy. That included the natural world too, which he celebrated as a precious gift from God.[20]

Francis of Assisi, *The Canticle of Brother Sun*

Most High, all-powerful, good Lord
Yours are the praises, the glory, the honor, and all blessing.
To you alone, Most High, do they belong,
and no one is worthy to mention Your name.

Praised be You, my Lord, with all your creatures, especially brother Sun,
Who is the day and through whom You give us light.
And he is beautiful and radiant with great splendor;
and bears a likeness of You, Most High One.

Praised be You, my Lord, through Sister Moon and the stars;
in heaven You formed them clear and precious and beautiful.
Praised be You, my Lord, through Brother Wind,
and through the air, cloudy and serene, and every kind of
weather, through which You give sustenance to Your creatures.

Praised be You, my Lord, through Sister Water,
which is very useful and humble and precious and chaste.
Praised be You, my Lord, through Brother Fire,
through whom You light the night
And he is beautiful and playful, and robust, and strong. . . .

Praised be You, my Lord, through those who give pardon for Your
love, and bear infirmity and tribulation.
Blessed are those who endure in peace
for by You, Most High, they shall be crowned.

Praised be You, my Lord, through our Sister Bodily Death,
from whom no living person can escape.
Woe to those who died in mortal sin.
Blessed are those whom death will find in Your most holy will,
for second death shall do them no harm.

Praise and bless my Lord and give Him thanks
and serve Him with great humility.

His impact was sensational. People could not get enough of him. "Men ran, and women too ran, clerics hurried, and religious hastened that they might see and hear the holy man of God who seemed to all to be a man of another world."[21] Francis won the admiration of people because he lived a Christlike life in the same world that ordinary people occupied. Francis lived in the city and invested his life in people, though avoiding all worldly pursuits. Thus, "in contrast with the new arbiters of society and their lust for gain, [he] would display total detachment, especially where money was concerned."[22]

Others began to follow Francis. In the spring of 1209 he wrote the first of several Rules, which outlined the principles of the order. Then he traveled to Rome, accompanied by his followers, to seek the pope's approval. They adopted the name Friars Minor or the "Little Brothers."[23] Their primary purpose was to reach the masses, living and preaching just as Jesus did. The order grew rapidly, far beyond Francis's ability to manage. So he retired from leadership. He continued, however, to serve as the ideal example to follow. "Therefore, every order, every sex, every age has in him a visible pattern of the way of salvation and has outstanding examples of holy works."[24] He never stopped reminding his followers of the original vision of the movement—absolute poverty, gospel preaching, sacrificial service and the imitation of Christ. Toward the end of his life he had a mystical experience in which he received the stigmata (the wounds of Christ). He died two years later. His influence and popularity, however, did not die with him. Laypeople championed him as an example of a true saint, though he was not a martyr, a bishop or a monk.

The Dominicans. Dominic started a similar order, though for slightly different reasons.[25] Born in Castile in 1170, which had only recently been liberated from the Moors, Dominic studied for the priesthood and became subprior of a cathedral chapter. While traveling to Denmark on a diplomatic mission, Dominic was exposed to popular heresy, which was capturing the allegiance of the laity. He observed that heretics often won a following because they set an example of sacrificial living and learned to communicate a simple, understandable message, however misguided that message was. A few years later Dominic traveled to Rome to ask the pope's permission to preach to heretics, pagans and ignorant Catholics. It became

Dominic and Francis meeting

his vocation.[26] Dominic believed that Catholics surrendered the doctrinal advantage they had, which in his mind was substantial, by failing to live like Jesus. He traveled to areas, therefore, where heretics appeared to be having the most success, and he recruited followers to assist him and share in the work. Together they pledged to live like Christ, serve the local bishop, win over heretics and instruct the faithful.

In 1216 Dominic appealed to the pope for approval of the order, which took the name Order of Preachers. He insisted that members of the order receive proper theological training, which was readily available at the new universities then emerging across Europe, learn reliable methods of preaching, live as good Christian examples and share life in community. Unlike the Franciscans, the Dominicans did not view poverty as an absolute good, though they valued it as a means of witness. Their orientation was always pragmatic. They were committed to train the laity, imparting traditional Christian teachings to the currents of ordinary life. The Dominicans were less popular than the Franciscans, but they were no less influential in shaping the religious life of medieval Europe, largely through their preaching and teaching.[27]

These mendicant movements posed problems for laypeople, of course, not the least of which was Francis himself, who set a standard that few could reach. His popularity was beyond question. But how many laypeople could embrace absolute poverty as fanatically as he did and manifest the love of Christ as lavishly as he did? Dominic actually served as a more realistic example because he was pragmatic. Even so, he was an intellectual and a preacher, not a banker, baker, merchant or lawyer. Still, Francis and Dominic started movements that sent the religious into the city. Mendicants entered the world of laypeople, preached in a language they could understand and explained the Christian faith to them in practical terms, even though they lived more like monks than like the laity. "The unique achievement of the friars," concludes Lester Little, "was their creation of new forms of religious expression specifically for the urban sector of society and those people dominant within it."[28]

LAY MOVEMENTS

The mendicant movement awakened a popular interest in spiritual things that took on a life of its own. In some cases laypeople took matters into their own hands, initiating movements that allowed them to live the Christian faith as active participants, not as passive spectators. They fought wars, practiced the spiritual disciplines, made money and gave it away, and did their common work, all in the name of God. In their minds ordinary life had dignity because God himself had become an ordinary human being.[29]

Lay saints. Beginning around 1200 the laity began to identify and elevate exceptionally holy laypeople from their own ranks to sainthood, whether or not the church hierarchy agreed, which forced church officials to seize control of the movement and canonize the most famous and worthy among them. Thus for the first time in the church's history sainthood became a possibility for laypeople. These "lay saints" lived like monks and nuns, though they chose to remain in the world. Ironically, their proximity to the world required a level of spiritual rigor that was rarely practiced even in monasteries. They *had* to practice rigorous self-discipline to protect themselves from worldly influence, which was literally right outside their door. "Whereas the monks of late antiquity were confronted by a corrupt society from which they fled," Richard Kieckhefer observed, these lay saints "made it their business to stay in that society, serve it in various capacities, and bear the inevitable afflictions patiently."[30] That they lived so sacrificially *as laypeople* only made their heroic feats seem all the more impressive. The city became their desert, a home served as their cave, the marketplace played the role of the devil's tempter.[31]

They deprived themselves of food and sleep; they shunned worldly honors; they avoided the company of others. They equaled, even surpassed, the austerity of the desert saints. Some practiced what was called "virginal marriage." At the marriage altar they vowed not only to remain faithful to their spouse but also to practice celibacy in marriage. Others pursued an alternative—"conjugal chastity." They had children first, perhaps to please their parents or to continue the family name, but then, once they had fulfilled their familial duty, they vowed to remain chaste for the rest of their married life. St. Hedwig of Silesia (d. 1243), for example, was married for fifty-three years, the last thirty of which were lived in chastity. In 1208 she and her husband made a solemn vow before the bishop that they would live as if they were widowed. This form of lay spirituality won the admiration of laypeople, who stood in awe of the feats of these lay saints, though admiration did not necessarily engender imitation. Most ordinary believers preferred living in the world, marrying, raising a family, working a secular job and enjoying the pleasures of life as a gift from God. They were looking for another alternative, something more relevant to life in the secular world.[32]

Beguines. Other lay movements emerged at the same time. The Beguines, for example, allowed lay women to pursue a more vigorous spiritual life without entering a monastery.[33] They operated independently from formal religious orders and maintained a loose organization, attracting women who wanted to live as genuine disciples, not by isolating themselves from society but by engaging society.[34] They committed themselves to the practice of prayer, fasting, poverty, manual labor and service to the needy. They looked to Jesus in his humanity as a model to follow, especially in his sufferings. Some became well known for their piety and charitable work. Jacques de Vitry, an early defender of the movement, wrote of their religious practices, "For we see many who, scorning the riches of their parents and rejecting the contemptible and wealthy husbands offered them, live in profound poverty, without anything but what they can acquire by spinning and working with their hands, content with vile clothes and modest food."[35]

An example of an early Beguine who achieved some notoriety was Mary of Oignies (1178-1213). She and her husband, who lived together in chastity, converted their home into a leper colony. Eventually she asked her husband for permission to withdraw to a cell and live in solitude. Three years later she reemerged to lead a small community of laypeople. They adopted a rule that provided guidelines for how they should live; they worshiped and worked together, and they distinguished themselves as people of prayer and sacrificial service. Mary's holiness of life, service to the poor and practical wisdom set the standard and attracted a wide following. Jacques de Vitry described her as the ideal. "So great was her longing for poverty that she took nothing but a bag in which to put any alms or food that might be given her, a cup to drink from, and clothed herself in rags. Those around her could not forbear to weep."[36]

Third-order movements. Various third-order or tertiary movements emerged at the same time. These constituted groups of laypeople who attached themselves to the Franciscans and Dominicans, though, for various reasons, they never became official members of either order. The "Order of Penitents," the first of several Franciscan third-order groups, sought to imitate the life of Jesus, which in Francis's mind provided a model for all Christians to follow, whether "religious" or lay. In 1221 Francis wrote a Rule that spelled out guidelines for these penitents. Francis believed that poverty served as the perfect symbol of Jesus' life, which expressed itself in active love and service, not morbid suffering, severe asceticism and complete withdrawal from society.

Third-order movements produced several saints that became famous in late medieval Europe. The story of Margaret of Cortuna (1247-1297), a Franciscan tertiary, serves as a good example. Repenting from a life of sexual promiscuity, she joined the Franciscans as a layperson and devoted herself to the mystical contemplation of Christ. She eventually decided to serve the needy. In 1286 she obtained a charter to found a hospital, which she called Mary of Mercy. She organized a congregation of Franciscan tertiaries to staff the hospital as nurses and administrators. The most famous Dominican tertiary was Catherine of Siena (1347-1380). As a young girl she pleaded with her parents to give her permission to become a Dominican tertiary. She joined the movement in 1365. Like Mary of Oignies, she lived in isolation and contemplation for several years. Then she began her vocation as a reformer. She purposed to reform herself, the church and the world, an admittedly ambitious undertaking. Eventually she was asked by the citizens of Florence to function as a mediator and arbitrator. She was dispatched to Avignon, France, where the papacy, dominated by French interests and consumed by material concerns, had been headquartered for over seventy years. She persuaded the pope to move the papacy back to Rome.

These women symbolized the beginning of a long, slow change of direction in the spiritual life of Europe. They maintained a commitment to traditional monastic virtues, like chastity (even though Mary of Oignies was married), poverty and fasting. But they also lived in the world. They worked with their hands, served the poor, functioned, unofficially at least, as leaders of the church, and attracted a following of both men and women. They demonstrated that laypeople could live with the same kind of conviction and passion as monks and nuns, though without having to withdraw completely from society.

Brethren of the Common Life. The Brethren of the Common Life followed a similar trajectory. The founder of the movement, Geert de Groote (1340-1384), grew up in Deventer, Holland, in the home of a wealthy merchant. Groote was educated at the Sorbonne, where he studied theology and law to prepare for an ecclesiastical career. He had worldly ambitions and broad interests, not all of them strictly orthodox (i.e., he delved into astrology and magic). He was something of a dandy too; he liked to dress in fancy clothes and impress people with his education and intelligence. Several friends warned him, however, that his soul was imperiled. As an early biographer writes, "frightened and filled with remorse, he began to take thought about saving his soul."[37] Then, in 1372, he became so ill that a priest decided to administer last rites, but only if Groote was willing to renounce magic and the black arts. Groote realized that he would someday have to face the judgment of God. He admitted his wrongdoing, repented of his sin, burned all of his questionable books and received the sacrament, only to recover almost immediately from his illness. Groote resolved to amend his way of life and renounce his worldly ambitions. He started to wear clerical garb, gave up his incomes and possessions, and joined a Carthusian monastery, where he prayed, fasted, labored, studied and attended daily Mass. But there was too much the activist and reformer in him to allow him to remain forever in a cloistered community. A sense of calling drove him from the monastery. He began to preach the faith and live an austere life among the masses.

Groote soon took up the cause of church renewal. He felt deep concern

Thomas à Kempis, *The Imitation of Christ*

"What good does it do, then, to debate the Trinity, if by a lack of humility you are displeasing to the Trinity? In truth, lofty words do not make a person holy and just, but a virtuous life makes one dear to God. I would much rather feel profound sorrow for my sins than be able to define the theological term for it. If you knew the whole Bible by heart and the sayings of all the philosophers, what good would it all be without God's love and grace? Vanity of vanities and all is vanity, except to love God and to serve only him. This is the highest wisdom: to see the world as it truly is, fallen and fleeting; to love the world not for its own sake, but for God's; and to direct all your effort toward achieving the kingdom of heaven."

about the worldliness of the church. Everywhere he saw evidence of inept priests, corrupt bishops and ignorant, superstitious laity. Bold and sometimes brash, he did not hesitate to criticize the abuses. He attracted a small following, mostly students and minor clergy. Nor surprisingly, he made enemies along the way too. Mendicants opposed him because the success of his movement exposed how much they had compromised Francis's vision, and clergy disliked him because he performed duties that belonged more properly to their office. He was eventually deprived of an opportunity to preach. He wrote several protests, all to no avail. He died of the plague in 1384. After his death one of his followers, Florentius Radwijns, gathered together his disciples and founded the Brethren of the Common Life. They formed a chapter in 1395 and wrote statutes in 1402. The movement grew to some thirty houses by 1424.

The Brethren lived together in private houses, usually located near a parish church, practiced the ascetic disciplines, worked trades (usually copying manuscripts) and pooled their income. Their community was "rooted in the model of the first apostles, without requiring them to leave town or church and without imposing any of the difficulties and obligations that come with taking vows and joining an order."[38] Especially important to them was the cultivation of virtue—humility, charity and service. The movement attracted ordinary people, "laymen and women and minor clergymen, from whom such 'devotion' would hardly have been expected, especially not in this 'modern age,' when so much else in the church seemed to suffer from indifference and corruption."[39] The most important book to come out of the movement, *The Imitation of Christ*, emphasized its two primary values—ascetic discipline and practical discipleship.

THE REFORMERS

These movements set the stage for the Reformation, which moved in a more radical direction. The Reformers closed down monasteries, defied the church hierarchy and urged ordinary believers to live as serious disciples of Christ in the world. They believed that true faith applied as much to secular life as it did to religious life.[40] For example, John Calvin, leader of the Reformation in Geneva, argued that, if viewed and treated properly, the world is God's gift to us, which we should receive with gratitude. "Let this be our principle," Calvin stated: "that the use of God's gifts is not wrongly directed when it is referred to that end to which the Author himself created and destined them for us, since he created them for our good, not for our ruin."[41] Martin Luther cited Christ as the primary example to follow, especially in the way he lived as an ordinary man. In a letter (dated March 31, 1521) to John Frederick, who would become the Duke of Saxony in 1532, Luther stated "that [Christ] always and in all things pleased his Father is true. His eating, drinking, and sleeping pleased his Father as much as his great miracles, for the Father sees not the works but the intent in the works."[42] Luther insisted that the one thing expected of believers is that they live by faith, even when doing distinctively secular activities. Only faith enables believers to live in the world as God intends.[43]

The Reformers addressed the needs, problems and responsibilities of ordinary people. They believed that the world belongs to God. No arena of activity falls outside God's redemptive purpose. Ordinary duties matter just as much to God as fasting, solitude and celibacy. Thus Luther argued that marriage is part of God's divine plan; it is not a temptation to be overcome or a burden to be endured but a calling to be embraced and a gift to be enjoyed. Surprising everyone, he chose to marry *as a priest*, to please his father and to spite the pope, as he put it. Luther was not "in love" before he married Katarina, but he certainly fell in love after he was married and enjoyed many years of marital happiness. That happiness included what appeared to be a lively physical relationship. When he could not attend the wedding of a friend, he jotted in a note:

> When you sleep with your Catherine and embrace her, think this—"This is a human being, the best little creature of God, and Christ has given her to me. Praise and glory to him." On the evening of the day when I calculate you will receive this letter, I will love my wife in the same way and have you in my memory and so we shall be together.[44]

He urged fellow monks to marry too. In a letter to Wolfgang Reissenbusch, a monk who was considering marriage, Luther wrote:

> It is a pity that men should be so stupid as to wonder that a man takes a wife, or to be ashamed of it, when no one wonders at his eating and drinking. Why should this necessity, which is based on human nature, be an object of doubt and wonder? It is best to comply with all our senses as soon as possible and give ourselves to God's Word and work in whatever he wishes us to do.[45]

Calvin viewed secular employment similarly. He argued that God assigns ordinary believers to a "sentry post," as he called it, in which they can use their gifts to serve God in the world. Such "secular" work is just as important to God as the work of the clergy, and it provides an opportunity for laypeople to contribute to God's kingdom work in the world. In this sense all work has dignity and purpose, no matter how mean and lowly, just as all work can bring glory to God. Consequently, "no task will be so sordid and base, provided you obey your calling in it, that it will not shine and be reckoned very precious in God's sight."[46] God calls, equips and uses ordinary people—bankers, teachers, government officials, janitors—for his extraordinary work. The Reformers reminded laypeople that they serve on the frontlines of God's kingdom.[47] The purpose of faith is not to require people to withdraw from the world (as monastic communities tended to do) or to enable people to succeed in the world (as modern self-help religion teaches), but to empower people to claim the world for God's kingdom.

A LAY SPIRITUALITY

How can ordinary believers begin to live in the secular world as serious followers of Christ? First, we can learn to view ordinary life as a legitimate arena of discipleship. In God's eyes there is no division between the secular and the sacred. All spheres of life belong to him. "Let a man sanctify the Lord God in his heart," writes spiritual writer A. W. Tozer, "and he can thereafter do no common act. All he does is good and acceptable to God through Jesus Christ. For such a man, living itself will be sacramental and the whole world a sanctuary."[48] The most mundane tasks we do—paying bills, running errands, doing laundry, cooking food and commuting to work—have a divine purpose to them. How can we turn these duties into holy activities? We can honor God with our best efforts, pray even as we work, love those around us, serve the common good of society, bear witness to our faith in Jesus Christ and thank God for every gift he has given to us. The apostle Paul is clear about this principle. "And whatever you do, in word or deed, do everything in the name of the Lord Jesus, giving thanks to God the Father through him" (Col 3:17).

Second, we can devote our resources to God, who has given us these things as gifts to invest in his kingdom work. Our time, possessions, talents and money belong to God; he calls us to be stewards of these gifts. That Christians in the West contribute so little time and money to charitable causes indicates that we have failed to grasp this principle. God owns everything; we own nothing. We are accountable to God for what belongs to him. Calvin gives good advice here. "Let this, therefore, be our rule for generosity and beneficence: We are the stewards of everything God has conferred on us by which we are able to help our neighbor, and are required to render account of our stewardship. Moreover, the only right stewardship is that which is tested by the rule of love." We serve God, Calvin said, when we surrender our resources to God and invest them in others. God has been generous with us; we should do the same with others.[49]

Third, we can cultivate what could be called, however misleadingly, "secular" disciplines that serve a spiritual purpose. The disciplines of the monastery include solitude, fasting, celibacy and meditation, which are useful habits because they discipline our appetites and quiet our hearts. But secular disciplines have value too, for they prepare and empower ordinary Christians to serve God in the secular world. For example, the discipline of hospitality welcomes the outsider into our homes as a cherished friend.

The discipline of service meets the practical needs of people who, for whatever reason, are unable to take care of themselves. The discipline of leadership envisions what can be accomplished for God's kingdom work in the world. These secular disciplines help the faithful to claim the world for God because the world *is* God's. This kind of spirituality will turn ordinary laypeople into extraordinary disciples.

Before his dramatic conversion to Christianity in the 1990s, Mazhar Mallouhi rejected traditional religion of every kind as hopelessly irrelevant to the needs of the modern world. Through the inspiration of Gandhi, however, he started to read the Bible and to study the life of Jesus, the only man, as Gandhi put it, who practiced what he preached. Though having no formal contact with a church or a Christian, Mallouhi surrendered his life to Jesus Christ. "This Christ is my Lord! Give me this new life you promise!" he wrote after his conversion. He purposed to devote himself to serve Jesus Christ. Word spread that he had become a Christian, eventually reaching Syrian officials, who threatened to kill him and his wife. He was forced to flee and live in exile. But no matter where he lived, Mallouhi would not compromise his commitment to live like Jesus. Paul Gordon Chandler, a missionary executive and friend of Mallouhi, was especially impressed with Mallouhi's commitment to hospitality.

> The result is a continual flow of people through their home, hundreds each week when they lived in Cairo. Everyone comes, from Muslim fundamentalist sheikhs, Catholic priests and nuns, Baptist pastors, Coptic Orthodox, Communists, Jewish rabbis, and Baha'is, to all kinds of Western expatriates. While living in Morocco, Mallouhi would bring home people he found in the street to feed them and help them.[50]

Mallouhi practiced the "secular" discipline of hospitality.

We still need saints, only of a different kind. The kind of saint needed today is the *secular saint*—the parent, the teacher, the coach, the lawyer, the politician, the neighbor, the volunteer, the executive—who believes that how Christians live in the world matters to God. Perhaps the era of bishops, monks and martyrs has passed, at least in the West, but the need for saints has not, and never will. Now more than ever the world needs people who treat secular life as part of God's rightful domain, which of course it is. The Christian faith cannot be confined to the church and religious activities without contradicting itself. Disciples are never content to keep faith at church. They cannot help but apply it to the world.

PRACTICES

- Read Matthew 6:25-34; Romans 12:1-13; Colossians 3:12-17.

- Consider in detail the ordinariness of your life. Perhaps you commute to work and have to do many repetitive activities while on the job. Or you care for three children under the age of eight. Or you have many chores to do every week, like shopping and cooking. How can you integrate these activities into your life as a disciple of Jesus Christ? Can you express gratitude for these activities? What is God's purpose for them? How can you pray for each activity? How can you commune with God as you do them? How is God working out his redemptive purposes in your life through them?

- Each morning before you begin the day, spend time visualizing the presence of God in your ordinary life. What do you see God doing? How can you respond in faith?

- At the end of the day thank God for the good work he has done in your life and the good God he is.

9

Word

The Spirituality of the Reformers

"Indeed, the word of God is living and active,
sharper than any two-edged sword, piercing until it divides
soul from spirit, joints from marrow;
it is able to judge the thoughts and intentions of the heart.
And before him no creature is hidden, but all are naked and laid bare to
the eyes of the one to whom we must render an account."

HEB 4:12-13

I have listened to at least three thousand sermons in my life thus far, with many more to come, I am sure. I remember only a few of them, usually the atrocious ones or the brilliant ones. I have forgotten the vast majority. Not that they were entirely forgettable. The brain can store only so much information, and my brain has decided not to store that many sermons. I do believe, however, that they have left an impression on me, doing their quiet work in the soul, just as the many words of instruction and advice I have received over the years from my parents, teachers and friends have influenced me, though I do not remember many of those words either. We are often shaped by truths we do not necessarily remember, a truth I wish pastors believed with greater conviction and confidence, especially as it applies to their preaching, for the discipline of preaching suffers from serious neglect in the contemporary church.

REFORMATION PREACHING

It was not so during the Reformation.[1] Today we know Martin Luther as that courageous and tenacious monk who ignited the Reformation. It is a reputation he certainly deserves. His personality, writing and leadership made him a giant even during his lifetime. But what is less well known is that in his own day Luther was renowned and beloved as a preacher too. His preaching, no less than his writing, won a huge following. That he was so committed to the pulpit represented a major shift in late medieval Christianity. During the Middle Ages the altar functioned as the center of worship, both in church architecture and in church practice, for it was there that the priest celebrated the Mass. In the Reformation the pulpit took the altar's place. Preaching the Word of God emerged as the centerpiece of Reformation worship, though not to the neglect of the sacraments, which made visible what preaching made understandable.[2]

Luther's church in Wittenberg is a prime example. The church held three public services on Sunday—one at 5 a.m., one at 10 a.m. and one in the afternoon. At each service the members of the congregation followed the liturgy, sang hymns, uttered their prayers and celebrated the Eucharist. They also listened to sermons, very long sermons. Even then, Sunday was not the only day for worship, nor the only day for sermons. On Mondays and Tuesdays pastors in Wittenberg preached on the catechism, Wednesdays on the Gospel of Matthew, Thursdays and Fridays on the apostolic letters, especially the letters of Paul, and Saturdays on the Gospel of John. Luther did the majority of the preaching. His workload was overwhelming. He often preached three times on Sunday, three or four times during the week and then again on special days of the church year, especially Advent and Christmas, which were his favorite seasons. During a five month period in 1528, Luther preached 195 sermons. Some 2,300 of his sermons have survived out of the more than 4,000 that he preached.[3]

He was not alone. Other reformers—Martin Bucer of Strasbourg, Ulrich Zwingli of Zurich, and John Knox of Scotland—preached as regularly as Luther did. John Calvin of Geneva exceeded them all.[4] He preached twice on Sundays and every day of alternate weeks. He devoted Sundays to the exposition of the New Testament and weekdays to the Old Testament, with the exception of Holy Week. Between March of 1555 and July of 1556, for example, Calvin preached two hundred sermons on the book of Deuteronomy alone, in addition to the sermons he preached on Sundays and the lectures he delivered during the week at the academy. A stenographer recorded nearly every sermon he preached between 1549 and 1564, which, when edited and compiled, ran to some forty-four volumes. His successor in Geneva, Theodore Beza, claimed that Calvin preached an average of 290 sermons a year![5] No wonder that historian Roland Bainton states, "The Reformation gave centrality to the sermon."[6]

It is hard for us to fathom the importance that the Reformers attached to the preaching of the Word. Pastors still preach sermons in countless churches around the world today, and some preach very well, informing and inspiring the faithful with a rich and steady diet of the Word of God. But preaching does not hold the place of prominence that it did during the Reformation, whether in the minds of pastors or in the minds of laypeople. It often gets crowded out by other demands and duties that seem far more pressing. Laypeople in particular expect churches to provide a wide variety of services, from youth groups to recovery groups. Not that these expectations are necessarily wrong. Churches face enormous pressure to fill the vacuum created by an increasingly secular society that no longer operates according to Christian belief and ethics, which was probably not the case five hundred or even two hundred years ago. But there is a price to be paid when we require churches—as well as pastors—to do so much for us. That price is neglect of biblical preaching. We might be missing more than we think.

The Reformers considered preaching their primary duty and highest calling, which in turn reflected their belief in the Word of God. This belief constitutes the essential feature of Reformation spirituality, their commitment to preaching the most obvious expression of that belief.[7] The Reformers believed that God, out of his infinite love and mercy, chose to reveal himself to us—for the sake of his glory and our salvation. The content of this self-revelation is known as the Word of God. The ultimate manifestation of the Word is Jesus Christ, God's Son, who is the Word made flesh, God's perfect self-portrait. The Word was also put to writing, telling

the story of salvation history, especially as it culminated in the coming of
Jesus Christ. Finally, the Word continues to speak to us even today
through the proclamation of the Word and the administration of the sacraments, both of which point to Jesus Christ, the incarnate Word of God.
Consequently, the Reformers held to a high view of preaching because of
their understanding of and commitment to the Word. In their minds the
sermon was the spoken and the sacraments the visible expression of the
Word of God. "Rather ought Christ to be preached," Luther stated,

> to the end that faith in him may be established, that he may not only be
> Christ, but be Christ for you and me, and that what is said of him and is
> denoted in his name may be effectual in us. Such faith is produced and pre-
> served in us by preaching why Christ came, what he thought and bestowed,
> and what benefit it is to accept him.[8]

The Reformers never assumed that the Word belonged to them alone.
Quite the opposite was the case. They wanted to get it out to the people,
which is why they not only preached the Word but also translated it into
the vernacular, explained it through the many pamphlets, confessions,
commentaries and catechisms they wrote, and encouraged laypeople to
read it on their own, thus taking advantage of the newly invented printing
press.[9] They believed that the Word of God is addressed to all of us, not
simply to a chosen few. We should take this Word seriously—study it diligently, ponder it day and night, believe it in the heart as well as the mind,
and surrender our lives to it, trusting that it is not *a* Word from God but
the Word of God. It is God's final revelation of himself to us, which came
to us in Jesus Christ, God's Son, and was recorded for us in Scripture and
continues to speak to us through proclamation and sacraments.

THE REFORMATION SETTING

The Reformation refers to a broad movement of religious reform that
flourished in sixteenth-century Europe.[10] Europe itself was undergoing
massive changes at the time. Political entities, both large scale (nation-
states) and small scale (city-states), were asserting their independence
from papal domination. The rise of urban culture produced a population
of people who demanded that the church do more to address their unique

needs and concerns, such as business and trade, marriage and family, travel and leisure. Many people throughout Europe became increasingly critical of the church's failures, which were simply too obvious to overlook. There was widespread agreement that the church desperately needed some kind of reform. There was less agreement, however, over what those reforms should be.

The Roman Catholic hierarchy—monks, clergy, bishops and professors—did not do much to help solve the problem; if anything, it was a major part of the problem. It often appeared remote, irrelevant, incompetent and corrupt. Monks followed a way of life that laity found unappealing, if not repulsive.[11] University professors, using a method of study known as scholasticism, explored theological questions that seemed silly and petty to the laity. Many parish clergy kept concubines, charged fees for services and demonstrated appalling ignorance of the Christian faith. Bishops and cardinals enjoyed the wealth and prestige of high office without actually having to perform their duties. But the biggest problem by far was the Renaissance papacy. Popes in the late fifteenth and early sixteenth centuries showed more interest in collecting art, building lavish cathedrals and living luxuriously than in providing spiritual leadership for the church. Their scandalous behavior was often lampooned and skewered, especially by acerbic humanists like Erasmus.[12] For these and other reasons the Reformation was an event just waiting to happen.

The outcome of the Reformation was as complex as its causes. Luther and Calvin might be the most familiar Reformers to us now, but they represented only one wing of the movement back then. This particular wing, called the Magisterial Reformation, relied on the power of political magistrates to help reform the church, emphasized the importance of correct doctrine and proclaimed that salvation comes through Christ, grace and faith alone, which we know through Scripture alone. Leaders of the Radical Reformation, such as Menno Simons (founder of the Mennonites), argued that Luther and Calvin did not go far enough. They wanted to follow *all* the teachings of the Bible, including the Sermon on the Mount, which led them to separate from society, embrace pacifism and refuse to take oaths or to hold any kind of political office. The English Reformation moved in still another direction. English reformers rejected the pope's authority over the church and made the crown the head of the church instead. Further, they struck a theological compromise, called the Middle Way, to please as many parties as they could and then tried to unify the Church of England around the liturgy, which was formulated in the *Book of Common Prayer*. But Catholic leaders did not sit idly by; they too took steps to reform the church, initiating the Catholic Reformation. Two Spanish mystics, Teresa of Ávila and John of the Cross, urged reform in Spain. The great archbishop, Contarini, attempted the same in Italy, though with less satisfying results. Ignatius of Loyola founded a new monastic order, the Society of Jesus, to win back territory that had been lost to Protestants. Finally, the papacy convened the Council of Trent, which met in three sessions from 1545 to 1563, to clarify Catholic doctrine and reform church practice.

Still, Martin Luther and John Calvin are the most well known of the Reformers. Martin Luther spent years in a monastery, that bastion of medieval culture, which he eventually left as a result of his conversion to the Reformation faith. John Calvin studied the liberal arts at one of the leading universities of his day, which set him on a course that also led to his conversion to the Reformation faith. Still, however different their journeys, in the end they arrived at the same destination; they both became preachers of the Word.

LUTHER'S SPIRITUAL JOURNEY

Martin Luther (1483-1546) grew up in the home of peasant parents whose fortunes were slowly rising.[13] His father, Hans, valued education and hoped his son would settle into a good profession, like law, which could support Hans in his old age. Luther was willing to comply too. But he changed vocational course when, caught in a violent thunderstorm, he promised his patron saint, Anne, that if she spared his life he would become a monk. Luther survived the storm and kept his word. He immediately joined an Augustinian monastery.

Luther was profoundly aware of his sinfulness, and he practiced penance with special vigor to conquer the problem. But however vigorously he practiced the discipline, it never seemed vigorous enough. He confessed sin for hours at a time, and he punished himself for the sins he kept committing. Ironically, penance accomplished the opposite for which it was intended; it only made Luther more aware of his sinfulness. Concerned about Luther's torment, his confessor, Johann von Staupitz, encouraged him to study the mystics. But study of the mystics actually exacerbated the problem, for in trying to love God, as the mystics stressed, Luther became more conscious of his lack of love for God.[14] If anything, he grew to hate God. His sense of unworthiness drove him to the edge of despair. Desperate for a remedy, Staupitz sent Luther off to graduate school to study theology. After receiving his degree Luther assumed a teaching post at the new university in Wittenberg, where he taught Bible and theology.

At Wittenberg Luther started to study Scripture in earnest, and he discovered ideas that surprised, comforted and terrified him.[15] Over time Luther's study of the Bible awakened him to a new truth. Reflecting on the experience years later, he claimed that the turning point came while he was studying Romans 1. One verse in particular—Romans 1:17—perplexed and vexed him. As he put it, "I was seized with the conviction that I must understand Paul's letter to the Romans . . . but to that moment one phrase in chapter 1 stood in my way." That phrase was "the righteousness of God." He had assumed that it refers to what he called God's *active* righteousness, that is, the standard by which God judges and punishes anyone who falls short of his perfect righteousness. Further, he thought that the phrase, "the righteous person shall live by faith," means that only righteous people can have faith. Luther knew that he was not righteous, which implied that he did not have faith and that he was therefore not saved. "I could not love the righteous God. . . . I hated the idea, 'in it the righteousness of God is revealed.' I hated the righteous God who punishes sinners."

But Luther continued to ponder the passage, "night and day," as he said, until he achieved a breakthrough. He discovered that "the righteousness of God" refers to God's *passive* righteousness, that is, the gift of righteousness that God graciously lavishes on sinners, and that "the righteous live by faith" means that faith makes people righteous, not that righteous people have faith. Luther was overwhelmed by the discovery.

> This immediately made me feel as though I had been born again and as though I had entered through open gates into paradise itself. From that moment, I saw the whole face of Scripture in a new light. . . . And now, where

I had once hated the phrase, "the righteousness of God," I began to love and extol it as the sweetest of phrases, so that this passage in Paul became the very gate of paradise to me.[16]

Over the next few years Luther began to teach Scripture to the faculty and students in Wittenberg, gradually winning them to his point of view. He also

Martin Luther

began to challenge abuses in the church, such as the sale of indulgences, which popes dispensed in order to reduce the number of years the faithful had to spend in purgatory. The indulgence system became a convenient way to raise money, which only added to Luther's fury. In 1517 Pope Leo X and Albert of Brandenburg developed a plan to hire a Dominican, Johann Tetzel, to sell indulgences in Germany. The two leaders intended to split the profits. Albert needed the money to pay off debts, Leo to finance the construction of St. Peter's Basilica in Rome. Tetzel was a master salesman, and he knew how to play on the fears and anxieties of people. "Listen to the voices of your dear dead relatives and friends, beseeching you and saying, 'Pity us, pity us. We are in dire torment from which you can redeem us for a pittance.' Remember that you are able to release them." He even used a little jingle to attract their business. "As soon as the coin in the coffer rings, the soul from Purgatory springs." Laypeople flocked to buy these indulgences from Tetzel.[17]

On October 31, 1517, Luther posted ninety-five theses that challenged the entire indulgence system and called for a debate. Luther rejected the system because he believed it reduced salvation to a sum of money. Over the next few years he developed a theology that emphasized salvation was a free gift through Christ's perfect sacrifice on the cross. He argued that

Christ, the perfect Mediator, died to pay the penalty for our sins. Having been raised from the dead, he offers forgiveness and eternal life to those who trust in him. Luther used the analogy of marriage to make his point. In marriage, what belongs to the husband becomes the wife's and what belongs to the wife becomes the husband's. In the same way our sin is given to Christ; his righteousness to us.

> By the wedding ring of faith [Christ] shares in the sins, death, and pains of hell which are his bride's. . . . Thus the believing soul by means of the pledge of its faith is free in Christ, its bridegroom, free from all sins, secure against death and hell, and is endowed with the eternal righteousness, life, and salvation of Christ its bridegroom.[18]

The gospel saves us from God's wrath; it saves us from sin and death and hell; it even saves us from ourselves—our feeble efforts and pathetic works.

> And this is the reason why our theology is certain: it snatches us away from ourselves and places us outside ourselves, so that we do not depend on our own strength, conscience, experience, person, or works but depend on that which is outside ourselves, that is, on the promise and truth of God, which cannot deceive.[19]

Luther's protest did not fall on deaf ears. It won supporters; it also attracted enemies. Eventually the hierarchy of the church took notice. Between 1517 and 1520 Luther attended a series of hearings and debates. Church leaders hoped to change his mind, but Luther became all the more adamant. In 1520 the pope excommunicated him; Luther responded to the news by burning the document. In 1521 Charles V, the Holy Roman Emperor, who was only twenty-one at the time, summoned Luther to appear at the Diet of Worms, where both emperor and papacy ordered him to recant. But he refused to bend when asked for a simple, straightforward answer. He would take his stand on Scripture and reason alone.

> Unless I am convinced by the testimony of Scripture or by clear reason, for I do not trust either in the pope or in councils alone, since it is well known that they have often erred and contradicted themselves, I am bound by the Scriptures I have quoted and my conscience is captive to the Word of God. I cannot and will not retract anything, for it is neither safe nor right to go against conscience. I cannot do otherwise; here I stand, may God help me. Amen.[20]

CALVIN'S SPIRITUAL JOURNEY

If Luther served as the major catalyst of the Reformation, John Calvin (1509-1564) became its primary theologian and organizer.[21] At an early age Calvin was exposed to the new humanist learning that was becoming the intellectual fashion. Humanist scholars cherished the wisdom of the ancient past and studied its classical literature.[22] No text was more important to them than the Bible. They studied the Bible with care and tried to

John Calvin

interpret it accurately, using the best scholarly tools then available to them, especially the languages of Hebrew and Greek. For example, Johannes Reuchlin (1455-1522), a German humanist, mastered Hebrew and published a Hebrew grammar and lexicon, which allowed other scholars to study the Old Testament in its original language. John Colet (1466-1519), dean of St. Paul's Cathedral in London, delivered a series of lectures on Paul's letters, advocating that they be used as a template by which to judge the church. His evaluation of the church of his day was far from complimentary. Erasmus of Rotterdam (1469-1536), the prince of the humanists, prepared and published the first critical edition and composite text of the Greek New Testament.[23] Like Colet, Erasmus leveled severe criticism against the church. But he did not leave the church, nor did most of his fellow humanists.

Calvin committed himself to the Reformation faith sometime in 1533 or 1534, a full twenty years after Luther. As Calvin testified, "God by a sudden conversion subdued and brought my mind to a teachable frame, which was more hardened in such matters than might have been expected from one at my early period of life."[24] At that point Calvin decided to become a Christian scholar. By 1536 he had already published the first edition of the *Institutes of the Christian Religion*, which received favorable reviews from many of the Reformers, some of whom urged him to become a leader in the movement. But he refused, "being of disposition somewhat unpolished and bashful," as Calvin described himself, "which led me always to love the shade and retirement."[25] To escape persecution in France, he traveled to Strasbourg (then located in Alsace, now in France), so that he could continue to pursue his scholarly interests.

Some time later Calvin left Strasbourg for Italy. A war in Switzerland forced him to take a detour through Geneva, which was in turmoil over the influence of Reformation ideas. Calvin only planned to spend one night there and then be on his way. But word reached William Farel (1489-1565), a Reformer living in Geneva, that Calvin was in town. He visited Calvin and tried to persuade him to remain and help push forward the reformation of the church. Calvin respectfully declined, but Farel persisted, saying, as Calvin reported later, that "God would curse my retirement, and the tranquility of the studies which I sought, if I should withdraw and refuse to give assistance, when the necessity was so urgent."[26] So Calvin relented. After the city council appointed him as the primary preacher of the city in 1536, Calvin set to work to reform the church. Not everyone, however, agreed with his strategy, appreciated his methods or warmed to his personality. Two years later the city council asked Calvin to leave.

Calvin chose to return to Strasbourg. Thus began the happiest three years of his adult life. He became the pastor of a congregation of French refugees and busied himself with his other interests. He wrote several important works of theology, developed deep friendships with a number of prominent Reformation leaders, including Martin Bucer, the beloved pastor of Strasbourg, and continued to form his own convictions about how the church should be organized. In 1540 he also married a widow, Idelette de Bure. He enjoyed nine years of marriage before she died of tuberculosis in 1549.

Meanwhile, life in Geneva began to deteriorate. In 1541 the city council became so desperate that it invited Calvin to return. At first he resisted, knowing that only hardship awaited him there. But in the end he chose duty over ease. "At length, however, a solemn and conscientious regard for my duty, prevailed with me to consent to return to the flock from which I had been torn; but with what grief, tears, great anxiety and distress I did this."[27] Calvin stayed there for the rest of his life and devoted himself to his work. As a pastor, he cared for the flock and exercised church discipline. As a theologian, he revised and expanded the *Institutes*, authored several important treatises, and wrote commentaries on almost every book of the Bible. As a friend, he carried on a vast correspondence with Reformers who lived throughout Western Europe, becoming a leading Reformation ecumenist. And as a leader, he organized the church in Geneva (and elsewhere), founded an academy to educate the youth and pursued various projects to serve the common good of the city. His productivity is truly astonishing. Still, what remained central to Calvin's life and work—his "true north"—was the exposition of the Word of God. Calvin came to this conviction *about* the Word through his study *of* the Word. The Word itself convinced him of its authority.

CALVIN ON THE WORD OF GOD

Like Luther, Calvin believed that God revealed himself to humanity through the Word. In this act of self-revelation God chose to "accommodate" himself to our human capacities, limited as they are, as if speaking in our earthly language.

> For who even of slight intelligence does not understand that, as nurses commonly do with infants, God is wont in a measure to "lisp" in speaking to us? Thus such forms of speaking do not so much express clearly what God is like as accommodate the knowledge of him to our slight capacity. To do this he must descend far beneath his loftiness.[28]

The culmination of God's self-revelation occurred in the incarnation.[29] Being both divine and human, Jesus is the perfect Mediator between God and humanity. "Hence it is clear," Calvin argued, "that we cannot trust in God save through Christ. In Christ God so to speak makes himself little, in order to lower himself to our capacity; and Christ alone calms our consciences that they may dare intimately approach God."[30]

But God did not stop there. Calvin argued that by his providence he guided the process by which the story of salvation was written down. The Scriptures too are the Word of God because they contain the record of God's saving activity in Jesus Christ. Thus God's self-revelation is both visible (in Jesus Christ) and written (in Scripture).[31] Though clearly subordinate to Christ, the revelation of God in Scripture is as certain and reliable as the revelation of God in Jesus Christ. In Scripture "God has bridged the infinite gulf between himself and humanity by condescending to speak and act in human forms."[32] Calvin used the example of spectacles or glasses to make his point. If you place a book in front of a person with bad vision, he might be able to recognize that it is a book, but he would "scarcely construe two words." But if you give him the right glasses to wear, he would be able to read the words. In the same manner Scripture, "gathering up the otherwise confused knowledge of God in our minds, having dispersed our dullness, clearly shows us the true God."[33]

Finally, Calvin believed the Holy Spirit provided inner testimony in the heart of believers to enable them to understand, believe and obey the Word, for there can be no higher or greater witness to God than God himself.[34] "Therefore, illumined by his power, we believe neither by our own nor by anyone else's judgment that Scripture is from God; but above human judgment we affirm with utter certainty . . . that it has flowed to us from the very mouth of God by the ministry of men."[35]

Not that Calvin ignored or dismissed evidence that confirms the reliability of the biblical record. If anything, he was well aware of external proofs that could reinforce what the inner testimony of the Holy Spirit reveals. He cited the antiquity of the Bible; the miracles that accompanied the witness of its authors; its preservation under opposition, persecution and apostasy; and the universal relevance of its message as examples of these proofs. But such evidence, however convincing, is of secondary importance. "Yet of themselves these are not strong enough to provide a firm faith, until our Heavenly Father, revealing his majesty there, lifts reverence to Scripture beyond the realm of controversy."[36]

THE BURDEN OF THE PREACHER

Both Luther and Calvin believed that the proclamation of the Word of God *is* the Word of God. "God does not wish to be heard," Calvin asserted, "but by the voice of His ministers."[37] It is a weighty responsibility, one that preachers should not take lightly. But it is also a noble calling and a great honor. That preachers feel inadequate makes no difference. If anything, it fits the pattern perfectly. God uses lowly things to accomplish a great purpose. The suffering of Christ and the simple, unadorned stories of Scripture fit this pattern perfectly. So also does the weakness and foolishness of preaching. "For since, in the wisdom of God," the apostle Paul wrote, "the world did not know God through wisdom, God decided, through the foolishness of our proclamation, to save those who believe" (1 Cor 1:21). Preaching is the means God uses to save the lost. "We who are ordained to preach the Gospel ought to know that God honored us when he willed that from our mouth the testimony of salvation should be given to men, that we should be witnesses of his truth, that we should present salvation to those who were formerly damned and lost."[38]

Luther went so far as to argue that preaching plays a role that not even Scripture can play, for preaching gives God an audible voice. The ears, he said, not the eyes, are the primary organ for receiving the Christian message. Hearing is more fundamental than seeing, for God, once visibly present on earth in Jesus Christ, has chosen to continue to reveal himself through the proclamation of the Word.[39] God calls people to himself through the preaching of the Word.

Martin Luther, "Sermon on the Lord's Supper"

"Therefore, do not be so cold toward it [the Lord's Supper or Eucharist]. We are not forcing you, but you ought to come of your own free will. It is my duty to instruct you as to the reason why you should come, namely, your need, not a command, for you feel the infirmity of your faith and your propensity to all evil. These perils should move you without any command whatsoever. It is not the pope, not the emperor, not the duke who compels me, but my own need compels me. . . . The need [which drives us to the sacrament] is that sin, devil, and death are always present. The benefit is that we receive forgiveness of sins and the Holy Spirit. Here, not poison, but a remedy and salvation is given, in so far as you acknowledge that you need it. Don't say: I am not fit today, I will wait a while. This is a trick of the devil. What will you do if you are not fit when death comes? Who will make you fit then? Say rather: Neither preacher, prince, pope, nor emperor compels me, but my great need and, beyond this, the benefit. First, the sacrament is Christ's body and blood in bread and wine comprehended in the Word. Secondly, the benefit is forgiveness of sins. This includes the need and the benefit. Thirdly, those who believe should come." (From Martin Luther: Selections from His Writings, *ed. John Dillenberger)*

If you ask a Christian what the work is by which he is made worthy of the name of Christian, he can give no other answer than hearing the word of God, which is faith. Thus the ears alone are the organs of a Christian man, because not by the works of any other member but by faith is he justified and judged a Christian.[40]

THE PREPARATION OF THE PREACHER

What preacher is capable of bearing such a heavy burden, considering the weightiness of preaching? The Reformers were aware of this problem. They had much to say, therefore, not only *about* preaching but also *to* preachers. They urged fellow preachers to become good stewards of the Word of God, which required the cultivation of certain disciplines. They considered faithfulness to the gospel as primary. Calvin reasoned that preaching is the Word of God only if the sermon itself actually proclaims the Word of God. Calvin used words like *ambassador* and *steward* to define the role of preachers. The authority is delegated, not inherent. "Now we must not find this strange, for when the servants of God speak thus, they attribute nothing to themselves, but show to what they are commissioned and what charge is given them; and thus they do not separate themselves from God."[41]

But competence mattered to them too. Everyone can read the Word, understand the Word and discuss the Word. Not everyone can preach the Word in worship. "Clearly not everyone is fitted to be a pastor," Calvin wrote. Preachers must know Scripture, understand doctrine, demonstrate godliness of character and possess the gift of teaching.[42] But even those qualities are not enough. Preachers also have to be conscientious students. Calvin regarded lack of preparation as a particularly dangerous and presumptuous fault.

If I should climb up into the pulpit without having deigned to look at a book and frivolously imagine, "Ah well! When I get there God will give me enough to talk about," and I do not condescend to read, or to think about what I ought to declare, and I come here without carefully pondering how I must apply the Holy Scripture to the edification of the people—well, then I should be a cock-sure charlatan and God would put me to confusion in my audaciousness.[43]

Calvin's pulpit

The Reformers were serious students, not only of the Word but also of the art of good communication or rhetoric. The first rule of rhetoric is that the medium should fit the message. How the Word is preached should correspond to what the Word says. Their style of preaching followed accordingly. Luther used an expository method of preaching. He looked for the central meaning of the text and then explained that meaning in light of the larger context. Calvin preached through the Bible one verse at a time, one book at a time (known as lectio continua); he covered an average of four verses a sermon. Both Luther and Calvin preached extemporaneously, refusing to read from a manuscript. They used a variety of rhetorical tools too. They retold biblical stories (Luther in particular was a master at this), rephrased Pauline passages and used words, illustrations, and metaphors that came from the ordinary life of his parishioners. Calvin considered eloquence a useful art. Still, if preachers erred, he believed that it should be on the side of simple exposition, not artful elocution.

> That eloquence, then, is neither to be condemned nor despised, which has no tendency to lead Christians to be taken up with an outward glitter of words, or intoxicate them with empty delight, or tickle their ears with its tinkling sound, or cover over the cross of Christ with its empty show as with a veil; but, on the contrary, tends to call us back to the native simplicity of the Gospel, tends to exalt the simple preaching of the Cross by voluntarily abasing itself, and, in fine, acts the part of a herald.[44]

THE CHARACTER OF THE PREACHER

The Reformers acknowledged that, however noble their calling, they were still human beings. They believed that their sermons had to speak first to the person doing the preaching. Calvin was adamant about this point. It was simply unacceptable to him that preachers would presume to expound the Word without applying it to themselves. "It would be better for him to break his neck going up into the pulpit if he does not take pains to be the first to follow God."[45] Calvin was terrified of the risk involved. He made sure he avoided the sin of presumption at all costs. "When I go up into the pulpit it is not only to teach others. I do not withdraw apart; for I must be a scholar and the word proceeding out of my mouth should be a service to me as well as to you; or woe is me!"[46]

Their sermons often had a humble, human quality to them. This was especially true of Luther. It is clear that he understood the human condition, which often surfaced in his sermons. During Passion Week in 1530, for example, he preached on the suffering of Christ, using it as an example of how believers should respond to their own suffering.

> When the suffering and affliction is at its worst, it bears and presses down so grievously that one thinks he can endure no more and must surely perish. But then if you can think of Christ, the faithful God will come and will help you, as he has always helped his own from the beginning of the world; for he is the same God as he always has been.[47]

Luther often pointed to the lowliness of Jesus as a source of comfort and encouragement. "To me there is no greater consolation given to mankind than this," he preached one Christmas day,

> that Christ became man, a child, a babe, playing in the lap and at the breasts of his most gracious mother. Who is there whom this sight would not comfort? Now is overcome the power of sin, death, hell, conscience, and guilt, if you come to this gurgling Babe and believe that he is come, not to judge you, but to save.[48]

Luther knew that his congregation comprised mostly ordinary people. In his mind it was not right to preach to the elites and ignore everyone else. He criticized fellow preachers who spoke to the educated and sophisticated but ignored the concerns of common people. "Good God," Luther exclaimed to a fellow minister, "there are sixteen-year-old girls, women, old men, and farmers in the church, and they don't understand lofty matters! . . . Someday I'll have to write a book against artful preachers."[49]

Though highly educated, Luther spoke in a way that ordinary people could understand, using idioms and illustrations that came from their world. "When I preach I regard neither doctors nor magistrates, of whom I have above forty in my congregation; I have all my eyes on the servant maids and on the children. And if the learned men are not well pleased with what they hear, well, the door is open."[50]

PASTORAL CARE

The Reformers were pastors, every one of them. They cared about the daily life of the people under their charge.[51] "Whatever others may think," Calvin wrote, "we do not regard our office as bound within so narrow limits that when the sermon is delivered we may rest as if our task was done. They whose blood will be required of us if lost through our slothfulness, are to be cared for much more closely and vigilantly."[52] The Reformers lived in the same world as their parishioners. Nearly every major Reformer chose to marry and have children; many suffered catastrophic losses and battled significant health problems; all of them faced almost constant opposition. We have a great deal of information about Luther's life because he was the most transparent and forthcoming. We know, for example, that he suffered the loss of two children. The death of his sweet daughter, Magdalene, who was only thirteen years old, was nearly unbearable for him. Luther devoted himself to her care. "I loved her very much," he wrote to a friend. "In the last thousand years God has given to no bishop such great gifts as he has given to me. I am angry with myself that I am unable to rejoice from my heart and be thankful to God, although I do at times sing a little hymn and thank God. Whether we live or die, we are the Lord's."[53] When his daughter drew near to death, he fell on his knees by her bed and, weeping bitterly, prayed that God might save her, if it be his will. A little while later she died in his arms. I am moved to tears every time I read the account of her death to my students. It turns the larger-than-life figure of Luther into an ordinary man.

Calvin's response to Idelette's death is equally powerful. "Though the death of my wife has been a very cruel thing for me, I try as much as possible to moderate my grief. . . . However, the few results that I obtain help very little. Actually, you know the tenderness or rather the softness of my soul."

He did not mitigate the severity of his loss. "Of course, the reason for my sorrow is not an ordinary one. I am deprived of my excellent life companion, who, if misfortune had come, would have been my willing companion not only in exile and sorrow, but even in death."[54] Calvin grieved when others suffered too. Referring to several deaths that his close friend, Charles Richebourg, experienced, he wrote to a friend, "These events bring me such sadness that they completely overwhelm my soul and break my spirit."[55]

Contrary to popular opinion, Calvin was beloved as a friend and pastor as much as he was admired as a scholar. Many respected him for the man he was, not simply for the mind he had. He was a superb pastor. For example, in a letter describing Calvin, one of his friends wrote to another:

> No words of mine can declare the fidelity and prudence with which he gave councel. The kindness with which he received all who came to him, the clearness and promptitude with which he replied to those who asked his opinion on the most important questions, and the ability with which he disentangled the difficulties and problems which were laid before him. Nor can I express the gentleness with which he could comfort the afflicted and raise the fallen and distressed.[56]

THE WORD OF GOD FOR US

The Reformers labored to preach well because they had a high view of the Word of God, whether incarnate, written, preached or made visible in the sacraments. How should we respond to this Word? First, we should make it our own, for it is in the written Word that we come to know the incarnate Word and God's saving work. The Bible tells a story of human resistance and God's persistence. The story is full of flawed heroes and strange twists of plot, of the wretchedness of evil and the triumph of good, which was accomplished in a way that no one could have predicted, namely, through the death and resurrection of Jesus Christ. It is a wonderful story; it is also a true story that speaks to the depths of the human condition. This story provides us with the truths we need to make sense of our own stories. What God accomplished then he can accomplish now because he is the same God who works in the same way. Even more, we come to realize that our stories are given meaning not because they are *our* stories but because they are located within *the* story of salvation history. The gospel invites us into a world that is bigger than our own.

Thus, for the sake of our own spiritual health, we must learn this story well by reading it time and again, not only to master the basic facts but also to understand it devotionally. Devotional reading requires that we not only learn the story but also apply it to our lives. I encourage my students to try to read through the entire Bible in one year, which enables them to grasp the larger whole of the redemptive story. I also challenge them to memorize important passages (for example, Ps 27; Is 55; Mt 5—7; Rom 8; Phil 3) and then meditate on these passages throughout the day. These disciplines change the students, for the story of the Bible becomes their story too.

Second, we must learn to *listen* to the Word, for "faith comes from what is heard, and what is heard comes through the Word of Christ" (Rom 10:17). Listening is different from reading. Listening uses the ears, reading the eyes; listening is a communal exercise, reading a solitary one. "Listening is an interpersonal act," observes author Eugene Peterson; "it involves two or more people in fairly close proximity. Reading involves one person with a book written by someone who can be miles away or centuries dead, or both. The listener is required to be attentive to the speaker and is more or less at the speaker's mercy."[57] In fact, what is contained in the written Word did not start out as a written word at all. The biblical story—the law, the prophets and the gospel—was passed on from teachers to people, masters to disciples, parents to children, over many generations. The story was spoken and heard, repeated and memorized, word for word, gesture for gesture, until it became lodged in the memory of the people of God. It functioned as an oral tradition long before it was put to writing. Even then, the Word was usually read aloud more often than it was read silently and privately because it was a Word for the entire community.

We need to recover the art of listening to the Word of God, allowing that Word to address us as if God were the speaker, we the hearers. When we read, we maintain control; when we listen, the Word has control.[58] We also need to learn how to listen to the preached Word. I do not believe that we will ever outgrow the need for the preaching of the Word of God. Many of us have never heard good preaching and thus do not know what we are missing. Nothing can be compared to the experience of listening to a good sermon in which God himself seems to be speaking. It awakens in us a deeper hunger for the Word of God. Laypeople should take the pulpit as seriously as pastors, if not more so, because their spiritual well-being depends on it. It is too easy for us to make an appearance on Sunday mornings with no sense of expectation that we are going to hear a word from God. Not every sermon, of course, is going to be profound, not every sermon funny or cathartic or erudite. But we can expect every sermon to be faithful to Scripture and applicable to life. The only truly bad sermon is one that fails to communicate Jesus Christ as the Word of God in a way that enables us to grow in faith and obedience.

If sermons fail to measure up, then we should prayerfully and humbly approach the pastor in private and speak our minds, making concrete suggestions for improvement. It is better to offend with honesty than to tolerate mediocrity, only to find ourselves chafing every time Sunday morning comes around or, worse, lowering our expectations until we expect nothing at all. We might be pleasantly surprised by the response. Most pastors I know want to become better preachers. If they dread something, it is not constructive criticism but indifference and dullness and dropouts. Preaching is a form of communication. Pastors do most of the talking. They need to hear from us too, whether it be appreciation or criticism. It is imperative, however, that we weigh our words carefully. I have heard many pastors tell stories of inane, rude, even cruel comments about their preaching that failed to distinguish between style and substance. If we approach our pastors, we should strive to be wise with our words and willing to live with the consequences of our suggestions. They might ask us to join a Tuesday morning study group to help them prepare for Sunday or ask us to protect their schedule so that they can devote more time to study and preparation.

Third, we should apply the written Word to life. In their preaching the Reformers did not confine the Word to private and personal matters only, nor did they go to the opposite extreme, striving to be relevant without anchoring their sermons in Scripture. They tried as best they could to explain what the Word teaches and then to apply it to the world of their parishioners. They did not hesitate to speak out about commerce, politics, popular entertainment, family life, suffering and social injustice. We would do well to imitate them at this point. When we study the Word, preach the Word and listen to the Word, we should do so with the needs of the world in mind, not simply our own personal problems, however pressing those might be. Karl Barth once said that when preparing for sermons, preachers should hold the Bible in one hand and the newspaper in the other. Laypeople should approach the Christian faith with that same principle in mind. The Bible does not tell us how to vote or how to reform the health care system or how to settle the civil war in the Sudan; but it does provide general principles for how we should live in the world. The Reformers were committed both to the supremacy of the Word and to Christian engagement with culture. We, their heirs, would be wise to follow their example.

Still, the primary value of the written Word of God is that it points to *the* Word of God, to Jesus Christ, God's Son and the world's Savior. The Reformers had much to say about how we should obey the Word, but in the end they had more to say about what we should *believe* about the Word. They confessed that God came into this world as the Word made flesh to win our salvation. There is more to the Christian faith than that, as the Reformers demonstrated time and again in their passionate and visionary preaching; but there is never less. In the end they kept returning to one central message—Jesus Christ is the very Word of God who came to reveal God and make us right with God.

PRACTICES

- Read Romans 1:16-17; Ephesians 2:1-10; 1 Timothy 4:6-10.
- Set a goal to read the following sections of the biblical story over the next two months: Genesis 1—11; 12—24; 37—50; Exodus 1—15; Joshua 1—2; Judges 6—16; Ruth; 1 Samuel 16—31; 1 Kings 1—12; Ezra; Nehemiah; Esther; Amos; Luke; Acts. As you read these narrative sections, think about how these passages could inform the way you view your own life story. Using their narratives as background, write your own story as you think God might describe it thus far.
- After you finish the above exercise, spend the next two months memorizing and meditating on several New Testament texts: Matthew 5:1-12; Romans 5:1-5; 8:1-8; Philippians 2:1-11; 3:7-14; Colossians 3:1-4. Try to meditate on each passage when you wake up in the morning, drive in your car and go to bed at night. Let these texts take root in your soul.

10

Conversion

The Spirituality of Evangelicals

"All authority in heaven and earth has been given to me.
Go therefore and make disciples of all nations,
baptizing them in the name of the Father and of the Son
and of the Holy Spirit, and teaching them to obey
everything that I have commanded you.
And remember, I am with you always, to the end of the age."

MT 28:18-20

No movement in the history of Christianity has been more energetic, creative, diverse and complex than evangelicalism. It has grown so dramatically over the past two hundred years that it now encircles the globe. Close to a billion Christians would identify themselves as evangelical. It includes a wide variety of denominations and movements too, from Puritanism to Pentecostalism. Still, however diverse, evangelicalism holds to one basic conviction—the necessity of a personal conversion to Jesus Christ (as we know of him through Scripture).[1] Evangelicals believe that true spirituality requires more than church attendance, liturgical practice, sacramental observance and creedal assent. These are important disciplines, to be sure; but they also tend to remain formal and external, which can easily engender nominal faith. Without denying the validity of these disciplines, evangelicals also emphasize the importance of personal experience and heartfelt response. At the heart of evangelical spirituality is the conversion of the whole of one's life to God.[2]

One biblical text comes to mind that captures the essence of evangelical spirituality. The Gospel of John records an account of a long conversation between Nicodemus and Jesus. The contrast between the two men could not be more startling. Nicodemus was the quintessential Jewish insider—a Pharisee, a ruler of the people and an esteemed teacher in Israel; Jesus was the outsider—a renegade rabbi, a miracle worker and a charismatic leader. During the course of their conversation Jesus said to Nicodemus, "Very truly, I tell you, no one can see the kingdom of God without being born from above." Though a powerful, well-educated Jew, Nicodemus did not understand the meaning of what Jesus said. "How can these things be?" Nicodemus inquired. "Are you a teacher of Israel," Jesus responded, "and yet you do not understand these things?" (Jn 3:3-10). There is always a new birth in evangelical spirituality, a "before" and an "after." As the parables of the lost sheep, lost coin and lost son keep repeating, what is "lost" must be "found," what is dead must be made alive. There must be a conversion.

THE ANATOMY OF A CONVERSION

No wonder that testimonies abound in evangelical circles. Evangelicals love to tell the stories of their conversions. One of the more famous is the story of John Newton's conversion.[3] It sums up much that is distinctive and good about evangelical spirituality. Newton was born in 1725 to a quiet, pious mother and a pompous, irreligious father who, as captain of a merchant ship, was away much of the time during Newton's early years. After his mother died in 1732, Newton spent the next several years in a boarding school before joining his father at sea as a cabin boy. He had shown some inclination toward religion as a child, but by the time he reached adolescence he seemed to have lost all interest.

The security Newton enjoyed under the protection of his father soon came to an end when his father retired from life at sea. He arranged that his son become an apprentice to another sea captain, Joseph Manesty. The arrangement lasted for a year. Then, while visiting Mary Catlett, a young woman to whom he had given his heart, Newton was seized by a "Press-Gang" of Navy sailors looking to conscript young, idle Englishmen, and they forced him to serve in the British Royal Navy on board the *Harwich*. Thus began his downward spiral into utter degradation. He became bitter about life and hostile toward Christianity. When Newton learned that the *Harwich* was about to embark on a five-year voyage around the world, he left the ship to ask his father to intervene on his behalf. A few sailors spotted him leaving the ship and, assuming he was deserting, dragged him back. The captain flogged him and demoted him from the quarterdeck, which meant that he lost his status as an officer in training. Several days later the ship departed for its circumnavigation of the globe. Newton's feeling of regret was so severe that he considered suicide. "When I could see [the English coastline] no longer," he wrote in his autobiography, "I was tempted to throw myself into the sea," which would have "put a period to all my sorrow at once."[4]

His life on board the *Harwich* was miserable; the captain hated him and fellow sailors taunted him. "My breast was filled with the most excruciating passions, eager desire, bitter rage, and black despair. Every hour exposed me to some new insult and hardship, with no hope of relief or mitigation, no friend to take my part or to listen to my complaint."[5] While the ship was sailing along the west coast of Africa, Newton was resourceful enough to negotiate his own release and land a position working for a British slave trader on Plantain Island, which was located off the African coast. The slave trader, who was often away on long journeys to buy slaves, charged his African wife with the responsibility to oversee Newton's work. In an ironic reversal of roles, Newton suffered horribly under her. She mocked, hounded and beat him almost incessantly. In effect, she treated him as her slave. In very short order Newton became gravely ill and almost died. This period proved to be the nadir of his life, not only physically but even more so spiritually. "My conduct, principles, and heart were still darker than my outward condition." Yet years later Newton would look back on the experience as God's gift to him. "It is a part of my daily employment to look back to Africa and to retrace the path by which the Lord has led me, for about forty-seven years, since he called me from infidelity and madness."[6]

His fortunes began to change for the better when he found work with another slave trader. Newton gradually settled into a life of comfortable dissipation. So indifferent did he become to the things once dear to him that when another British ship, the *Greyhound*, arrived and offered him passage home, he refused to board. Only the pleadings of the captain, who was a friend of Newton's father, and his love for Mary, which had remained strong, led him to change his mind. But the *Greyhound* was not heading straight for England. It had to sail first to Brazil and then to Newfoundland before turning for home. Newton sunk once more into abject irreligion and debauchery. His bad behavior was so egregious that even the captain of the ship—no paragon of virtue himself—was forced to rebuke him. Newton cursed the sailors, blasphemed God, drank himself into a stupor and agitated members of the crew. Twice over he barely survived accidents that were caused by his own stupidity. His heart had turned as hard as granite. "The admonition of conscience, which from successive repulses had grown weaker and weaker, at length entirely ceased. For a space of many months, if not for some years, I cannot recollect that I had a single check of conscience."[7]

Still, his long, slow turn toward the Christian faith began on that voyage. In May 1748 he happened upon a copy of the fifteenth-century classic *The Imitation of Christ* and began to read it. The message of the book cut him to the heart. He realized that if Thomas à Kempis's message was true, then he was doomed and damned. There was no other alternative. That very evening the ship ran into a severe storm that lasted for several days and almost sunk it. At one point the captain forced Newton to take the helm, which allowed him, even under such ferocious conditions, to examine his life. "I had here leisure and opportunity to think of my former religious professions, the calls, warnings, and deliverances I had met with, the licentious course of my life, particularly my unparalleled effrontery in making the gospel the subject of profane ridicule." His hours of reflection led to a sobering conclusion. "I thought . . . there never was, nor could be, such a sinner as myself. Then comparing the advantages I had broken through, I concluded at first that my sins were too great to be forgiven."[8] The ship survived the storm and managed to limp into an Irish port. While in Ireland Newton visited a church twice daily to pray; he also received his first

Communion. "This was not a formal, but a sincere surrender, under a warm sense of mercies recently received."[9] He would always point to this one experience at sea as the moment of his conversion, or at least the beginning of his conversion.

Upon returning to England Newton declared his intent to court Mary, promising her that he would live uprightly and secure a lucrative, respectable livelihood. Surprisingly, he found in the slave trade an occupation that met those conditions. He served as first mate on one voyage, after which he married Mary, and then as captain on three more. Though by then a Christian, Newton did not recognize—or at least did not acknowledge—the contradiction between his new faith and his new vocation. He felt no pangs of conscience, believing that it was his Christian duty, not to free the slaves but to treat them well.[10]

He discovered that it was not easy to live as a Christian on board a ship, even when serving as captain. He often slipped into old habits. In the mornings he would study the Bible and pray, tasting "the sweets of communion with God in the exercises of prayer and praise," but then spend his evenings "in vain and worthless company." The inconsistency tormented him. However hard he tried, he could not overcome the sinful inertia of his former way of life. He grew weary of the struggle. The vicious cycle in which he was caught underscored how desperately he needed grace. "I made no more resolves, but cast myself before the Lord to do with me as He should please. . . . The burden was removed from my conscience, and not only my peace but my health was restored. . . ."[11] It was grace that also enabled him to overcome the cycle of defeat that had plagued him for so long. "Now I began to understand the security of the covenant of grace, and to expect to be preserved, not by my own power and holiness, but by the mighty power and promise of God, through faith in an unchangeable Savior."[12]

Health problems finally forced him to retire from the slave trade. For the next nine years he served as a customs officer in Liverpool and involved himself in the growing evangelical movement in England. He also sought ordination in the Church of England. But the bishop denied his candidacy because he did not have a university education. Still, he persisted in his efforts. It was the publication of his conversion story, *An Authentic Narrative*, that opened the door to ordination.[13] The book was widely read and admired in evangelical circles. In 1764 Lord Dartmouth, a wealthy and influential evangelical who had read the autobiography, invited Newton to serve as rector of the church in Olney, the district over which Dartmouth had authority as a member of the landed aristocracy.

Newton proved to be an effective pastor of the 2,500 people who lived in the town. He visited church members at their places of work, distributed money and food to the poor, and taught the Bible to the children. He led a prayer meeting every Tuesday and delivered theological lectures every Thursday, both of which became very popular, and he invited parishioners to his home after worship on Sundays for a meal and conversation. In 1779 he published *Olney Hymns*, a collection of hymns that he and his good friend and neighbor, poet William Cowper, had written. Included in the collection was the hymn that would one day make his name famous around the world, "Amazing Grace."

John Newton

In 1780 he was invited to become rector of a prosperous Anglican church in London. His circle of friendships widened considerably; for example, he developed warm friendships with such luminaries as George Whitefield, John Wesley and Charles Wesley. Over time he emerged as a leader of the evangelical movement. His pastoral correspondence became so famous that it was collected, edited and published in book form. He became a good friend of William Wilberforce too, then a young, wealthy, witty and brilliant member of Parliament. Wilberforce asked Newton whether he should continue in politics after having been converted to Christ. Newton urged him to stay right where he was, maintain his former friendships, which included many rich and powerful people, and continue his work in Parliament. He reasoned that politics was as worthy a calling as pastoral work. Later he wrote to Wilberforce, "May the wisdom that influenced Joseph and Moses and Daniel rest upon you. Not only to guide you in the line of political duty but especially to keep you in the habit of dependence upon God, and communion with him, in the midst of all the changes and bustle around you."[14] Wilberforce remained in Parliament for the next forty-five years, becoming an advocate for moral reform in England and the leader of the abolitionist movement.

But Wilberforce also returned the favor. He challenged Newton to speak out publicly against slavery, arguing that his former life as a slaver gave him a visible platform on which to speak. Newton accepted the challenge. In 1788 he published *Thoughts upon the African Slave Trade*. It provided a devastating critique of slavery, which Newton called "iniquitous," "cruel," "oppressive," "destructive," "unlawful" and "disgraceful." As if finally admitting the horrible wrong he had done, he stated that he was "bound in conscience to take shame to myself by a public confession, which, however sincere, came too late to prevent or repair the misery and mischief to which I have, formerly, been accessory."[15] Later on he also served as an important witness in Parliamentary hearings on slavery.

During his years in London Newton's winsome personality, warm preaching, large circle of friends and well-known conversion story made him a virtual celebrity. He brokered his influence for the evangelical cause and tried his hardest to keep it united. He became something of an evangelical ecumenist. John Wesley marveled at his ability to transcend divisions and disputes without appearing spineless and obsequious. He once wrote to Newton, "You appear to be designed by divine providence for a healer of breaches, a reconciler of honest but prejudiced men, and a uniter of the children of God."[16] He finally retired from preaching and pastoral work in 1806, just one year before he died. By then he had earned a stellar reputation as a man of deep religious piety, conviction and influence. Still, Newton never forgot where he had come from, how unworthy he was and what grace had done for him. "So much forgiveness," he once wrote to a friend, "so little love. So many mercies, so few returns. Such great privileges, and a life so sadly below them." He wrote to another friend, "My memory is nearly gone, but I remember two things—that I am a great sinner, and that Christ is a great Savior." The epitaph on his gravestone, which he wrote several months before his death, says it all. "John Newton, clerk, once an infidel and libertine, a servant of slaves in Africa, was, by the rich mercy of our Lord and Savior Jesus Christ, preserved, restored, pardoned, and appointed to preach the faith he had long laboured to destroy."[17]

THE WHOLE OF OUR LIVES

Most people know him as the author of "Amazing Grace." The hymn is really Newton's testimony; it speaks of the wretchedness of his sin, his tempestuous journey to faith and the sweetness of his life in Christ. It shows how grace—and only grace—can transform a person from sinner to saint. It reflects the best in evangelical spirituality.

I value every one of the traditions of spirituality explored in this book. But evangelical spirituality runs deepest in me, and for a good reason. I experienced a conversion when I was twenty years old. Like Newton, I grew up in a Christian home and attended church regularly. I also dropped out of church when I was a teenager and lived a dissolute life. After two years of college I was hired to work as a camp counselor for the summer. During the week of staff orientation I met Tom Stark, a local pastor who had been invited to train us. In one of the training sessions he took a few moments to explain the gospel to us. I was shocked by his message, for I had never heard anything like it before. Later that evening I approached him and badgered him with questions. His answers only made the gospel message clearer to me. At the close of our conversation I said to him, "If that's what it means to be a Christian, I never want to be one." Over the next few weeks, however, Tom's words kept coming back to me. On a Friday night in late June I took a walk on the beach, fell on my knees and surrendered my life to Jesus. My soul was immediately flooded with inextinguishable joy. I did not come down from the "high" of that experience for many months.

I write this chapter, therefore, as an insider, which makes me more keenly aware of both the weaknesses and the strengths of this tradition. On the one hand, evangelicalism can easily trivialize the meaning of conversion. Over the years I have witnessed many superficial conversions. I know too many evangelicals whose conversion marked the end rather than the beginning of their spiritual pilgrimage, whose grasp of truth goes no deeper than knowledge of a handful of Bible verses and self-help formulas,

John Newton, "Amazing Grace"

Amazing grace! (how sweet the sound)
That saved a wretch like me!
I once was lost, but now am found,
Was blind, but now I see.

'Twas grace that taught my heart to fear,
And grace my fears relieved;
How precious did that grace appear,
The hour I first believed!

Through many dangers, toils and snares,
I have already come,
'Tis grace has brought me safe thus far,
And grace will lead me home.

The Lord has promised good to me,
His word my hope secures;
He will my shield and portion be,
As long as life endures.

Yes, when this flesh and heart shall fail,
And mortal life shall cease;
I shall possess, within the veil,
A life of joy and peace.

The earth shall soon dissolve like snow,
The sun forbear to shine;
But God, who called me here below,
Will be for ever mine.

and whose commitment to Christ requires little more than occasional church attendance. I feel an acute sense of embarrassment when I consider how often this great tradition has been abused or perverted. On the other hand, evangelicalism emphasizes a central truth that should never be compromised. The Bible makes it clear that we must be converted to Jesus

Christ. After hearing Peter's sermon on the Day of Pentecost, his Jewish listeners, cut to the heart, asked, "Brothers, what should we do?" To which Peter responded, "Repent, and be baptized every one of you in the name of Jesus Christ so that your sins may be forgiven; and you will receive the gift of the Holy Spirit" (Acts 2:37-38). In effect, he was calling them to conversion.

WHAT IS CONVERSION?

The idea of conversion suggests a turn, a change of direction, a new course for one's life. The word itself does not appear in the Bible, though several synonyms do. The two most important are *repentance*, which implies a change of heart, mind and direction, and *new birth*, which connotes a kind of second coming to life, this one spiritual in nature. Conversion can happen in a variety of ways too. It can be dramatic or quiet, emotional or thoughtful, sudden or drawn out.[18] What truly matters, however, is not *how* people are converted but *that* they are converted. The true test of its authenticity is the long-term results.[19]

Three seventeenth-century movements, all originating in Europe, emphasized the importance of results. These movements laid the foundation for modern evangelicalism.

Conversion as a process. The Puritans defined conversion as a process.[20] Puritanism first emerged in England as a reaction to the religious policy of Elizabeth I, who followed a moderate course of church reform—the "Middle Way," as it was called. Reformers had hoped that Elizabeth would continue the trajectory of reform set by her half brother, Edward VI. They soon realized that political expediency was more important to her than biblical fidelity. Still, they persisted in their efforts to purge the church of irreligion and to purify it according to the Word of God, which is why they came to be called "Puritans." They did not succeed as they had hoped. They were opposed by the crown, harassed by church authorities and wracked by disagreements and dissension from within their own ranks. By the early seventeenth century the movement began to fragment.

The Puritans produced many formidable theologians, writers and pastors, both in England and in the colonies. None became more famous than John Bunyan (1628-1688), the author of *The Pilgrim's Progress*, one of the most beloved books written in the English language.[21] A religious dissenter, Bunyan spent twelve years in the Bedford County jail for preaching without the crown's authorization. While in prison he wrote several books, including his autobiography, *Grace Abounding to the Chief of Sinners*. He also conceived of the plot and started to write *The Pilgrim's Progress*, which, upon its publication in 1678, became an immediate bestseller (there were over 100,000 copies in print by 1692).

The Pilgrim's Progress uses the literary device of an allegory to explore the nature of conversion. It traces the spiritual journey of the main character, Christian, as he travels from the City of Destruction to the Celestial City. Early on in the story Christian experiences a sudden, dramatic conversion. Evangelist tells Christian to follow the pathway of Salvation until he arrives at the Cross. Carrying the heavy burden of sin, Christian approached the cross. Gazing on it, "his burden loosed from off his shoulders, and fell from off his back, and began to tumble, and so continued to do, till it came to the mouth of the sepulcher where it fell in, and I saw it no more."[22]

But his experience at the foot of the cross marks only the beginning of his conversion. At that point he embarks on a long, perilous journey that continues the process. He faces many dangers along the way, which symbolize the various temptations and trials that all Christians face. There is the Hill of Difficulty, Vanity Fair and the Valley of the Shadow of Death. Christian meets wicked characters too, such as Mr. Worldly Wiseman, Pliable, Obstinate, Legality, Talkative and Ignorance, which represent errors into which believers are liable to fall if they do not live according to truth and trust in the promises of God. Still, these difficulties serve a divine purpose. Christian's companion, Hopeful, says to him toward the end of the journey, "These troubles and distresses that you go through in these waters are no sign that God hath forsaken you, but are sent to try you, whether you will call to mind that which heretofore you have received of His goodness, and live upon Him in your distresses."[23]

The Puritans believed that conversion sometimes happens in a moment of time. Many of them—John Bunyan included—experienced just such a conversion. But they also affirmed that conversion is a process that God uses to draw us ever closer to himself and to make us ever more like himself.[24] They called this process "owning the covenant." In their minds conversion has a kind of narrative quality to it, which is why, especially in the American colonies, Puritan pastors required candidates for church membership to provide a narrative of their conversion before they were allowed to become church members and receive the sacrament of communion. Pastors looked for more than an event; they wanted to see evidence of a *life* that had been converted to God.[25]

Conversion to holiness of life. As a process, therefore, conversion is supposed to have an effect—that is, engender holiness of life (or piety). The Pietist movement, which began in Germany in the seventeenth century, emphasized this particular aspect of conversion.[26] As devout Lutherans, Pietists believed that salvation comes through Christ alone, faith alone and grace alone, all of which we know through Scripture alone. But they did not stop there. Deeply aware of the problem of nominal religion that was rampant in the state church of Germany, especially after the bloody Thirty Years War (1618-1648), they also emphasized heartfelt faith and personal holiness. They believed that conversion *to* Christ implies living *for* Christ.

The most notable leader of the movement was Philipp Jakob Spener (1635-1705). Raised in a devout Lutheran home, Spener did not experience a dramatic conversion but instead imbibed the faith of his youth with little struggle or doubt. He eventually became a prominent minister in the German Lutheran church. His best known work, *Pia Desideria (Pious Desires)*, outlines his vision of the true Christian life. The Word of God was central to his vision. He believed that the Word should be put into the hands of laypeople, for it has power through the Holy Spirit to transform people's lives.[27] He also argued that laypeople should apply the teachings of the Bible to their daily lives. "The people must have impressed upon them and must accustom themselves to believing that it is by no means enough to have knowledge of the Christian faith, for Christianity consists rather of practice."[28] To encourage growth in personal holiness, he established *Collegia Pietas* ("Colleges of Piety") or small groups, which became one of the distinguishing features of the movement. Spener believed that true conversion requires more than assent to a creed; it mandates the cultivation of genuine faith and holiness of life.

Conversion to the world. Genuine conversion should inspire us to care about the world too, the world "for whom Christ died," as the apostle Paul put it. It is not simply *our* conversion that matters to God but the *world's* conversion. No group in the history of Christianity has taken this aspect of conversion more seriously than the Moravians, especially under the able leadership of Count Nicolaus Ludwig von Zinzendorf (1700-1760), a scion of one of the great families of Europe.[29] Like Spener, he showed signs of unusual devotion at a young age. After completing his formal education he embarked on a grand tour of Europe. During that tour he experienced a conversion of sorts, not to Christ, which he had already experienced, but to service. In the art museum of Düsseldorf he encountered Domenico Feti's famous painting *Ecce Homo* ("Behold, the man"), a portrait of Jesus wearing the crown of thorns. The inscription below the painting read, "I have done this for you; what have you done for me?" Zinzendorf knew that he had loved Jesus his whole life, but he realized in that moment that he had not served him yet.

In 1721 Zinzendorf purchased an estate in Saxony from his grandmother. By then his reputation as a devout Christian was already well known, which is probably what motivated Christian David, a Moravian refugee, to seek him out. He asked if Zinzendorf would grant him and a few fellow refugees asylum on his estate. Zinzendorf agreed to the request. In 1722 the first ten Moravians arrived and formed a community to which they gave the name Herrnhut. By 1726 their settlement—now including Catholics, Lutherans, separatists and Anabaptists as well as Moravians—had grown to three hundred members. Zinzendorf organized little "bands" for prayer and Bible study, drafted a constitution to regulate the life of the community and arranged for the election of twelve elders. Under Zinzendorf's leadership the community thrived and spread to other parts of Europe.

While visiting Copenhagen to attend the coronation of Christian VI, Zinzendorf met Anthony Ulrich, a former slave and new Christian from the island of St. Thomas, located in the West Indies. Ulrich pleaded with Zinzendorf to send missionaries to evangelize the slaves. Returning to Herrnhut, Zinzendorf shared the vision with the community and called them to earnest prayer and Bible study. A year later the community commissioned two missionaries, Leonard Dober and David Nitschman, to launch its first mission. By 1742, only ten years later, Herrnhut had already sent seventy missionaries to Greenland, the Guinea Coast of Africa, South

Africa, Algeria, Ceylon, Romania, and Constantinople, though the little community numbered only six hundred people. By 1760, the year Zinzendorf died, the Moravian Church had deployed 226 full-time missionaries around the world to preach the gospel and serve the needy.

Zinzendorf dedicated himself to obeying the Great Commission. Before being ordained into the ministry of the Lutheran church (he was later ordained as a minister in the Moravian Church too), Zinzendorf stated to the examining faculty of Tübingen:

> I shall go to distant nations, who are ignorant of Jesus and of redemption in His blood. I shall endeavor to imitate the labors of my brethren, who have the honor of being the first messengers to the heathen. . . . The love of Christ shall constrain me, and His cross refresh me. I will cheerfully be subject to the higher powers, and a sincere friend to my enemies.[30]

Like the Puritans, Zinzendorf understood conversion as a process, not simply an event. He learned from the Pietists that conversion should lead to holiness of life. But he also believed conversion called him—and the entire church—to the world.

These three movements—Puritanism, Pietism and Moravianism—established the foundation on which evangelical spirituality is built. Evangelicals call for personal commitment to Christ, though, unlike the Puritans, they often emphasize experience over process; they encourage holiness of life, though sometimes erring on the side of legalism; and, more than any other group in the history of Christianity, they pursue the task of world missions with unusual energy and conviction.

WHAT MAKES CONVERSION AUTHENTIC?

This emphasis on conversion, however, has created a problem in evangelical spirituality. How do we know what true conversion is? What makes it genuine? What if it fails to last? Many people who appear to have experienced a genuine conversion eventually return to their former way of life, as if they had experienced the spiritual equivalent of an adolescent romance that fades almost as quickly as it flares up. These reversals have forced evangelicals to clarify what makes a conversion authentic and why some conversions, though they appear to be sincere, fail to last.

One theologian in particular pondered this problem throughout his illustrious career. He became a major catalyst of the First Great Awakening in New England, which he subsequently reported on, analyzed, defended and explained to the wider public.[31] He is considered the greatest theologian America has produced. Born in 1703, Jonathan Edwards was the fifth of eleven children, and the only son.[32] He showed signs of deep religious devotion and keenness of intellect at a young age, and he experienced a conversion sometime after finishing his education at Yale College, which he recorded in his *Personal Narrative*.[33] After working as a tutor and pastor for several years, Edwards received a call in 1727 to the Congregational church of Northampton, Massachusetts, to serve as an assistant pastor under his famous grandfather, Solomon Stoddard, who had occupied the church's pulpit for fifty eight years. Edwards was soon asked to take his grandfather's place as the senior minister.

Edwards immediately set out to preach the gospel and call for conversion. A few years later he started to see dramatic changes in the church. Sobered by a few untimely deaths in the community, the members of his congregation began to take a serious interest in religion; they prayed more fervently, studied the Bible more diligently and conversed more freely about spiritual issues. Then, for six months, the church was swept up in a spiritual awakening. About three hundred people were converted in Edwards's church alone, and the awakening spread to other churches as well. Edwards continued to preach and provide pastoral care, doing his best to counsel the people who had been converted. But he also recorded his observations of the awakening, which he published in 1737 as *A Faithful Narrative of the Surprising Work of God*.

Edwards noted that people from all walks of life experienced conversion—young and old, rich and poor, wise and unwise, sober and dissolute. He also observed the pattern that the conversions seemed to follow—conviction of sin, commitment to live a better life, repeated failures, feelings of utter helplessness and guilt, and finally an experience of grace, which overwhelmed the converts with confidence, rapture and love. He was convinced that the awakening was the work of God.

This work of God, as it was carried on, and the number of true saints multiplied, soon made a glorious alteration in the town; so that in the spring and summer following, in 1735, the town seemed to be full of the presence of God: it never was so full of love, nor so full of joy; and yet so full of distress, as it was then. There was remarkable tokens of God's presence in almost every house.[34]

The awakening came to an abrupt end when Edwards's uncle committed suicide, two women in a nearby town went mad and people began to exhibit wild swings of emotion, from despair to elation. Criticism soon followed. Elites from Boston charged that the awakening was the product of religious "enthusiasm" (fanaticism or extremism), not genuine—that is, rational—faith. Edwards conceded that there were problems but still defended the awakening as genuinely supernatural. He wrote two subsequent books to clarify his position, *Distinguishing Marks of a Work of the Spirit of God* (1741) and *Some Thoughts Concerning the Present Revival of Religion in New England* (1742).

But even these books did not put the issue to rest for Edwards. The decline of zeal and eruption of conflicts in the church forced him to take up the question one last time. He wanted to define the nature of authentic conversion, or what he called "true religion." Why, he asked, do some people who seem to experience genuine conversion show so little evidence of it later on? Were they truly converted, he wondered, or did they just give the *appearance* of being converted? As a Calvinist, Edwards believed that salvation is, from beginning to end, God's work; God elects, calls, justifies, sanctifies and glorifies. Everything is the result of the divine initiative. Once saved, converts cannot lose their salvation, for God would not allow it. How could Edwards reconcile this belief with the disappointing aftermath of the awakening in Northampton? He wrote *Religious Affections* at least in part to answer this question.

His central argument is simple and elegant. "True religion, in large part, consists of holy affections."[35] Edwards defined the "affections" as a natural and intense reaction—whether positive or negative—to things of real consequence to us. We are thus strongly attracted to those things that are valuable to us; we are strongly repulsed by those things that are odious to us. By its very nature religion involves things that are profoundly significant and supremely consequential, for religion is concerned with the being of

God, who is ineffably glorious, beautiful and holy. It is impossible to claim to know such a being and not be overcome with delight, longing and love. Thus the only appropriate response is, as Edwards argued, "holy affections"—the intense inclination of the soul toward God. Such is the nature of true religion or conversion.

Edwards believed that these holy affections will be visible and obvious, like heat and light from a fire. But he was careful at this point to distinguish between signs that prove conversion is authentic and signs that prove nothing at all. Not all signs, however impressive, provide incontrovertible evidence of genuine conversion. This was true even in the case of

Jonathan Edwards, *Religious Affections*

"Gracious affections have efficacy, because of the transcendent excellence of divine things. These are intrinsic in themselves, and bear no conceived relation to self or to self-interest. It is this that causes men to be holy in all their practice. In turn this helps them to persevere all the time. For the nature of religion is invariably always the same, at all times, and through all changes. It never alters in any respect. The foundation of all holy affections is in moral excellence and the beauty of holiness. There is a love of holiness for its own sake that inclines people to practice holiness. Holiness is thus the main business that excites, draws, and governs all gracious affections. No wonder then that all such affections tend to holiness, for men will be united to and possessed by that which they love and desire."

the dramatic awakening in Northampton. On the one hand, Edwards identified intensity of emotion, "bodily exercises" (fainting or excessive weeping) and knowledge of doctrine as bogus signs, though he was quick to add that under certain circumstances these signs could still serve a useful purpose. On the other hand, Edwards identified sorrow over sin, delight in God, joy in life and endurance of faith, especially in the face of adversity, as legitimate signs. In the end, however, Edwards identified one sign as superior to all the rest. That sign is consistent *practice* of faith, which manifests itself in holiness of life, delight in God and love for neighbor. "Christian practice is much more to be preferred as evidence of salvation than sudden conversion, mystical enlightenment, or the mere experience of emotional comfort."[36] It is therefore the *outcome* of conversion—its impact on how we live, love and serve—that establishes the authenticity of conversion. "You will know them by their fruits," Jesus said.

Ironically, Edwards was not able to persuade his own congregation to accept his ideas. Many turned against him when he tried to exercise church discipline and protect the integrity of the Lord's Table. The conflict between Edwards and the congregation went on for several years, finally ending when the church asked him to leave. A year later, in 1751, he accepted a call to become a missionary to Indians in Stockbridge, Massachusetts. It was at this wilderness outpost that Edwards wrote his most mature works, including *Freedom of the Will* and *Original Sin*. By then his reputation as a great theologian was firmly established. In 1758 he was invited to serve as president of the College of New Jersey (later renamed Princeton). He died several months later from a smallpox vaccination.

WHO IS RESPONSIBLE FOR CONVERSION?

Edwards believed that he did not in any way plan or cause the awakening that swept through his church. He did nothing different in 1734 from what he had done in 1730 or would do in 1745. Yet something happened in those six months that transcended mere human effort. It was, as he said, a *surprising* work of God, the result of divine, not human, intervention. But many evangelicals who followed Edwards seemed to want less surprise. They turned conversion into a human enterprise, though never denying that it was a divine work too. Two changes occurred. First, evangelicals put increasing stress on the *experience* of conversion, believing that the intensity of the experience would somehow authenticate the reality of it. This led them to use methods that made conversion as predictable and convenient as possible. Second, they developed *strategies* to win and disciple converts, which turned evangelicalism in an entrepreneurial direction. Both experience and strategy became the distinguishing characteristics of evangelicalism in the nineteenth century.

Edwards probably saw the change coming. We catch a glimpse of his foresight in his evaluation of George Whitefield's preaching. While studying at Oxford, Whitefield (1714-1770) had fallen in with the Wesley brothers, joining their Holy Club. After experiencing a dramatic conversion at the age of nineteen, he began almost immediately to preach the gospel, often with dramatic results. It was not long before he expanded his evangelistic efforts to America (which he visited seven times). In 1740 Edwards invited the famous and flamboyant Whitefield to preach in his pulpit. By the time he arrived in Northampton, Whitefield was already well known throughout the colonies as a superb preacher and successful evangelist. He seemed to win countless people to Christ every time he opened his mouth. His impact in Northampton was sensational. Sarah Edwards

Whitefield preaching

mentioned the visit in her journal. "It is wonderful to see what a spell he casts over an audience. . . . I have seen upwards of a thousand people hang on his words with breathless silence, broken only by an occasional half-suppressed sob." Her husband agreed, noting, "the minds of the people in general appeared more engaged in religion, shewing a greater forwardness to make religion the subject of their conversation . . . and to embrace all opportunities to hear the Word preached."[37]

But Edwards had reservations too, which he expressed in a series of sermons he preached on the parable of the sower shortly after Whitefield had left. He noted that the transient nature of itinerancy tended to produce transient results—"sudden conversions are very often false," he said. He also expressed doubts about the spiritual efficacy of White-field's dramatic style because it drew too much attention to itself and appealed to those people—the "stony-ground," as Edwards called them—who embraced religion only when "exceedingly taken with the eloquence of the preacher" and "pleased with the aptness of expression, and with the fervency, and liveliness, and beautiful gestures of the preacher." Whitefield's style was apt to produce more hypocrites than true converts. In the end Edwards affirmed the role that Whitefield played, but his concerns anticipated changes in the evangelical movement that were about to occur.[38]

Experience. Whitefield's style appeared to prevail. His approach to ministry has influenced the evangelical movement ever since. Most of the well-known evangelists in the eighteenth and nineteenth centuries—including Whitefield—experienced dramatic conversions, which affected how they viewed conversion and how they operated as evangelists. Their autobiographical accounts reflect a highly experiential view of conversion. John Wesley's dramatic conversion became the prototype. John Wesley (1703-1791) grew up in a devout Anglican home.[39] He was ordained as an Anglican minister after studying at Oxford, where he and his brother organized Holy Clubs to encourage spiritual growth among the students. For close to ten years he preached, ministered to prisoners and served as a missionary in Georgia. Thus in every way he gave the impression of being a true Christian. But his conversion was still in the future.

While sailing to America, Wesley encountered a group of Moravians, who impressed him with their quiet, fervent faith. At one point during the voyage the ship ran into a squall that threatened to sink it. Everyone panicked, fearing death—except the Moravians, who calmly prayed and sang hymns. After arriving in Georgia he met Peter Boehler, also a Moravian, who became a spiritual mentor to him. Boehler observed Wesley's spiritual uneasiness and asked pointedly if he had assurance of faith. The question haunted Wesley. As he put it years later, he had gone to Georgia to save the Indians, but who, he asked, would save him? His failure in ministry and lack of victory over sin only exacerbated his doubts. "In this vile, abject state of bondage to sin," he wrote in his journal, "I was indeed fighting continually, but not conquering. . . . I fell, and rose, and fell again."[40]

The struggles continued after he returned to England. Once again, he looked to the Moravians for help. He experienced a conversion while listening to someone read from Luther's preface to the epistle to the Romans at a meeting of Moravians at Aldersgate (London). His conversion was sudden and emotional. "I felt my heart strangely warmed," he wrote in his journal. "I felt I did trust in Christ, Christ alone for salvation: And an assurance was given me, that he had taken away *my* sins, even *mine*, and saved *me*."[41] This kind of experience set the pattern for the millions of conversions that would follow. It is now commonplace for many—if not most—evangelicals to be able to identify the exact time and place of their conversion. They feel security and gain confidence because they have had an *experience* of conversion, which confirms the truthfulness of God's promise and the genuineness of their faith.

The importance of experience motivated the nineteenth-century American evangelist Charles G. Finney (1792-1875) to develop "new measures" to ensure that his evangelistic work would yield concrete results.[42] He conducted crusades in cities like Rochester, Philadelphia and New York that lasted up to six weeks. This prolonged exposure to the gospel created a sense of excitement that swelled the size of the crowds as the campaign progressed. He also dispatched volunteers to invite people to his crusades, reserved an "anxious bench" at the front of the auditorium for those who seemed ready to convert, and used laypeople—including women—to fill various leadership positions.[43] Finally, he urged converts to get involved in local churches after the campaign ended. In his famous book, *Lectures on Revivals of Religion*, he argued that a revival is not a miraculous occurrence, as Edwards had argued, but a natural one, the result of the proper use of the divinely ordained means. In short, he turned revivals into a scientific enterprise.

Strategy. Whitefield and his heirs used a variety of innovative techniques to win and disciple converts too. Whitefield led the way by becoming an itinerant, which proved to be an effective method of evangelism.[44] He turned the pulpit—or the platform, as was more often the case—into a kind of stage and captivated listeners with his dramatic style and winsome message. He was the first evangelical to try open-air preaching. It was not unusual for Whitefield to preach to crowds of five or even ten thousand people.[45]

Itinerancy suited Whitefield's personality and unusual gifts. But it also suited the evangelical movement. John Wesley spent fifty-three years traveling and preaching throughout England, often in open air. He preached some forty thousand sermons during his lifetime and traveled over a quarter million miles on horseback. He was a genius at making the gospel simple, understandable and compelling, which increased his effectiveness in reaching members of the English working class. His brother, Charles, advanced the cause by writing some 8,900 popular hymns. Together they built chapels and held midweek services to reach people who did not feel welcomed and comfortable in established churches.

John Wesley was a superb organizer as well. He adapted the structure of the Holy Club to nurture converts in the faith. Called "classes" in the Methodist movement, these small groups of twelve met regularly for confession of sin, Bible study, prayer, mutual accountability and strict discipline. Wesley was especially committed to the exercise of discipline. "Is it any wonder that we find so few Christians," he asked, "for where is Christian discipline? In what part of England is Christian discipline added to Christian doctrine? Now, wherever doctrine is preached, where there is no discipline, it cannot have its full effect upon its hearers." He even provided a list of questions that leaders were to use when members of the class gathered for their weekly meeting. "What known sins have you committed since our last meeting? What temptations have you overcome? How did God deliver you? What have you thought, said, or done that might be sinful?"[46]

Wesley appointed and trained laypeople to lead these classes, which generated a large supply of ready and able leaders as the movement expanded. Such was the *method* behind Methodism. In essence it turned his large-scale ministry of evangelism into a small-scale ministry of discipleship. Wesley also spelled out a theology of holiness that inspired new converts to mature in the faith; they in turn became willing volunteers for the various social reform societies that evangelicals founded in the early nineteenth century. These societies took up a wide range of benevolent causes—evangelism, foreign missions, Bible distribution, abolitionism, temperance, prison reform, suffrage, sabbath-day observance, care of wid-

ows and orphans, and so much more. In effect, Wesley and his followers
helped to build a kind of benevolent empire that expanded the ministry of
the church beyond its own narrow interests.[47]

EVANGELICAL SPIRITUALITY TODAY

The global impact of evangelical spirituality has been nothing short of astounding. Evangelicals have preached the gospel to literally hundreds of
millions of people, drawing many of them into the Christian fold, which
is why evangelicalism is the fastest growing Christian group in the world
today. At first Europeans (especially the British) and Americans dominated the movement. Throughout the nineteenth and early twentieth centuries they founded countless mission organizations to win the lost,
launched hundreds of voluntary societies to meet practical needs around
the world, inspired thousands of people—including many women—to use
their gifts for the cause of Christ, and supported the ministries of the high-
profile evangelists whose global impact epitomized the growing power of
evangelicalism. Dwight L. Moody became the most famous evangelist in
the late nineteenth century, preaching to tens of millions in England and
America; Billy Graham has been the most successful evangelist in history,
preaching to hundreds of millions around the world. We are profoundly
indebted to these European and American evangelicals for their courageous efforts. The Christian world will never be the same because of their
deep commitment to the truth of the gospel, to the authority of Scripture
and to innovative ministry.

But the movement has now gone global.[48] Since the early twentieth
century the most dynamic evangelical movement has been Pentecostalism,
which began at the Azusa Street revival (Los Angeles) in 1906 and now,
only one hundred years later, encircles the world. America produced the
seed of Pentecostalism, to be sure; but the world has become the soil. Pentecostalism has spawned thousands upon thousands of indigenous
churches in virtually every country around the globe. The growth of Pentecostalism demonstrates that non-Western Christians have in many ways
taken over leadership of the evangelical movement.

Two personal experiences illustrate this dramatic shift. In 2000 my children and I spent the summer in Nairobi, Kenya. I taught at a university

and my children did volunteer work at a Mother Teresa orphanage. On Sundays we worshiped at Nairobi Chapel, a thriving evangelical church that has, over the past decade, planted a dozen churches throughout the city and started other ministries, like medical clinics, in the city slums. The pastor, Oscar, told me that, while American Christians have money and organization, from which Africans can and do benefit, they are also materialistic, complacent and worldly. He wanted to set a course for his ministry that would avoid these problems.

In the winter of 2006 a leader of an evangelical ministry among the Kurds in Iraq visited the Whitworth University campus. He works cooperatively with Partners International, a mission agency headquartered in Spokane that develops strategic partnerships with indigenous ministries in areas of the world that are not always friendly to Westerners, especially to Americans. Pastor Yousif Matty experienced a dramatic conversion after serving in the Iraqi army during the Gulf War. Receiving a call from the Lord, he began to do evangelistic work among the Kurds. His ministry now plants churches, initiates community projects, operates Christian bookstores and runs three Christian schools. He is as zealous and entrepreneurial as that first generation of evangelicals, though he is not burdened with having to protect and preserve the future of Western civilization. Pastor Matty represents a new wave of evangelical leaders from the Majority World who are providing vision and energy for the evangelical movement.

Like Wesley and other early pioneers, this new generation of evangelicals is committed to conversion. It is not enough, they would say, to preach the message of salvation; we must also call people to *respond* to that message. But these leaders are equally committed to a holistic understanding of conversion, which is exactly what true conversion means. Conversion to Christ might be a singular event (say, at an evangelistic crusade). That is certainly where it often begins. But true conversion does not stop there. It demands that the whole of our lives—our marriages, our families, our minds, our pocketbooks, our schedules, our relationships, our jobs, our recreational interests, our struggles, our politics—be surrendered to God. It is an endless process. When Jesus called his disciples, he told them to deny themselves, take up the cross and follow him. As C. S. Lewis once wrote, God does not want something from us; he simply wants us. Once again, at the heart of evangelical spirituality is the conversion of the whole of our lives to God.

Newton's story illustrates the power of authentic conversion—his whole life was transformed by the gospel. His was a complete conversion, which is what conversion ought to be. Still, it was not something he could accomplish on his own, for it was beyond him. As he discovered, he could not achieve perfect genuineness or reach a point of total surrender or manifest the marks of "true religion." Nor did he have to. Newton's hymn, after all, is not about him, not even about conversion. It is about grace. God's grace found him, gave him sight, taught him to fear and relieved him of fear, delivered him from danger, and led him home. Grace promised him good and infused him with hope. Grace gave him the gift of eternal life. It was grace that converted him. Grace is powerful and perfect because it comes through Jesus Christ, God's Son, our Savior and our Lord.

PRACTICES

- Read John 3:1-21.
- Conversion should apply to the whole of our lives. C. S. Lewis once said that God does not want something *from* us; he simply wants us, *all* of us. Ponder the various dimensions of your life. What would it mean for you to surrender each of these areas to God? How would it affect your relationships? Use of money and time? Natural resources? Work and play?
- Meditate on Romans 12:1-2 every day for a week.

11

Risk

The Spirituality of Pioneer Missionaries

"Yet whatever gains I had, these I have come to
regard as loss because of Christ.
More than that, I regard everything as loss because of
the surpassing value of knowing Christ Jesus my Lord.
For his sake I have suffered the loss of all things, and I regard them as rubbish,
in order that I may gain Christ and be found in him."

PHIL 3:7-9

Pioneer missionaries are consummate risk-takers. They dare go to places the rest of us usually avoid, they reach out to groups the rest of us overlook, and they minister to needs the rest of us often ignore. They take these risks because of their single-minded devotion to Jesus Christ. They have a passion for Jesus and his kingdom that sets them apart. They love the God who took the ultimate risk by becoming a human being. God left the glory of his heavenly home and took up residence on earth, not as a great king but as a lowly baby. He identified so completely with humanity that most of his contemporaries had no idea who he really was. He sacrificed everything for us and our salvation, bridged the gap between heaven and earth, and translated divine truth into a language that all can understand. God not only acted on behalf of humanity; he also became human.[1] If we want to see the perfect example of risk-taking, all we have to do is read the Gospels.

The very idea of risk-taking brings to mind images of people who go to extreme measures to accomplish some great feat for God. We think of people who smuggle Bibles into countries hostile to Christianity or who found medical clinics in sprawling urban slums or who plant churches in remote areas of the world. This kind of work, we think, is for those fearless few who have a genetic predisposition for risky behavior. It certainly does not apply to those of us who prefer to live a quiet, normal life. I, for one, enjoy the comfort of my home, the love of friends who live close by and the security of a steady job. I am not very inclined to take risks.

But risk is inherent in the Christian faith, for Jesus himself commanded his followers to go into the world and to make disciples of all nations, which is bound to involve us in risky ventures, whether we travel to some remote part of the world to do mission work or cross the street to befriend a neighbor. A married, middle-aged colleague of mine recently started an evangelistic Bible study for several secular friends who want to know more about the Christian faith. Already he has become deeply involved in their lives. Likewise, a pastor friend decided a few years ago to explore the possibility of serving overseas for a summer. That set in motion a series of events that led his family not only to travel to Zambia for several months but also to adopt three Ethiopian children. If we take the Christian faith seriously, we will probably end up traveling somewhere or loving someone or trying something we would never have imagined at an earlier stage in our lives. It is simply what a life of discipleship requires.

A MISSIONARY FAITH

Christianity began as a missionary faith. Christ's entire mission was directed not only toward Jewish insiders but also toward Gentile outsiders. Jesus cared for the very people whom the Jewish leaders of his day dismissed or condemned, such as prostitutes, tax collectors and Samaritans.[2] When Jesus was accused of being a friend of tax collectors and sinners, he responded by telling the story of the lost sheep, lost coin and lost son (Lk 15). He reserved his sharpest criticism for Jewish leaders who refused to search for the lost. After his resurrection Jesus commanded his followers to carry on the same mission (Mt 28:16-20).

The church did not obey Jesus' command quickly or willingly. The first Christians were all Jews. Our earliest picture of the Christian movement in Jerusalem is of the first disciples huddled in the temple precinct, affiliating with Jewish culture, following Jewish customs and practicing Jewish rituals. It took persecution to force them out of Jerusalem, and even then it was Greek-speaking Jews (or Hellenists) who preached the gospel as they fled Jerusalem, not the Aramaic-speaking Jews, many of whom actually stayed behind. These Hellenists posed the greatest threat to traditional Judaism and proved to be the best missionaries to non-Jews. They started to evangelize people living outside Jerusalem, which included not only Jews but also Samaritans and Gentiles. Eventually they planted a church in Antioch, which became the center for Gentile Christianity. It was Barnabas, a Hellenist living in Antioch, who summoned Paul to help with the work there. Paul in turn became the most successful missionary in early Christianity. Reared in Tarsus, a Gentile city, yet trained in a rabbinic school in Jerusalem, Paul became the bridge between Jewish and Gentile cultures.

From what we can gather, the mission to the Gentiles challenged, even threatened, many Jewish Christians, who assumed that the mission would undermine the Jewish foundations on which Christianity was built. Hoping to keep the Christian movement in the womb of ancient Judaism, they wanted to force Gentile converts to become Jews first, which would have required them to submit to Jewish regulations like circumcision and dietary laws. Paul and his companions opposed these requirements, arguing that conversion to Jesus as Savior and Lord was enough. The two parties finally convened a Council in Jerusalem to decide as a community what was best for the church. Jewish leaders listened attentively—and probably skeptically—as Peter told the story of his work among the Gentiles and Paul reported the results of his missionary travels into Gentile territory. James, the Lord's brother and the leader of the church in Jerusalem, spoke for the consensus of those gathered when he argued that the gospel mandates only one conversion, which is to Christ. Conversion to Judaism was therefore unnecessary (Acts 15). This one decision set a trajectory for the entire movement. That people do not have to be converted to a dominant culture first before becoming Christians, be it Jewish, Roman or European, has allowed missionaries to adapt the gospel message to a wide variety of cultures.[3]

Christian missionaries have followed this principle for centuries.[4] They have tried to adapt the Christian faith to particular cultures by learning the local language, adjusting to cultural norms and presenting the Christian faith in a culturally accessible yet theologically uncompromising way. This missionary endeavor has continued for two millennia, unfolding in four basic phases.[5] The first phase began when pioneers introduced the Christian faith to Greco-Roman culture. The apostle Paul served as the primary catalyst. He and his coworkers planted dozens of churches in the Roman Empire. These fledgling churches continued to grow and multiply over the next few hundred years. By the middle of the second century Christianity began to attract the attention of pagan intellectuals who were curious about this peculiar, suspect faith. Luminaries like Justin Martyr, Clement of Alexandria and Origen found common ground (e.g., Greek philosophy) with pagan elites in order to explain the Christian faith in terms that made cultural sense to them. They laid the foundation for what is known today as the "orthodox" faith, which the Nicene Creed (A.D. 325, 381) and Chalcedonian formula (A.D. 451) summarize so well.[6]

The evangelization of Germanic and Viking tribal groups constitutes the second phase. In the year 410 the Visigoths marched through Italy and sacked the city of Rome. Over the next century these migrant groups conquered the empire. Another wave of invasions—this time led by the Vikings—occurred in the ninth and tenth centuries. Far from being intimidated or defeated, Christian missionaries launched a major campaign to win these groups to the faith. These efforts were spearheaded by monks who journeyed into hostile territory, built monasteries, learned languages, started schools and won whole tribes to Christianity. This process of evangelization took centuries. Europe became the new center of Christianity, and remained so for a millennium. We still see evidence of Christianity throughout Europe, especially in the number of church buildings that dominate the landscape, though many of these churches now stand virtually empty.[7]

The third phase began as a result of the Reformation, which turned the missionary task of the church into a competitive enterprise, pitting many

Christian groups against each other. Lutherans, Calvinists, Anabaptists, Anglicans and Roman Catholics all vied to win Europe to their cause. Competition motivated Christian groups to use more aggressive strategies to capture people's loyalty. It is no surprise, therefore, that the Reformers produced materials—pamphlets, sermons, confessions, catechisms, devotionals—that would help people to understand and believe the faith. These strategies became useful when Christian groups launched mission work in fields beyond Europe, an effort that was spearheaded by the Jesuits (on the Catholic side) and Moravians (on the Protestant side).

In the fourth phase the Christian movement became truly global, as it was at the very beginning. A handful of zealous and visionary leaders founded organizations—religious orders, in the case of the Roman Catholic Church, and voluntary societies, in the case of the Protestant church—to spread Christianity beyond the European world. In the sixteenth and seventeenth centuries Jesuits, Franciscans and Dominicans labored in many parts of the world to win non-Europeans to Christianity. They were especially successful in South America. Protestants embraced the same cause two hundred years later, largely as a result of the First and Second Great Awakenings in Britain and the United States. Protestant missionary entrepreneurs like William Carey and Hudson Taylor, both British, started dozens of "societies" (the Baptist Missionary Society, the London Missionary Society and China Inland Mission, to name only three) to win unreached people for Christ, especially in Africa and Asia.[8] Americans started similar kinds of organizations.[9] These societies recruited and deployed thousands of missionaries to travel to distant lands to plant churches, translate the Bible, start medical clinics and schools, and launch other ministries. Their efforts spawned hundreds of new indigenous denominations in Majority World countries that have long since become independent from the West. This indigenization process has been so significant that some missiologists believe it marks the fifth phase of the expansion of the Christian movement.

MISSIONARY DEVOTION

The willingness to take risks requires an unusual kind of devotion. How do pioneers sustain themselves in their work, considering the sacrifices they make, the isolation and loneliness they feel, and the misunderstandings that arise as a result of their mission work? Where do they find the courage to take so many risks and sacrifice so much? Not surprisingly, their risk-taking is inspired by a single-minded devotion to God. One man in particular, Ignatius of Loyola (d. 1556), the founder of the Jesuits, actually developed a set of spiritual practices that helped to cultivate such devotion.

Born and raised in Spain, Ignatius aspired to be a knight. While fighting in a battle he received a serious wound from which it took months to recover. During his convalescence he began to read the Bible, biographies of the saints and classics of spirituality, like *The Imitation of Christ*. These writings led him to devote his life to the service of Christ. Over the next several years he meditated on the life and teachings of Christ, repented of his sin and offered himself to God. He traveled too, finally ending up in Paris, where he studied for seven years. While living in Paris he began to

attract followers. They intended to go on a pilgrimage to the Holy Land, but circumstances would not allow it. So they traveled to Rome instead and submitted themselves to the pope. After careful negotiation and planning, the pope approved of the new religious order in 1540.

Religious orders in Ignatius's day used some variation of the Rule of St. Benedict, which applied to the settled life of the monastery. But Ignatius wanted to send people out. So he wrote a series of spiritual exercises for mis-

Ignatius

sionaries on the move. Ignatius designed them to be used as a manual for training that could be completed in four weeks. The focus of the first week is on confession and repentance, the second week on the life and teachings of Jesus, the third week on the events of Holy Week, the fourth week on the resurrection and the promise of heaven. The exercises make no mention of the Divine Office, traditional vows, corporate worship, liturgical prayers and monasteries. Instead, they provide instructions that a spiritual director can use to guide a disciple through a process of serious reflection and submission.[10]

Ignatius wanted to probe the depths of the soul so that "if such a soul has any inordinate inclinations or attachments, it will be most useful for it to work as forcefully as possible to attain the contrary of that to which the present attachment leads."[11] This strategy was intended to engender an unbendable, unalterable, unshakeable devotion to the will of God and to

The Spiritual Exercises of St. Ignatius

"In every good choice, in so far as it depends upon us, the direction of our intention should be simple. I must look only to the end for which I am created, that is, for the praise of God our Lord and for the salvation of my soul. Therefore, whatever I choose must have as its purpose to help me to this end. I must not shape or draw the end to the means, but the means to the end. Many, for example, first choose marriage, which is a means, and secondarily to serve God our Lord in the married state, which service of God is the end. . . . These individuals do not go straight to God, but want God to come straight to their inordinate attachments. Acting thus, they make a means of the end, and an end of the means, so that what they ought to seek first, they seek last. My first aim, then, should be my desire to serve God, which is the end, and after this, to seek a benefice or to marry, if it is more fitting for me, for these things are but means to the end. Thus, nothing should move me to use such means or to deprive myself of them except it be only the service and praise of God our Lord and the eternal salvation of my soul." (Trans. Anthony Mottola)

"the salvation of our soul."[12] The exercises he designed challenged would-be Jesuits to take their sin and God's gift of salvation with absolute seriousness, break them of bad habits and idolatry, and prepare them for a lifetime of sacrificial service. Ignatius wrote guidelines for decision-making too. In his mind, the most important decisions concern the basic direction of a person's life. In short, Ignatius hoped that his exercises would enable members of the order to organize their entire life around the will of God and to make their commitment to God absolute and resolute.

His vision succeeded beyond what anyone could have imagined. The biography of Jean de Brébeuf serves as a good example. Born and raised in France, Brébeuf (1593-1649) joined the Jesuits as a young man. In 1625 he was dispatched to North America to do mission work among the Huron natives. His work succeeded and thus attracted attention in Europe. Concerned that potential recruits might be seduced by the adventurous stories they were hearing, he wrote a letter to warn them about the dangers and difficulties they would face if they took up mission work among the Native American tribes. He tried to discourage anyone who had a romanticized view of the mission. Though the Huron, he said, would welcome them, "there is enough to greatly cast down a heart not well under subjection [to God]." Their readiness, he wrote, "does not shorten the road, does not smooth down the rocks, does not remove the dangers." Providing a detailed account of what daily life would be like for them, he said that in the summer the sun would burn them and mosquitoes, flies and fleas would drive them half mad; in the winter the cold would chill them to the bone. They would have to go without food for long periods of time and sleep on the ground, exposed to the elements. Once arriving at a village, they would have to live in a hut, "so mean that I have scarcely found in France one wretched enough to compare with it." It would take months, if not years, to learn the language, and even then they would know just enough to "stammer a little."[13]

Still, Brébeuf loved the Huron. In a second letter, therefore, he reminded recruits that the Huron were beloved of God. In language that is astonishingly tender (in spite of Brébeuf's use of the word *savage*), he wrote, "You must have sincere affection for the Savages,—looking upon them as ransomed by the blood of the son of God, and as our brethren, with whom we are to pass the rest of our lives." Brébeuf took his own counsel seriously. For years he faced unspeakable hardship, frustration and failure. But he carried on with perseverance, continued to serve the Huron and adapted to the culture. Eventually his efforts began to produce results. Many Huron were converted to the Christian faith. His work was cut short, however, when he was captured by the Iroquois, enemies of the Huron and the French, tortured and executed.[14]

MAKING SACRIFICES

Protestants exhibited that same kind of devotion when they began their work in the early nineteenth century. They took risks—often very costly—to introduce the Christian faith to peoples that stood outside the Christian fold.[15] The first and most obvious risk entailed the willingness to sacrifice what seemed most precious to them—the familiar world of home, family, friends, even country—to launch a new work. The stories of their sacrifices might offend our modern sensibilities, for many of these pioneers seemed all too willing (and even eager) to sacrifice marriage, children, friendships, health, wealth and reputation for the sake of their missionary work, which runs contrary to our inclination to see faith as an ally of those values. Consequently, it is natural for us to accuse them of being foolish and fanatical. If they were able to defend themselves, I am sure that they would say that they were only doing what Jesus did, who left his heavenly home to do his earthly ministry. Sacrifice, they would say, is inherent in the Christian faith, and they would quote the Bible to make their point, saying that true believers must be willing to give up houses, parents, brothers and sisters to follow Jesus.[16]

C. T. Studd was one such missionary. His life story provides a dramatic account of unspeakable sacrifice. Charles Thomas Studd (1862-1931)—always known as C. T. Studd—grew up with his two older brothers in English privilege.[17] He was considered the best English athlete of his day, and he traveled throughout the British Empire to compete. Cricket was his life, but it also became his idol, undermining his spiritual commitment. Attending a Dwight L. Moody crusade, however, he experienced a renewal of faith. "There the Lord met me again and restored to me the joy of His salvation."[18] Studd soon sensed he was called to serve as a missionary to China. His family opposed him, an experience that he likened to Moses' exile in the wilderness, but he forged ahead, committing himself, with six other high-profile Cambridge students, to become "Chinamen" for Christ. Known as "the Cambridge Seven," they became examples to thousands of students of choosing purpose over privilege.[19]

Studd journeyed into the interior of China, where he was forced to walk "with God alone" and use "native things only."[20] While in China he also inherited a small fortune, which his father's will had bequeathed to him when he reached the age of twenty-five. Following the example of his hero, Hudson Taylor, perhaps the greatest pioneer missionary to China, he gave away every shilling, trusting in God for the money he would need to do his missionary work. Studd also met his future wife in China, Priscilla Livingston Stewart, who was as devoted to missions as he was. Though passionately in love, they subordinated their relationship to their missionary calling because, as they said, "there is no abiding city." They married several months later on the coast of China in "a pilgrim's wedding." Their marriage took on a similar character.[21] Priscilla soon gave birth to five daughters. She refused to use a physician during the births because she did not want to interrupt the mission work, and she paid a price for it. But even the death of a daughter did not mitigate her commitment. "I made a covenant with my God that I was not going to let sorrow of any kind come into my life and ruin my life as a missionary. I was not going to let my husband see sorrow that would unhinge him. He never saw a tear when he came back."[22]

In 1900 the family moved to India, where Studd served as a pastor. They returned to England in 1908. Over the next year Studd became interested in what he called "the heart of Africa." Awakened by a clever and provocative advertisement in a newspaper—"Cannibals Want Missionaries!"—he sensed that God was calling him to be a missionary there. He had no organization, no money and no support, not even, at least initially, from his wife. Yet he sailed for Africa alone in 1910. (Priscilla did join him later, though not for long; she spent most of her time in England, running the home office.) Settling in southern Sudan, he launched an evangelistic ministry and founded a missionary organization, Heart of Africa (later renamed Worldwide Evangelization Crusade). It was grueling work. "Oh, the agony of it!" he wrote to his wife. "The being looked down upon by the world folk! The poverty! And have I not been tempted? Tempted to stop working for Christ! Doctors! Relatives! Family! Christians!"[23] Still, he ventured ever deeper into the interior of Africa, eventually eyeing the Belgian Congo as territory for his pioneering work. As if hearing God speak, Studd asked himself, "Dare you go back to spend the remainder of your days in England, knowing of these masses who have never heard of Jesus Christ? If you do, how will you meet Me henceforth before My Throne?"

He was filled with resolve. "That settled the matter. After such a word it was impossible to have the pluck to stay in England."[24]

Studd aspired to live what he described as a "reckless Christianity."[25] He relied on God to meet all his needs, even refusing to ask for money so that he would be forced to trust in God alone. Just before leaving for Africa he coined the phrase that would become the mission statement of his organization. "If Jesus Christ be God and died for me, then no sacrifice can be too great for me to make for Him." Every member of his team was required to pay the same price, including his wife. Aware of the sacrifices she was making, he wrote to her, "You little dream of how I know that you pay the greatest price, only I did not dare say so to you, but I do admire you, darling, and shall ever do so, and God will give us His hundredfold, and the result and honour must ever be according to the magnitude of the sacrifice."[26]

Studd's commitment to the mission was absolute and inflexible. No sacrifice was too great, not even the sacrifice of his own family. Over the last thirteen years of his life Studd saw his wife for only two weeks (three of his daughters joined him in Africa after they were married). At first Priscilla struggled with severe heart problems, perhaps masking the disappointment, even resentment, she felt toward her husband and the mission. She was confined to bed rest for months. But her husband showed little sympathy. After visiting England on a short furlough, he returned to Africa alone, leaving Priscilla at home, still bedridden. She experienced a deep renewal of faith the very next day, climbed out of bed and resolved to carry on the work of the mission at home.[27] She died in 1929, two years before her husband did. When Studd died, one of his sons-in-law, Norman Grubb, became the director of the mission.[28]

Studd seemed well suited for the work. He translated the Bible into local languages, planted a series of mission stations and adjusted quite easily to the harsh conditions of the jungle. He trekked thousands of miles, carried on a voluminous correspondence and preached several times a week. He lived as much like the native population as he could. When his health declined, he started to use morphine, to which he gradually became addicted. Toward the end of his life he hardly slept. It was not unusual for him to work eighteen-hour days, yet he refused to slow down. "Here is a land and a people to whom the Blessed Name has never been known throughout all time. Shall we leave them thus? We will not. We will sell our pottage and buy therewith our birthright to declare the glory of God to his people."[29]

But effort alone was not enough. He witnessed many failures and disappointments. Tribal people resisted the gospel, coworkers resented his demands, the home office accused him of fanaticism and mismanagement. The morale of the mission reached its nadir when Studd dismissed his own daughter and son-in-law, Edith and Alfred Buxton, from the mission because they did not appear to be committed. Studd referred to those years as his Gethsemane. His cross became "heavy beyond endurance." He was "fainting under it." "My heart seems worn out and bruised beyond repair, and in my deep loneliness I often wish to be gone."[30] But Studd would not yield or quit. If anything, he became ever more radical, even fanatical. He wrote a booklet on missions, "D.C.D.," which read in part, "I want to be one of those who *doesn't care a damn* except to give my life for Jesus and souls." One phrase, *Doesn't Care a Damn*, stirred quite a controversy at home, as did rumors of his addiction to morphine, his extremism and his intolerance.[31]

In 1925, however, the original vision of the mission was "reborn" at a prayer meeting. That prayer meeting became an important milestone in the history of the mission. "From that time to this there has been no check on the field to the unity, love, joy in sacrifice, zeal for the souls of the people, which has laid hold of the Crusades in the Heart of Africa."[32] The change was noticeable. The missionaries who still remained in the organization became as unflagging as Studd himself. The church grew too, in both numbers and depth of faith. His success seems unfathomable. He and his coworkers built churches that seated up to one thousand, and saw them filled. Upward of two thousand people would gather to hear "Bwana" preach when he was visiting a village. The organization expanded its operation into other countries, yet it never paid anyone a salary. Some forty missionaries joined the Crusade. But the strain was too much for Studd. His health continued to decline, though he worked to the very end. He died in 1931. Some two thousand natives attended his funeral. Yet the final word at the funeral was not about Studd but about the mission. "Never would we lower the standard shown in the Word! Never would we break the fellowship in the Gospel! Never would we cease our labours for the furtherance of the Gospel!"[33]

However extreme, Studd's story illustrates how much pioneer missionaries are willing to sacrifice. Studd failed to make much use of his prestigious education, gave up his inheritance and cultural privilege, and even abandoned his family because he was so devoted to the mission. His behavior seems—and probably was—fanatical. But in Studd's mind it was simply what pioneer work required. As a member of the first generation of missionaries working in the interior of Africa, he planted many churches in an area of the world that was both remote and exotic, at least in the eyes of the West. Such a feat is not unusual for zealous pioneers, no matter how great the cost, whether to themselves or to their loved ones. The second generation makes sacrifices too, but often in more measured ways, choosing instead to consolidate what the first generation started. Thus after Studd's death his son-in-law Norman Grubb inherited a mission that was in disarray, but he brought order and organization to it; he also imposed more realistic standards.

Studd's story raises a question about the role of sacrifice in the Christian faith. As Christians know, the greatest sacrifice has already been made— Christ's sacrifice on the cross, which has set us free from *having* to make sacrifices to earn our salvation but which also summons us to *want* to make sacrifices as an expression of gratitude to God and love for others. The degree of the sacrifice as well as the kind of sacrifice will vary, depending on context and calling. Some will work in the slums of Africa, others will raise a large family; some will take on a job that pays a low salary, others will make lots of money and give most of it away. There is no absolute rule to follow here, no perfect standard against which to measure both quality and quantity of sacrifice. Comparisons are simply out of the question. Only one truth applies to all: the ultimate sacrifice we make should be the whole of ourselves to God. And then we should simply let life take its course. "I appeal to you therefore, brothers and sisters, by the mercies of God, to present your bodies as a living sacrifice, holy and acceptable to God, which is your spiritual worship" (Rom 12:1).

CROSSING CULTURAL BARRIERS

A second risk involved building a bridge between cultures, which often made these Protestant pioneers feel like outsiders in both, cut off from home yet not entirely comfortable in the field. Consequently, they became like citizens who have no country, sojourners who have no home. The story of Mary Slessor provides an excellent example. On the one hand, she served as an effective bridge between British culture and tribal Africa; on the other hand, she became a virtual stranger to people in her native Scotland yet never became truly African either.

Mary Slessor (1848-1915) grew up in a working class home in Dundee, Scotland. Her father was an alcoholic, and he died when she was young. She was forced to quit school and work in a textile factory. Though a "wild lassie" during her childhood, as she described herself, she came to faith through the witness of a family friend who warned her of eternal judgment.[34] Slessor immediately became active in a street ministry. "Even then," her biographer, W. P. Livingston, notes, "she was unconventional in her methods and was criticized for it."[35] She visited homes, roused children to attend Sunday services and witnessed in the factory where she worked. People warmed to her almost immediately and came under the spell of her quiet charisma, though she was "only a working-girl, plain in appearance and in dress, diffident and self-effacing."[36]

During the fourteen years she worked in the factory, she became increasingly fascinated by a region in Africa known as Calabar (Nigeria), her eyes "fixed on the great struggle going on between the forces of light and darkness in the sphere of heathenism."[37] The original mission was planted there in 1846. Missionaries described the natives as bloody, savage, cruel, sensuous, devilish and cannibalistic. It was the perfect place for the fiery Slessor. "Not an attractive people to work amongst," comments W. P. Livingston, but then he adds, "Neither must the dwellers of earth have appeared to Christ who He looked down from heaven ere He took his place in their midst. And Mary Slessor shrank from nothing which she thought her Master would have done." She knew that her family and church needed her in Scotland, but she realized that "down in the slums of Africa there were millions who knew no more of the redemptive power of Christ than did the beasts of the field."[38] Her friends warned her that it was "the white man's grave," which was all the more reason, in Slessor's mind, for investing her life there. "Her reply to questioners was that Calabar was the post of danger, and was therefore the post of honour. Few would volunteer for service there, hence she wished to go, for it was there the Master needed her."[39] When her brother John, who was planning to serve as a missionary to Calabar, backed out due to fragile health (he died a few months later), Slessor volunteered and received approval from the mission board. She sailed in 1876.

She spent her first tenure of service on the coast. She was horrified by the brutality of the tribal social customs she observed—the virtual enslavement of women, twin murder (natives considered twins a sign of a demonic curse), polygamy, justice by ordeal. She believed that "it was the duty of the missionary to bring about a new set of conditions in which it would be pos-

Mary Slessor and adopted children

sible for the converts to live, and the thought influenced her whole after-career."[40] But she was equally concerned about, if not bitter toward, "the civilized countries that seek profit from the moral devastation of humanity."[41]

Still, she was not satisfied until she could penetrate ever deeper into the interior, where the Okoyong lived, a people from whom other missionaries had recoiled. Thus began the most important phase of her missionary work. For all practical purposes she became a virtual ruler among the various Okoyong tribes, mediating between the "civilized" West (British colonial rule) and "primitive" Africa (the tribes among whom she lived). She built a mission house, a school and a church, and she rescued dozens of abandoned, orphaned or endangered children, sometimes even adopting them. She often intervened on behalf of people falsely accused, cared for wives who were abused or neglected in the harem, confronted superstition and sorcery, opposed the use of alcohol, and combated tribal warfare. So adept was she at intervening in tribal affairs that the British government actually appointed her to supervise the tribal court. She introduced certain trades among the Okoyong too, which helped them establish a more economically lucrative relationship with the British.

Her contact with the British, however, did little to persuade her to change her way of life. She rarely wore hat and shoes, and she never boiled the water or used mosquito netting. She adjusted to the constant infestation of rats and ants, the presence of throngs of people, including her adopted children, and the threat of deadly disease. "These habits," explains Livingston:

> so seemingly eccentric to people lapped in the civilized order of things, had grown naturally out of the circumstances into which she had been forced in pursuit of the task she had set herself. She had deliberately given up everything for her Master, and she accepted all the consequences that the renunciation involved. . . . The one thing essential to her was her work, and anything that hampered her freedom of action was dropped.[42]

Slessor labored for nearly a decade before the first native, Akom, became a Christian. It was fifteen years before the first Communion service was held; even then only seven natives were received into the membership of the church. But her school began to produce young Christian leaders who taught in other mission schools. She attracted new missionaries too, predominantly female, who assumed leadership in mission stations that Slessor had started before moving deeper into the interior. Friends in Scotland begged her to return home, suggesting that she had done enough and needed to let others take over, "but she gazed into the interior, towards vast regions as yet unentered, and saw there the gleam of the Divine Light leading her on, and she turned with a happy sigh to follow it."[43]

If Slessor faced a frustration, it was not native resistance but the indifference of people back home who did not—and probably could not—grasp the significance of her work. She wondered why the lack of interest, especially among clergy, whom she found unwilling even to consider the mission field. "Oh Britain, surfeited with privilege! Tired of Sabbath and Church, would that you could send over to us what you are throwing away!"[44] Slessor did not realize how far and fast she had advanced, forcing the church back home to catch up. "It is a striking picture this, of the restless little woman ever forging her way into the wilderness and dragging a great Church behind her."[45]

In the last decade of her life she continued on the same course. But her health began to deteriorate, from both exhaustion and disease. She died on the mission field at the age of sixty-six, surrounded by her "bairns," the African children she had adopted. She started a movement that produced a church of ten thousand people, with a Communion roll of 3,400, to say nothing of a more prosperous economy, significant advances in the judicial system, peace among many of the tribes and new social customs that protected the lives of the innocent, such as twins and slaves.

Slessor played a unique missionary role. Part British, part African, she functioned as a bridge between cultures, yet never belonged to either one. She served as an evangelist, teacher, judge, diplomat and business entrepreneur, all roles that Europeans could recognize and endorse. But she lived like an African. She had changed too much to return to her homeland; yet she could never adapt enough to become truly African. Besides, her purpose was to *change* Africa, not conform to it, which required her to accommodate just enough to introduce Christian faith and values.

Slessor's experience is rare, but perhaps not as rare as it would seem. Many Christians function as a bridge between worlds, though often in settings much closer to home. Any time believers attempt to cross a cultural barrier for the sake of the gospel, they run the risk of living in a kind of cultural no man's land. A former student of mine works with street kids. For a time he spiked his hair, died it yellow, blue and red, and wore leather and chains. His behavior alienated people from his host church, yet he never quite managed to become a street kid either. Nor did he want to. Like Slessor, he entered their world to earn their trust and to win them to Christ.

TRANSLATING THE MESSAGE

A third risk involved the actual "translation" of the Christian message into terms people could understand, which required these pioneers to indigenize Christianity without at the same time compromising its essential message.[46] Such work was—and is—messy and complex, fraught with difficulty, and it often led to confusion and misunderstanding. It was easy for missionaries to disappoint everyone—supporters back home, who were inclined to evaluate missionaries in the light of their own cultural values, and the indigenous people they were trying to reach, who often rejected the Christian message, at least initially, because it appeared to threaten traditional cultural values. This kind of risk is inevitable whenever we take on the monumental task of translating the Christian message. That we should try is written into the very message itself, for the incarnation is the quintessential example of translation. That we will encounter difficulty along the way is bound to occur too. Even Jesus caused confusion; though he was God, he did not seem to be what people expected God to be.

William Carey (1761-1834) excelled in this task of cultural translation. Born into a lower-class English home, Carey received little formal education and suffered from poor health. He learned the cobbler's trade, married young and, when his wife, Dorothy, started bearing children, supplemented his income by tutoring poor, unruly students. He experienced an evangelical conversion in his late teen years, joined a Baptist church and served as a lay preacher. Early on in his life he became fascinated with exotic places. He began to learn languages (Greek, Latin, French, Dutch and Hebrew), to read books about faraway places (*Captain Cook's Voyages* was his favorite), to study world maps and to master the basic facts

William Carey

of world geography. He also developed the quality of being dogged and persistent. He once wrote to a cousin, "I can plod. I can persevere in any definite pursuit. To this I owe everything."[47]

His conversion to Christ and his interest in exotic places eventually converged, awakening in him a passion for world missions. He suggested to his Baptist colleagues that they form a missionary society. Much to his surprise, leaders in his own church opposed him. Said one elderly man to him—"Young man, sit down, sit down! You are an enthusiast. When God pleases to convert the heathen, he'll do it without consulting you or me"—to which Carey responded, "Was not the command given to the Apostles, to teach all nations, obligatory on all succeeding ministers to the end of the world, seeing that the accompanying promise was of equal extent?"[48] In 1792 he wrote "An Enquiry into the Obligations of Christians, to Use Means for the Conversion of Heathens . . ."—one of the earliest, clearest and greatest defenses of the Great Commission ever written. His efforts finally led to the founding of the Baptist Missionary Society, which in very short order commissioned Carey to serve as its first missionary to India. The obstacles he faced were formidable. He had no money, no organization, no formal education and no training. England's East India Company did not want missionaries there because mission work threatened to disrupt its commercial interests.[49] His father called him mad; his church objected; his wife, five months pregnant, refused to go.

But Carey left anyway. "Expect great things from God," he said. "Attempt great things for God."[50] He landed in Calcutta five months later. His first years in India were miserable. He (and his family, which joined him later on) suffered the ravages of disease and lived in virtual poverty. He had to work as a manager of an indigo plant to make money. A son died of dysentery and his wife, Dorothy, gradually slid into a depressed and delusional state from which she never fully recovered. But he persisted in faith and continued with the work. "Well, I have God, and his word is sure," he recorded in his journal. "For a long time my mouth has been shut, and my days have been beclouded with heaviness; but now I begin to be something like a traveler who has been almost beaten out in a violent storm, and who, with all his clothes about him dripping wet, sees the sky begin to clear."[51]

Other missionaries finally arrived, which allowed Carey to devote more time to the study of Indian languages and culture. He mastered Bengali and Sanskrit, and translated the Bible into those—and eventually other—languages. He started schools and a college, and he began to win a few converts who responded to Carey's winsome message about Christianity, which he portrayed as a positive alternative to the religions of India. Still, he paid a huge price for his work. He lost two of his wives and several children. A fire ravaged his library and printing business, wiping out much of his translation work. His mission board in England, far removed from the work, withdrew support on several occasions, and fellow missionaries betrayed him. It is a wonder that he remained in India as long as he did. Yet remain he did, for forty-one years, never once returning to England.

Carey decided that if his mission work was to succeed, he would have to study the culture before he tried to win it to Christ. So he became an "Orientalist," as it was called then, a scholar of Indian culture. He and his colleagues learned dozens of languages and translated the entire Bible into six of them—Bengali, Oriya, Marathi, Hindi, Assamese and Sanskrit—and parts of the Bible into twenty-nine others, an astounding achievement. "It is this breadth of vision of making God's Word available to all mankind in its own tongue," his biographer argues, "that is Carey's chief glory."[52] But his study of the culture went far beyond the mastery of languages. He read Indian literature and translated its most important pieces into Bengali, Sanskrit and English. Ironically, this self-educated man eventually received an appointment as a college professor because of his erudition. "It would not be an exaggeration to say," concludes Drewery, "that the Serampore missionaries [his team] contributed to the renaissance of Indian literature in the nineteenth century."[53]

Carey's strategy was risky. The Christianity he knew was European, defined by the Church of England and the Baptists, both English-born and English-bred denominations. The Bible he read was in English, the religious rituals he practiced were English, and the theological tradition he believed in was English. But he dared to engage Indian culture on its own terms. People who take on the task of translation often face significant opposition, and not always from the outsiders they are trying to reach either. Insiders are not always eager to engage in or accept the work of translation, for it requires a willingness to adapt to the needs of outsiders who would otherwise not fit in. Insiders must therefore evaluate—and perhaps change—how they worship, how they talk about God, how they define their belief system, how they live in the world. The work of translation, therefore, is often as disruptive and threatening to established communities of faith as it is to the outsider groups that pioneers are trying to win.

These early pioneer missionaries succeeded beyond their wildest dreams. For example, in 1800 roughly 2 percent of the world's Christians were non-European; today it is close to 70 percent. Western Christianity was dominant for centuries; but now non-Western Christianity is ascendant, while the West appears to be in decline.[54] Churches planted by Western missionaries have asserted their independence and have developed their own unique identity. Several non-Western countries, such as South Korea and India, have surpassed every country in the world in the size of their missionary force except the United States.

The ministry of Christian Outreach Fellowship (COF) is a good example. It was founded in Ghana in the 1980s to advance the gospel, not only in Ghana but also in Ivory Coast, Togo and Burkina Faso. COF missionaries plant churches, equip leaders, provide vocational training and initiate microenterprise projects. Over the past twenty-five years missionaries have planted over 250 churches and built 10 vocational training centers. Its new director, Emmanuel Anukun-Dabson, who was converted to the Christian faith from an animistic background, visited Whitworth University last year. Students were impressed by his passion for the gospel, joyful countenance, knowledge of the Bible and vision for ministry. They had never met anyone quite like him before. Emmanuel represents the new wave of pioneer missionaries from the Two-Thirds (or Majority) World who have not been affected—or infected—by the problems of Western theological controversies and cultural privilege. His ministry demonstrates that the indigenization process that began with the Jerusalem Council has prevailed. The Christian message is translatable; it can make—and in many cases has made—a home in every culture.[55] That has been true in every phase of the missionary movement; it is, in fact, inherent in the Christian worldview.

SINGLE-MINDED DEVOTION

What drove these missionaries to take such risks? What inspired them to sacrifice so much? If we want to understand the motivation of these pioneers, we must read their journals, which contain extensive reflections on their faith. Two pioneer missionaries come to mind, both of whom died young and left behind journals that reveal their innermost thoughts. David Brainerd (1718-1747) worked among indigenous peoples in

America. Ill health forced him to abandon the work when he was still in his twenties. He spent the final weeks of his life in the home of Jonathan Edwards. Edwards was so inspired by Brainerd's example that he wrote a brief biography of his life and edited his journal for publication. Living two hundred years later, Jim Elliot (1927-1956) labored for a brief period of time among the "Auca" Indians (properly called Huaorani) of Ecuador. He was martyred, along with four fellow missionaries, just after making contact with them. Elliot's young wife, Elisabeth, wrote his biography, which quotes extensively from his journal. After her husband's death, she decided to carry on his work. She too became a missionary to the Huaorani and witnessed the conversion of the very people who had murdered her husband.

Both men considered the salvation of the lost more important than their own comfort and security. Brainerd longed to see native tribes won to Christ. "Oh, that God would bring in great numbers of [non-Christians] to Jesus Christ!" wrote Brainerd. "I cannot but hope I shall see that glorious day."[56] Elliot carried the same burden. Consequently, he was willing to go wherever God called him and suffer whatever losses God willed. "But those generations passing away at this moment! They must hear of the Savior! How can we wait? O Lord of the Harvest, do send forth laborers! Here am I, Lord. Behold me. Send me. . . . God arouse us to care, to feel as He Himself does for their welfare."[57] He wanted to be the kind of man who would challenge people to make a choice, either for Christ or against Christ. "Father, make of me a crisis man. Bring those I contact to decision. Let me not be a milestone on a single road; make me a fork, that men must turn one way or another on facing Christ in me."[58]

Brainerd and Elliot were willing to sacrifice everything for the mission, even their own lives. "I hardly ever so longed to live to God," wrote Brainerd, "and to be altogether devoted to Him. I wanted to wear out my life in His service, and for His glory."[59] He understood such suffering as a natural and inevitable consequence of his identification with Christ. "I longed to be perpetually and entirely crucified to all things here below, by the cross of Christ."[60] Elliot was similarly motivated. "God, I pray Thee," he wrote in his journal, "light these idle sticks of my life that I may burn up for Thee. Consume my life, my God, for it is

Thine. I seek not a long life but a full one, like you, Lord Jesus."[61] This willingness to sacrifice their lives was borne out of their single-minded devotion to God.

SMALL RISKS EVERY DAY

I doubt that Jean de Brébeuf, C. T. Studd, Mary Slessor, William Carey, David Brainerd, Jim Elliot and, for that matter, Emmanuel Anukun-Dabson had any idea what would eventually become of their lives when they first began to entertain the thought of mission work. The work to which they gave themselves unfolded over a long period of time. Each decision, event, experience and sacrifice, which might have seemed small and insignificant at the time, prepared them for the next. The cumulative effect was great indeed, though I am not sure that it seemed that way when they were in the middle of it.

Perhaps that is the point. We read a brief synopsis of their stories, viewing the whole as if it were a landscape painting. We see the entirety of their lives in a single moment—de Brébeuf's journey from French Jesuit to American martyr, Studd's journey from British athlete to African evangelist, Slessor's journey from factory girl to tribal mediator, Carey's journey from a poor cobbler to a translator and professor. But they *lived* the story, day after day, year after year, not knowing how it would all turn out. Their work progressed slowly and unpredictably and mysteriously. They made little decisions every day to do the will of God as they knew it; they took little risks—as well as a few big ones—that set them on a course leading to adventure, achievement and influence; they chose to devote their time, talent and energy to God, refusing to put limits on what God would do with them.

Risk does not have to be grandiose. It can—and probably should—start small. Studd took a risk when he became involved in the student movement in England, Slessor when she started to work with street kids in Scotland, Carey when he began to serve as a lay preacher in England. They were not thinking at the time of traveling to some exotic place on the other side of the world, at least not at first. They believed that the world God loves and wants to redeem is just outside their front door. It is for us too. A number of years ago two students at Whitworth University took time to visit an old, seedy hotel located in downtown Spokane. They started to make a few sack lunches for the poor people who lived there. Soon other students joined them. Now, fifteen years later, this thriving ministry prepares and distributes hundreds of meals a week for residents who live in several run-down hotels that have been converted into one room apartments. They also befriend the residents, share the gospel, lead Bible studies and provide other services.

It begins, as all things do, with one small step. Only God knows where that step will lead. Thus we invite an unchurched neighbor to a backyard barbecue; a year later we are leading a neighborhood Bible study for "seekers." We volunteer to work at a Habitat for Humanity work site once a month; we end up getting so involved that we are asked to serve on the local board of directors. We assume the chair of a moribund mission committee at our church and innocently suggest at the first meeting that a few adults should consider working at an orphanage for two weeks during the summer; over the next two years we visit the orphanage so often that we decide to move there to spearhead the founding of other orphanages in the area. It always seems to work that way. Give God an inch and he takes a mile, though we hardly ever notice because we are actually walking that mile, one step at a time. We take one small risk; years later we look back and marvel at what has happened as a result.

God chose to risk everything in the incarnation; such a risk was costly beyond measure. But the incarnation also reminds us that the risk is worth taking. Our salvation is proof of that. God calls us to take risks too, following, however inadequately, the example that Jesus set. Nothing less than the world's salvation is the goal.

PRACTICES

- Read Matthew 28:16-20.
- William Carey wrote, "Expect great things from God; attempt great things for God." Consider a need, problem or concern that has been on your mind lately, for whatever reason. Perhaps it is a failing youth program at your church, a depressed colleague at work, a non-Christian neighbor you are just getting to know, a homeless person you see every day on your way to work, a neighbor whose marriage is dissolving or a

struggling orphanage in Nicaragua you know about. Spend time each day praying about the issue, asking for God's guidance.

- What is *one step* you can take to address this need? How can you seek the support of the church to help you?

Conclusion

Where Do We Go from Here?

*"Not that I have already obtained this or have already reached the goal;
but I press on to make it my own,
because Christ Jesus has made me his own."*

PHIL 3:12

All things are yours" (1 Cor 3:21) the apostle Paul wrote, including—
I think it is safe to say by now—the magnificent history of Christian spirituality, which provides us with a wide variety of traditions from which to
learn. The martyrs call us to proclaim Jesus as Lord and the desert saints
to fight against the world, the flesh and the devil. The early church challenges us to create a community of belonging for broken, displaced, disconnected people. Medieval monks invite us to abide by healthy rhythms,
mendicants to imitate the life of Christ and mystics to seek union with
God. The Reformers urge us to listen to the Word of God, evangelicals to
surrender our lives to it and missionaries to proclaim it to the world. The
stories of these saints are at our disposal to enlarge, enrich and warn us.
"There is more!" they tell us. "So much more."

None of these traditions is without fault. I could just as easily have written a book about their weaknesses. The history of Christian spirituality
does not always tell a happy story. Every person, movement and tradition

I have introduced has left an ambiguous legacy. I have chosen to dwell on the good part of the story, though I could have done the opposite. But I believe that failures and abuses do not nullify the value of these traditions. As I have already stated: *Abusus non tollit usus.*

Where do we go from here? Throughout the book I have described various disciplines that Christians have used in the spiritual life—lectio divina, wordless prayer and fasting, for example. I decided not explain them at length because I did not want to leave the impression that Christian spirituality is primarily concerned with technique, practice and discipline. Western culture holds self-help as a high value. We like to think that we can master anything we want if we simply put our mind to it and learn the right technique. We can create the perfect body, land the perfect job, raise perfect children and then enjoy a perfect retirement. We approach "spirituality" the same way. We assume that if we apply the right techniques, we will achieve perfect peace and prosperity.

The Christian faith does in fact require serious practice. The apostle Paul exhorted Timothy to "train yourself in godliness" (1 Tim 4:7) and he told believers living in Philippi to "work out your own salvation with fear and trembling" (Phil 2:12). Countless Christians face the frustration week after week of being told by their ministers what to believe but not how to put those beliefs into practice. Still, however important and necessary practice is, Christian spirituality transcends it. How we live as Christians grows out of what we believe about Jesus Christ, what we do as Christians out of who we are in Jesus Christ. The apostle Paul wrote, "So if anyone is in Christ, there is a new creation: everything old has passed away; see, everything has become new!" (2 Cor 5:17). Or again, "There is therefore now no condemnation for those who are in Christ Jesus. For the law of the Spirit of life in Christ Jesus has set you free from the law of sin and death" (Rom 8:1-2). What happens to us over a lifetime of Christian practice and growth amounts to nothing more than becoming what we already are in Jesus Christ. We *are* a new creation. It is for that reason that we can *become* a new creation. Paul captures this paradox perfectly: "Not that I have already obtained this or have already reached my goal; but I press on to make it my own, because Christ Jesus has made me his own" (Phil 3:12).

THE SOURCE

The traditions explored in this book are like refracted light that casts a rainbow of beautiful colors onto the landscape of our lives. The source of that light is Jesus Christ, who gathers all the brilliance of the divine radiance into a single beam that pierces the darkness of our world and sets our hearts on fire. Thomas Merton used the analogy of a magnifying glass to explore this idea. As a magnifying glass concentrates the rays of the sun into a beam of light and heat, "so the mystery of Christ in the Gospel concentrates the rays of God's light and fire to a point that sets fire to the spirit of man." The incarnation of Jesus Christ manifests the divine light to us, illuminating us, enlightening us and kindling in us a fiery passion for God. "Through the [magnifying] glass of His Incarnation God concentrates the rays of His Divine Truth and Love upon us so that we feel the burn, and all mystical experience is communicated to men through the Man Christ."[1]

Dorothy Day comes to mind as a modern saint who, just like her ancient counterparts—Perpetua, Antony, Augustine, Macrina, Benedict—lived in that light. Like the saints of old, she discovered that Jesus Christ is the source. A radical activist, she committed her life to work for social justice, which is why she joined the Communist Party, for she believed that it showed the greatest promise for establishing a just social order. But communism failed her. However lofty its goals, it did not—and could not—fulfill what it promised. In the wake of that disappointment she became a Christian. It was her commitment to Jesus Christ that made her one of the most tenacious Catholic social reformers in the twentieth century.

Though growing up as an Episcopalian, Dorothy Day (1897-1980) rejected the Christian faith during her early college years because she viewed it as entirely irrelevant to the problems of modern society, such as poverty, inadequate housing, chronic unemployment and exploitation of labor. She became a political radical instead. After finishing two years of college she moved to New York City and worked as a reporter for a socialist newspaper, joined the Industrial Workers of the World (the Wobblies), and agitated for the rights of the working class.

She was no mere armchair activist. She was arrested for the first time while marching in Washington, D.C., for the cause of suffrage. She spent

thirty days in jail, including ten days in solitary confinement, which dev-
astated her. "I lost all consciousness of any cause," she wrote in her autobiography. "I had no sense of being a radical, making protest against a government, carrying on a nonviolent revolution. I could only feel darkness
and desolation all around me." The experience marked her for life, awakening her to the evil of injustice. "I would never be free again, never free
when I knew that behind bars all over the world there were women and
men, young girls and boys, suffering constraint, punishment, isolation and
hardship for crimes of which all of us were guilty."[2]

Those ten days in solitary confinement also exposed how weak, shallow
and pretentious her supposedly "radical" convictions were. She lost all sense
of being smugly confident and indomitable. "I had instead a bitter awareness of the need of self-preservation, the need to escape, the need to endure
somehow through days of my imprisonment. I had an ugly sense of the fu-
tility of human effort, man's helpless misery, the triumph of might."[3] Desperate for hope and strength, she asked for a Bible and began to read it and
to pray. It was her first foray into Christianity. "I clung to the words of comfort in the Bible and as long as the light held out, I read and pondered." This
interest in religion, however, did not last long. Release from solitary confinement mitigated her sense of absolute need. "I had seen myself too weak
to stand alone, too weak to face the darkness of that punishment cell without crying out, and I was ashamed and again rejected religion that had
helped me when I had been brought to my knees by my suffering."[4]

After her release from prison she returned to New York City and indulged in the Bohemian lifestyle of the left-wing elite, which included a
smattering of anarchists, communists, socialists and artists. She stayed up
all night, drinking hard, debating politics and associating with luminaries
like Eugene O'Neill. She worked as a nurse for a year too, during which
time she fell in love, became pregnant and had an abortion, a decision she
regretted for the rest of her life. A second arrest, this time for living in a
"disorderly house," forced her to see herself for the impudent, careless and
immoral person she had become. If she wanted to serve the poor and defend the rights of the working class, she realized that she would have to
build her life on a sturdier foundation. She had the right cause but the
wrong worldview. This second arrest, she wrote:

was as ugly an experience as I ever wish to pass through, and a useful one. I do not think that ever again, no matter of what I am accused, can I suffer more than I did then of shame and regret, and self-contempt. Not only because I had been caught, found out, branded, publicly humiliated, but because of my own consciousness that I deserved it.[5]

Thus began her long and slow journey toward Christian faith.

In the late 1920s she moved to Staten Island, where she lived with her common-law husband, Forster, a fellow radical. For the first time in her life she experienced genuine happiness, which only increased when she gave birth to their child, Tamar Teresa. She started to attend a weekly Catholic Mass. She had Tamar baptized and decided to seek baptism for herself too. She knew that she would pay dearly for her conversion to Catholicism. Forster would surely leave her (which in fact he did); her radical friends too, would abandon her, for they thought the Catholic faith was far too conservative to be of any use to them. She wondered too, if conversion would erode her radical convictions, in effect domesticating her. She chose faith anyway.

Much to her surprise and delight, her new faith in Christ made her all the more earnest about the cause of social justice and service to the poor. "How our dear Lord must love them, I kept thinking to myself. They were His friends, His comrades, and who knows how close to His heart in their attempt to work for justice." Another trip to Washington—this time to participate in the Hunger March of the Unemployed (1932)—made her determined to continue her life's work, whether or not the church supported her. After the march she visited the National Catholic Shrine of the Immaculate Conception. "There I offered up a special prayer, a prayer which came with tears and with anguish, that some way would open up for me to use what talents I possessed for my fellow workers, for the poor."[6]

Upon her return to New York City she met Peter Maurin, a French peasant, social radical, devout Catholic and visionary. Together they founded the Catholic Worker Movement, an umbrella organization that published the *Catholic Worker* (a newspaper that agitated for the needs of the poor, the rights of labor and the cause of pacifism), established a network of hospitality houses to provide shelter and support for the destitute,

Dorothy Day

and organized farm communes and re-treat centers. The movement spread rapidly to cities across America. The hospitality houses became the lifeblood of the movement. Every day residents prayed together, read Scripture and spiritual classics, listened to spiritual instruction, served the poor, and enjoyed periods of silence.

Dorothy Day discovered in the Christian faith what communism clearly lacked. "If I could have felt that communism was the answer to my desire for a cause, a motive, a way to walk in, I would have remained as I was. But I felt that only faith in Christ could give the answer."[7] In Day's mind the incarnation embodied the essence of Christianity.

> We felt a respect for the poor and destitute as those nearest to God, as those chosen by Christ for His compassion. Christ lived among men. The great mystery of the Incarnation, which meant that God became man that man might become God, was a joy that made us want to kiss the earth in worship, because His feet once trod the same earth.[8]

Jesus dared to identify completely with fallen humanity. He was born in a stable, worked with his hands and associated with the poor. "He directed His sublime words to the poorest of the poor, to the people who thronged the towns and followed after John the Baptist, who hung around, sick and poverty-stricken at the doors of rich men."[9] In Christianity, Day found one truth that her years as a secular radical did not teach her—the power and beauty of sacrificial love. Love, she realized, reflects the very character of God as we know him in Jesus Christ.

The Christian faith also introduced her to certain spiritual practices— daily Mass, the Divine Office, regular prayer and solitude, for example— that enabled her to persist in the work, even when she felt exhausted and discouraged. At first rejecting Benedictine discipline as self-indulgent, she learned soon enough that she desperately needed to ask daily for God's help. She finally became an oblate in the Benedictine tradition to make the disciplines of study, solitude and prayer a regular part of her routine. "It is not only for others that I must have these retreats," she finally admitted. "It is because I too am hungry and thirsty for the bread of the strong. I too must nourish myself to do the work I have undertaken; I too must drink at these good springs so that I may not be an empty cistern and unable to help others."[10]

THE LANDSCAPE

If Jesus Christ is the source of light and we its recipients, then ordinary life is the landscape on which that light shines. "You are the light of the world," Jesus said.

> A city built on a hill cannot be hid. No one after lighting a lamp puts it under the bushel basket, but on the lamp stand, and it gives light to all in the house. In the same way, let your light shine before others, so that they may see your good works and give glory to your Father in heaven. (Mt 5:14-16)

Jesus lived as an ordinary person among ordinary people. He never separated sacred from secular, religion from daily life, and neither should we. The authenticity of our spiritual lives is tested not when we "do" formal religion, however earnest and devout we might be, but when we apply faith to ordinary life.

Brother Lawrence, a monk who lived in the seventeenth century, believed that it is possible to live a vital spiritual life while performing the most routine of tasks. He spent many hours every day as a monk doing tedious work in the monastery kitchen, which appeared to have no spiritual value whatsoever. But he did see value in it, and he often talked about it with his brothers. A fellow monk recorded his reflections, which were published after his death as *The Practice of the Presence of God*. According to Brother Lawrence, Christians do not become more mature by replacing mundane duties with more "spiritual" activities. Spirituality depends less on what we are doing and more on why and for whom we do it. "Our sanctification [does] not depend upon *changing* our works, but in doing that for God's sake which we commonly do for our own.

The most excellent method . . . of going to God [is] that of doing our common business without any view of pleasing men, and purely for the love of God."[11]

I regard Susanna Wesley (1669-1742) as a model of how to live for Jesus Christ in ordinary life. Susanna was the twenty-fifth child born into a Puritan household.[12] She eventually married Samuel Wesley, a rector in the Church of England, and became the matron of a busy household. She gave birth to nineteen children, ten of whom survived to adulthood, including two that achieved worldwide fame, John and Charles, the founders of the Methodist movement. Her initial and primary vocation was motherhood. For years she taught all of her children, sons and daughters alike, at home before sending some of them to Oxford. The curriculum included Bible, grammar, history, mathematics, geography, theology and languages (one daughter, Hetty, was able to read both Greek and Latin and possessed, as her brother John testified, a poetic genius). She met with each of her children weekly too, to give them special attention and to attend to their peculiar needs.

She maintained equilibrium in a home that suffered a number of calamities—two house fires, a daughter's ill-advised marriage and her husband's bouts with depression and financial mismanagement. Her secret? "Help me," she once prayed, "O Lord, to make a true use of all disappointments and calamities in this life, in such wise that they may unite my heart more closely with Thee. Cause them to separate my affections from worldly things and inspire my soul with more vigour in the pursuit of true happiness."[13]

But that is not all. She became a formidable religious leader in the Wesleyan movement. She led a Bible study in her home that attracted two hundred people. When questioned about this activity, she gave such a persuasive defense that her son John called her "a preacher of righteousness." She also wrote letters and a few theological treatises that reached a wide audience, and she supported inexperienced and unordained people when they wanted to test their gifts as preachers and leaders. Such use of laypeople became one of the central characteristics of the Methodist movement, allowing it to grow at the grassroots.

Her entire life was offered as a living sacrifice to God, as wife, mother, home manager, educator, letter writer, Bible study leader, servant of the poor and champion of others. She once prayed:

> Enable me, O God, to collect and compose my thoughts before an immediate approach to you in prayer. . . . You are infinitely too great to be trifled with, too wise to be imposed on by a mock devotion and abhor a sacrifice without a heart. Help me to entertain an habitual sense of your perfections, as an admirable help against cold and formal performances. Save me from engaging in rash and precipitate prayers and from abrupt breaking away to follow business or pleasure as though I had never prayed.[14]

Spiritual practices—what we do at church and in "the closet," as Susanna Wesley called it—puts us into postures to receive God's good gifts; daily life thrusts us into the arena where we can put them to good use. How we treat family, friends, neighbors and coworkers, how we use time and consume natural resources, how we perform daily tasks, and how we serve "the least of these" demonstrates the true value of our spiritual practices. If disciplines like lectio divina, wordless prayer and fasting do not affect daily conduct and attitude, then we do them in vain. They are not ends in themselves. Their purpose is to infuse us with love for God and love for neighbor.

DAILY WORK

Daily work is a case in point. Like most people, I spend many hours every day on the job, which in my case happens to be college teaching. I lecture, lead discussions, advise students, chair committees, attend meetings, grade papers, answer e-mail, read articles and books, and write. I love my work, and I work hard at it. My profession gives me an extraordinary opportunity to turn spiritual practice into a concrete good that benefits the small corner of the world I occupy. It is the perfect place for the light of Jesus Christ to shine through me. If spiritual discipline does not influence my work, then I am covering the light of Jesus Christ with the bushel of my own hypocrisy and selfishness.

Once again, history provides us with examples to study and follow. A few years ago I happened upon the story of a lawyer and activist who has since become something of a hero to me. Sadly, his story has been lost to popular historical memory, probably because he did not succeed in the noble cause to which he gave his life. Only scholars know about his life. But his story is worthy of being told and remembered, for this man worked tirelessly and heroically to honor God and serve the common good of society. The light of Jesus Christ shined through him during a very dark time.

Born in Vermont and educated at Yale, Jeremiah Evarts (1781-1831) practiced law and labored his entire adult life for various social reform causes. He was profoundly affected by the evangelical awakenings of the early nineteenth century. As a result, he became active in the American Board of Commissioners of Foreign Missions (one of the first evangelical mission societies founded in the United States), serving as its treasurer and then as its secretary from 1812 until his death. His evangelical piety affected both his private and public life. He prayed daily that he might "be preserved from rash and imprudent speeches in regard to the government, opposers of missions, or any other subject" and that he might "cultivate a temper universally mild and amiable towards all men." He also prayed that he might avoid all self-righteousness. "Whenever I hear of sinful actions, before I say a word by way of censure, [let me] remember how much I find to blame in myself, though under so great advantages."[15]

He devoted the last fifteen years of his life to defending the human rights of the Cherokees. He worked on two fronts. First, he made a public argument to oppose the forcible removal of the Cherokees from their native lands in Georgia. In his capacity as editor of the *Panoplist*, he wrote twenty-four essays to lay out his case. He argued that Cherokee removal violated natural law, undermined public morality and stained the reputation of the United States as one of the few nations on earth that actually guaranteed human rights in its Constitution. He cited previous treaties with the Cherokees as evidence that the integrity of the new nation was at stake. Would the United States uphold its laws and be true to its word? He also charged that forcible removal contradicted Old Testament law and New Testament teachings. The Cherokees were human beings, made in God's image, and they therefore had certain inalienable rights. Besides, they had built a civilized culture, which included farms, towns, schools, trade, transportation systems and a newspaper. Many Cherokees had also become Christians, and thus spiritual brothers and sisters to the majority of Americans. What would removal say about the soul of the nation? "Accustomed from his birth to feelings of entire equality and independence, [the Cherokee] would find himself, at a single stroke, smitten to the earth, and there held till manacles of a most degrading vassalage were fasted upon him."[16] Hundreds of thousands of American citizens read these essays, some of whom joined Evarts's cause.

Second, Evarts lobbied both the White House and Congress. He urged President John Quincy Adams to provide financial assistance to help the Cherokees continue to build their culture, which Adams consented to do. Later, he opposed President Andrew Jackson, who supported the Indian Removal Act of 1830. He also contacted members of Congress, pleading for their support, and initiated a public campaign of petitions, which resulted in the submission of hundreds of such petitions to Congress. The battle in Congress ensued in the spring of 1830. Neither side was able to prevail until President Jackson helped to turn the tide against the Cherokees by pressuring and intimidating members of Congress to vote for the Act. Not surprisingly, Congressmen from Georgia supported the Indian Removal Act too, arguing boldly that the right of conquest took precedence over the rights of the Cherokees. They even warned Evarts to withdraw from the conflict, for religion had no business, they argued, involving itself in politics.

Jackson and the state of Georgia finally prevailed. An appeal to the Supreme Court failed to reverse the decision. Evarts, who had been in Washington for most of the campaign, was crushed by the news. But he took solace in his faith in God. "My comfort is that God governs the world." Still, he was sorely tested.

> At times I am exceedingly cast down as to the result. It seems a most remarkable Providence, that the bill should pass, when a majority present showed themselves to be really and obstinately opposed to it; and that it passed by a majority of five, when the very next day . . . no one doubts that it would have been rejected. This strange state of things should make us stand astonished at the ways of Providence.[17]

Suffering from tuberculosis and exhaustion, Evarts died the next year. His death made it all but impossible to reverse the vote in Congress. In 1838 some twelve thousand Cherokees were forced to march all the way to Oklahoma in what is known as the Trail of Tears. Many died along the way, many more after they arrived. The entire incident became a sordid stain on America's constitutional principles and on its supposedly Christian character.

Evarts's story reminds us that God assigns all of us to a specific "post" of service, as Calvin called it. Evarts was a lawyer; I am a college professor. Someone else might be a stay-at-home parent or a police officer or a bank manager or preschool teacher or a regular volunteer at a soup kitchen. The position itself does not matter as much as what we do with it. Evarts used the legal profession to protect the rights of the Cherokees. I try to use the profession of college teaching to train leaders for church and society. Each of us has our own calling. God is the one who has called us to it; he expects that we honor him in what we do with it. The great tradition of Christian spirituality provides us with resources—texts, examples, insights, disciplines—that will help us do that well.

THE CHURCH

We cannot do it alone, which is why God also calls us to become members of his church. The church has often failed to fulfill its divine purpose. It has been slow to respond to obvious needs, too ingrown and complacent and institutionalized to do much of anything that requires steady and sacrificial action. But in spite of its many faults and failures, it can still play a major role in God's kingdom work in the world. History demonstrates that it is possible too. The early church created a community of love and service, which had a profound impact on the culture of its day. The monastic and mendicant movements did the same in the Middle Ages. The Anabaptists in the sixteenth century, the Pietists and Moravians in the seventeenth century, the Wesleyans in the eighteenth century, and revivalists in the nineteenth century did likewise. None of these communities was perfect. But they accomplished enough good—welcoming the outsider and outcast, seeking justice for the oppressed, caring for the poor and proclaiming the good news—to show the world something of the reality of God's kingdom.

The church is called to bear witness to Jesus Christ, not only by what it says but also by how it lives as a community of faith. Paul says as much in 1 Corinthians. "For just as the body is one and has many members, and all the members of the body, though many, are one body, so it is with Christ" (1 Cor 12:12). It is the last word—*Christ*—that is so startling. If Paul had followed the logic of his analogy, he should have inserted the word *church* instead. But he used *Christ* because he believed that the church is in fact the body of Christ on earth. As Christ is the incarnation of God, the church is the incarnation of Christ. Its community is the best form of witness the church has. "By this everyone will know that you are my disciples, if you have love for one another," Jesus said (Jn 13:35). God wills his church to be his body—his heart and hands, mind and muscle—on earth.

As individuals, we lack the resources required to influence the larger culture. Evarts was as courageous and tenacious as a person can be. Still, he needed the votes of members of Congress to achieve success. If only a few more Christians in Congress had been as conscientious as he was! As a community, however, we have the resources—the numbers, wealth, expertise and energy—to accomplish a great deal. What would happen if the sleeping giant of the church could be awakened, if service and sacrifice became the calling of the many rather than the few, and if ordinary Christians began to make small but significant changes in their efforts to live for the kingdom? What if local churches became as committed to the values of the kingdom of God as the saints, perhaps not as visibly and heroically but nevertheless as intentionally and persistently?[18]

I have been a churchman my entire adult life, first as a pastor, then as a college chaplain, and now as a professor of theology. I have taught Sunday school classes, organized youth retreats, sat on committees, attended Bible studies, participated in community work projects, and signed up for mission trips. I am no Pollyanna about the church. I am realistic about what the church is capable of accomplishing. I do not expect extraordinary things from the church. I will leave that to saints like Mother Teresa. Most of us will not rise to that level of sacrificial love, even if we wanted to. We simply have too much to do just to keep life going; the ordinary demands of life are quite enough for us. I receive appeals almost daily to join some worthy cause—to stop the war in Darfur, to rescue lost boys in Uganda, to reverse global warming, to provide decent and affordable housing for all God's children on earth. Even if I was rich, childless and unemployed, I would not be able to respond to all these appeals. As it is, I am middle class, a father of three and employed. I cannot do it all. No one can do it all, and no one should.

The church as a community, however, is capable of advancing the cause of the kingdom, if only just a little. Through sheer numbers alone that "little" can amount to "much." There are well over 150 million Christians in America (out of some two billion in the world), though of course not all are serious about their faith. What if just one third of those—50 million—began in modest ways to live more earnestly and deliberately for the kingdom? What if these believers consecrated their lives to God, began to practice spiritual discipline in earnest and committed themselves to serve God's kingdom? Just one hundred extra dollars a year would provide five billion dollars to help fight AIDS in Africa and battle sex trafficking in Asia. Just one hundred extra hours a year (only two a week!) would provide five billion volunteer hours to man soup kitchens in cities and pound nails for Habitat for Humanity. Just ten letters a year would send five hundred million pieces of mail to Washington to lobby for worthy causes. What if

Desmond Tutu

ordinary Christians used a little less water every day, consumed less energy and ate healthier food, recycled more conscientiously, purchased fair trade products, rode buses more often, and invested in just one cause outside their normal routine? Churches move slowly, just like glaciers, which is why activists so often become impatient. But when they do change, they can become as powerful as an advancing glacier that sweeps away everything in its path. In the end, slow, incremental, concrete change might be the most effective kind.

It will not happen easily and quickly. Thus we must also learn to live in hope. Bishop Desmond Tutu, who fought against apartheid in South Africa for decades before achieving some measure of victory, discovered that

Jesus himself is the reason why he—why all of us—can be hopeful. Jesus' ministry seemed to end in total failure when he died on the cross; but then the resurrection occurred, which changed everything. Suddenly, what had looked so hopeless became hopeful beyond measure. Death gave way to life, defeat to victory, despair to hope.

> Nothing could have been deader than Jesus on the cross on the first Good Friday. And the hopes of his disciples had appeared to die with his crucifixion. . . . And then Easter happened. Jesus rose from the dead. The incredible, the unexpected happened. Life triumphed over death, light over darkness, love over hatred, good over evil. That is what Easter means—hope prevails over despair. Jesus reigns as Lord of Lords and King of Kings. Oppression and injustice and suffering can't be the end of the human story.[19]

The apostle Paul wrote that hope does not become truly hopeful until there is no obvious reason for it. The intransigence of apartheid provided the occasion for Tutu's hope, the gospel the foundation for that hope, the Holy Spirit the power to remain hopeful. It was hope that kept Tutu faithful and persistent in his work.

God calls us to live in that same hope. Jesus has come; Jesus will come again. We live in the tension between the "already" and the "not yet." We know who God is in the face of Jesus Christ, what God has done through Jesus Christ to save and redeem the world, and what God has promised to do in us through the work of the Holy Spirit. We know that God commands us to serve his kingdom, no matter what the cost. Our task is to do the hard work of living for God day in and day out. He has not left us without resources. The rich history of Christian spirituality shows how our brothers and sisters from the past drew upon divine resources to live for God right where they were. They drank from the well of living water, and they call us to drink from that same well. Their voices continue to echo across the centuries, "There is more. So much more!"

Discussion Questions

CHAPTER 1: WITNESS

1. Why is early Christian martyrdom the proper place to begin a book on the history of Christian spirituality?

2. What common themes did you observe in the martyr stories retold in the chapter?

3. Why were the early Christians persecuted and martyred?

4. How do these reasons apply to today? In other words, how are Christians still misunderstood? How are they still perceived as a threat?

5. Rome was tolerant of new religions, but only if believers swore allegiance to Rome. The Christian commitment to the lordship of Christ challenged this claim. What are the counterparts to "Rome" in our culture?

6. The early Christians confessed that Jesus is Lord, and many suffered for it. What does it mean to confess Jesus as Lord today? What is the price you might have to pay?

7. Considering that you will probably not suffer martyrdom, how is this chapter relevant to you?

CHAPTER 2: BELONGING

1. Have you ever experienced a deep sense of belonging? Describe the experience.

2. How did the early Christian community provide a sense of belonging in the ancient world?

3. What made Christian community so attractive to the pagan population of the Roman world?

4. What would make Christian community attractive to irreligious people living in the modern world?

5. Why is it so difficult for churches to provide that kind of community?

6. What can your church do to become that kind of community?

CHAPTER 3: STRUGGLE

1. Can eccentricity actually teach us important lessons about the Christian faith? Can you think of biblical examples? Historical examples? Examples from your own personal experience?

2. Why did the desert saints withdraw into the wilderness? What was life like for them there? Why is the desert such an important place for Christian spirituality?

3. What "sayings" of the desert saints did you find most intriguing and provocative in the chapter? Why?

4. Who was Evagrius? What does *logismoi* mean? Identify the eight deadly *logismoi* and define each one.

5. What is the difference between committing the sin of gluttony and *thinking* gluttonously? Between acting out lust and *thinking* lustful thoughts? Which one is deadlier—committing a sinful act or simply thinking about it? Why?

6. Define *ascesis*. What appetites are most deadly in modern society? Why?

7. What are the five "disciplines of deprivation" mentioned in the chapter? What is the purpose behind each one? How could we translate these disciplines into modern society?

8. Define *apatheia*. What does it mean to practice *apatheia* in modern society?

9. Define *agape*. What expressions of *agape* would have the most impact in modern society? Why?

CHAPTER 4: RHYTHM

1. How do you schedule your time? What does that say about how you view time and use time?

2. What makes monastic rhythm so unique? What is the difference between consuming or wasting time, on the one hand, and actually *living* in time, on the other?

3. Why were monasteries founded in the early Middle Ages?

4. How did monasteries contribute to the common good of society?

5. Describe the monastic practice of prayer and work. How could you apply that to your circumstances?

6. How do we view work in modern society? Why do we find it so difficult to integrate work and prayer? How can you begin to practice the rhythm of prayer and work in your life?

CHAPTER 5: HOLY HEROES

1. Who are the heroes in modern culture? What kind of impact do they have?

2. Who are your heroes? Why them?

3. What does *theosis* mean? Why is it an important concept in Eastern Orthodoxy?

4. What makes icons so unusual as an art form? What do icons convey? What is the spiritual value they hold?

5. What did you learn from the strange spiritual biography of Melania the Younger? What is the value of studying the lives of the saints?

6. Why is it important to listen to the voices of the saints of the past? Did any of the Chrysostom quotes speak to you? Which other "saints" have spoken to you?

7. What biblical stories (e.g., Joseph, Ruth, Esther) are meaningful to you? Why?

8. What would it mean for you to see your "situations" in life as God's divine workshop?

CHAPTER 6: WINDOWS

1. What makes Gothic architecture such a fitting symbol of a sacramental view of the Christian life?

2. How do we view the material world in modern society?

3. What is the significance of the incarnation for our understanding of the sacraments?

4. Identify the seven sacraments of the medieval Roman church. What is the purpose of each?

5. What is the significance of pilgrimage? Of relics?

6. Can you think of some reasons why these expressions of spiritual devotion might have a good effect?

7. What is the church year? What role did it play in the Middle Ages?

8. Could you adapt the church year to your circumstances? Is so, how?

9. How can you begin to practice a more sacramental faith? What kind of impact might it have on you?

CHAPTER 7: UNION

1. Why do you pray? Describe how you pray. Is it a meaningful discipline to you?

2. What is the essence of mystical spirituality? What important questions does it raise about how we claim to know God?

3. What contributions did Plato, Plotinus and Dionysius make to mystical spirituality?

4. What is the significance of purgation? What are its limitations?

5. What is the way of illumination? What is unique about the Christian understanding of illumination?

6. What are the two alternative meanings of union? What is the significance of the difference?

7. How did Bernard and Julian define union with God?

8. Do you see any evidence in modern culture of the longing to know God? What do these longings tell us about modern society? What do the mystics have to teach us about these longings?

CHAPTER 8: ORDINARINESS

1. Has religious life and ordinary life become divided in our society? Can

you think of examples? What happens when that occurs?

2. How do you view your ordinary life? What is it like? What is its value?

3. Trace the ways that medieval religion began to affect the lives of ordinary people.

4. What contributions did the mendicant movement make? Lay religious orders?

5. How did the Reformers change the way people viewed ordinary life?

6. How can you live your ordinary life for God? How would this affect your view and use of time and resources? How would it shape your attitude about to-do lists? Interruptions? Mundane tasks?

7. What does it mean to do all tasks to the glory of God?

CHAPTER 9: WORD

1. How did the Reformers define the Word of God?

2. How did this definition affect their view of ministry?

3. What role did the Word of God play in the spiritual journeys of Luther and Calvin?

4. How did Luther and Calvin preach the Word of God?

5. The Word of God tells a story of God's self-revelation in history, which culminated in the incarnation, life, death and resurrection of Jesus. We know it as God's redemptive story. What is the value of knowing this story as it is told in the Bible?

6. How can you understand your own story in light of the redemptive story?

CHAPTER 10: CONVERSION

1. What does John Newton's story say about conversion?

2. What does it mean to have the whole of one's life converted to God?

3. How did the Puritans, the Pietists and the Moravians contribute to the evangelical idea of conversion?

4. How did the Great Awakening affect how conversion is understood?

5. How did Jonathan Edwards explain the true nature of conversion?

What "signs" are neutral? Genuine? Should we even think in terms of signs?

6. What role did George Whitefield play in shaping our understanding of conversion?

7. What happened in the nineteenth century that changed the way evangelicals understand conversion? How would you evaluate that change?

8. How important do you think conversion is in the Christian life?

9. Can you think of areas of your life that need to be converted to God?

CHAPTER 11: RISK

1. What kinds of risks have you taken in your life? How did they turn out? If you have chosen not to take many risks, why?

2. Recall the four biographies recounted in the chapter. What kinds of risks did these pioneers take?

3. What "little" decisions did these missionaries make that had such big implications, though they could not have foreseen it at the time?

4. Can you think of examples in your own life in which you made small decisions that had big implications?

5. Do you think Christians should be risk-takers? What is the difference between faith and presumption? What characterizes wise risk? Foolish risk?

6. Are Western Christians too comfortable and secure? How can that begin to change?

7. How can *you* begin to take risks for God?

CONCLUSION

1. What chapters in this book were most meaningful, memorable and helpful to you? Why?

2. How have you changed your beliefs and behaviors as a result of this book?

3. This final chapter states that Christian growth consists of nothing more than becoming what we already are in Christ. What does that mean?

4. Reflect on Dorothy Day's spiritual journey. What did she discover about the Christian faith that made her a more effective and devout activist?

5. Is it really possible to live for God in ordinary life? How did Susanna Wesley do it? How can you begin to do it?

6. Most people spend many hours a day working a job. Others spend many hours laboring at home. How can you do your work "as unto the Lord"?

7. How can your church begin to play a more significant role in serving God's kingdom? What kind of leadership can you provide?

8. What does it mean to live in hope?

Annotated Reading List

It took me many years to burrow into the literature of the history of Christian spirituality. The number of books is massive, though that should not intimidate readers, whether new to the field or well-read veterans. There is no end to reading good books. It is best, then, to enjoy the journey, which will never end anyway. The following reading list is organized by chapter. I chose to provide one or two introductory books on the subject (if good ones are available) and to suggest several good primary sources. It is always best, after all, to read the original writers rather than to read those of us who write about them.

INTRODUCTION

Augustine. *The Confessions.* Hyde Park, N.Y.: New City Press, 1997. There are many editions of this classic work. I would recommend using this one.

McGrath, Alister. *Christian Spirituality: An Introduction.* London: Blackwell, 1999. A good topical approach to the subject of Christian spirituality.

Maas, Robin, and Gabriel O'Donnell, eds. *Spiritual Traditions for the Contemporary Church.* Nashville: Abingdon, 1990. A useful history of spirituality that contains contemporary application.

Tyson, John R. *Invitation to Christian Spirituality: An Ecumenical Anthology.* New York: Oxford, 1999. A superb collection of spiritual writings, from early Christianity to the twentieth century.

CHAPTER 1: WITNESS

Arnold, Eberhard, ed. *The Early Christians in Their Own Words.* Farmington, Penn.: Plough, 1997. A collection of quotes, many of them addressing martyrdom, from early Christianity.

Eusebius. *The History of the Church from Christ to Constantine.* New York: Penguin, 1965. One of the first histories of Christianity, which contains many martyr stories, written by a bishop and close friend of Constantine.

Frend, W. H. C. *Martyrdom and Persecution in the Early Church.* Garden City, N.Y.: Anchor Books, 1967. The best volume on persecution.

Hefley, James, and Marti Hefley. *By Their Blood: Christian Martyrs of the Twentieth Century.* Grand Rapids: Baker, 1996. A collection of twentieth-century martyr stories. Inspiring and convicting.

Wilken, Robert Louis. *The Spirit of Early Christian Thought.* New Haven, Conn.: Yale University Press, 2003. An absolutely superb introduction to how the church fathers came to their theological conclusions.

CHAPTER 2: BELONGING

Brown, Peter. *The World of Late Antiquity: AD 150-750.* New York: Harcourt Brace Jovanovich, 1971. An excellent historical introduction to the world in which Christianity grew up.

Hippolytus. *On the Apostolic Tradition.* Crestwood, N.Y.: St. Vladimir's Seminary Press, 2001. An invaluable source, written in A.D. 215, on early Christian church life.

Richardson, Cyril C., ed. *Early Christian Fathers.* New York: Touchstone, 1996. A primary source collection of early Christian writers, such as Athenagorus and Justin Martyr.

Stark, Rodney. *The Rise of Christianity.* Princeton, N.J.: Princeton University Press, 1996. A historical and sociological analysis of how and why the early Christian movement succeeded.

CHAPTER 3: STRUGGLE

Athanasius. *The Life of Antony.* New York: Paulist Press, 1980. The best spiritual biography of the greatest of the desert saints, written by the tenacious fourth-century bishop of Alexandria.

Bamberger, John, ed. *Evagrius Ponticus: The Praktikos and Chapters on Prayer.* Spencer, Mass.: Cistercian Publications, 1970. A short volume of the best of Evagrius, the great fourth-century philosopher and psychologist of the desert.

Chadwick, Owen, ed. *Western Asceticism*. Philadelphia: Westminster Press, 1958. An excellent collection of the sayings of the desert saints, as well as the complete text of *The Rule of St. Benedict* and excerpts from John Cassian's *Conferences*.

Chryssavgis, John. *In the Heart of the Desert: The Spirituality of the Desert Fathers and Mothers*. Bloomington, Ind.: World Wisdom, 2003. A useful introduction to the spirituality of the desert saints.

Smith, Allyne, ed. *Philokalia: The Eastern Christian Spiritual Texts*. Woodstock, Vt.: Skylight Paths, 2006. A convenient compilation, arranged by topic, of the massive five volumes of Eastern Orthodox spiritual writings.

Swan, Laura, ed. *The Forgotten Desert Mothers*. New York: Paulist Press, 2001. A collection of the sayings of the greatest of the desert mothers.

CHAPTER 4: RHYTHM

Knowles, David. *Christian Monasticism*. New York: McGraw-Hill, 1969. A short introduction to monasticism, written by the venerable scholar of monasticism.

Leclercq, Jean. *The Love of Learning and the Desire for God: A Study of Monastic Culture*. New York: Fordham University Press, 1982. A classic book on the difference between purely "academic" learning and "monastic" learning.

Meisel, Antony C., and M. L. del Mastro, eds. *The Rule of St. Benedict*. New York: Doubleday, 1975. An excellent introduction accompanies the text.

Norris, Kathleen. *The Cloister Walk*. New York: Riverhead, 1997. A bestselling book on contemporary monasticism, written by an oblate.

CHAPTER 5: HOLY HEROES

Athanasius. *On the Incarnation*. Crestwood, N.Y.: St. Vladimir's Seminary Press, 1993. The most important early defense of the incarnation, written by Athanasius in the early fourth century when he was only nineteen years old.

John Chrysostom. *On Marriage and Family Life*. Crestwood, N.Y.: St. Vladimir's Seminary Press, 1986; and *On Living Simply*. Liguori, Mo.:

Liguori Publications, 1996. The former is a collection of Chrysostom
sermons, the latter a collection of sermon quotes.

John of Damascus. *Three Treatises on the Divine Images.* Crestwood, N.Y.:
St. Vladimir's Seminary Press, 2003. The classic defense of the use of
icons in worship, written by the great eighth-century theologian.

Ware, Timothy. *The Orthodox Church.* New York: Penguin, 1997. Simply
the best introduction to this fascinating tradition.

White, Carolinne, ed. and trans. *Early Christian Lives.* New York: Penguin, 1998. A collection of early Christian biographies.

CHAPTER 6: WINDOWS

Osborne, Kenan B. *Sacramental Theology: A General Introduction.* New
York: Paulist Press, 1988. A Catholic view of the sacraments.

Pfatteicher, Philip H. *Liturgical Spirituality.* Valley Forge, Penn.: Trinity
Press International, 1997. A solid exploration of the spirituality of worship.

Scott, Robert A. *The Gothic Enterprise: A Guide to Understanding the Medieval Cathedral.* Berkeley: University of California Press, 2003. A
short, accessible introduction to these architectural wonders.

Vander Zee, Leonard. *Christ, Baptism and the Lord's Supper: Recovering the
Sacraments for Evangelical Worship.* Downers Grove, Ill.: InterVarsity
Press, 2004. A recent Protestant perspective on the sacraments.

Wagner, Mary Anthony. *The Sacred World of the Christian: Sensed in Faith.*
Collegeville, Minn.: Liturgical Press, 1993. An introduction to the importance of the senses in sacramental theology.

CHAPTER 7: UNION

Colledge, Edmund, and James Walsh, eds. *Julian of Norwich: Showings.*
New York: Paulist Press, 1978. Reflections on her sixteen visions. Insightful, gentle and beautiful.

Cousins, Ewart, ed. and trans. *Bonaventure: The Soul's Journey into God,
The Tree of Life, The Life of St. Francis.* New York: Paulist Press, 1978. A
major figure in medieval mysticism, combining the best of Augustine,
Francis and Pseudo-Dionysius.

Evans, G. R., ed. *Bernard of Clairvaux: Selected Works.* New York: Paulist

Press, 1987. An excellent collection from this magnificent mystic, preacher and poet.

Louth, Andrew. *The Origins of the Christian Mystical Tradition.* New York: Oxford, 1981. A very dense but informative book on mysticism from Plato to Pseudo-Dionysius.

MacQuarrie, John. *Two Worlds Are Ours: An Introduction to Christian Mysticism.* Minneapolis: Fortress Press, 2004. A historical overview of mysticism focusing primarily on major figures.

Penrose, Mary E. *Refreshing Waters from Ancient Wells: The Wisdom of Women Mystics.* Mahwah, N.J.: Paulist Press, 2004. An excellent collection of the writings of women mystics, which includes short biographical sketches of each person.

Peters, E. Allison, ed. *John of the Cross: Dark Night of the Soul.* New York: Doubleday, 1959. An often-cited classic from the period of the Reformation.

CHAPTER 8: ORDINARINESS

Armstrong, Regis, and Ignatius Brady, eds. and trans. *Francis and Clare: The Complete Works.* New York: Paulist Press, 1982. All of their writings in one volume.

Armstrong, Regis J., J. A. Wayne Hellman and William J. Short, eds. *The Francis Trilogy of Thomas of Celano.* Hyde Park, N.Y.: New City Press, 2004. A delightful exposure to Francis of Assisi through the eyes of his close friend and first biographer.

Chesterton, G. K. *St. Francis of Assisi.* Garden City, N.Y.: Image, 1957. A lively and entertaining portrait of the great saint.

Tappert, Theodore G., ed. *Luther: Letters of Spiritual Counsel.* Philadelphia: Westminster Press, 1955. Luther at his pastoral best.

Thomas à Kempis. *The Imitation of Christ.* Notre Dame, Ind.: Ave Maria Press, 1989. The fourteenth-century classic that has influenced so many.

CHAPTER 9: WORD

Bainton, Roland H. *Here I Stand: A Life of Martin Luther.* New York: Abingdon-Cokesbury, 1950. One of the best religious biographies ever written.

Calvin, John. *Golden Booklet of the True Christian Life*. Grand Rapids: Baker, 1952. A section from Calvin's *Institutes* that addresses how Christians should practice faith in ordinary life.

Dillenberger, John, ed. *John Calvin: Selections from His Writings*. New York: Anchor Books, 1971. A collection of Calvin's writings, including sections from the *Institutes of the Christian Religion* and some of his letters.

———. *Martin Luther: Selections from His Writings*. Garden City, N.Y.: Anchor Books, 1961. A wide variety of sources from the pen of Luther.

Parker, T. H. L. *John Calvin: A Biography*. Philadelphia: Westminster Press, 1975. The best of several good biographies of Calvin.

CHAPTER 10: CONVERSION

Bunyan, John. *Grace Abounding to the Chief of Sinners*. New York: Penguin, 1987. Bunyan's autobiography.

———. *The Pilgrim's Progress*. New York: Penguin, 1964. The classic allegory, from the hand of the Baptist Puritan master.

Edwards, Jonathan. *Religious Affections*. Minneapolis: Bethany House, 1996. His groundbreaking work on conversion.

Jeffrey, David Lyle, ed. *A Burning and a Shining Light: English Spirituality in the Age of Wesley*. Grand Rapids: Eerdmans, 1987. An excellent collection of primary sources.

Smith, John E., Harry S. Stout and Kenneth P. Minkema, eds. *A Jonathan Edwards Reader*. New Haven, Conn.: Yale University Press, 1995. A useful collection of Edwards sources.

Whaling, Frank, ed. *John and Charles Wesley: Selected Prayers, Hymns, Journal Notes, Sermons, Letters and Treatises*. New York: Paulist Press, 1981. A collection of diverse Wesley writings.

CHAPTER 11: RISK

Anderson, Courtney. *To the Golden Shore: The Life of Adoniram Judson*. Grand Rapids: Zondervan, 1956. A biography of the first great American foreign missionary who inspired many to follow in his wake.

Elliot, Elisabeth. *Shadow of the Almighty: The Life & Testament of Jim Elliot*. San Francisco: Harper & Row, 1958. A biography of her husband, Jim Elliot, who was martyred in South America in 1956.

George, Timothy. *Faithful Witness: The Life & Mission of William Carey.* Birmingham, Ala.: New Hope, 1991. A recent biography of this intrepid missionary to India.

Grubb, Norman P. *C. T. Studd: Athlete and Pioneer.* Grand Rapids: Zondervan, 1933. An unusual biography about an unusual man.

Ignatius of Loyola. *The Spiritual Exercises of St. Ignatius,* translated by Anthony Mottola. New York: Image, 1964. Ignatius's manual to prepare Christians for a life of rigorous discipleship.

Livingston, W. P. *Mary Slessor of Calabar: Pioneer Missionary.* New York: George H. Doran, n.d. A fascinating account of this courageous woman.

Taylor, Howard, and Mrs. Howard Taylor. *J. Hudson Taylor: God's Man in China.* Chicago: Moody Press, 1965. A moving biography of this great pioneer and founder of the China Inland Mission.

Tucker, Ruth A. *From Jerusalem to Irian Jaya.* Grand Rapids: Zondervan, 1983. An accessible biographical history of Christian missions.

CONCLUSION

Brother Lawrence. *The Practice of the Presence of God.* New York: Barbour, 1993. The classic from the monk who came to know God in the kitchen.

Day, Dorothy. *The Long Loneliness.* San Francisco: HarperSanFrancisco, 1952. An excellent autobiography from the woman who converted from Communism to Catholicism.

Merton, Thomas. *New Seeds of Contemplation.* New York: New Directions, 1961. From the modern Catholic mystic.

Tutu, Desmond. *Crying in the Wilderness: The Struggle for Justice in South Africa.* Grand Rapids: Eerdmans, 1982. A moving account of Tutu's grueling ministry in South Africa.

Illustration Credits

Introduction: There Is More!

Image: Saint Augustine by Antonello da Messina (?1430-1479). Galleria Nazionale, Palermo, Italy
Credit: Scala/Art Resource, NY

Chapter 1: Witness

Image: The Christian Martyr's Last Prayer, 1863-1883 (oil on canvas) by Jean Leon Gerome (1824-1904)
Credit: © Walters Art Museum, Baltimore, USA/The Bridgeman Art Library

Image: Saint Perpetua, detail from vault mosaic. Archbishop's Palace, Ravenna, Italy
Credit: Scala/Art Resource, NY

Image: Polycarp, Bishop of Smyrna
Credit: ©Mary Evans Picture Library/The Image Works

Chapter 2: Belonging

Image: Our Lady of Humility, detail of women in prayer. Church of the Oratorio, Montecchio, Brescia Darfo Boario Terme, Italy
Credit: ©Seat Archive/Alinari Archives/The Image Works

Image: Distribution of the Goods of the Community and Death of Ananias by Masaccio (Maso di San Giovanni). Brancacci Chapel, S. Maria del Carmine, Florence, Italy
Credit: Scala/Art Resource, NY

Image: Baptism Scene. From Lungotevere, Rome. Museo Nazionale Romano (Terme di Diocleziano), Rome, Italy
Credit: Erich Lessing/Art Resource, NY

Chapter 3: Struggle

Image: St Anthony tormented by devils, c. 1475-c. 1500. From the "Sforza Hours." British Library, London
Credit: HIP/Art Resource, NY

Image: Stone desert on the approach to Mount Sinai. Location: Sinai Desert, Egypt
Credit: Erich Lessing/Art Resource, NY

Image: Abba Moses
Credit: Holy Transfiguration Monastery, Brookline, Massachusetts

Image: The sermon of St. Anthony Abbot to the hermits, by Lodovico Carracci (1555-1619). Location: Pinacoteca di Brera, Milan, Italy
Credit: Erich Lessing/Art Resource, NY

Chapter 4: Rhythm

Image: Saint Pachomius
Credit: ©Mary Evans Picture Library/The Image Works

Image: Story of Saint Benedict: detail of the monks dining in the refectory. By Giovanni Antonio Bazzi Sodoma, called Il (1477-1549). Location: Abbey, Monte Oliveto Maggiore, Italy
Credit: Scala/Art Resource, NY

Chapter 5: Holy Heroes

Image: Macrina
Credit: Holy Transfiguration Monastery, Brookline, Massachusetts

Image: Pantocrator
Credit: Holy Transfiguration Monastery, Brookline, Massachusetts

Image: Melania the Younger
Credit: Holy Transfiguration Monastery, Brookline, Massachusetts

Image: John Chrysostom
Credit: Holy Transfiguration Monastery, Brookline, Massachusetts

Chapter 6: Windows

Image: Chartres Cathedral façade. Location: Chartres, France
Credit: Vanni/Art Resource, NY

Image: The Savior by Juan de Juanes. Location: Museo del Prado, Madrid, Spain
Credit: Erich Lessing/Art Resource, NY

Image: Psalter map, c. 1250. Location: British Library, London
Credit: HIP/Art Resource, NY

Image: Saint Theobald the Hermit by Master Francois. From Le Miroir Historial
by Vincent de Beauvais, vol. III. France, 15th C.E. Photo: R. G. Ojeda. Location:
Musee Conde, Chantilly, France.
Credit: Réunion des Musées Nationaux/Art Resource, NY

Chapter 7: Union

Image: Saint Thomas Aquinas, by Gentile de Fabriano (1385-1427). Location:
Pinacoteca di Brera, Milan, Italy
Credit: Scala/Art Resource, NY

Image: Saint Catherine Monastery. Mount Sinai, Sinai Desert, Egypt
Credit: Erich Lessing/Art Resource, NY

Image: Julian of Norwich
Credit: Br. R. Lentz, OFM, 1995/Trinity Stores, trinitystores.com

Chapter 8: Ordinariness

Image: Francis of Assisi
Credit: Br. R. Lentz, OFM, 1995/Trinity Stores, trinitystores.com

Image: The meeting of St. Francis of Assisi and St. Dominic, by Benozzo Gossoli
(1420-1497). Location: S. Francesco, Montefalco, Italy
Credit: Scala/Art Resource, NY

Chapter 9: Word

Image: Engraving of Martin Luther posting ninety-five theses on the castle
church door at Wittenberg
Credit: Foto Marburg/Art Resource, NY

Image: John Calvin
Credit: Library of Congress, Prints & Photographs Division

Image: Calvin's pulpit in Geneva
Credit: Courtesy of Mark A. Gstohl, Ph.D., Asst. Professor of Theology, Xavier
University of Louisiana

Chapter 10: Conversion

Image: John Newton
Credit: The Image Works

Image: George Whitefield preaching in the open air, c. 1750. Wood engraving c. 1870. Ann Ronan Picture Library, London
Credit: HIP/Art Resource, NY

Chapter 11: Risk

Image: Ignatius of Loyola
Credit: Br. R. Lentz, OFM, 1995/Trinity Stores, trinitystores.com

Image: Mary Slessor and adopted children
Credit: Wikipedia/Dundee City Library

Image: William Carey
Credit: Wikipedia/John Brown Myers; London 1887

Conclusion: Where Do We Go from Here?

Image: Famed editor and reformer Dorothy Day attending planning session of anti-Vietnam war activists
Credit: Lee Lockwood//Time Life Pictures/Getty Images

Image: Desmond Tutu
Credit: Wikipedia/ Benny Gool

Notes

Introduction: There Is More!

[1]Augustine, *The Confessions* (Hyde Park, N.Y.: New City Press, 1997), p. 143.

[2]Ibid., pp. 68-69.

[3]C. S. Lewis, introduction to *St. Athanasius: On the Incarnation* (Crestwood, N.Y.: St. Vladimir's Seminary Press, 1993), p. 5.

[4]The word *spirituality* is a recent addition to the theological lexicon, surfacing only some two hundred years ago. Almost from the beginning it had a more heterodox connotation, reflecting what we now understand as the modern fascination with spiritual things outside the boundaries of historic orthodoxy. The Transcendentalists, for example, preferred a word like *spirituality* over *piety* and *holiness* because it reflected, in their minds, an open, experimental attitude, one less tied to tradition. Their use of the term set a trend that has continued to this day. Many Americans now claim to be "spiritual" but not "religious." They like to sample, borrow and experiment with a wide variety of religious beliefs and practices, as if creating a kind of "designer" religion that fits their unique interests and concerns. I have chosen to use the term because it is so widely accepted but also to tether it to a more traditional understanding of the Christian faith.

[5]There are dozens of titles dealing with the history of Christian spirituality. See, for example, Thomas M. Gannon and George W. Traub, *The Desert and the City: An Interpretation of Christian Spirituality* (Chicago: Loyola University Press, 1984); Margaret R. Miles, *Practicing Christianity: Critical Perspective for an Embodied Spirituality* (New York: Crossroad, 1988); Lawrence S. Cunningham and Keith J. Egan, *Christian Spirituality: Themes from the Tradition* (New York: Paulist Press, 1996); Alister McGrath, *Christian Spirituality: An Introduction* (London: Blackwell, 1999); Urban T. Holmes, *A History of Christian Spirituality* (Minneapolis: Seabury Press, 1980); Michael Cox, *Handbook of Christian Spirituality* (San Francisco: Harper & Row, 1983); Cheslyn Jones, Geoffrey Wainwright and Edward Yarnold, eds., *The Study of Spirituality* (New York: Oxford, 1986); Robin Mass and Gabriel O'Donnell, eds., *Spiritual Traditions for the Contemporary Church* (Nashville: Abingdon, 1990); Gordon Mursell, ed., *The Story of Christian Spirituality: Two Thousand Years, from East to West* (Minneapolis: Fortress Press, 2001); Luke Timothy Johnson, *Faith's Freedom: A Classic Spirituality for Contemporary Christians* (Minneapolis: Fortress, 1990); Philip Sheldrake, *Spirituality and History* (New York: Crossroad, 1992); Rowan Williams, *The Wound of Knowledge: Christian Spirituality from the New Testament to St. John of the Cross* (Boston: Cowley, 1991); John Macquarrie, *Paths in Spirituality,* 2nd

ed. (Harrisburg, Penn.: Morehouse, 1992); Bradley C. Holt, *Thirsty for God: A Brief History of Christian Spirituality* (Minneapolis: Augsburg Press, 1993).

[6]"In the Christian understanding of the divine activity, salvation comes not only *in* history but *through* history; history is, as it were, the stuff, the material in which salvation takes place. Salvation is centered in the Christ event; yet even in the simplest forms of Christian affirmation, that event does not stand alone. It takes place as the climax of a long period of preparation; it leads to a long sequel" (Andrew F. Walls, "Globalization and the Study of Christian History," in *Globalizing Theology: Belief and Practice in an Era of World Christianity,* ed. Craig Ott and Harold A. Netland [Grand Rapids: Baker, 2006], p. 70).

[7]Robert Louis Wilken explains Augustine's idea in his excellent book, *The Spirit of Early Christian Thought.* Augustine argued that we must "believe" before we can understand something. By belief he does not mean complete trust or mindless submission but a willingness to let the subject have its way with us first. Only then will we be able to understand it well enough to respond, whether approvingly or critically. See Robert Louis Wilken, *The Spirit of Early Christian Thought* (New Haven, Conn.: Yale University Press, 2003), pp. 166-80.

[8]C. S. Lewis, "Meditation in a Toolshed," *God in the Dock* (Grand Rapids: Eerdmans, 1970), pp. 212-15.

[9]Lamenting such forgetfulness, Alister McGrath writes, "One of the greatest tragedies that has beset Protestant churches in the present century is a loss of corporate, long-term memory, in favor of a time-scale that spans at best a generation. When you're trying to get somewhere, it helps to know where you've come from. Hindsight leads to foresight, as an enhanced awareness of possibilities dawn" (Alister McGrath, *Roots That Refresh: A Celebration of Reformation Spirituality* [London: Hodder & Stoughton, 1991], p. 21).

[10]Rowan Williams, archbishop of Canterbury, argues that a willingness to engage with the "strangeness" of the past will help us to understand our own strangeness too. Conversely, an unwillingness to learn from the past will cause us "to shrink the historical by ignoring or deliberately editing out what is strange, and so to leave us in our modern isolation" (Rowan Williams, *Why Study the Past? The Quest for the Historical Church* [Grand Rapids: Eerdmans, 2005], p. 24).

[11]Augustine, *Confessions*, p. 178.

[12]The debate about the nature of God was resolved for the most part at the Council of Nicea (A.D. 325), which was elaborated on at the Council of Constantinople (A.D. 381). The debate about the nature of Christ as both divine and human was resolved at the Council at Chalcedon (A.D. 451), though certain wings of the church did not accept the teachings of Chalcedon and chose to separate. The two most important dissenting churches were the Monophysites and the Nestorians, both of which exist to this day. See Wilken, *Spirit of Early Christian Thought,* chaps. 4-5; William C. Placher, *A History of Christian Theology: An Introduction* (Philadelphia: Westminster Press, 1983), chap. 6; Jaroslav Pelikan, *The Christian Tradition: A History of the Development of Doctrine,* vol 1, *The Emergence of the Catholic Tradition (100-600)* (Chicago: University of Chicago Press, 1971), chaps. 4-5. For excellent primary source collections on the debate, see William G. Rusch, ed., *The Trinitarian Controversy* (Minneapolis: Fortress Press, 1980); Richard A. Norris Jr. and William

G. Rusch, eds., *The Christological Controversy* (Minneapolis: Fortress Press, 1980).
[13]Augustine, *Confessions,* pp. 282-83.

Chapter 1: Witness

[1]Robin Lane Fox, *Pagans and Christians* (New York: Alfred A. Knopf, 1989), p. 420.

[2]"The intransigence of the braver Christians made a great impression on their brethren and also impressed itself on pagans" (ibid., p. 421).

[3]Paul could be combative about this issue too. He often referred to his own suffering to counter the evil influence of "false apostles" who were undermining his work, especially in Corinth. Paul used his experience of suffering to validate his calling as an apostle. See 2 Corinthians 11.

[4]See Christopher Bryan, *Render to Caesar: Jesus, the Early Church, and the Roman Superpower* (New York: Oxford University Press, 2006); Ivor J. Davidson, *Birth of the Church: From Jesus to Constantine, AD 30-312* (Grand Rapids: Baker, 2004); Larry W. Hurtado, *Lord Jesus Christ: Devotion to Jesus in Earliest Christianity* (Grand Rapids: Eerdmans, 2003).

[5]Recent scholarship has focused on the role martyr accounts played in the early Christian community. See, for example, Daniel Boyarin, *Dying for God: Martyrdom and the Making of Christianity and Judaism* (Stanford, Calif.: Stanford University Press, 1999); Judith Perkins, *The Suffering Self: Pain and Narrative Representation in the Early Christian Era* (London: Routledge, 1995); Elizabeth A. Castelli, *Martyrdom and Memory: Early Christian Culture Making* (New York: Columbia University Press, 2004); Robin Darling Young, *In Process Before the World: Martyrdom as Public Liturgy in Early Christianity* (Milwaukee: Marquette University Press, 2006).

[6]We have many examples that have come down to us. Early church histories, like Eusebius's, for example, contain lengthy accounts of martyrdoms. Eusebius includes pages and pages of quoted material which he lifted, sometimes word for word, from, say, a bishop's letter to a church. Some of these are highly embellished, to be sure. But many are reliable. We must therefore take them on a case-by-case basis. The most famous stories of early martyrdoms—Polycarp, Justin Martyr, Perpetua, Blandina, Cyprian—are clearly reliable, containing much eyewitness material. For an ancient source, see Eusebius, *The History of the Church from Christ to Constantine* (New York: Penguin, 1965). For a scholarly edition of early martyr stories, see Herbert Musurillo, ed., *The Acts of the Christian Martyrs* (New York: Oxford University Press, 1972). Musurillo's book provides an English translation of every story, but also includes the original ancient language source. It is an invaluable resource. Most of these early stories are short. They contain the facts, but they also provide a kind of spiritual commentary as well.

[7]W. H. C. Frend, *Martyrdom and Persecution in the Early Church* (Garden City, N.Y.: Anchor Books, 1967), p. 67. See also his magnum opus, *The Rise of Christianity* (Philadelphia: Fortress Press, 1984).

[8]Justin Martyr, in *The Early Christians in Their Own Words,* ed. Eberhard Arnold (Farmington, Penn.: Plough, 1997), p. 103.

[9]Carpus and Papylus, in Arnold, *Early Christians in Their Own Words,* pp. 73-75.

[10]Henry Bettenson, ed., *Documents of the Christian Church,* 2nd ed. (London: Oxford Uni-

versity Press, 1963), pp. 3-4. Pliny served as governor of Bithynia for two years before he died in A.D. 113. He traveled extensively throughout the territory that fell under his jurisdiction in order to learn better how to rule it. He observed that Christians were causing trouble, and for two reasons. First, Christians were affecting the economy of the region because converts were no longer visiting the temples and buying idols. Second, pagans were charging them with the crime of being disloyal to Rome. Pliny interrogated a number of Christians, including two women deaconesses, tortured some of them and even executed a few. He wrote to ask the emperor for advice.

[11]The word *pagan* literally means "from the country," and it refers to those who practiced traditional Roman religions and thus resisted conversion to Christianity. Obviously the term applies to more than those who lived in the country, though people living in rural areas, whether they were poor peasants or owners of large country estates, were the least open to Christianity. I use the term in these first chapters to refer to people living in the Roman world who adhered to traditional religions or to oriental cults.

[12]John D. Ziziouslas, "The Early Christian Community," in *Christian Spirituality: Origins to the Twelfth Century,* ed. Bernard McGinn and John Meyendorff (New York: Crossroads, 1987), p. 41.

[13]Musurillo, *Acts of the Christian Martyrs,* pp. 63-85.

[14]Athenagoras, *A Plea Regarding Christians,* in *Early Christian Fathers,* ed. Cyril C. Richardson (New York: Touchstone, 1996), pp. 334-40.

[15]"The martyr is the conduit of divine presence who vindicates the claim to another citizenship" (Rowan Williams, *Why Study the Past? The Quest of the Historical Church* [Grand Rapids: Eerdmans, 2005], p. 39).

[16]We have a number of documents from the second and third centuries that serve as good examples. Hippolytus, a teacher in Rome, wrote *The Apostolic Tradition* in the early third century to provide a manual for baptismal instruction and church leadership. It provides invaluable information about early Christian belief and practice. Tertullian, a lawyer and adult convert to Christianity, wrote diatribes against popular Roman culture. His descriptions of the Roman games and other forms of entertainment could be applied with equal force and relevance to much of popular culture today.

[17]See Bettenson, *Documents of the Christian Church,* pp. 1-2. Tacitus made this comment when he was telling the story of the fire of Rome. It was rumored the emperor, Nero, had started it. So Nero used the Christians as a scapegoat. Tacitus charged that they were "haters of the human race," which meant that they appeared to be anti-Roman. It appears that this was a common charge in early Christianity. Minucius Felix, a lawyer converted to Christianity, wrote that pagans often complained about lack of Christian participation in and support for Roman institutions. Pagan critics, he said, complain that Christians "do not go to our shows, you take no part in our processions, you are not present at our public banquets, you shrink in horror from our social games." Again, quoting pagan complaints, he said that Christians "despise temples as if they were tombs. They disparage the gods and ridicule our sacred rites. They look down on our priests although they are pitiful themselves. They despise titles of honor and the purple robe of high government office" (see Arnold, *Early Christians,* pp. 90-91).

[18]For the entire account see Musurillo, "The Martyrdom of Saints Perpetua and Felicitas," *Acts of the Christian Martyrs,* pp. 107-31.

[19]Cicero, quoted in Robert Louis Wilken, *The Christians as the Romans Saw Them* (New Haven, Conn.: Yale University Press, 1984), p. 57.

[20]"There could be skepticism about particular gods and particular rites," historian W. H. C. Frend notes, but the religion of empire, "representing the truths behind them, was inviolable. The gods in their totality were the guardians of Rome. . . . Roman religion was therefore less a matter of personal devotion than of national cult" (Frend, *Martyrdom and Persecution,* pp. 78-79. See also S. R. F. Price, *Rituals and Power: The Roman Imperial Cult in Asia Minor* [New York: Cambridge University Press, 1984]).

[21]Musurillo, *Acts of the Christian Martyrs,* pp. 38-41.

[22]Athenagoras, *A Plea Concerning Christians,* in *Early Christian Fathers,* ed. Cyril C. Richardson (New York: Touchstone, 1996), p. 301.

[23]Tertullian, in Arnold, *Early Christians,* p. 92.

[24]"This universality of claim, this aggressiveness of temper, this consciousness from the first of world-wide dominion . . . was the inevitable cause of Roman persecution" (Herbert B. Workman, *Persecution in the Early Church* [New York: Oxford University Press, 1980], p. 32). He concludes, "But how can a man serve two Emperors, be enrolled under two flags, live in two camps, or go on two different campaigns at the same time? Does not one exclude the other?" (p. 75).

[25]Stephen Benko, *Pagan Rome and the Early Christians* (Bloomington: Indiana University Press, 1984), p. 59.

[26]Eusebius, *History,* pp. 119-22.

[27]James Edwards has written a superb book exploring this topic. See James Edwards, *Is Jesus the Only Savior?* (Grand Rapids: Eerdmans, 2005).

[28]Celsus, quoted in Wilken, *Christians as the Romans Saw Them,* p. 102.

[29]Ibid., pp. 104-5.

[30]Ibid., p. 96. "Everywhere they speak in their writings of the tree of life and of resurrection of the flesh by the tree—I imagine because their master was nailed to a cross and was a carpenter by trade. So that if he had happened to be thrown off a cliff, or pushed into a pit, or suffocated by strangling, or if he had been a cobbler or stonemason or blacksmith, there would have been a cliff of life above the heavens, or a pit of resurrection, or a rope of immortality, or a blessed stone or an iron of love, or a holy hide of leather. Would not an old woman who sings a story to lull a little child to sleep have been ashamed to whisper such tales as these?"

[31]Porphyry, quoted in Wilken, *Christians as the Romans Saw Them,* p. 160.

[32]Ibid., p. 163.

[33]Ibid., p. 145.

[34]In a recent cover story of *Newsweek,* a magazine that does not represent or promulgate a Christian perspective, Jon Meacham writes, "Without the Resurrection, it is virtually impossible to imagine that the Jesus movement of the first decades of the first century would have long endured. A small band of devotees might have kept his name alive for a time, even insisting on his messianic identity by calling him Christ, but the group would have

been just one of the many sects of first-century Judaism" (Jon Meacham, "From Jesus to Christ," *Newsweek,* March 28, 2005, pp. 40-48, quote p. 42).

[35]The martyrs were willing to sacrifice their very bodies to Christ in the arena not because they disparaged their bodies or longed for release from them but because they believed their bodies would be raised as surely as Jesus' body had been. It is not surprising to observe, therefore, that the eternal perfection of the resurrected body "was stressed as a reward for such sacrifice or that the terror of execution was allayed by the suggestion that a sort of anesthesia of glory might spill over from the promised resurrection in to the ravaged flesh of the arena, making its experience bearable," argues historian Carolyn Walker Bynum (*The Resurrection of the Body in Western Christianity, 200-1336* [New York: Columbia University Press, 1995], p. 46).

[36]Wilken, *Christians as the Romans Saw Them,* p. 63.

[37]Justin Martyr, in Arnold, *Early Christians in Their Own Words,* p. 162.

[38]Not that such obstinacy was always the product of perfect motives. Not all martyrs were as noble and humble as Polycarp and Perpetua. Some rushed into martyrdom, wanting the glory of it. They bore witness to themselves more than they bore witness to the gospel. This obsession with martyrdom caused early Christian leaders to establish standards for martyrdom, so that only those who were called to it, against their natural wishes, were given the title "martyr." In this way they hoped to uphold the purpose of martyrdom, which was to bear witness to the truth of the gospel and not to the heroism of a person.

[39]For reliable accounts of modern martyrdom, see James Hefley and Marti Hefley, *By Their Blood: Christian Martyrs of the Twentieth Century* (Grand Rapids: Baker, 1996); and Steve Cleary et al., eds., *Extreme Devotion* (Nashville: Word Publishing, 2001).

[40]David Barrett, "Status of Global Mission, 2007, in the Context of 20th and 21st Centuries," Gordon-Conwell Theological Seminary <www.gordonconwell.edu/ockenga /globalchristianity/resources.php>.

Chapter 2: Belonging

[1]Rodney Stark, *Cities of God: The Real Story of How Christianity Became an Urban Movement and Conquered Rome* (San Francisco: HarperSanFrancisco, 2006), pp. 63-83.

[2]See Robert Louis Wilken, *The Christians as the Roman Saw Them* (New Haven, Conn.: Yale University Press, 1984), pp. 1-66 for excellent information on Pliny's view of early Christianity.

[3]Pliny wrote to Trajan: "There is no shadow of doubt that the temples, which have been almost deserted, are beginning to be frequented once more, that the sacred rites which have been long neglected are being renewed, and that the sacrificial victims are for sale everywhere, whereas, till recently, a buyer was rarely to be found" (Henry Bettenson, ed., *Documents of the Christian Church* [New York: Oxford University Press, 1963)], p. 4).

[4]Ibid., p. 3.

[5]"Letter to Diognetus," in *Early Christian Fathers,* ed. Cyril C. Richardson (New York: Touchstone, 1996), p. 217.

[6]Wayne A. Meeks, *The Origins of Christian Morality: The First Two Centuries* (New Haven, Conn.: Yale University Press, 1993), p. 109.

[7]Aristides, *Apology,* in *The Early Christians in Their Own Words,* ed. Eberhard Arnold (Farmington, Penn.: Plough, 1970), pp. 109-11. The second-century lawyer Tertullian made similar observations: "We are bound together by a common religious conviction, by one and the same divine discipline and by the bond of hope. We form a permanent society and come together for communal gatherings as if forming an army around God and besieging him with our prayers" (pp. 116-18).

[8]Tertullian, *Apologeticus,* in *The Early Christian Fathers,* ed. Henry Bettenson (New York: Oxford University Press, 1956), p. 165.

[9]Julian, quoted in Rodney Stark, *The Rise of Christianity* (Princeton, N.J.: Princeton University Press, 1996), pp. 83-84.

[10]Tatian, "Address to the Greeks," in Arnold, *Early Christians in Their Own Words,* p. 90.

[11]Celsus, quoted in Ramsey MacMullen, *Christianizing the Roman Empire* (New Haven, Conn.: Yale University Press, 1984), p. 37.

[12]See Peter Coleman, *Christian Attitudes to Marriage: From Ancient Times to the Third Millennium* (London: SCM Press, 2004), pp. 120-47.

[13]For recent scholarship on the ordination and ministry of women in early Christianity, see Kevin Madigan and Carolyn Osiek, eds., *Ordained Women in the Early Church: A Documentary History* (Baltimore: Johns Hopkins University Press, 2005); Carolyn Osiek, Margaret Y. MacDonald and Janet H. Tulloch, eds., *A Woman's Place: House Churches in Earliest Christianity* (Minneapolis: Fortress, 2005); Beverly Mayne Kienzle and Pamela J. Walker, eds., *Women Preachers and Prophets Through Two Millenia of Christianity* (Berkeley: University of California Press, 1998). Wayne Meeks argues, "Both in terms of their position in the larger society and in terms of their participation in the Christian communities, then, a number of women broke through the normal expectations of female roles" (*Origins of Christian Morality,* p. 71).

[14]Tertullian, quoted in Carl A. Volz, *Pastoral Life and Practice in the Early Church* (Minneapolis: Augsburg, 1990), p. 78.

[15]Tertullian, quoted in Stark, *Rise of Christianity,* p. 123.

[16]O. M. Bakke, *When Children Became People: The Birth of Childhood in Early Christianity,* trans. Brian McNeil (Minneapolis: Fortress, 2005). Bakke argues that the ancient world had no clear conception of childhood as we would understand that concept today. He shows that the early Christian movement honored children as valuable to God and treated them with special care and concern. In short, early Christianity created the concept of childhood.

[17]See David Batson, *The Treasure Chest of the Early Christians: Faith, Care, and Community from the Apostolic Age to Constantine the Great* (Grand Rapids: Eerdmans, 2001), and Abraham J. Malherbe, *Social Aspects of Early Christianity* (Minneapolis: Fortress Press, 1983).

[18]Athenagoras, "A Plea Regarding Christians," in *Early Christian Fathers,* ed. Cyril C. Richardson (New York: Touchstone, 1996), pp. 310-11.

[19]Ibid., p. 301.

[20]Justin Martyr, quoted in Meeks, *Origins of Christian Morality,* p. 35.

[21]Meeks, *Origins of Christian Morality,* p. 110.

[22]"The Christian church offered a new way of living in this world," concludes Peter Brown (*The World of Late Antiquity: AD 150-750* [New York: Harcourt Brace Jovanovich, 1971], p. 65).

[23]See John E. Stambaugh, *The Ancient Roman City* (Baltimore: Johns Hopkins University Press, 1988); Wayne A. Meeks, *The First Urban Christians* (New Haven, Conn.: Yale University Press, 1983); Meeks, *Origins of Christian Morality;* Karl P. Donfried and Peter Richardson, eds., *Judaism and Christianity in First-Century Rome* (Grand Rapids: Eerdmans, 1998); Stark, *Rise of Christianity;* Peter Brown, *Poverty and Leadership in the Later Roman Empire* (Waltham, Mass.: Brandeis University Press, 2001).

[24]As Peter Brown observes, mobility meant "wider horizons and unprecedented opportunities for travel, . . . the erosion of local differences through trade and emigration, and the weakening of ancient barriers before new wealth and new criteria of status" (*World of Late Antiquity*, p. 60).

[25]Ibid., p. 62.

[26]"Any accurate portrait of Antioch in New Testament times," sociologist Rodney Stark comments, "must depict a city filled with misery, danger, despair, and hatred. A city where the average family lived a squalid life in filthy and cramped quarters. . . . A city filled with hatred and fear rooted in intense ethnic antagonisms and exacerbated by a constant stream of strangers. A city so lacking in stable networks of attachments that petty incidents could prompt mob violence. A city where crime flourished and the streets were dangerous at night" (Stark, *Rise of Christianity,* pp. 160-61).

[27]Joseph H. Hellerman notes that this sense of family made the Christian community "attractive to displaced and fragmented urbanites in antiquity." The individual Christian, "whether slave or free, Roman or barbarian, could count on her brothers and sisters in the faith to provide the affective and material support necessary for survival in the ancient world" (Joseph H. Hellerman, *The Ancient Church as Family* [Minneapolis: Fortress, 2001], p. 220). He challenges the idea that the language of brother and sister in the New Testament and in early Christianity served only to reinforce the dominance of bishops. See also Rowan A. Greer, *Broken Lights and Mended Lives: Theology and Common Life in the Early Church* (University Park: Pennsylvania State University Press, 1986).

[28]Brown, *World of Late Antiquity*, p. 68. See also Bonnie Thurston, *Spiritual Life in the Early Church* (Minneapolis: Augsburg/Fortress, 1993)

[29]Stambaugh, *Ancient Roman City*, p. 135.

[30]Tertullian, *Apology* 39, 40, in Arnold, *Early Christians in Their Own Words*, p. 117.

[31]Hellerman concludes, "Rather, those who had the most to gain from the image of the church as a family were the poor, the hungry, the enslaved, the imprisoned, the orphans, and the widows. For brother-sister terminology in antiquity had nothing to do with hierarchy, power, and privilege, but everything to do with equality, solidarity, and generalized reciprocity" (*Ancient Church as Family*, p. 221).

[32]Eusebius, *The History of the Church* (New York: Penguin, 1965), p. 237.

[33]Pontus, *Life of St. Cyprian*, quoted in *Early Christian Biographies*, ed. Roy J. Deferrari (New York: Fathers of the Church, 1952), p. 14. William H. McNeill notes, "Another advantage Christians enjoyed over pagans was that the teaching of their faith made life

meaningful even amid sudden and surprising death. . . . Christianity was, therefore, a system of thought and feeling thoroughly adapted to a time of troubles in which hardship, disease, and violent death commonly prevailed" (*Plagues and Peoples* [Garden City, N.Y.: Doubleday, 1976], p. 108).

[34]Stark, *Rise of Christianity,* pp. 86-87.

[35]Dionysius, quoted in Eusebius, *History of the Church,* p. 237.

[36]MacMullen, *Christianizing the Roman Empire,* p. 28.

[37]Robert Louis Wilken, "Christian Formation in the Early Church," *Educating People of Faith: Exploring the History of Jewish and Christian Communities,* ed. John Van Engen (Grand Rapids: Eerdmans, 2004), pp. 48-62.

[38]John Chrysostom, quoted in Volz, *Pastoral Life,* p. 141.

[39]Origen, quoted in Volz, *Pastoral Life,* p. 168.

[40]Gregory of Nazianzus, quoted in Volz, *Pastoral Life,* p. 144.

[41]Justin Martyr, *First Apology,* in *Early Christian Fathers,* ed. Cyril C. Richardson (New York: Touchstone, 1996), p. 287.

[42]Cyril of Jerusalem, quoted in Clinton E. Arnold, "Early Church Catechesis and New Christians' Classes in Contemporary Evangelicalism," *Journal of the Evangelical Theological Society,* March 2004, pp. 39-54.

[43]*Didache,* in *Early Christian Fathers,* p. 173.

[44]Hippolytus, *On the Apostolic Tradition* (Crestwood, N.Y.: St. Vladimir's Seminary Press, 2001).

[45]Tertullian, *A Glimpse at Early Christian Life* (Tyler, Tex.: Scroll Publishing, 1991), pp. 21-23.

[46]John D. Ziziouslas comments, "The deeper meaning of baptism for Christian existence involved on the one hand a death of the 'old person,' that is, of the way in which personal identity was acquired through biological birth; on the other hand it involved a birth, that is, the emergence of an identity through a set of relationships, those provided by the church as the communion of the Spirit" ("The Early Christian Community," in *Christian Spirituality: Origins to the Twelfth Century,* ed. Bernard McGinn and John Meyendorff [New York: Crossroad, 1987], p. 28).

[47]Hippolytus, *Apostolic Tradition.*

[48]Virginia De Leon, "Church's Size Can't Hurt Willow," *Spokeman-Review,* December 12, 2005, pp. A1, 9.

Chapter 3: Struggle

[1]Owen Chadwick, ed., *Western Asceticism* (Philadelphia: Westminster Press, 1958), pp. 128-29. *The Sayings of the Desert Fathers* have come to us in two forms: sayings arranged according to topic, as we find in Chadwick's book, and sayings arranged according to the original source, namely, the Abba to whom the saying is attributed. For examples of the former, see Owen Chadwick, *Western Asceticism;* Benedicta Ward, ed., *The Desert Fathers: Sayings of the Early Christian Monks* (New York: Penguin, 2003); and Thomas Merton, ed., *The Wisdom of the Desert* (New York: New Directions, 1960). For examples of the latter, see Benedicta Ward, trans., *The Sayings of the Desert Fathers: The Alphabetical Collection*

(Kalamazoo, Mich.: Cistercian Publications, 1975); and Laura Swan, *The Forgotten Desert Mothers* (New York: Paulist Press, 2001). For a general introduction to the literature, see William Harmless, *Desert Christians: An Introduction to the Literature of Early Monasticism* (New York: Oxford University Press, 2004). The Eastern Orthodox Church has also compiled a four-volume collection of the sayings of Eastern spiritual masters. For two examples, see G. E. H. Palmer, Philip Gherrard and Kallistos Ware, eds., *The Philokalia*, vol. 1 (London: Faber and Faber, 1983) and vol. 4 (1999).

[2]St. Mark the Ascetic, "On the Spiritual Law," in *The Philokalia*, vol. 1, ed. G. E. H. Palmer, Philip Gherrard and Kallistos Ware (London: Faber and Faber, 1983), p. 123.

[3]"The world" refers to the perversion of human dominion over the world, such as exploitation of the earth or excessive desire for power; "the flesh" connotes the perversion of pleasure, usually in the form of some self-indulgence; "the devil" concerns the influence of spiritual evil that seeks to undermine God's plan for the world.

[4]Chadwick, *Western Asceticism*, pp. 61-62.

[5]Anselm Greun, *Heaven Begins Within You: Wisdom from the Desert Fathers* (New York: Crossroad, 1999), p. 38.

[6]Chadwick, *Western Asceticism*, p. 65.

[7]Ibid., pp. 84-85.

[8]Ibid., p. 111.

[9]Ibid., p. 117

[10]James Cowan, *Desert Father: In the Desert with Saint Antony* (New York: Shambhala, 2004).

[11]Athanasius, *The Life of Antony and The Letter to Marcellinus* (New York: Paulist Press, 1980), p. 32. For other collections of biographies of the desert saints, see Tim Vivian, ed., *Journeying into God: Seven Early Monastic Lives* (Minneapolis: Fortress, 1996); Robert T. Meyer, ed., *Palladius: The Lausiac History* (Westminster, Md.: Newman Press, 1965); *The Lives of the Saints of the Holy Land and the Sinai Desert* (Buena Vista, Colo.: Holy Apostles Convent, 1988); Norman Russell, ed., *The Lives of the Desert Fathers* (Kalamazoo, Mich.: Cistercian Publications, 1980); Swan, *Forgotten Desert Mothers*. John Eviratus (John Moschos) collected similar stories from the sixth and seventh centuries after traveling in an arc from Asia Minor to Egypt. See John Moschos, *The Spiritual Meadow* (Kalamazoo, Mich.: Cistercian Publications, 1992). In the 1990s a travel writer retraced John's steps to provide an account of what the geographical and spiritual landscape of the desert tradition looks like today (see William Dalrymple, *From the Holy Mountain: A Journey Among the Christians of the Middle East* [New York: Henry Holt, 1997] for this fascinating account.)

[12]David Brakke, *Demons and the Making of the Monk: Spiritual Combat in Early Christianity* (Cambridge, Mass.: Harvard University Press, 2006).

[13]Athanasius, *Life of Antony*, p. 36.

[14]Ibid., pp. 42, 46.

[15]Ibid., pp. 66-67.

[16]The terms used to describe this movement can be confusing. *Ascetic* refers to those who practiced extreme forms of self-denial. *Monk* initially denoted those who fled into the desert to live in solitude, but it later became associated with the monastic movement; thus

today a monk is one who lives in a monastery. *Hermit* and *anchorite* describe ascetics who live alone, *cenobite* those who live in a community. The movement of the desert saints includes these various expressions of ascetic spirituality.

[17]Antony, quoted in John Chryssavgis, *In the Heart of the Desert: The Spirituality of the Desert Fathers and Mothers* (Bloomington, Ind.: World Wisdom, 2003), p. 84.

[18]Karl Barth notes that the withdrawal into the wilderness was "a highly responsible and effective protest and opposition to the world, and not least to a worldly Church, a new and specific way of combating it, and therefore a direct address to it " (Karl Barth, *Church Dogmatics* 4/2, ed. G. W. Bromiley and T. F. Torrance, trans. G. W. Bromiley [Edinburgh: T & T Clark, 1958], p. 13). See also Jan Willem Drijvers and John W. Watt, eds., *Portraits of Spiritual Authority: Religious Power in Early Christianity, Byzantium and the Christian Orient* (Leiden, U.K.: Brill, 1999).

[19]The desert saints intended to respond with greater depth "to the immense love that God showed us by sending his Son, who became human like us, suffered and died to save us" (Lucian Regnault, *The Day-to-Day Life of the Desert Fathers in Fourth-Century Egypt* [Petersham, Mass.: St. Bede's, 1999], pp. 8-9).

[20]Chyssavgis, *Heart of the Desert*, p. 50.

[21]See Rowan Williams, *The Wound of Knowledge* (London: Darton, Longman & Todd, 1979), pp. 90-94.

[22]Rodney Stark, *The Rise of Christianity* (Princeton, N.J.: Princeton University Press, 1996), chap. 1.

[23]Eusebius, *The History of the Church from Christ to Constantine* (New York: Penguin, 1965). See also H. A. Drake, *Constantine and the Bishops: The Politics of Intolerance* (Baltimore: Johns Hopkins University Press, 2000); and Peter Brown, *Power and Persuasion in Late Aniquity: Towards a Christian Empire* (Madison: University of Wisconsin Press, 1992).

[24]Even before the last great persecution had begun several church leaders noted with alarm that the growth and popularity of Christianity threatened to undermine the high standards of discipleship that the martyrs had established. The great Christian intellectual Origen, who died in 253, noted that the church had not always been so soft. In his youth he had witnessed the martyrdom of his own father, which reminded him that being a Christian had at one time demanded a costly commitment. "Those were the days when Christians really were faithful, when the noble martyrdoms were taking place, when, after conducting the martyrs' bodies to the cemeteries, we returned thence to meet together, and the entire church was present without being afraid. . . . Then there were true believers, few in number, but faithful, treading the straight and narrow way which leads to life." In his mind the church had changed for the worse, largely because of the cessation of persecution. "But now, when we have become many, out of the multitude which profess piety there are extremely few who are attaining to the election of God and to blessedness." Origen himself died a few years later of wounds he had received while under torture for his faith (Origen, quoted in Margaret R. Miles, *Fullness of Life: Historical Foundations for a New Asceticism* [Philadelphia: Westminster Press, 1981], pp. 20-21).

[25]Archimandrite Aimilianos, abbot of the Holy Monastery of Simonopetra, writes that the spirit of martyrdom has always informed the ascetic calling of the desert saints. "The el-

ement, however, which is never absent from any monastic vocation, the one which clearly, emphatically and totally arouses and excites the whole being of those longing for monasticism is the martyr spirit, the passion for passion or suffering, the willingness to persevere, to suffer, to sacrifice oneself, to die for love of God or to express the innermost impulses of one's soul and the quest for the ever-sought-after God." He argues that martyrs practiced a form of asceticism, not only when they died but also in preparation for their death. In his mind what martyrs performed the night before they died (through fasting and praying), monks now perform over a lifetime. "The instrument of this martyrdom is asceticism" (*The Authentic Seal* [Halkidiki, Greece: Ormylia, 1999], p. 251).

[26]Thomas M. Gannon, and George W. Traub, *The Desert and the City* (Chicago: Loyola University Press, 1969), p. 23.

[27]Aideen M. Hartney, *Gruesome Deaths and Celibate Lives: Christian Martyrs and Ascetics* (Exeter, U.K.: University of Exeter Press, 2005).

[28]Elizabeth Clark, *Reading Renunciation: Asceticism and Scripture in Early Christianity* (Princeton, N.J.: Princeton University Press, 1999).

[29]Andrew Louth, *The Wilderness of God* (Nashville: Abingdon, 1991), p. 45.

[30]Gannon and Traub, *Desert and the City*, pp. 26-27.

[31]Douglas Burton-Christie, *The Word of the Desert: Scripture and the Quest for Holiness in Early Christian Monasticism* (New York: Oxford University Press, 1993). Burton-Christie writes persuasively of the central role that Scripture played in the movement. This will become obvious in various places in the rest of the chapter.

[32]Chadwick, *Western Asceticism*, p. 42.

[33]Ibid., p. 43.

[34]The life story of Thomas Merton illustrates the point. Living for years as a Bohemian intellectual in New York City, Merton was converted to the Roman Catholic faith in his early adult years. But he did more than convert; he also became a monk, joining perhaps the strictest order of his day, the Trappists. A few years after his conversion Merton received permission from his superiors to write an autobiography chronicling his journey from city to monastery, from bohemian to monk, from socialite to hermit, which he published under the title *The Seven Storey Mountain*. It became a sensational bestseller in the late 1940s, and it continues to sell at a steady pace to this day. Its popularity is telling. The book does not contain lurid details about his wanton years in New York. The reason for its success lies elsewhere. It explores Merton's *interior* journey from darkness to light. That journey has captured the attention of millions who appear to have found inspiration in his story to evaluate the direction of their own lives. "It is in this darkness," writes Merton, "when there is nothing left in us that can please or comfort our own minds, when we seem to be useless and worthy of all contempt, when we seem to have failed, when we seem to be destroyed and devoured, it is then that the deep and secret selfishness that is too close for us to identify is stripped away from our souls. It is in this darkness that we find true liberty. It is in this abandonment that we are made strong. This is the night which empties us and makes us pure" (*New Seeds of Contemplation* [New York: New Directions, 1972], p. 258).

[35]For a brief biography of Evagrius, see John Bamberger, ed., *Evagrius Ponticus: The Praktikos and Chapters on Prayer* (Spencer, Mass.: Cistercian Publications, 1970). Roberta

Bondi explores the theology of Evagrius at some length. She explains the difference between his view of passion, which in his mind is always bad, and his view of positive emotions, like love. She also expounds on his understanding of the *logismoi* or thoughts that characterize fallen humanity, and she shows how these surface as gluttony and avarice and all the rest. See Roberta C. Bondi, *To Love as God Loves: Conversations with the Early Church* (Philadelphia: Fortress, 1987). See also Anselm Gruen, *Heaven Begins Within You* (New York: Crossroad, 1999); and Louth, *Wilderness of God*. We are indebted to Evagrius for his insight concerning the human inclination toward evil. But not everything he argued was orthodox. He tended to neglect the centrality of Christ in his mystical view of contemplative prayer, for example. For a good critique of his theology, see Gannon and Traub, *Desert and the City*, chap. 1.

[36]Bamberger, *Evagrius Ponticus*, p. 17.

[37]Ibid., pp. 16-20.

[38]Ibid., p. 25.

[39]Ibid., p. 24.

[40]Ibid., p. 36.

[41]Swan, *Forgotten Desert Mothers*, p. 47.

[42]Thomas Merton, ed., *The Wisdom of the Desert: Sayings from the Desert Fathers of the Fourth Century* (New York: New Directions, 1960), p. 62.

[43]For books on asceticism in early Christianity, see Margaret Miles, *Fullness of Life: Historical Foundation for a New Asceticism* (Philadelphia: Westminster Press, 1981); and Vincent Wimbush and Richard Valantasis, eds., *Asceticism* (New York: Oxford University Press, 1995).

[44]Merton, *Wisdom of the Desert*, p. 74.

[45]For a useful book on sexual renunciation in early Christianity, see Peter Brown, *The Body and Society: Men, Women, and Sexual Renunciation in Early Christianity* (New York: Columbia University Press, 1988). See also Susanna Elm, *"Virgins of God": The Making of Asceticism in Late Antiquity* (Oxford: Clarendon Press, 1994).

[46]Syncletica, quoted in *Journeying into God*, ed. Tim Vivian (Minneapolis: Fortress, 1996), p. 48.

[47]Ibid., p. 49.

[48]Ibid.

[49]Ibid., p. 51.

[50]Several books describe the daily life of the desert saints. See, for example, Lucian Regnault, *The Day-to-Day Life of the Desert Fathers in Fourth-Century Egypt* (Petersham, Mass.: St. Bede's, 1999); Derwas J. Chitty, *The Desert a City* (New York: Oxford University Press, 1966); Philip Rousseau, *Ascetics, Authority, and the Church in the Age of Jerome and Cassian* (New York: Oxford University Press, 1978); Jacques LaCarriere, *Men Possessed by God: The Story of the Desert Monks of Ancient Christendom* (Garden City, N.Y.: Doubleday, 1964); James E. Goehring, *Ascetics, Society, and the Desert: Studies in Early Egyptian Monasticism* (Harrisburg, Penn.: Trinity Press, 1999); Marcel Driot, *Fathers of the Desert: Life and Spirituality* (New York: St. Paul Publications, 1992); Louth, *Wilderness of God*; Brown, *Body and Society*.

[51]For books on the importance of community in the desert tradition, see Graham Gould, *The Desert Fathers on Monastic Community* (Oxford: Clarendon Press, 1993); and Carolinne White, *Christian Friendship in the Fourth Century* (Cambridge: Cambridge University Press, 1992).

[52]Several books include a chapter or section on the desert methods of training disciples. See Chryssavgis, *Heart of the Desert;* Rousseau, *Ascetics, Authority, and the Church;* LaCarriere, *Men Possessed by God;* Regnault, *Day-to-Day Life of the Desert Fathers.*

[53]Chadwick, *Western Asceticism,* p. 100.

[54]Esias of Scetis, quoted in Rousseau, *Ascetics, Authority, and the Church,* p. 24.

[55]See Harmless, *Desert Christians.*

[56]John Cassian's writings exercised significant influence in the Middle Ages. They were read in most monasteries; Thomas Aquinas read them every day. See Colm Luibheid, trans., *John Cassian: Conferences* (New York: Paulist Press, 1985).

[57]For an excellent study of these great bishops, see Andrea Sterk, *Renouncing the World Yet Leading the Church: The Monk-Bishop in Late Antiquity* (Cambridge, Mass.: Harvard University Press, 2004). Sterk devotes individual chapters to a number of late fourth-century bishops, including Basil of Caesarea, Gregory of Nyssa, Gregory of Nazianzus and John Chrysostom. See also Conrad Leyser, *Authority and Asceticism from Augustine to Gregory the Great* (Oxford: Clarendon Press, 2000).

[58]Patricia Ranft, *Women and Spiritual Equality in Christian Tradition* (New York: St. Martin's Press, 1998).

[59]This fanaticism sometimes reflected cultural values that departed sharply from Christianity. For example, the philosophy of Platonism drew a sharp line between heaven and earth, spiritual and material, soul and body. To attain heaven, the desert saints sometimes neglected earth; to become spiritual, they sometimes rejected the material; to attend to the soul, they sometimes denied the body. Stoicism taught them that passion of whatever kind was evil. True spirituality required perfect passionlessness *(apatheia)* or perfect "equilibrium," as Antony demonstrated. These various philosophical traditions, highly defused in the culture of the Roman world, exercised some degree of influence, not always positive, over the movement.

[60]Chadwick, *Western Asceticism,* p. 130.

[61]Ibid., pp. 119-20.

[62]Ibid., p. 115.

[63]Ibid., p. 126.

[64]*Philokalia,* 1:107-8.

[65]Ibid., p. 188.

[66]Ibid., p. 125.

[67]Ibid., p. 171.

[68]Ibid., p. 162.

[69]Merton, *Wisdom of the Desert,* p. 37.

[70]Chadwick, *Western Asceticism,* p. 185.

[71]Ibid., pp. 144-45.

[72]St. Mark the Ascetic, "Of Those Who Think They Are Made Righteous by Works," in *The Philokalia,* 1.145.

[73]Peter Brown makes the point that in Syria the desert saints, known as "Holy Men," became the principal advisers and mediators in society because people trusted them as impartial and fair-minded. See Peter Brown, "The Rise and Function of the Holy Man in Late Antiquity," *Journal of Roman Studies* 61 (1971): 80-101.

[74]Merton, *New Seeds of Contemplation,* p. 206.

[75]Chadwick, *Western Asceticism,* p. 40.

Chapter 4: Rhythm

[1]Philip H. Pfatteicher writes, "Whether we live in the city or in the country, whether we work by day or by night or not at all, we are still subject to the deeply evocative symbols of night and day, darkness and light. Daily Prayer is rooted in those primal experiences of all creatures. There is a fundamental rhythm in the world. The rhythm of activity and rest, working and sleeping" (*Liturgical Spirituality* [Valley Forge, Penn.: Trinity Press International, 1997], p. 34).

[2]Peter Levi, *The Frontiers of Paradise: A Study of Monks and Monasteries* (New York: Weidenfeld & Nicolson, 1987), pp. 19-20. Kathleen Norris has also written about the relevance of monasticism for contemporary life. See Kathleen Norris, *The Cloister Walk* (New York: Riverhead Books, 1997).

[3]The apostle Paul, however, raised questions about how far the Christian community should go. He deferred to the Jews at some points, but he also warned about a legalistic attachment to "new moons and festivals," and the like. "Therefore do not let anyone condemn you in matters of food and drink or of observing festivals, or new moons, or sabbaths. These are only a shadow of what is to come; but the substance belongs to Christ" (Col 2:16-17).

[4]There is a huge body of literature on the church year. See, for example, C. Jones et al., eds., *The Study of Liturgy,* rev. ed. (New York: Oxford University Press, 1992); F. E. Brightman, *Liturgies Eastern and Western* (New York: Oxford University Press, 1985); J. G. Davies, *Holy Week: A Short History* (Richmond, Va.: John Knox Press, 1963); and Thomas J. Talley, *The Origins of the Liturgical Year* (New York: Pueblo, 1986).

[5]Many secondary sources explore the emergence and historical development of the monastic movement. See, for example, Christopher Nugent Lawrence Brooke, *The Age of the Cloister: The Story of Monastic Life in the Middle Ages* (Mahwah, N.J.: HiddenSpring, 2003); Jennifer L. Hevelone-Harper, *Disciples of the Desert* (Baltimore: Johns Hopkins, 2005); Peter King, *Western Monasticism* (Kalamazoo, Mich.: Cistercian Publications, 1999); Philip Rousseau, *Pachomius: The Making of a Community in Fourth-Century Egypt* (Berkeley: University of California Press, 1985); C. H. Lawrence, *Medieval Monasticism: Forms of Religious Life in Western Europe in the Middle Ages* (New York: Longman, 2001); David Knowles, *Christian Monasticism* (New York: McGraw-Hill, 1969); Marilyn Dunn, *The Emergence of Monasticism: From the Desert Fathers to the Early Middle Ages* (Oxford: Blackwell, 2000); Derwas J. Chitty, *The Desert a City: An Introduction to the Study of Egyptian and Palestinian Monasticism Under the Christian Empire* (Crestwood, N.Y.: St. Vladimir's Seminary Press, 1966); Mayeul de Dreuille, *Seeking the Absolute Love: The Founders of Christian Monasticism* (New York: Crossroad, 1999); and Mayeul de Dreuille,

A History of Monasticism from East to West (New York: Crossroad, 1999); George A. Hillery, *The Monastery* (Westport, Conn.: Greenwood, 1992). For an older but still insightful book, see Herbert B. Workman, *The Evolution of the Monastic Ideal* (London: Epworth Press, 1913).

[6]Knowles, *Christian Monasticism,* p. 12.

[7]It is no surprise that the first monasteries were founded in Egypt, where Alexandrian Christianity exercised such significant influence, even in regions far removed from that great city. It embodied a series of tensions that provided a rich theological resource for the architects of the monastic movement: an affirmation of the incarnation and rejection of worldliness, service to the needy and withdrawal from the world, theological orthodoxy and openness to Greek ideas, ascetic practice and mystical experience. Alexandrian Christianity engendered a climate of creativity and experimentation. The emergence of monasticism was one result. See Rousseau, *Pachomius,* p. 31.

[8]Ibid., pp. 58-61

[9]Ibid., pp. 75-76.

[10]Knowles, *Christian Monasticism,* p. 10.

[11]Pachomius, quoted in Rousseau, *Pachomius,* pp. 128-29.

[12]Ibid., p. 146.

[13]Douglas J. McMillan and Kathryn Smith Fladenmuller, *Regular Life: Monastic, Canonical, and Mendicant Rules* (Kalamazoo, Mich.: Medieval Institute Publications, 1997). See also Hugh Feiss, ed. and trans., *Essential Monastic Wisdom: Writings on the Contemplative Life* (San Francisco: HarperSanFrancisco, 1999).

[14]For several concise biographical accounts of Basil, see Hans Von Campenhausen, *The Fathers of the Greek Church* (New York: Pantheon, 1955); Dunn, *Emergence of Monasticism;* Anthony Meredith, *The Cappadocians* (Crestwood, N.Y.: St. Vladimir's Seminary Press, 1995); Andrea Sterk, *Renouncing the World Yet Leading the Church: The Monk-Bishop in Late Antiquity* (Cambridge, Mass.: Harvard University Press, 2004).

[15]Basil the Great, *On the Holy Spirit* (Crestwood, N.Y.: St. Vladimir's Seminary Press, 2001).

[16]For an introduction to the Shorter Rule and Longer Rule, with excerpts, see McMillan and Fladenmuller, *Regular Life.*

[17]Basil, quoted in Dunn, *Emergence of Monasticism,* pp. 38-40.

[18]Ibid.

[19]Anthony C. Meisel and M. L. del Mastro, eds., *The Rule of St. Benedict* (New York: Doubleday, 1975), p. 14. I will be using this edition of the Rule throughout this chapter.

[20]The earliest biography of Benedict was written by Gregory the Great, who served as pope from 590 to 604 (see Carolinne White, ed., *Early Christian Lives* [New York: Penguin, 1998], pp. 161-204). It is impossible to determine how much of the biography provides reliable historical information, for Gregory was clearly motivated to present Benedict as an ideal figure. For a modern biography, see Carmen Acevedo Butcher, *Man of Blessing: A Life of St. Benedict* (Brewster, Mass.: Paraclete Press, 2006).

[21]For sources on Benedictine spirituality, see Esther De Waal, *Seeking God: The Way of St. Benedict* (Collegeville, Minn.: Liturgical Press, 2001); Columba Stewart, *Prayer and Com-*

munity: The Benedictine Tradition (Maryknoll, N.Y.: Orbis, 1998); Peter-Damian Belisle,
The Language of Silence: The Changing Face of Monastic Solitude (Maryknoll, N.Y.: Orbis,
2003).

[22]Benedict, in Meisel and Mastro, *Rule of St. Benedict,* pp. 48-50.

[23]Meisel and Mastro, *Rule of St. Benedict,* pp. 70-72.

[24]Ibid., pp. 78-79.

[25]Benedict, in ibid., pp. 76-77.

[26]Meisel and Mastro, *Rule of St. Benedict,* pp. 54-61.

[27]For a history of the Divine Office, see Paul F. Bradshaw, *Daily Prayer in the Early Church:
A Study of the Origin and Early Development of the Divine Office* (New York: Oxford University Press, 1982); Robert Taft, *The Liturgy of the Hours in East and West: The Origins of
the Divine Office and Its Meaning for Today* (Collegeville, Minn.: Liturgical Press, 1986).

[28]There is a growing interest in the practice of lectio divina in the American church today.
Laypeople are attending lectio retreats and using lectio as a discipline in small group Bible
studies. Lectio encourages a complete engagement in the text of Scripture. Practitioners
pay close attention as the text is read; they try to listen for the voice of God.

[29]Jean Leclercq, *The Love of Learning and the Desire for God: A Study of Monastic Culture*
(New York: Fordham University Press, 1982), p. 18.

[30]Ibid., p. 19.

[31]Ibid., p. 22.

[32]Meisel and Mastro, *Rule of St. Benedict,* p. 32.

[33]Richard Fletcher, *The Barbarian Conversion: From Paganism to Christianity* (New York:
Henry Holt & Co., 1997); Ian Wood, *The Missionary Life: Saints and the Evangelisation
of Europe, 400-1050* (Essex, U.K.: Pearson Education Limited, 2001).

[34]For the impact of monasticism on the Western intellectual tradition, see Marcia L. Col-
ish, *Medieval Foundations of the Western Intellectual Tradition: 400-1400* (New Haven,
Conn.: Yale University Press, 1997).

[35]See Barbara H. Rosenwein, *Rhinoceros Bound: Cluny in the Tenth Century* (Philadelphia:
University of Pennsylvania Press, 1982). See also Joan Evans, *Monastic Life at Cluny, 910-
1157* (New York: Oxford University Press, 1931).

[36]See Esther DeWaal, *The Way of Simplicity: The Cistercian Tradition* (Maryknoll, N.Y.: Orbis, 1998). Though not the founder of the Cistercians, Bernard of Clairvaux was clearly
its most prominent leader. See Jean Leclercq, *Bernard of Clairvaux and the Cistercian Spirit*
(Kalamazoo, Mich.: Cistercian Publications, 1976); G. R. Evans, *Bernard of Clairvaux*
(New York: Oxford University Press, 2000).

[37]For a description of daily life in a modern monastery, see George A. Hillery, Jr., *The Monastery: A Study in Freedom, Love, and Community* (Westport, Conn.: Praeger, 1992).

[38]Susan J. White, *The Spirit of Worship: The Liturgical Tradition* (Maryknoll, N.Y.: Orbis,
1999), p. 21.

[39]"The natural rhythms of work and rest, prayer and conversion," writes Benedictine scholar
Columba Stewart, "are basic to human fulfillment. Worry about time and its use easily
preoccupies modern people who feel that they have less and less of it." Stewart believes
that work has become the first priority of modern society, prayer merely optional. To re-

verse that trend, prayer "needs space each day," so that it is protected from the encroachment of all-consuming work. "Benedict ensures that protection by making the schedule of prayer fundamental, with everything else keyed to that basic rhythm." Such a commitment to prayer will actually become "deeply subversive of attempts to put other things first" (Columba Stewart, *Prayer and Community: The Benedictine Tradition* [Maryknoll, N.Y.: Orbis, 1998], pp. 120-21).

Chapter 5: Holy Heroes

[1]Many books have been written over the past few decades to explain this rich and complex tradition to outsiders. Perhaps the best introduction to this fascinating faith tradition is Kallistos Ware, *The Orthodox Church*, rev. ed. (New York: Penguin, 1993). See also Demetrios J. Constantelos, *Understanding the Greek Orthodox Church: Its Faith, History and Practice* (Boston: Seabury Press, 1988); and Elisabeth Behr-Sigel, *The Place of the Heart: An Introduction to Orthodox Spirituality* (Torrance, Calif.: Oakwood, 1992). For the best introductory books on the spirituality of Eastern Orthodoxy, see John Chryssavgis, *Light Through Darkness: The Orthodox Tradition* (Maryknoll, N.Y.: Orbis, 2004); and John Anthony McGuckin, *Standing in God's Holy Fire: The Byzantine Tradition* (Maryknoll, N.Y.: Orbis, 2001).

[2]The Western church is familiar with such terms as *sanctification* and *holiness*, the former a favorite term of John Calvin, the latter of John Wesley and the Methodists. But while in the Western church the term *deification* tends to connote a narrow piety, however inaccurate that might be, in the Eastern tradition it connotes something far more grandiose—the complete transformation of one's life. For example, see John Meyendorff, *Byzantine Theology: Historical Trends and Doctrinal Themes*, 2nd ed. (New York: Fordham University Press, 1983); and Vladimir Lossky, *The Mystical Theology of the Eastern Church* (Crestwood, N.Y.: St. Vladimir's Seminary Press, 1976).

[3]Athanasius, *On the Incarnation* (Crestwood, N.Y.: St. Vladimir's Seminary Press, 1993), p. 41.

[4]Robert Louis Wilken, *The Spirit of Early Christian Thought* (New Haven, Conn.: Yale University Press, 2003), p. 239. "Because of the Incarnation Christianity posits an intimate relation between the material things and the living God." Later in the same chapter Wilken quotes John of Damascus (c. 675-c. 749): "Look how matter is honored" (p. 245). Wilken says of John of Damascus's argument: "His point is that matter has within itself the capacity to become a resting place for God, to become something other while remaining what it is" (p. 248).

[5]The definition of the Second Nicene Council reads: "For the more these are kept in view through their iconographic representation, the more those who look at them are lifted up to remember and have an earnest desire for the prototypes" (Daniel J. Saha, *Icon and Logos: Sources in Eighth-Century Iconoclasm* [Toronto: University of Toronto Press, 1986], p. 179).

[6]John of Damascus, the great apologist of icons, makes a distinction between the results (iconic image) and the process (story behind the image). "I venerate the image of Christ, as God incarnate; of the mistress of all, the Mother of God, as the mother of the Son of

God; of the saints, of the friends of God, who, struggling against sin to the point of blood, have both imitated Christ by shedding their blood for him, who shed his own blood for them, and lived a life following his footsteps. I set down in a record their brave feats and their sufferings, as ones who have been sanctified through them and as a stimulus to zealous imitation" (John of Damascus, *Three Treatises on the Divine Images* [Crestwood, N.Y.: St. Vladimir's Seminary Press, 2003], pp. 34-35).

[7]Gregory of Nyssa, Macrina's younger brother, wrote a biography of her life. See Joan M. Peterson, ed., *Handmaids of the Lord: Contemporary Descriptions of Feminine Asceticism in the First Six Christian Centuries* (Kalamazoo, Mich.: Cistercian Publications, 1996), pp. 39-86.

[8]For short and useful introductions to icons as they developed in Eastern Orthodoxy, see Jaroslav Pelikan, *The Christian Tradition: A History of the Development of Doctrine: The Spirit of Eastern Orthodoxy (600-1700)* (Chicago: University of Chicago Press, 1974), pp. 91-133, and Wilken, *Spirit of Early Christian Thought*, pp. 237-61. For sympathetic treatments of icons, see Egon Sendler, *The Icon: Image of the Invisible: Elements of Theology, Aesthetic and Technique* (Los Angeles: Oakwood, 1988); Henry Maguire, *The Icons of Their Bodies: Saints and Their Images in Byzantium* (Princeton, N.J.: Princeton University Press, 1996); John Baggley, *Doors of Perception: Icons and Their Spiritual Significance* (Crestwood, N.J.: St. Vladimir's Seminary Press, 1988); Michel Quenot, *The Icon: Window on the Kingdom* (Crestwood, N.J.: St. Vladimir's Seminary Press, 2002); Leonid Ouspensky and Vladimir Lossky, *The Meaning of Icons* (Crestwood, N.J.: St. Vladimir's Seminary Press, 1982); Leslie Brubaker and Robert Ousterhout, eds., *The Sacred Image of East and West* (Chicago: University of Chicago Press, 1995); and Anthony Ugolnik, *The Illuminating Icon* (Grand Rapids: Eerdmans, 1988).

[9]Wilken, *Spirit of Early Christian Thought*, p. 257. Wilken quotes Theodore of Studios, an iconodule who lived a century after John of Damascus. "There would not be a prototype [that is, no Christ] if there were no image. . . . If Christ cannot exist unless his image exists in potentiality, and if the image subsists in the prototype before it is produced artistically, then anyone who does not acknowledge that His image is also venerated in Him destroys the veneration of Christ" (ibid.).

[10]John of Damascus, *Three Treatises*, p. 29.

[11]Leonid Ouspensky and Vladimir Lossky, two contemporary Eastern Orthodox writers, explain, "If the Divine Hypostasis of the Son of God became man, our case is the reverse: man can become god, not by nature, but by grace" (Ouspensky and Lossky, *Meaning of Icons*, p. 34).

[12]Again, Ouspensky and Lossky write, "The grace of the Holy Spirit penetrates into his nature, combines with it, and fills and transfigures it. Man grows, as it were, into the eternal life, already here on earth acquiring the beginning of this life, the beginning of deification, which will be made fully manifest in the life to come" (ibid., p. 35).

[13]Ibid., p. 38.

[14]Ibid., p. 37. "Both in icons and in the lives of saints, the first thing that emerges is not the individuality but its subordination to that of which it is the bearer" (ibid.).

[15]Ibid. "Therefore, the icon perforce shows the nature of the service of a saint, whether he be an Apostle, a bishop, a martyr . . . and reproduces with particular care his characteristic, distinctive traits" (ibid.).

[16]Ibid., p. 41. "A man stands, as it were, at the start of a pathway which is not concentrated on some point in depth, but which unfolds itself before him in all its immensity" (ibid.).

[17]John of Damascus, quoted in Margaret R. Miles, *Fullness of Life: Historical Foundations for a New Asceticism* (Philadelphia: Westminster Press, 1981), p. 109.

[18]For sources on the spirituality of icons, see Gennadios Limouris, *Icons: Windows on Eternity: Theology and Spirituality in Color* (Geneva: World Council of Churches, 1990); and Jim Forest, *Praying with Icons* (Maryknoll, N.Y.: Orbis, 2000).

[19]For an excellent source for stories of early martyrdoms, see Herbert Musurillo, ed. and trans., *The Acts of the Christian Martyrs* (New York: Oxford University Press, 1972). For the stories of the early desert saints, see Robert T. Meyer, ed. and trans., *Palladius: The Lausiac History* (Westminster, Md.: Newman Press, 1965). See also Norman Russell, ed. and trans., *The Lives of the Desert Fathers* (Kalamazoo, Mich.: Cistercian Publications, 1980). For an example of a biography of a bishop, see Robert T. Meyers, ed. and trans., *Palladius: Dialogue on the Life of St. John Chrysostom* (New York: Newman Press, 1985). See also Roy J. Deferrari, ed., *Early Christian Biographies in the Fathers of the Church* (New York: Fathers of the Church, 1952); and Carolinne White, ed. and trans., *Early Christian Lives* (New York: Penguin, 1998).

[20]Lawrence Cunningham, *The Meaning of Saints* (San Francisco: Harper & Row, 1980), p. 13. Renate Blemenfeld-Kosinski and Timea Szell argue similarly: "Yet since ordinary Christians turn to saints precisely because of an acknowledged lack of mental and religious competence, commemorating these holy heroes entails above all invoking their names in time of distress, rather than imitating, or meditating on, their virtues" (*Images of Sainthood in Medieval Europe* [Ithaca, N.Y.: Cornell University Press, 1991], p. 16). See also Peter Brown, *The Cult of the Saints: Its Rise and Function in Latin Christianity* (Chicago: University of Chicago Press, 1981); Michael Plekon, *Living Icons: Persons of Faith in the Eastern Church* (Notre Dame, Ind.: University of Notre Dame Press, 2002); Thomas Head, *Hagiography and the Cult of Saints* (New York: Cambridge University Press, 1990).

[21]For a critical introduction to her life, as well as to Gerontius's biography, see Peterson, *Handmaids of the Lord*, pp. 281-362.

[22]Elizabeth A. Clark, ed. and trans., *The Life of Melania the Younger* (Lewiston, N.Y.: Edwin Mellen, 1984). Clark makes the point that Gerontius may have been motivated, at least in part, to write the biography of Melania to defend her orthodoxy, which was being called into question because of her association with Origenists like Evagrius. "She had such zeal for the name of our Lord Jesus Christ and the orthodox faith that if she heard that someone was a heretic, even in name, and advised him to make a change for the better, he was persuaded. . . . But if he was not persuaded, she would in no way accept anything from him to give for the service of the poor" (p. 46). Melania's endowment of monasteries also indicates the high value of monastic expressions of spirituality during this period.

[23]Ibid., p. 65.

[24]Ibid., p. 26.

[25]Ibid., p. 77.

[26]Ibid., p. 34.

[27]Ibid., p. 40.

[28]Ibid., p. 48.

[29]The first spiritual biography of Chrysostom was written by his friend Palladius. See Robert T. Meyer, ed., *Palladius: Dialogue on the Life of St. John Chrysostom* (New York: Newman Press, 1985). The best modern biographies come from the pens of J. N. D. Kelly's *Golden Mouth: The Story of John Chrysostom—Ascetic, Preacher, Bishop* (New York: Cornell University Press, 1995); and of Pauline Allen, *John Chrysostom* (London: Routledge, 1999). An excellent book on Chrysostom as preacher and pastor is by R. A. Krupp, *Shepherding the Flock of God: The Pastoral Theology of John Chrysostom* (New York: Peter Lang, 1991). Andrea Sterk also has an excellent chapter on how the experience of solitude influenced his work as a bishop. See her *Renouncing the World Yet Leading the Church: The Monk-Bishop in Late Antiquity* (Cambridge, Mass.: Harvard University Press, 2004), pp. 141-62.

[30]Robert A. Krupp, "Golden Tongue and Iron Will," *Christian History* 44 (1994): 7.

[31]Robert Payne, "Preaching to Dread and Panic," *Christian History* 44 (1994): 13.

[32]Krupp, "Golden Tongue and Iron Will," p. 10.

[33]John Chrysostom, quoted in Krupp, *Shepherding the Flock of God,* pp. 51-52.

[34]Ibid., p. 176.

[35]John Chrysostom, quoted in Carl A. Volz, "The Genius of Chrysostom's Preaching," *Christian History* 44 (1994): 26. Chrysostom wrote a book on pastoral care too. It is still in print today, which says something about its timelessness. See *Six Books on the Priesthood* (Crestwood, N.Y.: St. Vladimir's Seminary Press, 1964).

[36]Chrysostom, quoted in Robert A. Krupp, "Golden Tongue and Iron Will," *Christian History* 44 (1994): 10.

[37]Ibid., p. 7.

[38]John Chrysostom, *On Wealth and Poverty* (Crestwood, N.Y.: St. Vladimir's Seminary Press, 1997), p. 40.

[39]Ibid., pp. 49-50. For other collections of Chrysostom sermons, see *On Marriage and Family Life* (Crestwood, N.Y.: St. Vladimir's Seminary Press, 1986); and *On Living Simply,* comp. John Van de Weyer (Liguori, Mo.: Liguori Publications, 1996).

[40]Adelphios, quoted in John Moschos, *The Spiritual Meadow,* trans. John Wortley (Kalamazoo, Mich.: Cistercian Publications, 1992), p. 106.

[41]Michael Quenot, a scholar of icons, comments, "Iconography has embraced the entire concept of those Gospel teachings like the Sermon on the Mount, which completely reverse our secular, earthly values" (*The Icon*, p. 106).

[42]C. S. Lewis, *Mere Christianity* (New York: Macmillan, 1952), pp. 172-74.

[43]Peter J. Kreeft, *Heaven: The Heart's Deepest Longing* (San Francisco: Harper & Row, 1980), pp. 108-9.

Chapter 6: Windows

[1]For an introduction to the history and style of Gothic architecture, see Otto von Simson, *The Gothic Cathedral: Origins of Gothic Architecture and the Medieval Concept of Order* (Princeton, N.J.: Princeton University Press, 1956); Robert A. Scott, *The Gothic Enterprise: A Guide to Understanding the Medieval Cathedral* (Berkeley: University of California

Press, 2003); Robert Branner, *Gothic Architecture* (New York: George Braziller, 1961); Charles M. Radding and William W. Clark, *Medieval Architecture, Medieval Learning: Builders and Masters in the Age of Romanesque and Gothic* (New Haven, Conn.: Yale University Press, 1992); Christopher Wilson, *The Gothic Cathedral: The Architecture of the Great Church, 1130-1530* (London: Thames & Hudson, 1990); Paul Frankl, *Gothic Architecture* (New Haven, Conn.: Yale University Press, 1962).

[2]Von Simson, *Gothic Cathedral,* p. 133.

[3]Ibid., pp. 38-39.

[4]"If the architect designed his sanctuary according to the laws of harmonious proportion, he did not only imitate the order of the visible world, but conveyed an imitation of the perfection of the world to come" (ibid., p. 37).

[5]Scott, *Gothic Enterprise,* p. 125.

[6]H. W. Janson, *History of Art,* rev. Anthony F. Janson, 3rd ed. (Englewood Cliffs, N.J.: Prentice-Hall, 1986), p. 302.

[7]The Roman Catholic Church made its official decision at the Council of Florence in 1430, though the church administered the seven sacraments long before they became official. In short, the seven sacraments had functional authority before they had official authority. Protestants observe two sacraments, arguing that Christ himself instituted only those two, baptism and the Eucharist. I agree with Protestants at this point, though I would add that Catholics have a more "sacramental" view of the spiritual life, for they celebrate how God uses his material creation to communicate grace to us.

[8]"We have to accept that as long as we live, we shall be constantly involved in the tension between spiritual and material, soul and body, sacred and secular. To live in these tensions is the condition in which God has placed us, and we must see a right balance between the polarities" (John Macquarrie, *A Guide to the Sacraments* [New York: Continuum, 1997], pp. 3-4).

[9]"The Church's use of the material things of creation as sacramental puts emphasis upon the goodness of matter when such things are used in Christian religious services, whether that be bread and wine, water and oil, incense, color, or lights. All make an appeal to the senses and are used to praise God and help humankind on toward salvation" (Mary Anthony Wagner, *The Sacred World of the Christian: Sensed in Faith* [Collegeville, Minn.: Liturgical Press, 1993], pp. 122-23).

[10]"To create an image of God runs the risk of constructing something which we ourselves have generated." Consequently, "every image which we generate could become an idol" (Alister E. McGrath, *Christian Spirituality: An Introduction* [Oxford: Blackwell, 1999], p. 111).

[11]Kenan B. Osborne, *Sacramental Theology: A General Introduction* (New York: Paulist Press, 1988), p. 120. He is one of many modern theologians who explain the meaning of the sacraments by starting with the incarnation. He borrows extensively from Edward Schillebeeckx, who states, "Religion is behind all our human capabilities. Only by grace, and not in virtue of our own merits, can we truly serve God as person to person. Personal communion with God is possible only in and through God's own generous initiative in coming to meet us in grace" (*Christ the Sacrament of the Encounter with God* [New York: Sheed & Ward, 1963], p. 4).

[12]"It allows us to visualize God in a manner of which God approves. It is not as if we have decided to treat Jesus as if he were an image of the invisible God. It is that we have been told that Jesus is indeed an image of that God, and we are meant to act upon that knowledge" (McGrath, *Christian Spirituality*, p. 113).

[13]Several prominent Roman Catholic and even Protestant theologians call the incarnation of Jesus Christ the "primordial sacrament." I will not use such language because it misconstrues the meaning of the incarnation. Christ's life, death and resurrection is the means of salvation for all those who believe. The sacraments are effectual, however we understand that, through the work of Christ. But Christ himself is not a sacrament. Christ is more than that; Christ is God. See, for example, Karl Rahner, *The Church and the Sacraments* (New York: Herder & Herder, 1963); Edward Schillebeeckx, *Christ the Sacrament of the Encounter with God* (New York: Sheed & Ward, 1963); Osborne, *Sacramental Theology*; and Leonard Vander Zee, *Christ, Baptism and the Lord's Supper: Recovering the Sacraments for Evangelical Worship* (Downers Grove, Ill.: InterVarsity Press, 2004). For example, Kevin W. Irwin writes, "The unity of the human and the divine (one of the aspects of the task involved in Christian spirituality) has been accomplished in Christ, and it is this irrevocable union of humanity and divinity in Christ that makes Christian spirituality that process of living out the implications of this mystery in our own lives." Irwin then uses the incarnation to explain the meaning and purpose of the sacraments and the liturgy of the church (*Liturgy, Prayer and Spirituality* [New York: Paulist Press, 1984], p. 47).

[14]Vander Zee, *Christ, Baptism and the Lord's Supper*, p. 45.

[15]Ibid., p. 46.

[16]Cyprian, quoted in Jaroslav Pelikan, *The Emergence of the Catholic Tradition (100-600)*, The Christian Tradition: A History of the Development of Doctrine, 5 vols. (Chicago: University of Chicago Press), 1:291.

[17]Cyprian, quoted in O. M. Bakke, *When Children Became People: The Birth of Childhood in Early Christianity*, trans. Brian McNeil (Minneapolis: Fortress Press, 2005), p. 71.

[18]For fascinating details of what medieval life was like, see Joseph and Frances Gies, *Life in a Medieval Village* (New York: Harper, 1990), and *Life in a Medieval City* (New York: Harper, 1969).

[19]For example, the Anglican rite reads, "Do you here, in the presence of God and of this congregation, renew the solemn promise and vow that was made in your name at your baptism; ratifying and confirming the same in your own persons, and acknowledging yourselves bound to believe and to do all those things which your sponsors then undertook for you?" (Macquarrie, *Guide to the Sacraments*, p. 83).

[20]Ibid., p. 89.

[21]Jaroslav Pelikan, *The Christian Tradition*, vol. 3, *The Growth of Medieval Theology (600-1300)* (Chicago: University of Chicago Press, 1978), p. 212.

[22]Gies and Gies, *Life in a Medieval Village*, pp. 127-28.

[23]For a fascinating account of liturgies for the sick and the dead, see Frederick S. Paxton, *Christianizing Death: The Creation of a Ritual Process in Early Medieval Europe* (Ithaca, N.Y.: Cornell University Press, 1990).

[24]"During the Middle Ages it was a pious commonplace that pilgrimage was in itself a mer-

itorious act, closely allied with and symbolic of every man's journey towards the heavenly kingdom" (Margaret Wade Labarge, *Medieval Travellers* [New York: W. W. Norton, 1982], p. 68).

[25]For critical translations of her account and an introduction to her life, see John Wilkinson, ed. and trans., *Egeria's Travels*, 3rd ed. (Warminster, U.K.: Aris & Phillips, 1999); George E. Gingras, trans., *Egeria: Diary of a Pilgrimage* (New York: Newman Press, 1970); Amy Oden, ed., *Her Story: Women's Writings in the History of Christian Thought* (Nashville: Abingdon, 1994); and Patricia Wilson-Kastner, et al., eds., *A Lost Tradition: Women Writers of the Early Church* (Washington, D.C.: University Press of America, 1981). For interpretations of her pilgrimage, see Marcel Poorthuis and Joshua Schwartz, eds., *Saints and Role Models in Judaism and Christianity* (Boston: Brill, 2004); Maribel Dietz, *Wandering Monks, Virgins, and Pilgrims: Ascetic Travel in the Mediterranean World, A.D. 300-800* (University Park: Pennsylvania State University Press, 2005), pp. 43-54; E. D. Hunt, *Holy Land Pilgrimage in the Later Roman Empire, AD 312-460* (Oxford: Clarendon Press, 1982); and Lee I. Levine, ed., *Jerusalem: Its Sanctity and Centrality to Judaism, Christianity, and Islam* (New York: Continuum, 1999).

[26]Cyril, quoted in J. G. Davies, *Holy Week: A Short History* (Richmond, Va.: John Knox Press, 1963), p. 36.

[27]For a sympathetic account of the history and the pilgrimage itself, see Walter Starkie, *The Road to Santiago: Pilgrims of St. James* (London: John Murray, 1957). See also Jonathan Sumption, *Pilgrimage: An Image of Medieval Religion* (Totowa, N.J.: Rowman & Littlefield, 1975); Victor Turner and Edith Turner, *Image and Pilgrimage in Christian Culture: Anthropological Perspectives* (New York: Columbia University Press, 1978); and Labarge, *Medieval Travellers*.

[28]Quoted in Sumption, *Pilgrimage*, p. 22.

[29]Cyril of Jerusalem, quoted in Sumption, *Pilgrimage*, p. 23.

[30]"A fantastic assortment of bones, stray bits of timber, thought to be fragments of the True Cross, and the like, were reverently preserved as relics. Their possession brought to the church the protection of the saint and attracted pilgrims hoping for favours and miracles" (Brooke, *Popular Religion*, p. 14).

[31]John of Salisbury, quoted in Brooke, *Popular Religion*, pp. 40-41.

[32]As the incarnation of God in Jesus Christ became a concentrated and localized manifestation of the power of God, asserts Margaret Miles, "the sanctity of particular living or dead human beings, of particular places, and of particular objects" acted like a "lightning rod to collect and communicate God's power" (Margaret R. Miles, *Fullness of Life: Historical Foundations for a New Asceticism* [Philadelphia: Westminster Press, 1981], p. 82).

[33]Richard Kieckhefer, "Major Currents in Late Medieval Devotion," in *Christian Spirituality: High Middle Ages and Reformation*, ed. Jill Raitt (New York: Crossroad, 1988), p. 89. See also Jaroslav Pelikan, *Mary Through the Centuries* (New Haven, Conn.: Yale University Press, 1996); Carl E. Braaten, ed., *Mary: Mother of God* (Grand Rapids: Eerdmans, 2004); Luigi Gambero, ed., *Mary and the Fathers of the Church: The Blessed Virgin in Patristic Thought* (New York: Ignatius, 1991); and Rachel Fulton, *From Judgment to Passion: Devotion to Christ & the Virgin Mary, 800-1200* (New York: Columbia University Press, 2002).

[34]"This development was the more encouraged by Church leaders because it provided a practical means of presenting the facts of the Gospel to the larger number of nominal Christians who flocked into the Church in the wake of Constantine. Here was a method whereby the life of Christ could be set before the worshippers week by week, year in, year out. Through the liturgical cycle, the birth, ministry, death and resurrection of Jesus were brought home to the semi-pagan masses. Time itself was to be sanctified" (Davis, *Holy Week*, pp. 15-16).

[35]Gregory of Nazianzus, "Oration 38, on the Birthday of Christ, AD 380," in *S. Cyril of Jerusalem, S. Gregory Nazianzen*, trans. Edward Hamilton Gifford et al., vol. 7, series 2 of *Nicene and Post-Nicene Fathers*, ed. Philip Schaff and Henry Wace, 14 vols. (Peabody, Mass.: Hendrickson, 1994), p. 346.

[36]Philip H. Pfatteicher, *Liturgical Spirituality* (Valley Forge, Penn.: Trinity Press, 1997), p. 108. Liturgical spirituality has evolved into a branch of the broader study of spirituality. See also Gordon W. Lathrop, *Holy Things: A Liturgical Theology* (Minneapolis: Fortress Press, 1998); Mary Anthony Wagner, *The Sacred World of the Christian: Sensed in Faith* (Collegeville, Minn.: Liturgical Press, 1993); Kevin W. Irwin, *Liturgy, Prayer and Spirituality* (New York: Paulist Press, 1984); Susan J. White, *The Spirit of Worship: The Liturgical Tradition* (Maryknoll, N.Y.: Orbis, 1999); Thomas J. Talley, *The Origins of the Liturgical Year* (New York: Pueblo, 1986); Michael D. Whalen, *Seasons and Feasts of the Church Year* (New York: Paulist Press, 1993); and Robert Gantoy et al., *Days of the Lord: The Liturgical Year* (Collegeville, Minn.: Liturgical Press, 1991).

Chapter 7: Union

[1]For information about his life, theology and mystical experience, see Hans Küng, *Great Christian Thinkers* (New York: Continuum, 2004); Brian Davies, *Aquinas* (New York: Continuum, 2002); and Josef Pieper, *The Silence of St. Thomas* (New York: Pantheon, 1957). Some scholars, like Davies, suggest that Thomas might have had a stroke or mental breakdown, which explains why he stopped writing. But other scholars, like Pieper, disagree. It is hard to understand why Thomas referred to it as a mystical experience if he had only had some kind of stroke.

[2]Plotinus, quoted in Andrew Louth, *The Origins of the Christian Mystical Tradition: From Plato to Denys* (New York: Oxford University Press, 1981), p. 38.

[3]Plotinus, quoted in Michael Cox, *Handbook of Christian Spirituality* (San Francisco: Harper & Row, 1983), p. 39.

[4]Plotinus, quoted in Louth, *Origins of the Christian Mystical Tradition*, p. 46.

[5]Dionysius wrote four major works, *The Celestial Hierarchy, The Ecclesiastical Hierarchy, The Divine Names* and *Mystical Theology*. For excellent introductions to the Pseudo-Dionysius, see Paul Rorem, "The Uplifting Spirituality of Pseudo-Dionysius," in *Christian Spirituality: Origins to the Twelfth Century*, ed. Bernard McGinn and John Meyendorff (New York: Crossroad, 1987); Louis Bouyer, *The Spirituality of the New Testament and the Fathers* (New York: The Seabury Press, 1982), pp. 395-421; Jaroslav Pelikan, *The Christian Tradition*, vol. 2, *The Spirit of Eastern Christendom (600-1700)* (Chicago: University of Chicago Press, 1974), pp. 30-36; Rowan Williams, *The Wound of Knowledge: Christian Spiri-

tuality from the New Testament to Saint John of the Cross (Cambridge: Cowley, 1979), pp.
127-32; Vladimir Lossky, *The Mystical Theology of the Eastern Church* (Crestwood, N.Y.:
St. Vladimir's Seminary Press, 2002); Louth, *Origins of the Christian Mystical Tradition*,
pp. 164-78; Andrew Louth, *Denys the Areopagite* (Wilton, Conn.: Morehouse-Barlow,
1989); Hans Urs Von Balthasar, *The Glory of the Lord: A Theological Aesthetics*, vol. 2, *Studies in Theological Style: Clerical Styles* (San Francisco: Ignatius Press, 1984), pp. 144-210;
Mark A. McIntosh, *Mystical Theology: The Integrity of Spirituality and Theology* (Oxford:
Blackwell, 1998), pp. 44-56. For the best primary source collection of the Pseudo-Dionysius's writings, see Paul Rorem, ed., *Pseudo-Dionysius: The Complete Works* (New York:
Paulist Press, 1987).

[6] Pseudo-Dionysius, quoted in Louth, *Origins of the Christian Mystical Tradition*, p. 167.

[7] Pseudo-Dionysius, "The Celestial Hierarchy," in *Pseudo-Dionysius: The Complete Works*,
ed. Paul Rorem (New York: Paulist Press, 1987), pp. 146-47.

[8] Pseudo-Dionysius, "The Divine Names," in Rorem, *Pseudo-Dionysius*, p. 53.

[9] Pseudo-Dionysius, "The Mystical Theology," in Rorem, *Pseudo-Dionysius*, p. 139.

[10] Ibid. A number of other medieval mystical authors argued similarly. All of them came under the influence of Pseudo-Dionysius, either directly or indirectly. Perhaps the most famous of these medieval mystics is the author of *The Cloud of Unknowing*, who says that in
order to know God we must unknow everything first. See James Walsh, ed., *The Cloud of
Unknowing* (New York: Paulist Press, 1981).

[11] Pseudo-Dionysius, quoted in Louth, *Origins of the Christian Mystical Tradition*, p. 168.

[12] Paul Rorem, "The Uplifting Spirituality," in *Pseudo-Dionysius*, p. 139.

[13] For the most recent biography of John Climacus, see John Chryssavgis, *John Climacus:
From the Egyptian Desert to the Sinaite Mountain* (London: Ashgate, 2004).

[14] Colm Luibheid and Norman Russell, eds., *John Climacus: The Ladder of Divine Ascent*,
The Classics of Western Spirituality (New York: Paulist Press, 1982), p. 12.

[15] John Climacus, quoted in *John Climacus: The Ladder of Divine Ascent*, ed. Colm Luibheid
and Norman Russell (New York: Paulist Press, 1982), p. 158.

[16] Ibid., p. 162.

[17] Ibid., p. 165.

[18] Ibid., p. 81.

[19] Ibid., pp. 91-92.

[20] Ibid., p. 83.

[21] Ibid., p. 231.

[22] Ibid., p. 237.

[23] Thomas Merton, *New Seeds of Contemplation* (New York: New Directions, 1962), pp.
256-57.

[24] Bonaventure, *Bonaventure: The Soul's Journey into God, The Tree of Life, The Life of St.
Francis*, trans. Ewert Cousins (New York: Paulist Press, 1978), p. 54. This collection of
some of his most important spiritual writings contains an excellent introduction to his life
and work. See also Balthasar, *The Glory of the Lord*, 2:260-362.

[25] Bonaventure, *Soul's Journey*, p. 67.

[26] Ibid., p. 98.

[27]Ibid., p. 97.

[28]*The Tree of Life*, for example, offers an extended meditation on the life of Christ, interspersing Gospel stories with poems that he wrote. See *The Tree of Life*, pp. 119-75.

[29]Bonaventure, quoted in von Balthasar, *Glory of the Lord*, 2:275-76.

[30]Bonaventure, *Soul's Journey*, p. 88.

[31]Ibid., p. 106.

[32]Karl Barth, *Church Dogmatics* 4/2, ed. G. W. Bromiley and T. F. Torrance, trans. G. W. Bromiley (Edinburgh: T & T Clark, 1962), p. 539.

[33]See Jn 6:48; 8:12; 10:11; 8:58; and 10:30.

[34]For accessible works on Bernard of Clairvaux, see Jean Leclercq, *Bernard of Clairvaux and the Cistercian Spirit* (Kalamazoo, Mich.: Cistercian Publications, 1976); Jean Leclercq, "The School of Citeaux," in Jean Leclercq, François Vandenbroucke and Louis Bouyer, *A History of Christian Spirituality II: The Spirituality of the Middle Ages* (New York: Seabury Press, 1982); G. R. Evans, *Bernard of Clairvaux* (New York: Oxford University Press, 2000); Adrian Bredero, *Bernard of Clairvaux: Between Cult and Culture* (Grand Rapids: Eerdmans, 1996); James I. Wimsatt, "St. Bernard, the Canticle of Canticles and Mystical Poetry," in *An Introduction to the Medieval Mystics of Europe*, ed. Paul E. Szarmach (Albany: State University of New York Press, 1984). For primary sources, see G. R. Evans, ed., *Bernard of Clairvaux: Selected Works* (New York: Paulist Press, 1987); James M. Houston, ed., *The Love of God and Spiritual Friendship* (Portland, Ore.: Multnomah Press, 1983); M. Basil Pennington, ed., *Bernard of Clairvaux: A Lover Teaching the Way of Love* (Hyde Park, N.Y.: New City Press, 1997).

[35]"Many of his pages are simply mosaics of scriptural expressions, skillfully chosen, compared and arranged, one casting light on the other" (Leclercq, *Bernard of Clairvaux*, p. 21).

[36]"What had previously"—and perhaps most accurately—"been merely a warlike expedition for political ends," comments LeClercq on Bernard's support of the Crusade, "became with him and under his influence and example an act of penance, a step toward conversion" (ibid., p. 67).

[37]Bernard, "On Conversion," in Evans, *Bernard of Clairvaux*, p. 74.

[38]Ibid., p. 76.

[39]Bernard, "On Loving God," quoted in James M. Houston, ed., *The Love of God and Spiritual Friendship* (Portland, Ore.: Multnomah Press, 1983), p. 157.

[40]Ibid., p. 159.

[41]Williams, *Wound of Knowledge*, p. 110.

[42]For the best text of her major work, *Showings*, see *Julian of Norwich: Showings*, trans. Edmund Colledge and James Walsh (New York: Paulist Press, 1978). Julian wrote a "short text" and a "long text" of *Showings*, the latter written twenty years after the former. I will always indicate which text I am using. "ST" refers to the short text: "LT" to the long text. For excellent introductions to Julian's life and theology, see Grace Jantzen, *Julian of Norwich: Mystic and Theologian* (New York: Paulist Press, 1987); Denise Nowakowski Baker, *Julian of Norwich's Showings: From Vision to Book* (Princeton, N.J.: Princeton University Press, 1994); Ritamary Bradley, "Julian of Norwich: Writer and Mystic," in *An Introduction to the Medieval Mystics of Europe*, ed. Paul Szarmach (Al-

bany: State University of New York Press, 1984), pp. 195-216.

[43]The *Ancrene Riwle*, a medieval manual for anchorites, states, "Ye Anchorites have taken to yourselves Mary's part, and Mary's part is quietness and rest from all the world's din, that nothing may hinder her from hearing the voice of God" (quoted in Grace M. Jantzen, *Julian of Norwich: Mystic and Theologian* [New York: Paulist Press, 1987], p. 31).

[44]Again, the *Ancrene Riwle* reads, "Wear no iron, nor haircloth, nor hedge-hog skins; and do not beat yourselves therewith, nor with a scourge of leather thongs, nor leaded; and do not with holly nor with briars cause yourselves to bleed without leave of your confessor; and do not, at one time, use too many flagellations" (ibid., p. 41).

[45]Julian, *Showings*, p. 130 (ST).

[46]Ibid., p. 342 (LT).

[47]Ibid., p. 229.

[48]Ibid., p. 343.

[49]Ibid., p. 248.

[50]Ibid., p. 249.

[51]Merton, *New Seeds of Contemplation*, pp. 1-6.

[52]John of the Cross *Ascent of Mount Carmel* 1.4, Christian Classics Ethereal Library <http://ccel.wheaton.edu>

[53]Ibid., 2.3.

[54]See Cynthia Bourgeault, *Centering Prayer and Inner Awakening* (Cambridge, Mass.: Cowley, 2004).

Chapter 8: Ordinariness

[1]Tertullian, quoted in Jacques Fontaine, "The Practice of Christian Life: The Birth of the Laity," in *Christian Spirituality: Origins to the Twelfth Century*, ed. Bernard McGinn and John Meyendorff (New York: Crossroad, 1987), p. 459.

[2]Feudalism prevailed in much of Western Europe during the early Middle Ages. It was essentially hierarchical in nature. The nobility owned the land. They rented out large portions of it to vassals, who built their own estates. Vassals swore homage to the local lord and often served as knights in his army. Peasants worked the land. They lived off what they produced; they also paid vassals in produce and labor. The church fit nicely into this system, especially monasteries, which became large fiefs under the domination and protection of the nobility. Not all monks, abbots and bishops were so rigid in their thinking, noted Hugh of Lincoln, a twelfth-century monk-bishop: "the kingdom of God is not confined only to monks, hermits, and anchorites. When, at the last, the Lord shall judge every individual, he will not hold it against him that he has not been a hermit or a monk, but will reject each of the damned because he had not been a real Christian ("A Devoted Life," *Christian History* 93 [Winter 2007]: 4).

[3]Abbo of Fleury, quoted in André Vauchez, *The Laity in the Middle Ages: Religious Beliefs and Devotional Practices* (Notre Dame, Ind.: University of Notre Dame Press, 1993), p. 41.

[4]Vauchez, *Laity in the Middle Ages*, p. 12

[5]Ibid. See also Yves Congar, *Lay People in the Church* (Westminster, Md.: Newman Press, 1957), p. 384. "Medieval Christianity," Congar writes, "was the result of two factors:

namely, an innate logic which forced it to direct all worldly activities toward the goal of eternal salvation, and the historical circumstances of its development under the influence of austere monasticism. It inspired a spirituality which was monastic through and through. . . . It imitated the characteristics which were peculiar to monastic life, such as the orientation of life toward eternity and an absence of any evaluation of earthly realities and achievements for their own sake and in themselves" (ibid., p. 384).

[6]Lester Little has written an excellent book about the interaction between the emergence of the profit economy and new spiritual movements in the Middle Ages. See Lester K. Little, *Religious Poverty and the Profit Economy in Medieval Europe* (Ithaca, N.Y.: Cornell University Press, 1978).

[7]"For it was an increasingly independent public that theology had to address, and one that was no longer satisfied with the monastic, hierarchical, and authoritative spirituality of conventional Christendom" (Lucien Joseph Richard, *The Spirituality of John Calvin* [Atlanta: John Knox Press, 1974], p. 137).

[8]The most prominent of these movements included the Cistercians, the Premonstratensians, the Carthusians and the Augustinian Canons. But there were many others.

[9]Fellow Cistercian Peter Celle warned about the dangers of a university education. The monastery, he said, would provide a much better setting for study, one that would nurture piety and protect them from worldly temptation. "No book has to be bought there, the master of the scriptorium does not get paid, there is no onslaught in disputations, no weaving of sophistries; it is free of passing judgment on all questions, free from involvement in all reasoning and argument" (quoted in Little, *Religious Poverty*, p. 93). Not that the Cistercians contributed nothing to the richness of the spiritual life of the Middle Ages. Far from it. Cistercian spirituality left an indelible mark on the medieval church. Bernard of Clairvaux's writings were widely read. Thomas Merton, who died in 1968, was a member of the Cistercian order. Many people, both religious and nonreligious, have read his spiritual writings with a deep sense of appreciation. See, for example, Esther De Waal, *The Way of Simplicity: The Cistercian Tradition* (Maryknoll, N.Y.: Orbis, 1998).

[10]Guido, quoted in Little, *Religious Poverty*, p. 87.

[11]There is a huge body of literature on Francis and the Franciscan movement. For biographies of St. Francis, see Jay M. Hammon, *Francis of Assisi: History, Hagiography and Hermeneutics in the Early Documents* (Hyde Park, N.Y.: New City Press, 2004); Lawrence S. Cunningham, *Francis of Assisi: Performing the Gospel Life* (Grand Rapids: Eerdmans, 2004); Julien Green, *God's Fool: The Life and Times of Francis of Assisi* (San Francisco: Harper & Row, 1985); Arnaldo Fortini, *Francis of Assisi* (New York: Crossroad, 1981); and Omer Englebert, *St. Francis of Assisi: A Biography* (Chicago: Franciscan Herald Press, 1965).

[12]Thomas of Celano, *St. Francis of Assisi*, in *St. Francis of Assisi, Writings and Early Biographies: English Omnibus of the Sources for the Life of St. Francis*, ed. Marion A. Habig, 3rd ed. (London: SPCK, 1973), p. 304. In addition to the biographies written about him, Francis left behind a small collection of writings: two Rules, Admonitions, Prayers and other pieces. The best source for this huge collection of primary sources is Habig's *St. Francis of Assisi;* and Regis Armstrong and Ignatius Brady, trans., *Francis and Clare: The Complete*

Works (New York: Paulist Press, 1982). In the several pages that follow, I will be quoting from the Habig collection of early Franciscan writings.

[13]Celano, *St. Francis of Assisi,* p. 230.

[14]Ibid., p. 234.

[15]Bonaventure, *Bonaventure: The Soul's Journey into God, The Tree of Life, The Life of St. Francis,* trans. Ewert Cousins (New York: Paulist Press, 1978), p. 194.

[16]Celano, *St. Francis of Assisi,* p. 329.

[17]Ibid., p. 266.

[18]Ibid., p. 288.

[19]Ibid., p. 243.

[20]Francis wrote "The Canticle of Brother Sun" as an expression of his deep love for and identification with nature. A few lines read, "Praised be You, my Lord, with all your creatures, especially sir Brother Sun, Who is the day and through whom You give us light. . . . Praised be You, my Lord, through Sister Moon and the stars, in heaven you formed them clear and precious and beautiful."

[21]Celano, *St. Francis of Assisi,* p. 259.

[22]Lazaro Iriarte, *Franciscan History: The Three Orders of St. Francis of Assisi* (Chicago: Franciscan Herald Press, 1982), p. 9.

[23]For books on the history of the Franciscan order, see Cajetan Esser, *Origins of the Franciscan Order* (Chicago: Franciscan Herald Press, 1970); Lazaro de Aspurz Iriarte, *The Franciscan Calling* (Chicago: Franciscan Herald Press, 1974); Lazaro de Aspurz Iriarte, *Franciscan History: The Three Orders of St. Francis of Assisi* (Chicago: Franciscan Herald Press, 1982); John R. H. Moorman, *St. Francis of Assisi: Writings and Early Biographies* (London: SPCK, 1979); John R. H. Moorman, *A History of the Franciscan Order from Its Origins to 1517* (London: SPCK, 1968). For books on Franciscan spirituality, see Brother Ramon, *Franciscan Spirituality: Following Francis Today* (London: SPCK, 1994); and William J. Short, *Poverty and Joy: The Franciscan Tradition* (Maryknoll, N.Y.: Orbis, 1999).

[24]Celano, *St. Francis of Assisi,* p. 305.

[25]M. H. Vicarre, *St. Dominic and His Times* (New York: McGraw-Hill, 1964); Simon Tugwell, ed., *Early Dominicans: Selected Writings* (New York: Paulist Press, 1982); and Simon Tugwell, *The Way of the Preacher* (Springfield, Ill.: Templegate, 1979); William A. Hinnebusch, *A History of the Dominican Order: Origins and Growth to 1550* (New York: Alba House, 1965). See also Thomas M. Gannon, and George W. Traub, *The Desert and the City* (Chicago: Loyola University Press, 1969); Jill Raitt, ed., *Christian Spirituality: High Middle Ages and Reformation* (New York: Crossroad, 1988); and Jean Leclercq et al., *A History of Christian Spirituality II: The Spirituality of the Middle Ages* (New York: Seabury Press, 1982). These books also include excellent material on the Franciscans as well as on the Brethren of the Common Life.

[26]Dominic "seemed to have more zeal than anyone else for the salvation of the human race," André Vauchez observes; "his charity and his compassion were extended not only to the faithful, but also to the infidels, the pagans, and even the damned in hell" (Vauchez, *Laity in the Middle Ages,* p. 99).

[27]For sources on Dominican spirituality, see Richard Woods, *Mysticism and Prophecy: The Dominican Tradition* (Maryknoll, N.Y.: Orbis, 1998); Benedict M. Ashley, *The Dominicans* (Collegeville, Minn.: Liturgical Press, 1990); and Simon Tugwell, *The Way of the Preacher* (Springfield, Ill.: Templegate, 1979).

[28]Little, *Religious Poverty*, p. 173. Vauchez agrees, arguing that "all forms of concrete action in the world aimed at bringing it into conformity with the evangelical ideal." These "grew in importance in the twelfth and thirteenth centuries, in the context of an incarnational Christianity which exalted God's humanity" (Vauchez, *Laity in the Middle Ages*, p. xviii).

[29]"Beyond any particular sets of circumstances that might be offered in explanation, the growth of the laity's role in the church seems to me to be related above all to the rehabilitation of the active life in Christian spirituality. Whether it be holy wars or works of charity, the practice of poverty or the exercise of justice, all forms of concrete action in the world aimed at bringing it into conformity with the evangelical ideal grew in importance in the twelfth and thirteenth centuries, in the context of an incarnational Christianity which exalted God's humanity" (ibid.).

[30]Richard Kieckhefer, *Unquiet Souls: Fourteenth-Century Saints and Their Religious Milieu* (Chicago: University of Chicago Press, 1984), p. 88.

[31]"The harsh asceticism they took upon themselves," Kieckhefer concludes, "their thoroughgoing absorption in prayer, and their alienation from the world about them all grew out of the monastic tradition. . . . While the context of lay piety was secular, its substance was essentially that of the cloister" (ibid., p. 15). Vauchez comes to the same conclusion. "There was no need to flee the world to win salvation: it was better to live within it, not to sanctify oneself by turning profane realities (family and professional life, for example) to religious ends but to be a living example of absolute detachment and devotion to God in the midst of men, slaves to their passions" (Vauchez, *Laity in the Middle Ages*, p. 182; see also André Vauchez, *Sainthood in the Later Middle Ages* [Cambridge: Cambridge University Press, 1997]).

[32]See George Duby, *Love and Marriage in the Middle Ages* (Chapel Hill: University of North Carolina Press, 1994); and Karen A. Winstead, *Virgin Martyrs* (Ithaca, N.Y.: Cornell University Press, 1997).

[33]For information about the Beguines and other lay movements, especially for women, see Patricia Ranft, *Women and the Religious Life in Premodern Europe* (New York: St. Martin's Press, 1996), pp. 61-94; Caroline Walker Bynum, "Religious Women in the Late Middle Ages," in *Christian Spirituality: High Middle Ages and Reformation*, ed. Jill Raitt (New York: Crossroad, 1988); François Vandenbroucke, "New Milieux, New Problems: From the Twelfth to the Sixteenth Century," in Leclercq et al., *History of Christian Spirituality II*, pp. 141-67; Fiona Bowie, *Beguine Spirituality* (New York: Spiritual Classics, 1989); Saskia Murk-Jansen, *Brides in the Desert: The Spirituality of the Beguines* (Maryknoll, N.Y.: Orbis, 1998); Walter Simons, *Cities of Ladies* (Philadelphia: University Press, 2001).

[34]"It seems as though the traditional communities of the Church, valid for all, were no longer sufficient to nourish their Christian life; as though they found, in the practices of their associations, a better means of access to God's word and his grace" (François Van-

denbroucke, "Laity and Clergy in the Thirteenth Century," in Jean Leclercq et al., *A History of Christian Spirituality II*, p. 353).

[35]Jacques de Vitry, quoted in Ranft, *Women and the Religious Life*, p. 72. For an excerpt of his biography of Mary of Oignies, see Bernard McGinn, ed., *The Essential Writings of Christian Mysticism* (New York: Random House, 2006), pp. 60-65.

[36]Jacques de Vitry, quoted in Vandenbroucke, "Laity and Clergy in the Thirteenth Century," p. 358.

[37]Theodore P. van Zijl, *Gerard Groote, Ascetic and Reformer (1340-1384): A Dissertation* (Washington, D.C.: Catholic University of America Press, 1963), p. 74.

[38]John Van Engen, ed., *Devotio Moderna: Basic Writings* (New York: Paulist Press, 1988), p. 23.

[39]Ibid., p. 35. For other sources on Groote and his movement, see Albert Hyma, *The Christian Renaissance: A History of the Devotio Moderna*, 2nd ed. (New York: Archon, 1965); Regnerus R. Post, *The Modern Devotion* (Leiden, The Netherlands: Brill, 1968); and Mark S. Burrows, "Devotio Moderna: Reforming Piety in the Later Middle Ages," in *Spiritual Traditions for the Contemporary Church*, ed. Robin Maas and Gabriel O'Donnell (Nashville: Abingdon, 1990), pp. 109-32. The most widely known and read book that came out of this movement was Thomas à Kempis, *The Imitation of Christ*, trans. William C. Creasy (Notre Dame, Ind.: Ave Maria Press, 1989). It reflects the general features we have just explored.

[40]For a useful introduction to lay movements during the Reformation period, see Carl R. Trueman, "Reformers, Puritans, and Evangelicals: The Lay Connection," in *The Rise of the Laity in Evangelical Protestantism*, ed. Deryck W. Lovegrove (London: Routledge, 2002), pp. 17-35.

[41]John Calvin, *Institutes of the Christian Religion*, ed. John T. McNeill, trans. Ford Lewis Battles (Louisville, Ky.: Westminster John Knox Press, 1960), p. 720.

[42]Martin Luther, *Luther: Letters of Spiritual Counsel*, The Library of Christian Classics 18, ed. Theodore G. Tappert (Philadelphia: Westminster Press, 1955), p. 114.

[43]"The aim is not to get people to do certain things—fasting, going on a pilgrimage, becoming a monk, doing 'good works,' even receiving the sacrament—so much as it is to get people to have faith and to exercise the love which comes from faith" (Tappert, *Luther*, p. 15).

[44]Martin Luther, quoted in Owen Chadwick, *The Early Reformation on the Continent* (New York: Oxford University Press, 2003), pp. 140-41.

[45]Martin Luther, *Luther*, p. 274.

[46]Calvin, *Institutes*, p. 725.

[47]Eventually several Catholic writers—Brother Lawrence and Francis de Sales among them—joined the chorus of voices, arguing that God can be served just as well in the kitchen, factory, classroom and office as in the church or monastery.

[48]A. W. Tozer, *The Pursuit of God* (Harrisburg, Penn.: Christian Publications, 1948), p. 127.

[49]Calvin, *Institutes*, pp. 695-96.

[50]Paul-Gordon Chandler, "Mazhar Mallouhi: Gandhi's Living Christian Legacy in the Muslim World," *International Bulletin of Missionary Research* 27, no. 2 (2003): 54-59.

Chapter 9: Word

[1]"While printing was the novel means of communication," writes Lewis W. Spitz, "it would be a mistake to underestimate the power of the spoken word, the influence of preaching, for the pulpit carried with it great authority. While pamphlets could soften up a public for the reception of reform ideas, the pattern was that evangelical preachers would come or be called to a town, would rally the burghers, who with the guilds would put pressure on the reluctant city council in favor of reform" (Lewis W. Spitz, *The Protestant Reformation, 1517-1559* [New York: Harper & Row, 1985], p. 93).

[2]Hughes Oliphant Old makes the point that the Reformation created a distinct school of preaching but did not necessarily rediscover it. There was much good preaching in the Middle Ages, especially during certain periods, such as the Mendicant movement. "There was a tremendous amount of preaching in the Middle Ages, and much of it was of a high quality. It was done with both learning and devotion. We would be terribly misled if we imagined that the Protestant Reformers rediscovered preaching." See Hughes Oliphant Old, *The Reading and Preaching of the Scriptures in the Worship of the Christian Church,* vol. 4, *The Age of the Reformation* (Grand Rapids: Eerdmans, 2002). For another excellent source on the history of preaching, see O. C. Edwards, *A History of Preaching* (Nashville: Abingdon, 2004).

[3]Edwards, *History of Preaching,* p. 294.

[4]For information on Calvin's preaching besides Edwards and Old, see T. H. L. Parker, *Calvin's Preaching* (Louisville, Ky.: Westminster John Knox Press, 1992); Richard Stauffer, *The Humanness of John Calvin,* trans. George H. Shriver (Nashville: Abingdon, 1971); John Leith, "Calvin's Doctrine of the Proclamation of the Word and Its Significance for Today," in *John Calvin and the Church: A Prism of Reform,* ed. Timothy George (Louisville, Ky.: Westminster John Knox Press, 1990); Leroy Nixon, *John Calvin: Expository Preacher* (Grand Rapids: Eerdmans, 1950); Ronald S. Wallace, *Calvin, Geneva and the Reformation* (Eugene, Ore.: Wipf & Stock, 1998); W. Fred Graham, *The Constructive Revolutionary: John Calvin and His Socio-Economic Impact* (Atlanta: John Knox Press, 1971); Serene Jones, *Calvin and the Rhetoric of Piety* (Louisville, Ky.: Westminster John Knox Press, 1995).

[5]Edwards, *History of Preaching,* p. 313. See also T. H. L. Parker for fascinating details about Calvin as a preacher. Most of these volumes were lost; only some have since been found. The importance of these sermons was eclipsed by Calvin's theological writings and commentaries.

[6]Roland H. Bainton, *Here I Stand: A Life of Martin Luther* (New York: Abingdon-Cokesbury, 1950), p. 348.

[7]For introductions to Reformation spirituality, see T. Hartley Hall IV, "The Shape of Reformed Piety," in *Spiritual Traditions for the Contemporary Church,* ed. Robin Maas and Gabriel O'Donnell (Nashville: Abingdon, 1990), pp. 202-34; Howard Hageman, "Reformed Spirituality," in *Protestant Spiritual Traditions,* ed. Frank C. Senn (New York: Paulist Press, 1986), pp. 55-79; Alister McGrath, *Roots That Refresh: A Celebration of Reformation Spirituality* (London: Hodder & Stoughton, 1991); Howard L. Rice, *Reformed Spirituality: An Introduction for Believers* (Louisville, Ky.: Westminster John Knox Press, 1991); Carter Lindberg, ed., *The Reformation Theologians: An Introduction to Theology in*

the Early Modern Period (Oxford: Blackwell, 2002).

[8]Martin Luther, "Freedom of the Christian," in *Martin Luther: Selections from His Writings,* ed. John Dillenberger (Garden City, N.Y.: Anchor Books, 1961), p. 66.

[9]See Gerald Strauss, *Luther's House of Learning: Indoctrination of the Young in the German Reformation* (Baltimore: Johns Hopkins University Press, 1978). Strauss argues that, however intentional and methodical the catechetical training in Germany, it did not have the effect that was hoped for.

[10]For a thorough discussion of late medieval religion and its impact on the Reformation, see Lewis W. Spitz, *The Protestant Reformation, 1517-1559* (New York: Harper & Row, 1985); Harold J. Grimm, *The Reformation Era, 1500-1650* (New York: Macmillan, 1973); Heiko Oberman, *Forerunners of the Reformation: The Shape of Late Medieval Thought Illustrated by Key Documents* (Philadelphia: Fortress Press, 1981); Owen Chadwick, *The Reformation* (New York: Penguin, 1964); and J. Huizinga, *The Waning of the Middle Ages* (New York: Doubleday Anchor, 1949).

[11]Consequently, "a monastically derived lay piety with prominent clerical ideals of obedience and sexual purity seemed incongruous to an increasingly literate, socially mobile urban laity, who prized simplicity, directness, and respectful treatment in all spheres of their lives" (Steven Ozment, *The Age of Reform, 1250-1550: An Intellectual and Religious History of Late Medieval and Reformation Europe* [New Haven, Conn.: Yale University Press, 1980], p. 220).

[12]Perhaps the most notable example was Erasmus's famous *Praise of Folly,* which openly mocked the church hierarchy, including popes, cardinals, bishops, professors and monks.

[13]For two excellent Luther biographies, see Bainton, *Here I Stand;* and Heiko Oberman, *Luther: Man Between God and the Devil,* trans. Eileen Walliser-Schwarzbart (New York: Doubleday, 1992).

[14]Ozment, *Age of Reform,* p. 242.

[15]"Discovering the Scriptures was a process fraught with surprises and not infrequently with perplexities. He kept finding new passages that spoke to him in the voice of the living God. Scholarship alone would neither have provided this challenge nor would it have been able to cope with it" (Oberman, *Luther,* p. 158).

[16]Ibid., p. 165.

[17]Ibid., p. 176.

[18]Luther, "Freedom of the Christian," in Dillengerger, *Martin Luther,* p. 61.

[19]Martin Luther, quoted in Jared Wicks, *Luther and His Spiritual Legacy* (Wilmington, Del.: Michael Glazier, 1983), pp. 136-37.

[20]Luther, quoted in Ozment, *Age of Reform,* p. 245.

[21]For biographies of Calvin, see T. H. L. Parker, *John Calvin: A Biography* (Philadelphia: Westminster Press, 1975); Alister McGrath, *A Life of John Calvin* (Oxford: Blackwell, 1990); François Wendel, *Calvin: The Origins and Development of His Religious Thought* (New York: Harper & Row, 1950); John T. McNeill, *The History and Character of Calvinism* (New York: Oxford University Press, 1954).

[22]For more information on humanism, see William J. Bousma, "Humanism: The Spirituality of Renaissance Humanism," and James D. Tracy, "Humanism: Ad Fontes. The Hu-

manist Understanding of Scripture as Nourishment for the Soul," in *Christian Spirituality: High Middle Ages and Reformation,* ed. Jill Raitt (New York: Crossroad, 1987), pp. 236-51; Jean Leclercq, François Vandenbroucke and Louis Boyer, *The Spirituality of the Middle Ages* (New York: Seabury Press, 1982), pp. 506-16; John F. D'Amico, *Renaissance Humanism in Papal Rome: Humanists and Churchmen on the Eve of the Reformation* (Baltimore: Johns Hopkins University Press, 1983); Roland H. Bainton, *Erasmus of Christendom* (New York: Crossroad, 1969); and Philip Edgcumbe, *Lefevre: Pioneer of Ecclesiastical Renewal in France* (Grand Rapids: Baker, 1984).

[23]The Bible was more than an ancient book to Erasmus. He was deeply committed to its usefulness and authority. "There is no temptation so strong, no onslaught of the enemy so vehement, that the ardent study of Sacred Scripture does not easily repel, no adversity so full of grief that it does not render bearable" (see Tracy, "Humanism: Ad Fontes," p. 253). For this reason he urged clergy to preach the Scriptures faithfully. "What good is it to be baptized," Erasmus asked, "if one has not been catechized, what good to go to the Lord's Table if one does not know what it means?" (Edwards, *History of Preaching,* p. 275).

[24]John Calvin, "The Author's Preface to the Commentary on the Book of Psalms," in *John Calvin: Selections from His Writings,* ed. John Dillenberger (New York: Anchor Books, 1971), p. 26.

[25]Ibid.

[26]Ibid., p. 28.

[27]Ibid., p. 29.

[28]John Calvin, *Institutes of the Christian Religion* 1.13.1, ed. John T. McNeill, trans. Ford Lewis Battles (Louisville, Ky.: Westminster John Knox Press, 1960).

[29]"At the center of God's accommodating Himself to human capacity is His supreme act of condescension, the giving of His only Son to reconcile a fallen world to Himself" (Ford Lewis Battles, "God Was Accommodating Himself to Human Capacity," in *Readings in Calvin's Theology,* ed. Donald K. McKim (Eugene, Ore.: Wipf & Stock, 1998), pp. 23-24.

[30]Calvin, quoted in Battles, "God Was Accommodating," p. 42.

[31]"Patiently God, through history accommodates His ways of revelation to our condition. Thus, par excellence, the Word made flesh and the written Word from which He speaks are God accommodating Himself to us" (Battles, "God Was Accommodating," p. 38).

[32]Donald K. McKim, "Calvin's View of Scripture," in *Readings in Calvin's Theology,* ed. Donald K. McKim (Eugene, Ore.: Wipf & Stock, 1998), p. 54.

[33]Calvin *Institutes* 1.6.2.

[34]"For as God alone is a fit witness of himself in his Word, so also the Word will not find acceptance in men's hearts before it is sealed by the inward testimony of the Spirit. The same Spirit, therefore, who has spoken through the mouths of the prophets must penetrate into our hearts to persuade us that they faithfully proclaimed what had been divinely commanded" (ibid., 1.7.4).

[35]Ibid., 1.7.5.

[36]Ibid., 1.8.13.

[37]Ronald S. Wallace, *Calvin's Doctrine of the Word and Sacrament* (Grand Rapids: Eerdmans,

1957), p. 83. "Among the many noble endowments with which God has adorned the human race one of the most remarkable is, that He deigns to consecrate the mouths and tongues of men to His service, making His own voice to be heard in them" (ibid., p. 84).

[38]Quoted in Parker, *Calvin's Preaching*, p. 46.

[39]Luther thought of God "as a speaking God, of the gospel as a tale or spoken message, of the Bible not as a book but as preaching, and of the church as a gathering of people who listen to the Word of God being spoken to them" (Wilhelm Pauck, *The Heritage of the Reformation* [New York: Free Press, 1961], p. 106). Vilmos Vajta adds to this perspective in his classic book on Luther and worship. "The pulpit stands between the lectern and the pew. It applies the Bible truths of old to the congregation of today. It is in the sermon that the letter which kills becomes the Spirit which gives life.... After all, the Bible itself witnesses to the importance of the oral gospel in the early church. The sermon does not supercede scripture but 'uses' it." (Vilmos Vajta, *Luther on Worship* [Philadelphia: Muhlenberg Press, 1958], pp. 77-78.)

[40]Martin Luther, in *Luther: Early Theological Works*, ed. and trans. James Atkinson (Philadelphia: Westminster Press, 1962), pp. 194-95.

[41]John Calvin, quoted in Edwards, *History of Preaching*, p. 315.

[42]Ibid.

[43]Calvin, quoted in Parker, *Calvin's Preaching*, p. 81.

[44]Calvin, quoted in Edwards, *History of Preaching*, pp. 315-16.

[45]Calvin, quoted in Parker, *Calvin's Preaching*, p. 40.

[46]Ibid.

[47]Martin Luther, "Sermon at Cobert on Cross and Suffering, 1530," *Luther's Works*, ed. John W. Doberstein, vol. 51 (Philadelphia: Fortress Press, 1959), p. 200.

[48]Luther, quoted in Bainton, *Here I Stand*, p. 355.

[49]Luther, quoted in Edwards, *History of Preaching*, p. 292.

[50]Martin Luther, quoted in *Christian History* 34 (1992): 27.

[51]"The people around Calvin in Geneva required not only spiritual comfort and assurance, they also required guidance as to how each individual in the practice of daily life should respond to the grace of God through a life of faith and obedience" (Wallace, *Calvin, Geneva, and the Reformation*, p. 185). See Elsie Anne McKee, ed., *John Calvin: Writings in Pastoral Piety* (New York: Paulist Press, 2001) for excerpts from Calvin's pastoral writing.

[52]John Calvin, quoted in Wallace, *Calvin, Geneva, and the Reformation*, p. 173.

[53]"Table Talk Recorded by Casper Heydenreich," in Theodore E. Tappert, ed., *Luther: Letters of Spiritual Counsel* (Philadelphia: Westminster Press, 1960), pp. 50-51.

[54]John Calvin, quoted in Stauffer, *Humanness of John Calvin*, p. 45.

[55]Ibid., p. 41.

[56]Quoted in Wallace, *Calvin, Geneva and the Reformation*, pp. 180-81.

[57]Eugene H. Peterson, *Working the Angles: The Shape of Pastoral Integrity* (Grand Rapids: Eerdmans, 1987), p. 88.

[58]Peterson has also written an excellent book on how to read the Bible so that we learn to listen to it too. See Eugene H. Peterson, *Eat This Book: A Conversation in the Art of Spiritual Reading* (Grand Rapids: Eerdmans, 2006).

Chapter 10: Conversion

[1]David Bebbington, a leading scholar of evangelicalism, argues that evangelicalism is founded on four basic principles: the authority of Scripture, the centrality of the crucifixion, the necessity of conversion and the importance of activism. I believe that the first two convictions originated during the Reformation period, which evangelicals have also embraced. I believe that the latter two are at the heart of evangelical spirituality, though activism grows out of conversion. See David W. Bebbington, *The Dominance of Evangelicalism: The Age of Spurgeon and Moody* (Downers Grove, Ill.: InterVarsity Press, 2005).

[2]For the best source on evangelical spirituality, see James M. Gordon, *Evangelical Spirituality: From the Wesleys to John Stott* (London: SPCK, 1991). Gordon provides biographical sketches of evangelical luminaries. See also Douglas A. Sweeney, *The American Evangelical Story: A History of the Movement* (Grand Rapids: Baker Academic, 2005); Keith T. Hardman, *The Spiritual Awakeners: American Revivalists from Solomon Stoddard to Dwight L. Moody* (Chicago: Moody Press, 1983); Ian Randall, *What a Friend We Have in Jesus: The Evangelical Tradition* (Maryknoll, N.Y.: Orbis, 2005); P. Adams, *Roots of Contemporary Evangelical Spirituality* (Bramcote, U.K.: Grove, 1988); J. Cockerton, *Essentials of Evangelical Spirituality* (Bramcote, U.K.: Grove, 1994); G. M. Ditchfield, *The Evangelical Revival* (London: UCL Press, 1998); D. K. Gillett, *Trust and Obey: Explorations in Evangelical Spirituality* (London: DLT Press, 1993). For a collection of primary sources, see David Lyle Jeffrey, ed., *A Burning and a Shining Light: English Spirituality in the Age of Wesley* (Grand Rapids: Eerdmans, 1987). InterVarsity Press is publishing a five-volume history of evangelicalism. Three volumes have already been released. These volumes provide a great deal of information about evangelical spirituality. See Mark A. Noll, *The Rise of Evangelicalism: The Age of Edwards, Whitefield and the Wesleys* (Downers Grove, Ill.: InterVarsity Press, 2003); John Wolffe, *The Expansion of Evangelicalism: The Age of Wilberforce, More, Chalmers and Finney* (Downers Grove, Ill.: InterVarsity Press, 2007); David W. Bebbington, *The Dominance of Evangelicalism: The Age of Spurgeon and Moody* (Downers Grove, Ill.: InterVarsity Press, 2005). See also D. M. Lewis, *Christianity Reborn: The Global Expansion of Evangelicalism in the 20th Century* (Grand Rapids: Eerdmans, 2004). In the past decade scholars have also become interested in the trans-Atlantic nature of evangelicalism. See Richard Carwardine, *Trans-Atlantic Revivalism: Popular Evangelicalism in Britain and America, 1790-1865* (Westport, Conn.: Greenwood Press, 1978); Mark A. Noll, David W. Bebbington and George Rawlyk, eds., *Evangelicalism: Comparative Studies of Popular Protestantism in North America, the British Isles, and Beyond, 1700-1990* (New York: Oxford University Press, 1994); W. R. Ward, *The Protestant Evangelical Awakening* (Cambridge: Cambridge University Press, 1992).

[3]For resources on John Newton's life, see Steve Turner, *Amazing Grace: The Story of America's Most Beloved Song* (New York: HarperCollins, 2002); John Pollock, *Amazing Grace: John Newton's Story* (San Francisco: Harper & Row, 1981); D. Bruce Hindmarsh, *John Newton and the English Evangelical Tradition Between the Conversions of Wesley and Wilberforce* (Oxford: Clarendon Press, 1996); James M. Gordon, *Evangelical Spirituality* (London: SPCK, 1991), pp. 67-92. The magazine *Christian History* (Winter 2004) has devoted an entire issue to the life of John Newton; it contains maps, timelines, articles and visuals.

[4]John Newton, *The Life and Spirituality of John Newton* (Vancouver, Canada: Regent College Publishing, 1998), p. 31.

[5]Ibid., p 31.

[6]Quoted in Turner, *Amazing Grace*, p. 29.

[7]Newton, *Life and Spirituality*, p. 52.

[8]Ibid., p. 56.

[9]Ibid., p. 65.

[10]Ibid. On his last voyage as the captain of a slave ship Newton did not lose one slave, which was virtually unheard of. No doubt he was proud of the accomplishment and considered it a manifestation of his Christian concern for the slaves. Only later in life did he confess that the system itself was morally bankrupt.

[11]Newton, *Life and Spirituality*, p. 70.

[12]Quoted in Turner, *Amazing Grace*, p. 65.

[13]Now available under the title *The Life and Spirituality of John Newton* (Vancouver, B.C.: Regent College Publishing, 1998).

[14]Quoted in Turner, *Amazing Grace*, p. 97.

[15]Ibid., p. 100.

[16]Ibid., p. 109. For an essay on Newton as an ecumenical leader, see Bruce Hindmarsh, "'I Am a Sort of Middle-Man': The Politically Correct Evangelicalism of John Newton," in *Amazing Grace: Evangelicalism in Australia, Britain, Canada, and the United States*, ed. George A. Rawlyk and Mark A. Noll (Grand Rapids: Baker Books, 1993).

[17]Turner, *Amazing Grace*, p. 110.

[18]"Sometimes the fact and experience of conversion," observe Hugh T. Kerr and John M. Mulder, "are related to the search for intellectual truth or the longing for moral purity and goodness." In their minds, this kind of conversion is the more placid one. At other times, however, "deep emotional earthquakes out of the past shatter the present, and make way for a new tomorrow" (*Conversions: The Christian Experience* [Grand Rapids: Eerdmans, 1983], p. ix).

[19]Walter Conn argues that conversion should be understood as a psychological phenomenon (see *Christian Conversion: A Developmental Interpretation of Autonomy and Surrender* [New York: Paulist Press, 1986]). He follows the work of the great William James's *The Varieties of Religious Experience: A Study in Human Nature* (New York: Penguin, 1982); originally published in 1902. James uses the Puritan John Bunyan as a case study in the book.

[20]For an introduction to English Puritanism, see William Haller, *The Rise of Puritanism* (Philadelphia: University of Pennsylvania Press, 1938). See also Patrick Collinson, *The Elizabethan Puritan Movement* (London: Jonah Cope, 1967).

[21]For Bunyan's autobiography see *Grace Abounding to the Chief of Sinners* (New York: Penguin, 1987). For secondary sources, see Robert L. Greaves, *John Bunyan* (Grand Rapids: Eerdmans, 1969), and John Kelman, *The Road: A Study of John Bunyan's* Pilgrim's Progress, vols. 1-2 (Port Washington, N.Y.: Kennikat Press, 1970).

[22]John Bunyan, *The Pilgrim's Progress* (New York: Penguin, 1964), p. 41.

[23]Ibid., p. 144.

[24]See Bruce Hindmarsh, *The Evangelical Conversion Narrative: Spiritual Autobiography in Early Modern England* (New York: Oxford University Press, 2005).

[25]For books on Puritan piety, preaching and conversion, especially in America, see Leland Ryken, *Worldly Saints: The Puritans as They Really Were* (Grand Rapids: Zondervan, 1986); Charles Lloyd Cohen, *God's Caress: The Psychology of Puritan Religious Experience* (New York: Oxford University Press, 1986); Patricia Caldwell, *The Puritan Conversion Narrative: The Beginnings of American Expression* (Cambridge: Cambridge University Press, 1983); Norman Pettit, *The Heart Prepared: Grace and Conversion in Puritan Spiritual Life* (New Haven, Conn.: Yale University Press, 1966); Charles E. Hambrick-Stowe, *The Practice of Piety* (Chapel Hill: University of North Carolina Press, 1986); Owen C. Watkins, *The Puritan Experience* (London: Routledge & Kegan Paul, 1972).

[26]For an introduction to pietism, see Dale Brown, *Understanding Pietism* (Grand Rapids: Eerdmans, 1978); Ted A. Campbell, *The Religion of the Heart: A Study of European Religious Life in the Seventeenth and Eighteenth Centuries* (Columbia: University of South Carolina Press, 1991); Ernest F. Stoeffler, *The Rise of Evangelical Pietism* (Leiden, The Netherlands: E. J. Brill, 1971); Ernest F. Stoeffler, *German Pietism During the Eighteenth Century* (1973); G. T. Halbrooks, ed., *Pietism* (Nashville: Broadman, 1981).

[27]"If we succeed in getting the people to seek eagerly and diligently in the book of life for their joy, their spiritual life will be wonderfully strengthened and they will become altogether different people" (Philipp Jakob Spener, "Pia Desideria," in *Pietists: Selected Writings*, ed. Peter C. Erb (New York: Paulist Press, 1983), p. 34.

[28]Ibid., p. 36.

[29]For sources on the Moravians and Zinzendorf, see J. Taylor Hamilton and Kenneth G. Hamilton, *A History of the Moravian Church* (Bethlehem, Penn.: Moravian Church of America, 1967); Anthony J. Lewis, *Zinzendorf: The Ecumential Pioneer* (Philadelphia: Westminster, 1962); John R. Weinlick, *Count Zinzendorf* (Nashville: Abingdon, 1956).

[30]Nicolas Ludwig von Zinzendorf, quoted in "The Rich Young Ruler Who Said Yes," *Christian History* 1, no.1 (1982): 35.

[31]There were other important leaders too, among them Theodore Freylinghuysen, a member of the Dutch Reformed Church, and Gilbert Tennant, a Presbyterian.

[32]There is a huge body of scholarly literature on Edwards. For the most recent scholarly biography, see George M. Marsden, *Jonathan Edwards: A Life* (New Haven, Conn.: Yale University Press, 2003).

[33]Jonathan Edwards, "Personal Narrative," in *A Jonathan Edwards Reader*, ed. John E. Smith, Harry S. Stout and Kenneth P. Minkema (New Haven, Conn.: Yale University Press, 1995).

[34]Jonathan Edwards, "A Faithful Narrative of the Surprising Work of God," in *A Jonathan Edwards Reader*, ed. John E. Smith, Harry S. Stout and Kenneth P. Minkema (New Haven, Conn.: Yale University Press, 1995), p. 63.

[35]Jonathan Edwards, *Religious Affections*, ed. James M. Houston (Minneapolis: Bethany House, 1996), p. 5.

[36]Ibid., p. 179.

[37]Jonathan Edwards, quoted in Ava Chamberlain, "The Grand Sower of the Seed: Jonathan Edwards's Critique of George Whitefield," *New England Quarterly*, September 1997, p. 380.

[38] Ibid.

[39] Stephen Tomkins, *John Wesley: A Biography* (Grand Rapids: Eerdmans, 2003); Robert G. Tuttle Jr., *John Wesley: His Life and Theology* (Grand Rapids: Zondervan, 1978); Richard P. Heitzenrater, *The Elusive Mr. Wesley* (Nashville: Abingdon, 1984); Charles Yrigoyen Jr., *John Wesley: Holiness of Heart and Mind* (Nashville: Abingdon, 1996); Thomas C. Oden, *John Wesley's Spiritual Christianity: A Plain Exposition of His Teaching on Christian Doctrine* (Grand Rapids: Zondervan, 1994).

[40] John Wesley, *The Journal of John Wesley: A Selection,* ed. Elisabeth Jay (New York: Oxford University Press, 1987), p. 32. For a compilation of Wesley's various writings, see Frank Whaling, ed., *John and Charles Wesley: Selected Prayers, Hymns, Journal Notes, Sermons, Letters and Treatises* (New York: Paulist Press, 1981).

[41] Wesley, *Journal of John Wesley,* pp. 34-35.

[42] Charles E. Hambrick-Stowe, *Charles G. Finney and the Spirit of American Evangelicalism* (Grand Rapids: Eerdmans, 1996); Keith J. Hardman, *Charles Grandison Finney, 1792-1875: Revivalist and Reformer* (Syracuse, N.Y.: Syracuse University Press, 1987); Lewis A. Drummond, *Charles G. Finney and the Birth of Modern Evangelicalism* (London: Hodder & Stoughton, 1983)

[43] Evangelicalism in nineteenth-century America, in fact, allowed women to use their gifts in a variety of ways, including preaching. See Catherine A. Brekus, *Female Preaching in America: Strangers and Pilgrims, 1740-1845* (Chapel Hill: University of North Carolina Press, 1998); Marilyn J. Westerkamp, *Women and Religion in Early America, 1600-1850: The Puritan and Evangelical Traditions* (London: Routledge, 1999).

[44] See Timothy D. Hall, *Contested Boundaries: Itinerancy and the Reshaping of the Colonial American Religious World* (Durham, N.C.: Duke University Press, 1994).

[45] Harry S. Stout, *The Divine Dramatist: George Whitefield and the Rise of Modern Evangelicalism* (Grand Rapids: Eerdmans, 1991).

[46] Charles Edward White, "Spare the Rod and Spoil the Church," *Christian History* 69 (2001): 28-30.

[47] David Hempton, *The Religion of the People: Methodism and Popular Religion, c. 1750-1900* (London: Routledge, 1996); Richard P. Heitzenrater, *Wesley and the People Called Methodists* (Nashville: Abingdon, 1994); J. Kent, *Wesley and the Wesleyans: Religion in Eighteenth-Century Britain* (New York: Cambridge University Press, 2002); David W. Bebbington, *Evangelicalism in Modern Britain: A History From the 1730s to the 1980s* (London: Routledge, 1989); John H. Wigger, *Taking Heaven by Storm: Methodism and the Rise of Popular Christianity in America* (New York: Oxford University Press, 1998); H. B. McGonigle, *Sufficient Saving Grace: John Wesley's Evangelical Arminianism* (Carlisle, U.K.: Paternoster, 2001); H. D. Rock, *Reasonable Enthusiast: John Wesley and the Rise of Methodism* (London: Epworth Press, 1989).

[48] See D. M. Lewis, ed., *Christianity Reborn: The Global Expansion of Evangelicalism in the Twentieth Century* (Grand Rapids: Eerdmans, 2004).

Chapter 11: Risk

[1] "Incarnation," Andrew Walls states, "is translation. When God in Christ became man,

Divinity was translated into humanity, as though humanity were a receptor language." "In the light of the frustrations inherent in the translation process," Walls continues, "it is the more astonishing that God chose translation as his mode of action for the salvation of humanity. Christian faith rests on a divine act of translation: 'the Word became flesh and dwelt among us' (John 1:14)" (*The Missionary Movement in Christian History: Studies in the Transmission of Faith* [Maryknoll, N.Y.: Orbis, 1996], p. 26).

[2]The Gospel of Luke in particular tells many stories of the way Jesus reached out to women, Gentiles and other outsiders.

[3]Scholars argue that the Jerusalem Council marks a turning point in the history of Christianity, for it set missionaries free to adapt the Christian faith to non-Jewish cultures.

[4]See, for example, Lamin Sanneh, *Translating the Message: The Missionary Impact on Culture* (Maryknoll, N.Y.: Orbis, 2004); Lamin Sanneh, *Whose Religion Is Christianity?* (Grand Rapids: Eerdmans, 2003); and Lesslie Newbigin, *Foolishness to the Greeks: The Gospel and Western Culture* (Grand Rapids: Eerdmans, 1986).

[5]I am indebted to several noteworthy books for this short section. Kenneth Scott Latourette has written the standard work on the history of missions. Andrew Walls has written a superb book on how missionaries have actually functioned throughout history, with special attention given to the modern period. Stephen Neill's book provides a concise and detailed summary of the history of Christian missions. Ruth Tucker's book tells the story of missions largely from a biographical perspective. W. H. C. Frend provides almost exhaustive information on early Christian missions, and Rodney Stark adds a sociological perspective to the same period. Ian Wood covers the early medieval period. See Kenneth Scott Latourette, *A History of the Expansion of Christianity*, 7 vols. (New York: Harper & Brothers, 1937-1945); Andrew Walls, *The Missionary Movement in Christian History: Studies in the Transmission of Faith* (Maryknoll, N.Y.: Orbis, 1996); Stephen Neill, *A History of Christian Missions* (New York: Penguin, 1964); Ruth A. Tucker, *From Jerusalem to Irian Jaya: A Biographical History of Christian Missions* (Grand Rapids: Zondervan, 1983); W. H. C. Frend, *The Rise of Christianity* (Philadelphia: Fortress, 1984); Rodney Stark, *The Rise of Christianity* (Princeton, N.J.: Princeton University Press, 1996); Ian Wood, *The Missionary Life: Saints and the Evangelisation of Europe, 400-1050* (Essex, U.K.: Pearson Education, 2001); Gerald H. Anderson, ed., *Biographical Dictionary of Christian Missions* (New York: Simon & Schuster, 1998).

[6]Written in 325 and revised in 381, the Nicene Creed explains that God is one in community, or a triunity; the Chalcedonian formula asserts that Christ is one person with two natures, a divine nature and a human nature.

[7]See J. N. Hillgarth, ed., *Christianity and Paganism, 350-750: The Conversion of Western Europe* (Philadelphia: University of Pennsylvania Press, 1986); and Richard Fletcher, *The Barbarian Conversion: From Paganism to Christianity* (Berkeley: University of California Press, 1997).

[8]Andrew Porter, *Religion vs. Empire? British Protestant Missionaries and Overseas Expansion, 1700-1914* (Manchester, U.K.: Manchester University Press, 2004). See also Brian Stanley, ed., *Missions, Nationalism, and the End of Empire* (Grand Rapids: Eerdmans, 2003).

[9]William R. Hutchison, *Errand to the World: American Protestant Thought and Foreign Missions* (Chicago: University of Chicago Press, 1987); Joel A. Carpenter and Wilbert R. Shenk, eds., *Earthen Vessels: American Evangelicals and Foreign Missions, 1880-1980* (Grand Rapids: Eerdmans, 1990); Wilbert R. Shenk, ed., *North American Foreign Missions, 1810-1914: Theology, Theory, and Policy* (Grand Rapids: Eerdmans, 2004); Dana L. Robert, *American Women in Mission* (Atlanta: Mercer University Press, 1997).

[10]John W. O'Malley, *The First Jesuits* (Cambridge, Mass.: Harvard University Press, 1993), chap. 1. For an excellent book on Jesuit spirituality, see David Lonsdale, *Eyes to See, Ears to Hear: An Introduction to Ignatian Spirituality* (London: Darton, Longman & Todd, 1990).

[11]Ignatius Loyola, *The Spiritual Exercises of St. Ignatius*, trans. Anthony Mottola, (New York: Doubleday, 1964), p. 41.

[12]Ignatius Loyola, quoted in O'Malley, *First Jesuits*, p. 37.

[13]Edwin S. Gaustad, ed., *A Documentary History of Religion in America: To the Civil War* (Grand Rapids: Eerdmans, 1982), pp. 75-78.

[14]Ibid. See also Francis Parkman, *The Jesuits in North America*. The Jesuits left a lengthy record of their work in the New World that ran to over seventy volumes. For examples of those documents see R. G. Thwaites, ed., *Jesuit Relations and Allied Documents* (Cleveland: Burrows, 1896-1901). For a short history of the founder of the Jesuits, see John Patrick Donnelly, *Ignatius of Loyola: Founder of the Jesuits* (New York: Longman, 2004.) For a history of the early years of the order, see O'Malley, *First Jesuits*.

[15]I have chosen to use the biographies of only a few great pioneer missionaries. I could have used dozens of others. Most of these works would not be considered "critical" biographies that look objectively at a missionary's life. While they do not intentionally distort the facts, these biographies aim to inspire, convict and recruit readers to the cause of world missions. In addition to the biographies mentioned in the following notes, see Courtney Anderson, *To the Golden Shore: The Life of Adoniram Judson* (Grand Rapids: Zondervan, 1956); Jim Cromarty, *It Is Not Death to Die: A New Biography of Hudson Taylor* (Fearn, U.K.: Christian Focus, 2001); Elisabeth Elliot, *A Chance to Die: The Life and Legacy of Amy Carmichael* (Old Tappan, N.J.: Revell, 1987); Rosalind Goforth, *Goforth of China* (Grand Rapids: Zondervan, 1937); Howard Taylor and Mrs. Howard Taylor, *Hudson Taylor's Spiritual Secret* (Chicago: Moody Press, 1989); Howard Taylor and Mrs. Howard Taylor, *J. Hudson Taylor: God's Man in China* (Chicago: Moody Press, 1965); Mrs. Howard Taylor, *Borden of Yale* (Minneapolis: Bethany House, 1988); Mrs. Howard Taylor, *Pastor Hsi* (Singapore: Overseas Missionary Fellowship, 1900); Catherine B. Allen, *The New Lottie Moon Story* (Nashville: Broadman, 1980).

[16]I have read a number of unpublished missionary biographies or autobiographies too, of which there are thousands, stored away in archives and family libraries, most of which will never be read. The manuscripts I have read only confirm what published biographies say. In one case I read about a missionary couple that often lived in substandard housing, lost several children to disease, faced constant setbacks and suffered ill health. Yet they told their story matter-of-factly, always emphasizing that the mission was worth the sacrifices.

[17]Studd's son-in-law and successor, Norman P. Grubb, wrote his biography, partly to ex-

plain to critics that Studd was the ideal missionary and thus far from being the fanatic that many thought. He recorded Studd's story—often letting Studd speak for himself by quoting extensively from Studd's letters and journals—to achieve a spiritual goal, for "the convictions which dominated C. T.'s life are also my convictions" and thus "this book has been written with my heart as well as with my head." Studd "lived to glorify his Saviour. The object of this book is likewise to glorify Him as He is seen at work in and through this utterly surrendered life" (Norman P. Grubb, *C. T. Studd: Athlete and Pioneer* [Grand Rapids: Zondervan, 1933]).

[18]Ibid., p. 30.

[19]As Studd asked dramatically, when before had the world seen such men "standing side by side renouncing the careers in which they had already gained no small distinction, putting aside the splendid prizes of earthly ambition, taking leave of the social circles in which they shone with no mean brilliance, and plunging into that warfare whose splendours are seen only by faith, and whose rewards seem so shadowy to the unopened vision of ordinary men?" (ibid., p. 46).

[20]Ibid., p. 49.

[21]Ibid., pp. 79, 81.

[22]Ibid., p. 88.

[23]Ibid., p. 119.

[24]Ibid., p. 123.

[25]Ibid., p. 149.

[26]Ibid., pp. 129-30.

[27]Many missionary biographies very often do not speak with clarity about the suffering of missionary families. Many did suffer too. One notable exception is the biography of Bob Pierce, founder of World Vision, written shortly after his death by his daughter, Marilee Pierce Dunker. It is a painful book to read. On the one hand, the reader cannot help but stand in awe of the vision and energy of Bob Pierce, who founded an organization that has done so much good around the world, especially in founding orphanages and assisting in relief efforts. But Pierce was an abusive husband and absent father, and he suffered for it (see Marilee Pierce Dunker, *Man of Vision, Woman of Prayer* [Nashville: Thomas Nelson, 1980]).

[28]That son-in-law, Norman Grubb, took over leadership of an organization that was in shambles, placed it on firmer ground and helped to expand its operation to reach around the world. It is amazing, considering how virtually abusive Studd was to his own family members, that his daughters and sons-in-law remained so loyal to him and carried on the work after he died.

[29]Grubb, *C. T. Studd*, p. 144.

[30]Ibid., p. 196.

[31]After Priscilla's death the home mission committee took control of the organization, removed Studd from leadership, with two of his sons-in-law, David Munro and Norman Grubb, and prepared to launch a new organization. Desperate, Studd broke into the mission headquarters, taking records to keep them in his possession. Norman Grubb was later reinstated after Studd's death and helped the mission return to its original glory. In 1970

it supported over five hundred missionaries. See Tucker, *From Jerusalem to Irian Jaya*, pp. 266-67. Tucker provides many colorful sketches of pioneer missionaries, and she offers a perspective often ignored or dismissed by biographers. She suggests that what led to Studd's "downfall," if it is even appropriate to speak of it in those terms, was his extremism and fanaticism, which resulted from his single-minded devotion to the mission. Norman Grubb's biography does not ignore this darker side to Studd, but it does tend to mitigate the severity of it, or to use it to illustrate the depth of Studd's commitment to the work.

[32]Grubb, *C. T. Studd*, p. 199.

[33]Ibid., p. 238.

[34]W. P. Livingston, *Mary Slessor of Calabar: Pioneer Missionary* (New York: George H. Doran, n.d.), p. 5.

[35]Ibid., p. 10.

[36]Ibid., p. 11.

[37]Ibid., p. 13.

[38]Ibid., p. 16.

[39]Ibid., p. 19.

[40]Ibid., p. 27.

[41]Ibid., p. 31.

[42]Ibid., p. 134.

[43]Ibid., p. 193.

[44]Ibid., p. 216.

[45]Ibid., p. 224.

[46]See Lamin Sanneh, *Translating the Message: The Missionary Impact on Culture* (Maryknoll, N.Y.: Orbis, 1997).

[47]William Carey, quoted in Mary Drewery, *William Carey: A Biography* (Grand Rapids: Zondervan, 1979), p. 25. For other sources on Carey, see Timothy George, *Faithful Witness: The Life & Mission of William Carey* (Birmingham, Ala.: New Hope, 1991); Basil Miller, *William Carey* (Minneapolis: Bethany, 1985); Terry G. Carter, ed., *The Journal and Selected Letters of William Carey* (Macon, Ga.: Smyth & Helwys, 2000).

[48]Carey, quoted in Drewery, *William Carey*, p. 31.

[49]Carey did not question those interests either. Instead, he turned it into motivation for the mission. "It only requires," he wrote, "that we should have as much love to the souls of our fellow-creatures . . . as they have for the profits arising from a few otter-skins" (ibid., p. 37).

[50]Ibid., p. 39.

[51]Ibid., p. 74.

[52]Drewery, *William Carey*, p. 156.

[53]Ibid., p. 159.

[54]Philip Jenkins explores this theme in his groundbreaking book on the growth of non-Western Christianity. See Philip Jenkins, *The Next Christendom* (New York: Oxford University Press, 2003).

[55]"The faith of Christ," concludes Andrew Walls, "is infinitely translatable; it creates 'a place to feel at home.' But it must not make a place where we are so much at home that no one

else can live there. Here we have no abiding city. In Christ all poor sinners meet, and in finding themselves reconciled with him, are reconciled to each other" (Walls, *Missionary Movement*, p. 25).

[56]David Brainerd, quoted in Jonathan Edwards, *Life and Dairy of David Brainerd* (Chicago: Moody Press, 1949), p. 77.

[57]Jim Elliot, quoted in Elisabeth Elliot, *Shadow of the Almighty: The Life & Testament of Jim Elliot* (San Francisco: Harper & Row, 1958), p. 70.

[58]Ibid., p. 59.

[59]Brainerd in Edwards, *Life and Dairy*, p. 81.

[60]Ibid., p. 155.

[61]Elliot, quoted in Elliot, *Shadow of the Almighty*, p. 55.

Conclusion: Where Do We Go from Here?

[1]Thomas Merton, *New Seeds of Contemplation* (New York: New Directions, 1961), p. 150.

[2]Dorothy Day, *The Long Loneliness* (San Francisco: HarperSanFrancisco, 1952), p. 78. For books by or about Dorothy Day, see Dorothy Day, *Selected Writings: By Little and By Little*, ed. R. Ellsberg (Maryknoll, N.Y.: Orbis, 1992); Dorothy Day, *On Pilgrimage* (Grand Rapids: Eerdmans, 1999); Dorothy Day, *Loaves and Fishes* (Maryknoll, N.Y.: Orbis, 1997); Brigid O'Shea Merriman, *Searching for Christ: The Spirituality of Dorothy Day* (Notre Dame, Ind.: University of Notre Dame Press, 1994); Jim Forest, *Love is the Measure: A Biography of Dorothy Day* (Maryknoll, N.Y.: Orbis, 1994); Deborah Kent, *Dorothy Day: Friend to the Forgotten* (Topeka, Kans.: Sagebrush Education Resources, 2003); and Anne Klejment and Nancy L. Roberts, *American Catholic Pacifism: The Influence of Dorothy Day and the Catholic Worker* (Westport, Conn.: Praeger, 1996).

[3]Day, *Long Loneliness*, p. 79.

[4]Ibid., pp. 81, 83.

[5]Ibid., p. 100.

[6]Ibid., pp. 165-66.

[7]Ibid., p. 141.

[8]Ibid., p. 204.

[9]Ibid., pp. 204-5.

[10]Ibid., p. 263.

[11]Brother Lawrence, *The Practice of the Presence of God* (New York: Barbour, 1993), pp. 27-28.

[12]See Arnold A. Dallimore, *Susanna Wesley: The Mother of John & Charles Wesley* (Grand Rapids: Baker, 1993).

[13]Cheri Fuller, "Susanna Wesley: Creating a Spiritual Legacy," <http://www.navpress.com/epubs/displayarticle/2/2.44.3.html>.

[14]Quoted in Michael Counsell, ed., *2000 Years of Prayer* (Harrisburg, Penn.: Morehouse Publishing, 1999), p. 312.

[15]Jeremiah Evarts, quoted in John G. West Jr., *The Politics of Revelation and Reason: Religion and Civic Life in the New Nation* (Lawrence: University Press of Kansas, 1996), p. 175. I am indebted to West for introducing me to this fascinating, largely forgotten hero in American history. For other sources on Evarts and his work on behalf of the Cherokees,

see William G. McLoughlin, *Cherokees and Missionaries, 1789-1839* (New Haven, Conn.: Yale University Press, 1984); John Ehle, *Trail of Tears: The Rise and Fall of the Cherokee Nation* (New York: Doubleday, 1988); John A. Andrew III, *From Revival to Removal: Jeremiah Evarts, the Cherokee Nation, and the Search for the Soul of America* (Athens: University of Georgia Press, 1992). For an early memoir of Evarts, see E. C. Tracy, *Memoir of the Life of Jeremiah Evarts, Esq.* (Boston: Crocker & Brewster, 1845).

[16]Evarts, quoted in West, *Politics of Revelation*, p. 181. For the entire collection of Evarts's essays, see Francis Paul Prucha, ed., *Cherokee Removal: The "William Penn" Essays and Other Writings of Jeremiah Evarts* (Knoxville: University of Tennessee Press, 1981).

[17]Evarts, quoted in West, *Politics of Revelation*, p. 197.

[18]Ron Sider addressed both the potential and the difficulty of awakening the evangelical wing of the church in his *The Scandal of the Evangelical Conscience* (Grand Rapids: Baker, 2005).

[19]Desmond Tutu, *Crying in the Wilderness: The Struggle for Justice in South Africa* (Grand Rapids: Eerdmans, 1982), pp. 82-83.

Subject Index

Abbo of Fleury, 190
abbot, 107-8
abolitionism, 237, 252
acedia, 115-16
agape, 85, 91-93
Alcuin of York, 113
Aldersgate, 251
"Amazing Grace," 236, 238-39
anchorite (anchoress), 180
Antioch (of Syria), 61-62
Antony of Egypt, St., 75-79, 81, 89, 94
apatheia, 85, 88-91
apophatic theology, 169
Apostolic Tradition, On the, 66
Aristides, 54-55
Athanasius of Alexandria, St., 45-46, 75-
    76, 88, 120
ascesis, 85-88
asceticism, 74-81, 85-88, 127, 171-73,
    194-96, 199-200, 204
Athenagoras, 40, 59-60
Augustine of Hippo, St., 15-17, 20, 22-23,
    66, 88, 105-6, 127
Baptist Missionary Society, 274
Barth, Karl, 177, 230, 324n. 18
Basil of Caesarea, St., 103-4, 122
Bede, the Venerable, 112-13
Beguines, 200-204
Benedict of Nursia, St., 106-7
Benedictines, 106-11, 286
Bernard of Clairvaux, St., 114, 178-80,
    192
Beza, Theodore, 211-12
Bible translation, 212, 266, 272-76
bloodless martyr, 78-81
Bonaventure, John, 173-76, 194-95
Bonhoeffer, Dietrich, 69
Boniface of Germany, St., 112
Brainerd, David, 276-78
Brébeuf, Jean de, 263-64
Brethren of the Common Life, 202-4

Brother Lawrence, 287-88
Bucer, Martin, 210, 219
Bunyan, John, 240-42
Calabar (Nigeria), 269-71
Calvin, John, 204-6, 210-11, 214, 218-27
Cambridge Seven, 264
Canons Regular, 105, 114
Canticle, The (Francis of Assisi), 196
Carey, William, 273-76
Cassian, John, 88-110
Catherine of Siena, 201-2
Catholic Worker Movement, 285-87
Catholic Worker (Dorothy Day), 285
Celsus, 44, 57
Chalcedon, Council of, 23, 122-23, 259
Charlemagne, 105, 113
Cherokees, 290-91
church, 292-94
church year, 100, 157-58
    Christmas, 157-58
    Epiphany, 157
    Holy Week, 157
    Lent, 157
    Pascha, 157
Cicero, 39
Cistercians, 113-14, 173, 192
Cluny, 113, 190
Confessions, The (Augustine), 15-17, 22-23
Colet, John, 218
Collegia Pietas, 242
Conferences, The (Cassian), 88, 110
Constantine (Roman emperor), 32-33, 79-
    80, 101
Constantinople, 128, 132-34
conversion, 232-33, 238-53, 273
Cyprian of Carthage, St., 63-64
Cyril of Jerusalem, St., 155-56
Dark Night of the Soul (John of the Cross),
    184-85
Day, Dorothy, 283-86
deification, 119-21, 136-38

desert, 81-83, 93-95
Didache, the, 67
Diocletian (Roman emperor), 79-101
Diognetus, Letter to, 54-55
Divine Office, 110-11, 113, 286
Dominic, St., 197-99
Dominicans, 197-99, 260
Eastern Orthodoxy, 118-38
Edict of Milan, 80
Edwards, Jonathan, 244-50, 277
Edwards, Sarah, 249
Egeria, 152-54
Elizabeth I, 240
Elliot, Jim, 277-78
Erasmus, 213, 218
Evagrius Ponticus, 83-85, 89, 115
evangelicalism, 232-33, 238, 253-54
Evarts, Jeremiah, 290-92
Eusebius of Caesarea, 80
*Faithful Narrative of the Surprising Work of
   God* (Edwards), 245-46
Farel, William, 219
Finney, Charles G., 251
First Great Awakening, 244-52, 260
Florentius Radwigns, 203
Francis of Assisi, St., 48, 173, 193-97, 201,
   203
Franciscans, 173, 193-97, 201, 260
Friars Minor, 193-97
Geneva, 219-20
gothic cathedrals, 139-43
Graham, Billy, 253
Great Commission, The, 257-58, 274
Gregory of Nazianzus, St., 66
Gregory of Nyssa, St., 122
Gregory the Great (Pope), 106
Groote, Geert de, 202-3
Guido (Carthusians), 192-93
hagiography, 121, 126-30
Herrnhut, 243-44
Hippolytus of Rome, 66-67
Holy Club, 250-51
Holy Land, 152-53

Holy Spirit, 17, 19, 23, 59-60, 104, 119,
   123-24, 221, 242, 295
humanism, 218-19
Iconoclastic Controversy, 122-23
iconography, 124-26
icons, 121-26
Ignatius of Loyola, 214, 261-63
illumination, 142, 170, 173-76
Imitation of Christ, The (Thomas a'
   Kempis), 203-4, 234
indulgences, 216
incarnation
   in the desert saints, 79, 81
   in early Christianity, 44-46
   in Eastern Orthodoxy, 119-20, 122
   in missions, 256-57, 273, 279
   in mysticism, 169, 177-78
   in Reformation preaching, 211-12,
      220-21, 225, 230
   in medieval sacramentalism, 144-47
   in social activism, 285-86
   in spiritual theology, 22-23
Institutes of the Christian Religion (Calvin),
   218-19
itinerancy, 251-52
Jacques de Vitry, 200-201
Jerusalem Council, 258
John Chrysostom, St., 65-66, 88, 130-36
John Climacus, 170-73
John of Damascus, 122-23, 125
John of the Cross, 184-85, 214
Julian of Norwich, 180-84
Julian the Apostate (Roman emperor),
   56
Justin Martyr, 33-34, 40-41, 46, 60
Ladder of Divine Ascent, The (John
   Climacus), 170-73
laity, 188-93, 198-200, 203-7, 224-27
lectio divina, 96, 110, 330n. 28
Lectures on Revivals of Religion (Finney),
   251
Lewis, C. S., 18, 20, 136-37
logismoi, 84-85

Luther, Martin, 95, 204-5, 210, 214-18, 221-26
Macarius the Great, Abba, 86, 90-91
Macrina the Younger, 103-5, 121-24
Margaret of Cortuna, 201
Mark the Ascetic, St., 74-92
marriage and family
    in early Christianity, 57-58, 62-63
    in the desert saints, 86-87
    in the Reformation, 204-5, 226-27
    virginal, 200
Mary of Oignies, 200-201
Mary, the Virgin, 156-57
martyrdom
    definition of, 27-31, 47-48
    in the desert saints, 78
    reasons for, 28, 30-31, 33-34, 39-41, 47
    stories of, 34-43
"Martyrs of Lyons," 34-36
Maurin, Peter, 285-86
Melania the Younger, 126-29
mendicants, 193-99
Merton, Thomas, 94, 172, 183-84, 283, 325n. 35
Methodist movement, 252-53
missions, 259-60, 276
monasteries, 96-98, 101-14, 190, 192, 204
monasticism
    Benedictine, 106-11
    common labor, 108-9
    missions, 112-13
    prayer and work, 110-11, 114-16
    role of the Rule, 103-11
    scholarship and education, 110-13
Monte Cassino, 106
Moody, Dwight L., 253, 264
Moravians, 242-45, 250-51, 260
Moses, Abba, 83-90
New Measures, 251
Newton, John, 232-39, 254-55
Nicaea, First Council of, 22-23, 259
Nicaea, Second Council of, 122-23
Ninety-five Theses, 216-17

Olney Hymns (Newton), 236
On Loving God (Bernard), 179-80
order of preachers, 197-99
Origen, 66, 324n. 24
Pachomius, 101-3
Panoplist, The (Evarts), 290
pastoral care
    in early Christianity, 65-67
    in the Reformation, 224-27
Paul the apostle, St., 29-30, 52-53, 55, 258-59
Pentecostalism, 253
Perpetua, Vibia, 37-39
persecution, biblical view of, 29-30
Peterson, Eugene, 228
Pia Desideria (Spener), 242
Pietism, 242
pilgrimage, 152-55
Pilgrim's Progress, The (Bunyan), 240-41
plagues, 63-65
Plato, 166
Pliny the Younger, 34, 47, 50-52
Plotinus, 166-67
pluralism, 43-47
Poemen, Abba, 75, 87, 89-90
Polycarp, Bishop of Smyrna, 41-43, 155
Porphyry, 44-45
Practice of the Presence of God, The (Brother Lawrence), 287
prayer, 101, 110-11, 114-16, 182-85, 190-91
preaching
    John Chrysostom, 132-35
    evangelical, 248-52
    mendicant, 193-99
    Reformation, 210-12, 220-27, 228-30
profit economy, 191-92
Pseudo-Dionysius, 167-70
purgation, 170-73
Puritanism, 240-42
Reformation, the, 204, 212-27, 259-60
relics, 155-57
Religious Affections (Edwards), 246-48

Reuchlin, Johannes, 218
Roman Empire, 27-28, 31-32, 36, 41, 43-
    47, 60-62, 79-80
Rule of St. Augustine, 105
Rule of St. Benedict, The, 106-11
sabbath, 99-100
sacraments, 142-62
    baptism, 68, 148-49
    confirmation, 149
    penance, 149-50, 214-15
    Eucharist, 88, 143, 145, 150
    ordination, 151
    marriage, 150-51
    extreme unction, 151-52
    Reformation view, 212
sainthood, 119-24, 199-200, 207-8
salvation history, 17-21, 23-24, 227-28
Santiago de Compostela, 154-55
Sayings of the Desert Fathers, 88
Scripture (in Reformation), 211-12, 220-
    21
Serapion, Abba, 91
Seven Deadly Sins, 84
Showings (Julian), 180-84
Silvanus, Abba, 89
Simeon the Stylite, 78, 93
Slessor, Mary, 269-73
Society of Jesus (Jesuits), 214, 260-63
Soul's Journey to God, The (Bonaventure),
    173-74
Spener, Philipp Jakob, 242
spiritual discipline, 67, 75-78, 88, 91-92,
    94
Spiritual Exercises, The (Ignatius of
    Loyola), 261-63
spirituality, definition of, 18, 23, 48, 282-
    83
Stigmata, 173, 197
Studd, Charles Thomas, 264-68
Suger, Abbot, 113, 141-42
Syncletica, Amma, 85-86

Tacitus, 36
Tatian, 56-57
Teresa of Ávila, 184, 214
Tertiaries (Third Order), 201-2
Tertullian, 40-41, 56, 58-59, 62-63, 67-
    68, 188-89
Tetzel, Johann, 216
Theosis, 119-21, 136-38
Thomas Aquinas, 164-65
Thomas of Celano, 194-95
Trajan (Roman emperor), 50-52
Trent, Council of, 214
Trinity, the, 17-19, 22-23, 59-60
Tutu, Bishop Desmond, 294-95
union (with God), 166-70, 176-84
virtue, 203
    Benedictine, 109-10
    hospitality, 92, 206-7, 285-86
    humility, 91
    love, 92-93
vocation, 205
voluntary societies, 252, 260
Wesley, Charles, 236, 252
Wesley, John, 236-37, 250-52
Wesley, Susanna, 288-89
Whitefield, George, 236, 248-51
widows, 57-60, 132
Wilberforce, William, 236-37
Wittenberg, 210, 215
women, role of
    in early Christianity, 57-58
    in evangelicalism, 253
    in the desert tradition, 86-88, 129
Word of God, 211-12, 220-23, 227-30
world, the flesh, and the devil, the, 74, 77,
    83, 93, 95, 126
Worldwide Evangelist Crusade, 265-66
Worms, Diet of, 217
Zinzendorf, Nicolaus Ludwig von, 243-44